ECONOMICS IN A CHANGING WORLD
Volume 2 Microeconomics

This is IEA Conference Volume Number 108

ECONOMICS IN A CHANGING WORLD

Congress Editor: Anthony B. Atkinson

Economics in a Changing World

Proceedings of the Tenth World Congress of the International Economic Association Moscow

Congress Editor: Anthony B. Atkinson

Volume 2 MICROECONOMICS

Edited by

Beth Allen

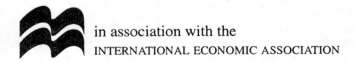

in association with the
INTERNATIONAL ECONOMIC ASSOCIATION

First published in Great Britain 1996 by
MACMILLAN PRESS LTD
Houndmills, Basingstoke, Hampshire RG21 6XS
and London
Companies and representatives throughout the world

UNESCO Subvention 1992/93/SHS/SES/68/SUB/16

A catalogue record for this book is available
from the British Library.

ISBN 0–333–60124–6

 First published in the United States of America 1996 by
ST. MARTIN'S PRESS, INC.,
Scholarly and Reference Division,
175 Fifth Avenue,
New York, N.Y. 10010

ISBN 0–312–15929–3

Library of Congress Cataloging-in-Publication Data
(Revised for vol. 2)
Economics in a changing world
(I.E.A. conference volume : no 108.)
Includes bibliographical references.
ISBN 0–312–15929–3
Contents: —v.3. Public policy
and economic organization / edited by Dieter
Bös—   —v. 5. Economic growth and
capital and labour markets / edited by
Jean-Paul Fitoussi—   —v.2. Microeconomics
/ edited by Beth Allen.
1. Economic policy—Congresses.
I. Atkinson, A. B. (Anthony Barnes).
II. Series.
HD73.I575   1996   330   93–1789
ISBN 0–312–10182–1 (v.3)   CIP
ISBN 0–312–12468–6 (v.5)
ISBN 0–312–15929–3 (v.2)

10   9   8   7   6   5   4   3   2   1
05   04   03   02   01   00   99   98   97   96

Printed in Great Britain by
The Ipswich Book Company Ltd, Ipswich, Suffolk

Contents

Preface

Anthony B. Atkinson

The World Congress of the International Economic Association held
in Moscow in August 1992 was the tenth in a series which began in
Rome in 1956 and which had been held most recently in New Delhi
in 1986 and Athens in 1989. Each of the previous congresses has had
its distinctive features, but the Tenth Congress was undoubtedly special because it took place against a background of historic changes in
the Russian economy and society. To quote from the letter sent by
Jacques Delors, President of the Commission of the European Communities, which co-sponsored the Congress:

> The former Soviet society is facing a period of enormous changes,
> the results of which are of global significance. The huge and urgent
> tasks to be accomplished call for a sound analysis of the progress
> of economic transformation, to be carried out by Eastern as well as
> Western experts. The Tenth World Congress of the IEA will offer
> the opportunity for them to have discussions together, start collab-
> oration and develop a common language.

Those who were present at the Moscow Congress will know that there
was indeed lively discussion of the choices facing Russian economic
policy, and that it provided first-hand insight into the problems of transition to a market economy. The Congress represented an unprecedented
opportunity for contacts, both formal and informal, between economists
from East and West.

At the same time, the 1992 Congress was not solely concerned with
the problems of economic transformation. Like the Ninth Congress in
Athens, it covered in principle all fields of economics. While the historic changes taking place in Russia and Eastern Europe were in the
forefront of everyone's mind, the Congress was not limited to this
subject. There were several reasons for this. The first is that, with a
meeting only every three years, it is important that all economists should
feel free to attend, whatever their fields of specialism. As my predecessor, Amartya Sen, remarked in his Preface to the Athens Congress

vii

volumes, 'it seems unreasonable to make economists of particular specialisation wait many multiples of three years for their turn to come up'. Secondly, while there were indeed important sessions on economic transformation, it was the hope of the Programme Committee that sessions in all areas would be of interest to Russian economists and others whose economies are in transition. Subjects such as Public Finance, the Economics of Financial Markets, Business History, and the Economics of Health, just to take some examples, are very relevant to what is happening in the Russian economy and in Eastern Europe.

Thirdly, the IEA is an *international* association, and while meeting in Russia it was most important that we did not lose sight of the economic issues which confront other parts of the world. It would be easy for the economics profession to become immersed in the issues of transition from communism to a market economy and to neglect the enduring problems of Africa, Asia and Latin America. In this context I should draw attention to the sessions on the development problems of Latin America and China, on economic policy with particular reference to Africa, and on the Indian economy. The last of these sessions was organized in honour of Sir Austin Robinson. Unfortunately he could not attend the Congress, but he continued to play an active role in the Association's affairs, as he had since its creation more than 40 years ago, right up to his death in 1993. He is much missed.

The Congress programme consisted of five plenary lectures (by Professor A. Blinder, Academician O. Bogomolov, Professor B. Grodal, Professor D. Patinkin and the Presidential Address), of four panel sessions (chaired by Professors K.J. Arrow, B. Csikós-Nagy, J. Drèze, and Mr S. Wright), twenty-nine half-day sessions, and seventeen full-day sessions, with invited and contributed papers. The programme was organized on a decentralized basis, as was perhaps appropriate in the new Russian circumstances, with each session being organized by one or two Programme Committee members. To them were sent the more than 400 papers submitted, and they arranged for the Invited Speakers. On the final programme were 67 invited papers and 241 contributed papers. Those taking part were drawn from more than 50 countries.

The full list of the Programme Committee is as follows:

A.G. Aganbegyan, Academy of National Economy, Moscow, Russia
B. Allen, University of Minnesota and Federal Reserve Bank of Minneapolis, USA
M. Aoki, Stanford University, USA
K.J. Arrow, Stanford University, USA

E.L. Bacha, Pontifícia Universidade Católica do Rio de Janeiro, Brazil

K. Basu, Delhi School of Economics, India

O. Blanchard, Massachusetts Institute of Technology, USA

O. Bogomolov, Academy of Sciences, Moscow, Russia

D. Bös, University of Bonn, Germany

B. Csikós-Nagy, Hungarian Economic Association

J.-P. Danthine, University of Lausanne, Switzerland

P.A. David, Stanford University, USA

A.S. Deaton, Princeton University, USA

J.-P. Fitoussi, Observatoire Français des Conjonctures Economiques, Paris, France

M. Germouni, Rabat, Morocco

J. Le Grand, London School of Economics, UK

J.-M. Grandmont, Centre d' Études Prospectives d'Économie Mathématiques Appliquées à la Planification, Paris, France

L. Hannah, London School of Economics, UK

A. Heertje, University of Amsterdam, Holland

M. Hoel, University of Oslo, Norway

B. Holmlund, Uppsala University, Sweden

J. Humphries, University of Cambridge, UK

Y.M. Ioannides, Virginia Polytechnic Institute, USA

A.P. Kirman, University of Marseille, France

A. Krueger, Stanford University, USA

D. Kumar, University of Delhi, India

Y. Luo, Beijing University, China

M.I. Mahmoud, African Centre for Monetary Studies, Senegal

P. Maillet, University of Lille, France

J. Malcomson, University of Southampton, UK

E. Maskin, Harvard University, USA

J. Melitz, Institut Nationale de la Statistique et des Études Économiques, Paris, France

P.-A. Muet, Observatoire Français des Conjonctures Économiques, Paris, France

I. Musu, Venice University, Italy

T. Negishi, University of Tokyo, Japan

L. Phlips, European University Institute, Florence, Italy

R. Portes, Centre for Economic Policy Research, London, UK

B.M.S. van Praag, Erasmus University, Holland

J. Sachs, Harvard University, USA

P. Saunders, University of New South Wales, Australia

C. Schmidt, Laboratoire d'Économie et de Sociologie des Organisations de Défence, Paris, France
S. Scotchmer, University of California, Berkeley, USA
A.K. Sen, Harvard University, USA
M.R. Sertel, Boğaziçi University, Turkey
T. Smeeding, Syracuse University, USA
K. Stahl, University of Mannheim, Germany
O. Stark, Harvard University, USA
P. Temin, Massachusetts Institute of Technology, USA
H. Tulkens, Centre for Operations Research and Econometrics, Belgium
J. Vinals, Committee of European Community Central Bankers, Switzerland
A.D. Woodland, University of Sydney, Australia
R.D. Worrell, Central Bank of Barbados
S. Wright, University of Cambridge, UK
S. Zamagni, University of Bologna, Italy

The plenary lectures and invited papers are being published in five volumes. Each of the volumes has a separate editor and IEA editor:

Vol. 1: *System Transformation: Eastern and Western Assessments*, edited by Abel Aganbegyan, Oleg Bogomolov and Michael Kaser (M. Kaser editing for IEA);
Vol. 2: *Microeconomics*, edited by Beth Allen (N. Watts editing for IEA);
Vol. 3: *Public Policy and Economic Organization*, edited by Dieter Bös (R. Maurice editing for IEA);
Vol. 4: *Development, Trade and the Environment*, edited by Edmar Bacha (M. Hadfield editing for IEA);
Vol. 5: *Capital and Labour Markets and Economic Growth*, edited by Jean-Paul Fitoussi (L. Cook editing for IEA).

I take this opportunity of thanking the editors of the volumes, Michael Kaser, who is the Association's General Editor, and the IEA editorial team, for their work in producing these conference proceedings.

The situation of the Russian economy in 1992 undoubtedly made the Congress of great interest. It also added to the difficulties of organization, and I should like to put on record the Association's deep appreciation to all those who have made it possible. First of all, our Russian hosts, Academicians Agenbegyan and Bogomolov, invited the Association and inspired us with their confidence that the Congress could be achieved. The Local Organizing Committee, headed by Vice Prime Minister A. Shokhin, and managed by Vice Rector A.A. Modin, undertook all the hard work to make the Congress a reality in very difficult circumstances. We appreciate the hospitality of the Academy of National Economy and the Russian Academy of Sciences, and the participation of other institutions. It is not possible to refer to all of the Academy staff by name, but I would like to assure them that all the participants from outside Russia were very grateful.

The organization has also involved much work for the Association's staff. I would like to thank the Secretary-General, Jean-Paul Fitoussi, whose contribution has been absolutely essential in ensuring that the Congress took place. In Paris, the Administrative Secretary, Elisabeth Majid, has worked tirelessly, together with her colleagues, on travel, visa and financial aspects. For Elisabeth, it was her last IEA Congress, and I would like to put on record the Association's appreciation of all her work. In London, Jacky Jennings as Programme Secretary has taken a great deal of responsibility, and it has been a pleasure to work with her. Alistair McAuley of the University of Essex helped with initial contacts in Moscow. My predecessor, Amartya Sen, and other members of the IEA Executive Committee have been a constant source of help and sound advice.

Before concluding these prefatory remarks, I should express my warm gratitude to the bodies which have funded the Congress. In addition to the co-sponsorship of the Commission of the European Communities to which reference has already been made, the generosity of (in alphabetical order) the Austrian National Bank, the Bank for International Settlements, the British Academy, the Carnegie Corporation, the European Bank for Reconstruction and Development, the Ford Foundation, the Credit-Anstalt, Vienna, Deutsche Bundesbank, the McArthur Foundation, and the Soros Foundation (which made possible the participation of Eastern European economists) is very much appreciated.

The International Economic Association

A non-profit organization with purely scientific aims, the International Economic Association (IEA) was founded in 1950. It is a federation of national economic associations and presently includes fifty-eight such professional organizations from all parts of the world. Its basic purpose is the development of economics as an intellectual discipline. Its approach recognizes a diversity of problems, systems and values in the world and also takes note of methodological diversities.

The IEA has, since its creation, tried to fulfil that purpose by promoting mutual understanding of economists from the West and the East, as well as from the North and the South, through the organization of scientific meetings and common research programmes, and by means of publications on problems of current importance. During its forty years of existence, it has organized one hundred round-table conferences for specialists on topics ranging from fundamental theories to methods and tools of analysis and major problems of the present-day world. The ten triennial World Congresses have regularly attracted the participation of a great many economists from all over the world.

The Association is governed by a Council, composed of representatives of all member associations, and by a fifteen-member Executive Committee which is elected by the Council. The Executive Committee (1989–92) at the time of the Moscow Congress was

President: Professor Anthony B. Atkinson, UK
Vice-President: Professor Luo Yuanzheng, China
Treasurer: Professor Alexandre Lamfalussy, Belgium
Past President: Professor Amartya Sen, India
Other Members: Professor Abel Aganbegyan, USSR
Professor Kenneth J. Arrow, USA.
Professor Edmar Lisboa Bacha, Brazil
Professor B.R. Brahmananda, India
Professor Wolfgang Heinrichs,
   German Federal Republic
Professor Edmond Malinvaud, France
Professor Takashi Negishi, Japan

Professor Don Patinkin, Israel
Professor Agnar Sandmo, Norway
Professor Erich Streissler, Austria
Professor Stefano Zamagni, Italy
Advisers: Professor Oleg T. Bogomolov, USSR
Professor Karel Dyba, Czechoslovakia
Professor Mohammed Germouni, Morocco
Secretary-General: Professor Jean-Paul Fitoussi, France
General Editor: Professor Michael Kaser, UK
Adviser to
General Editor: Professor Sir Austin Robinson, UK (since deceased)

The Association has also been fortunate in having secured the following outstanding economists to serve as President: Gottfried Haberler (1950–3), Howard S. Ellis (1953–6), Erik Lindahl (1956–69), E.A.G. Robinson (1959–62), G. Ugo Papi (1962–5), Paul A. Samuelson (1965–8), Erik Lundberg (1968–71), Fritz Machlup (1971–4), Edmond Malinvaud (1974–7), Shigeto Tsuru (1977–80), Victor L. Urquidi (1980–3), Kenneth J. Arrow (1983–6), Amartya Sen (1986–9). Professor Michael Bruno took office at the conclusion of the Moscow Congress.

The activities of the Association are mainly funded from the subscriptions of members and grants from a number of organizations, including continuing support from UNESCO.

List of Contributors

Professor Dilip Abreu, Department of Economics, Princeton University, Princeton, New Jersey, USA

Professor Beth Allen, Department of Economics, University of Minnesota, Minneapolis, Minnesota, USA, and Federal Reserve Bank of Minneapolis, Minneapolis, Minnesota, USA

Professor Masahiko Aoki, Department of Economics, Stanford University, Stanford, California, USA

Professor Abhijit Banerjee, Department of Economics, Harvard University, Cambridge, Massachusetts, USA

Professor Kenneth Binmore, Department of Economics, University College London, UK

Professor Jean-Michel Grandmont, Centre d'Études Prospectives d'Économie Mathématique Appliquées à la Planification, Paris, France

Professor Birgit Grodal, Institute of Economics, University of Copenhagen, Denmark

Professor Oliver Hart, Department of Economics, Harvard University, Cambridge, Massachusetts, USA

Professor Alan Kirman, GREQAM, EHESS, and University of Aix – Marseille III, France

Professor Andreu Mas-Colell, Department of Economics, Harvard University, Cambridge, Massachusetts, USA

Professor John McMillan, Graduate School of International Relations and Pacific Studies, University of California at San Diego, La Jolla, California, USA

Professor Christos H. Papadimitriou, Department of Computer Science and Engineering, University of California at Berkeley, California, USA

Professor Louis Phlips, Department of Economics, European University Institute, San Domenico di Fiesole, Italy

Professor Suzanne Scotchmer, Graduate School of Public Policy, University of California at Berkeley, Berkeley, California, USA

Professor Christian Schmidt, Laboratoire d'Économie et de Sociologie des Organisations de Défence, University of Paris IX-Dauphine, Paris, France

Dr Nina Smith, Centre for Labour Market and Social Research, Aarhus, Denmark

Professor Sanjay Srivastava, Graduate School of Industrial Administration, Carnegie-Mellon University, Pittsburgh, Pennsylvania, USA

Professor Ian Walker, Department of Economics, Keele University, Staffordshire, UK

Professor Jörgen W. Weibull, Department of Economics , Stockholm School of Economics, Stockholm, Sweden

Professor Niels Westergård-Nielsen, Centre for Labour Market and Social Research, Aarhus, Denmark

Introduction

Beth Allen[1]

This volume contains invited papers in the broadly defined area of microeconomic theory that were presented to the IEA Tenth World Congress in Moscow. These papers are generally more technical than those from sessions in other areas. Moreover, these papers tend not to reflect the Russian location of the meeting as much as those from other sessions; issues of transition economies and comparative systems are noticeably absent (compared to some of the other conference volumes). Within microeconomics, however, a wide range of topics are represented here – from the foundations of economic choice through strategic behaviour, multiple market interactions, and asymmetric information, to applications in such diverse areas as the internal organization of firms, patent policy, product markets, and labour supply, finishing with a piece on the history of oligopoly theory.

Specifically, this volume contains Birgit Grodal's plenary lecture on profit maximization in the theory of Cournot competition, plus invited lectures from nine separate sessions. These sessions are as follows: Rationality, Game Theory and Implementation, General Equilibrium, Information, Internal Structure of the Enterprise, Intellectual Property, Empirical Product Markets, Microeconomics of the Household, and History of Economic Thought. We have printed some of the discussants' comments from the sessions on Rationality and Internal Structure of the Enterprise. However, we have chosen not to include any of the contributed papers from the nine sessions, despite the fact that some contributed research pieces were certainly excellent and worthy of publication. I decided to exclude all contributed papers due to the difficult logistics of selecting only a small number of such contributions from the programme in a way that would provide equal access to the conference volume for all authors of good papers without the necessity of contacting all speakers to invite them to submit their work.

In Part I of this volume, the microeconomics portion of the Moscow proceedings begins with the text of Birgit Grodal's plenary lecture, entitled 'Profit Maximization and Imperfect Competition' (Chapter 1). This chapter re-examines several significant aspects from the theory of equilibrium behaviour by profit-maximizing firms under perfect competition. In particular, in an imperfectly competitive general equilibrium model with quantity-setting firms, Grodal points out that some important conclusions no longer hold. In a Cournot oligopoly model, the price normalization rule has surprising real effects. Different choices of numeraire and different normalization rules can lead to essentially any production plan – including inefficient production plans – being obtained as equilibrium plans. Even the existence or non-existence of equilibrium can depend on the way in which prices are normalized. This contrasts sharply with the perfectly competitive (general equilibrium) framework. There the choice of numeraire good or an economist's decision, for example, to normalize prices so that they belong to the unit simplex (i.e., to divide all prices by the same strictly positive scalar so that they add up to precisely one) or the unit sphere (i.e., to divide each price by the sum of the squared prices so that they lie on the surface of the unit ball in the price space) is completely inconsequential. For perfectly competitive economies with commodity endowments and no money, both household demands and firm net supply relations satisfy homogeneity of degree zero in all prices. This is because, in the standard model, utility functions do not depend on prices whereas budget sets are unchanged when all prices are multiplied by the same strictly positive constant. For firms, cost-minimizing and profit-maximizing production plans are similarly homogeneous of degree zero in all prices (although costs and profits are themselves first-degree homogeneous in all prices). Grodal further shows that even in the limit as the number of firms increases and all firms become small relative to the market, these features, which are pathological relative to the perfectly competitive paradigm, persist. She next considers alternative objective functions for firms. With one owner, maximization of the single owner's utility is generally not equivalent to profit maximization by a Cournot oligopoly. With many owners, the analogous objective function is not defined, although there may exist firm-specific price normalization rules that cause all shareholders to agree to maximize the profits of a quantity-setting firm. The overall conclusion from Grodal's analysis is that price normalization fails to remain innocuous in any general equilibrium model in which quantity-setting firms have nontrivial market power. One suspects that recognized limitations of 'general equilibrium theory *à la* Cournot' become even more severe whenever the stockholders of firms can trade shares in (complete or incomplete) asset markets, whenever firm decision-making is carried out according to majority rule of shareholders, and whenever the objectives of firms' managers need not coincide with shareholders' objectives. It remains to examine this set of issues in models with differentiated products, price-setting firms, and dynamic intertemporal features.

The Rationality in Economics full-day session included more than the usual number of invited presentations. Part II of this volume includes three of these papers, with discussants' comments for two of them. The session covered many different concepts of 'rationality' in economic theory. Decision-theoretic, philosophical, and game-theoretic approaches were discussed, extending to aggregation, social choice, income inequality, and learning behaviour and rational expectations. Throughout the session, both individual and group rationality appeared, sometimes within the same paper.

The first paper printed here, by Ken Binmore (Chapter 2), focuses on how 'rational' players should play the prisoners' dilemma game. His chapter is organized around fallacies appearing in the literature, such as the restriction to symmetric strategies and coordinated deviations in symmetric non-cooperative games, the appeal to factors (such as enforcement of commitments, disutility of breaking promises, and externalities) not modelled as part of the game's description, and various misinterpretations of Axelrod's experiment. The chapter begins with a discussion of preferences or choices (instead of payoffs) as primitive concepts and assumes a variant of Savage's sure-thing principle: if A is preferred to B when P is true and if A is preferred to B when P is false, then A is preferred to B when the validity of P is uncertain. The chapter emphasizes the necessity of completely and precisely formulating game-theoretic models, including the strategy sets. Games with no players are introduced to clarify some concepts.

In Chapter 3, Jean-Michel Grandmont relates aggregation and learning to rationality in individual actions by utility-maximizing households. Beginning from the seminal result of Sonnenschein (as extended by Debreu, McFadden, Mantel, Mas-Colell, and Richter) that 'almost anything' can be generated as the aggregate excess demand function of traders with well-behaved preferences, Grandmont demonstrates that suitable heterogeneity of a particular form can nevertheless lead to strong restrictions on aggregate economic relations. The key insight is roughly that heterogeneity leads to aggregate expenditures that are approximately independent of prices and hence tend to satisfy the weak axiom of revealed preference and gross substitutability; competitive equilibria are unique and stable. Moreover, in a partial-equilibrium Cournot variant of the model, consumer heterogeneity yields concave revenue functions for firms, so that existence (and uniqueness) of Nash equilibrium is assured in the non-cooperative game played among profit-maximizing quantity-setting firms. Then the dynamic rational expectations hypothesis is questioned based on the observation that learning leads to local instability, especially when expectations matter significantly. Alan Kirman's discussion of Grandmont's presentation stresses that the form of heterogeneity assumed here constitutes a severe restriction on the distribution of consumers' preferences around some underlying basic preference relations; aggregation over these transformed preferences yields a total demand that resembles the demand generated by a single Cobb–Douglas consumer. Thus, Grandmont analyzes the outcome of a very particular sort of heterogeneity; he does not obtain the desired general conclusion that heterogeneity itself necessarily helps the problem. Turning to the expectational stability issues, Kirman argues that we need an economic theory of learning how to learn about endogenous variables as well as a study of the impact of memory length on rational expectations. Kirman's comments also point out some relationships to the literature on general equilibrium in smooth economies and on learning rational expectations.

Finally, in Chapter 4, Abhijit Banerjee and Jörgen Weibull survey evolutionary game theory and its relationship to rationality-based solution concepts. They wish to substitute rationality for arguments centred on Nash equilibrium and other non-cooperative solution concepts and to generalize evolutionary games to incorporate boundedly rational adaptive behaviour. They establish a connection between attractors of evolutionary processes and Nash equilibrium in generalized environments. In addition, they show that even when the evolutionary process does not converge, continuous-time evolution eventually eliminates dominated and iteratively dominated strategies.

Ken Binmore's discussion of the chapter by Banerjee and Weibull stresses their reliance on the principle that rationality should be common knowledge in evolutionary games. However, Binmore is sceptical about the extent to which their conclusions can be generalized. He points out that discrete time dynamics or noisy processes can exhibit quite different behaviour – for example, strictly dominated strategies need not disappear.

Overall, the session provided a tantalizing taste of the variety of problems in microeconomic theory which may be fruitfully re-examined from the viewpoint of some form of rationality. In the future, this research area is likely to give interesting and surprising answers to many important open questions in economic theory and game theory.

The Game Theory and Implementation session (which begins Part

III of this volume) was much more tightly focused. It contained two invited surveys by individuals working at the forefront of two distinct and important problems in implementation theory. Briefly, implementation concerns the attainment of a desired outcome or set of outcomes as the equilibrium of some game, which is considered to be (perhaps optimally) chosen according to certain rules by the planner or mechanism designer in a decentralized society. A *mechanism* is a (measurable) mapping from players' messages to (randomized) feasible allocations or outcomes. It defines a non-cooperative game with strategy sets defined to be the message spaces and payoffs equal to the (expected) utilities of allocations or outcomes. The implementation problem then reduces to the question of finding a mechanism in the desired class (that is, those mechanisms satisfying linearity or an incentive compatibility requirement) for which the resulting non-cooperative game gives the desired feasible allocations or outcomes as its equilibria. *Equilibrium* may refer to Nash equilibria, one of its refinements (such as strong equilibria or perfect equilibrium), or some other non-cooperative game-theoretic solution concept. Dilip Abreu (Chapter 5) examines implementation in iteratively undominated strategies under both complete and incomplete information; many of the results reported here appear in the series of articles on virtual implementation by Dilip Abreu and Hitoshi Matsushima, while others first appeared in the joint work of Dilip Abreu and Arunava Sen. Chapter 6, by Sanjay Srivastava, summarizes recent incomplete information implementation results, including the characterization of exchange economy allocations that can be implemented as Bayesian Nash equilibria. Much of this material has appeared in joint work with Tom Palfrey.

The General Equilibrium session contained two rather different papers. My paper, Chapter 7, attempts a very broad survey of general equilibrium theory, with formal details provided only for static pure-exchange economies. I chose to emphasize a number of current research areas and open questions that I consider interesting. In the final section of my chapter, I also discuss the extension of general equilibrium theory to dynamic models. The other paper (Chapter 8) from this session, by Andreu Mas-Colell, takes an alternative tack and focuses on the determinacy of equilibria. While we know from microeconomic theory that we can't expect competitive equilibrium to be unique, a pathbreaking paper by Gerard Debreu, published about a quarter of a century ago, proved that equilibria are locally unique and finite in number, at least for a generic smooth economy. Andreu Mas-Colell re-examines the contribution of this piece of research and suggests an elementary proof of Debreu's result which does not rely on Sard's Theorem, while stressing the more general contribution made by Debreu's introduction of methods from differential topology into the toolbag of modern general equilibrium theorists.

Similarly, the session on Information included two very different papers. Chapter 9, by Christos Papadimitriou, is quite theoretical in spirit. He exposits some recent research in computer science and relates it to problems in economic theory and game theory. More specifically, two distributed scheduling problems are considered; one problem uses expectations, whereas the other emphasizes the worst possible case. Both problems involve decisions by multiple agents in a team having a common objective function and making their choices based on observation of a subset of the variables of interest; the optimum (expected or maximin) value is interpreted as the value of information and communication. In Chapter 10, the second paper from this session, Oliver Hart examines the capital structure of firms from the perspective of agency theory or managerial discretion. He argues that the conflict of interest between a firm's management and its shareholders is not only inherent but also critical for the explanation of capital structure. In particular, the observed features of (optimal) capital structure – including the common utilization of senior or secured debt – cannot be justified solely by such considerations as taxes, asymmetric information, and incomplete markets. This chapter has a much more applied flavour than the one by Papadimitriou and, in fact, would have fitted equally well into the applications-oriented part of this volume.

Part IV of this volume begins with the Internal Structure of the Enterprise session. In Chapter 11 Masahiko Aoki surveys the recent literature in applied microeconomic theory that addresses the internal organization of firms. His viewpoint is that of comparative systems, albeit his specialization in the Pacific-rim countries – especially Japan – lends a somewhat unusual flavour to this piece. After a critique of the way that the revelation principle has been applied, he discusses teams, transaction costs, multiple hierarchies and the principal–agent problem, with particular emphasis on the explanation of alternative observed structures of firms and the recent need for workers to exhibit integrative skills. John McMillan's discussion of this chapter focuses on transition economies – in particular, the evolving Chinese institutions of community-owned firms and auctions that sell the right to manage a firm.

Suzanne Scotchmer's paper in the Intellectual Property session examines patent policy from the perspective of the theory of incentives (Chapter 12). She explicitly assumes that (successful) research and development projects will be rewarded through monopoly revenues and that the extent of patent protection cannot depend on the particular project. She considers isolated product inventions (both by a single innovator and by interacting firms), cumulative inventions (accessories, applications, and improvements), and imitation. In addition to the competitive approach that this research area has until recently taken almost exclusively, the chapter discusses the cooperative approach, as exemplified by research joint ventures.

The Empirical Products session contained a joint paper by Alan Kirman and Louis Phlips (Chapter 13). Excluding work dealing with multiple industries, they survey empirical studies of markets for single products. After discussing the definition of a market, these authors cover conjectural variation as a parameter to measure the discrepancy between the behaviour of a firm and perfectly competitive behaviour, price discrimination (including cost allocation rules based on the Aumann–Shapley value), dynamic game theory, adverse selection, and auctions. They explain that game-theoretic dynamic models are very difficult to treat empirically because of the need for very long-run precise data and because of the complications caused by endogenously timed discrete price changes and by contracts that may lead to particular collusive equilibria in, for instance, the Folk Theorem. (This is the result claiming that any feasible and individually rational payoffs are equilibrium outcomes in an infinitely repeated non-cooperative game.) An extended discussion of testing for lemon effects in the used-truck market raises questions about which variables should be included as controls and the extent to which dealer warranties have solved the asymmetric information problem. Kirman and Phlips regret the large gap between theory and empirical work in industrial organization; they conclude by blaming the gap on data difficulties and the shortcomings of theory.

The Microeconomics of the Household session is represented by Chapter 14 by Nina Smith, Ian Walker, and Niels Westergård-Nielsen. They examine the labour supply behaviour of single mothers in Denmark and the United Kingdom and find that the presence of pre-school children has opposite effects in these two countries. Cross-section data are used in a bivariate probit model in which the labour force participation decision is followed by a choice between part-time and full-time work. Policy conclusions are drawn based on the changes in net income inequality that would result from replacing the welfare system by (equally costly) lump-sum transfers.

Finally, the History of Thought session features a paper by Christian Schmidt (Chapter 15) that re-examines Cournot's contribution to economics. The author argues that previous interpretations (beginning with Bertrand and including Shubik's retrospective) of Cournot's duopoly model are biased and misleading. In particular, he credits Cournot with introducing mathematical analysis into economics and with recognizing the distinction between complements and substitutes.

The collection of papers represented here strongly suggests that microeconomics remains an active and challenging research area in many countries. Different approaches are taken, including a healthy re-examination of the fundamentals of economic behaviour. However, perhaps the general technical level of the surveys is misleading, in that current research articles tend to be considerably more formal mathematically, while still focusing on the sorts of economic questions addressed in this volume. Despite such minor qualifications regarding the representativeness of this collection, my overall impression is that microeconomic theory is indeed thriving as a fascinating and useful central part of economic science.

Note

1. This work was supported, in part, by the National Science Foundation, the Curtis Carlson Professorship in Economics of the University of Minnesota, and the Federal Reserve Bank of Minneapolis. The views expressed herein are those of the author and not necessarily those of the Federal Reserve Bank of Minneapolis or the Federal Reserve System.

Part I

Plenary Lecture

1 Profit Maximization and Imperfect Competition

Birgit Grodal[1]

UNIVERSITY OF COPENHAGEN

1.1 INTRODUCTION

In most economic literature, firms are assumed to maximize profits. If there is perfect competition and a complete market structure in the economy, this objective of firms has a sound economic interpretation. Profit maximization is well defined, it serves the needs of the shareholders, and shareholders unanimously instruct the managers of firms to maximize profits.

The purpose of this Chapter is to prove that profit maximization becomes an arbitrary objective when imperfect competition prevails in the economy. In particular, the profit maximization hypothesis is not justified by the preferences of shareholders. An overview of the different approaches to imperfect competition in general equilibrium theory can be found in Hart (1985). We use the model of imperfect competition à la Cournot (introduced by Gabszewicz and Vial, 1972), where the quantity-setting firms are assumed to have full knowledge about the price implications of their choices of production plans. However, one should emphasize that the arbitrariness of profit maximization is generally true also in models with competition à la Bertrand, and in models of imperfect competition based on subjective demand functions.

Most general equilibrium models give rise to relative prices only, without determining the price level. However, in order to define the profit functions of the firms, the absolute prices must be known. When perfect competition prevails, the price normalization (e.g. the choice of numeraire) does not have any real effect, but when firms are able to influence the relative prices via their choice of production plans and the firms maximize profits, the equilibria depend crucially on the way prices are normalized. The dependence of Cournot–Walras equilibria on the prices normalization was also noticed by Gabszewicz and Vial (1972).

Grodal (1984) showed that not only do the equilibria depend on the normalization of prices, but also that essentially any profile of production plans, efficient or not, can be obtained as an equilibrium by a suitable choice of price normalization. We shall repeat the argument in this Chapter. Recently Böhm (1990) has published similar observations.

This indeterminacy of the equilibria implies that even the most basic feature of the economy, the existence of an equilibrium, may change according to which normalization rule is used (see Dierker and Grodal, 1986).

Roberts (1980) has analyzed the limits of Cournot–Walras equilibria when all firms become arbitrarily small relative to the entire economy. We show that the price normalization may even affect the limit. Indeed, we give a non-pathological example of an economy where the set of limit points depends on the normalization rule which is followed.

Clearly these results demonstrate that firms should not maximize profits using an arbitrary normalization rule. Profits are significant only when measured in relation to their purchasing power. When firms, by their strategic behaviour, influence the price system, they also influence the prices confronting their shareholders.

If a firm has only one shareholder, the firm has a natural objective – namely maximizing the utility of the owner. Therefore, if every firm has just one owner, one can define an equilibrium based on the utility functions of the owners. Such equilibria are well defined and are, of course, independent of how prices are normalized (see Dierker and Grodal, 1986).

If a firm has many shareholders, there is generally no natural way to deduce the objective of the firm from the preferences of the shareholders. In the last part of the Chapter we briefly discuss assumptions which imply that a firm can find a way of normalizing the prices such that maximization of profits using this normalization is justified by the preferences of its shareholders.

1.2 PERFECT COMPETITION AND COMPLETE MARKETS

Consider a private ownership economy with commodity space $\mathbb{R}^\ell$, n firms and m consumers. Each firm $j = 1,\ldots,n$ has a compact and convex production set $Y_j \subset \mathbb{R}^\ell$. Each of the m consumers has a convex and closed consumption set $X_i \subset \mathbb{R}^\ell$ and a continuous, monotone, and strictly quasiconcave utility function $u_i \colon X_i \to \mathbb{R}$. Moreover, we assume there is private ownership, i.e. each consumer has a vector of initial resources $\omega_i \in X_i$ and shares in the firm

$$(\theta_{ij})_{j=1}^n, \text{ where } \theta_{ij} \geq 0 \text{ and } \sum_{i=1}^m \theta_{ij} = 1 \text{ for all } j = 1, \ldots n$$

Let us assume all consumers and producers take the prices of the commodities as given, and there is a complete set of markets. We can then define an equilibrium in the economy – a Walras equilibrium – as a state $(x_i^*)_{i=1}^m$, $(y_j^*)_{j=1}^n$ and a price system $p^* \in \mathbb{R}_+^\ell 1\{0\}$ such that

1. for all firms $j = 1, \ldots, n$,
   y_j^* maximizes profits measured in the price system p^*;
2. for all consumers $i = 1, \ldots, m$,
   x_i^* is the consumption plan which gives the maximal utility, when the utility function u_i is maximized over the budget set determined by p^* and the income

$$w_i(p^*) = p^*\omega_i + \sum_{j=1}^n \theta_{ij} p^* y_i^*;$$

3. for all the commodities supply is equal to demand.

In such an economy only relative prices matter. Indeed, if y_j maximizes profits when the price system is p, the same will be the case if prices are λp, where $\lambda > 0$. (Of course, the profit will be multiplied with λ.) Also for the consumers. If x_i maximizes utility when the price system is p then, due to the private ownership, x_i will also maximize utility when prices are λp.

Therefore if $((x_i^*)_{i=1}^m, (y_j^*)_{j=1}^n, p^*)$ is an equilibrium, then for any $\lambda > 0$, $((x_i^*)_{i=1}^m, (y_j^*)_{j=1}^n, \lambda p^*)$ is also an equilibrium. Thus, in an equilibrium only the relative prices are determined. One might say that the model is incomplete. However, it is crucial to note that it does not matter how one closes the model, that is how one determines the absolute prices from the relative prices. This will have no real effect.

In the equilibrium we have demanded that y_j^* should be a profit-maximizing production plan for the firm j. This can be justified on two quite different grounds. First, we know that when firms maximize profits with respect to the same price system the outcome will be efficient. However, more important, profit maximization can be justified internally in the model. Let us consider any shareholder in the firm j, $(\theta_{ij} > 0)$. Since the shareholder and the firm take the same price system as given, the shareholder will insist that the firm chooses a production plan which maximizes profits. Any production plan which does not maximize profits will be strictly worse for the shareholder. Consequently, shareholders unanimously instruct the manager of the firm to choose a production plan which maximizes profits. Finally, we know that under the assumption of perfect competition and the existence of a complete set of commodity markets, as assumed above, there is no need for trading assets in the firms. The price of a firm will, in equilibrium, be identical to the maximal profit it can obtain. With these asset prices all the consumers can just as well use the complete set of commodity markets: i.e. the market for assets is redundant.

The purpose of this chapter is to show that the above conclusions change drastically when imperfect competition prevails in the economy. We use a model where firms influence prices *à la* Cournot, but parallel conclusions can be drawn in most models of imperfect competition.

1.3 IMPERFECT COMPETITION *À LA* COURNOT

We shall assume the same basic model as before, but now assume that firms can influence the price system in the economy via their choice of production plans. We then prove that when firms maximize profits, the outcome is entirely dependent on how prices are normalized.

General equilibrium theory does not give any insight into how prices are normalized. However, even if we had a theory determining the absolute prices (e.g. money prices or prices in relation to a consumption index) it might, as we shall see, be very 'irrational' for the firm to maximize profits with respect to these absolute prices.

We shall define a normalization rule for the price systems as a function which determines the absolute prices from the relative prices. Formally, letting $\Delta = \{p \in \mathbb{R}_+^\ell \mid \sum_{h=1}^{\ell} p_h = 1\}$, we define:

Definition 1 *A normalization rule is a continuous mapping* $\alpha: \Delta \to \mathbb{R}_+^\ell \setminus \{0\}$, *such that for all* $p \in \Delta$,

$$\frac{1}{\sum_{h=1}^{\ell} \alpha_h(p)} \alpha(p) = p$$

In the spirit of Gabszewicz and Vial (1972) we shall define imperfect competition à *la* Cournot in the following way. When a firm j is considering which production plan to choose, it imagines the price systems which will emerge when the other firms have chosen some fixed production plans $\bar{y}_k$, $k \neq j$, and the firm j itself chooses different production plans $y_j \in Y_j$. Indeed, it imagines the equilibrium price systems, which can emerge in the pure exchange economy defined by the m price taking consumers each endowed with the initial resources

$$\omega_i (\bar{y}_1, \ldots, y_j, \ldots, \bar{y}_n) = \omega_i + \sum_{k \neq j} \theta_{ik} \bar{y}_k + \theta_{ij} y_j$$

Firm j will then, after having imagined the consequences of all the production plans $y_j \in Y_j$, choose a production plan $\bar{y}_j$ such that its profits are maximized.

It should be noted that we could also have used this thought process to define a Walras equilibrium for the economy. Indeed, the state $((x_i^*)_{i=1}^m, (y_j^*)_{j=1}^n)$ and the price system p^* is a Walras equilibrium if and only if p^* is an equilibrium price system in the pure exchange economy defined by $\omega_i(y_1^*, \ldots, y_j^*, \ldots, y_n^*)$, $i = 1, \ldots, m$ and moreover, y_j^* maximizes profit with respect to the fixed price system p^* for all firms j.

Assumptions which guarantee that there exists an equilibrium in a pure exchange economy have been intensively studied (see, e.g., Debreu, 1982), and we shall in the present context not worry about existence of equilibria in the imagined pure exchange economies. Let $W(y_1, \ldots, y_n)$ denote the relative price systems $p \in \Delta$, which are equilibrium price systems when firms respectively choose the production plans $y_j \in Y_j$ and notice that $W(y_1, \ldots, y_n)$ typically consists of finitely many price systems (see Debreu, 1970). Only in very special examples will there be a unique price system in $W(y_1, \ldots, y_n)$. (Compare Figure 1.1, where for convenience we have used the relative prices $p = (p_1, p_2, \ldots, 1)$).

We therefore define a *price selection* as a function $p : \prod_{j=1}^{n} Y_j \to \Delta$ such that $p(y_1, \ldots, y_n) \in W(y_1, \ldots, y_n)$ for all production profiles

$(y_1, \ldots, y_n) \in \prod_{j=1}^{n} Y_j$.

In order to define firms' profit functions for a given price selection p, we still have to define the absolute price system corresponding to the

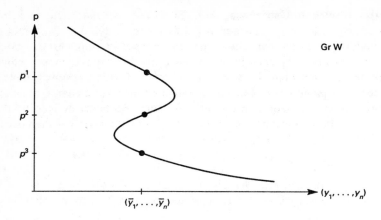

Figure 1.1

relative price system $p(y_1,\ldots,y_n) \in \Delta$, for all $(y_1,\ldots,y_n) \in \prod\limits_{j=1}^{n} Y_j$, i.e

we have to specify a normalization rule α.

The price function corresponding to the price selection p and the normalization rule α is the function p^α: $\prod\limits_{j=1}^{n} Yj \to \mathbb{R}_+^\ell$, where

$$p^\alpha(y_1,\ldots,y_n) = \alpha(p(y_1,\ldots,y_n)).$$

We can now make the following definition:

Definition 2 *The n production plans $\bar{y}_1 \in Y_1,\ldots,\bar{y}_n \in Y_n$ is a Cournot – Walras equilibrium associated with the price selection p and the normalization rule α if for all firms $j = 1,\ldots, n$*

$$p^\alpha(\bar{y}_1,\ldots,\bar{y}_j,\ldots,\bar{y}_n) \cdot \bar{y}_j \geq p^\alpha(\bar{y}_1,\ldots,y_j,\ldots,\bar{y}_n) \cdot y_j$$
for all $y_j \in Y_j$.

In a Cournot–Walras equilibrium associated with the price selection p and the normalization rule α the firms imagine that the price system changes according to the function p^α, and they maximize profits given the production plans of the other firms.

1.3.1. Indeterminacy

As mentioned in Section 1.2., when there is perfect competition in the economy it does not matter how prices are normalized. However, when imperfect competition prevails, almost all production profiles – efficient or not – can be rationalized as a Cournot–Walras equilibrium for a given price selection just by changing the normalization rule.

The reason for this is simple. Let us compare the profit functions for firm j, using two different normalization rules. Let $\bar{\alpha}$ be defined by $\bar{\alpha}(p) = p$ for all p, i.e. prices are normalized such that $\sum_{h=1}^{\ell} p_h = 1$.

Secondly, consider the normalization rule $\alpha(p) = \left(1, \dfrac{p_2}{p_1}, \ldots, \dfrac{p_\ell}{p_1}\right)$ i.e. prices are normalized using the first commodity as numéraire commodity. If we compare the corresponding two profit functions for firm j we see that these are quite different. Indeed

$$\pi_j^{\bar{\alpha}}(\bar{y}_1, \ldots, y_j, \ldots, \bar{y}_n) = \sum_{h=1}^{\ell} p_h(\bar{y}_1, \ldots, y_j, \ldots, \bar{y}_n)\, y_{jh}, \text{ and}$$

$$\pi_j^{\alpha}(\bar{y}_1, \ldots, y_j, \ldots, \bar{y}_n) = \sum_{h=1}^{\ell} \frac{p_h(\bar{y}_1, \ldots, y_j, \ldots, \bar{y}_n)}{p_1(\bar{y}_1, \ldots, y_j, \ldots, \bar{y}_n)}\, y_{jh}$$

$$= \frac{\pi_j^{\bar{\alpha}}(\bar{y}_1, \ldots, y_j, \ldots, \bar{y}_n)}{p_1(\bar{y}_1, \ldots, y_j, \ldots, \bar{y}_n)}$$

Clearly, maximizing $\pi_j^{\bar{\alpha}}(\bar{y}_1, \ldots, \bar{y}_{j-1}, \cdot, \bar{y}_{j+1}, \ldots, \bar{y}_n)$ over Y_j is generally different from maximizing $\pi_j^{\alpha}(\bar{y}_1, \ldots, \bar{y}_{j-1}, \cdot, \bar{y}_{j+1}, \ldots, \bar{y}_n)$ over Y_j. Therefore the Cournot–Walras equilibria associated with p and α will generally be different from the Cournot–Walras equilibria associated with p and $\bar{\alpha}$.

Now let p be a price selection from W and consider some arbitrary production plans $\bar{y}_1, \ldots, \bar{y}_n$ for the firms and let $\bar{p} = p(\bar{y}_1, \ldots, \bar{y}_n)$. We shall say that the production plans $(\bar{y}_1, \ldots, \bar{y}_n)$ are *p-dominated* if for one of the firms there exist convergent sequences $(y_j^n)_n$ and $(q_j^n)_n$, $y_j^n \in Y_j$, $q_j^n \in \Delta$, such that $q_j^n = p(\bar{y}_1, \ldots, y_j^n, \ldots, \bar{y}_n)$, $\lim_n q_j^n = \bar{p}$, and $\lim_n q_j^n y_j^n > \bar{p}\, \bar{y}_j$. Thus the production plans $(\bar{y}_1, \ldots, \bar{y}_n)$ are *p-dominated* if for one of the firms there exists a convergent sequence of production plans, such that the corresponding sequence of price systems coverges to $\bar{p}$ (the price system corresponding to $\bar{y}_j$) and the production plans in the limit give a higher profit than $\bar{y}_j$. If the price selection $p(\cdot)$ is continuous, then this condition simplifies. Indeed, the production plans $(\bar{y}_1, \ldots, \bar{y}_n)$ are p-dominated, if for one of the firms there exists a production plan $y_j \in Y_j$ such that $p(\bar{y}_1, \ldots, y_j, \ldots, \bar{y}_n) = \bar{p}$ and $\bar{p} y_j > \bar{p} \bar{y}_j$. Thus the production plans $(\bar{y}_1, \ldots, \bar{y}_n)$ are p-dominated, if for one of the firms there exists a production plan $y_j \in Y_j$, which gives exactly the same relative price system *and* a higher profit. Clearly, production plans $(\bar{y}_1, \ldots, \bar{y}_n)$, which are p-dominated, can never be obtained as a Cournot–Walras equilibrium associated with the price selection p.

To assume that production plans are not p-dominated puts very few restrictions on the production plans. For example, if $p(\bar{y}_1, \ldots, y_j, \ldots, \bar{y}_n)$: $Y_j \to \Delta$ is injective for all firms, then $(\bar{y}_1, \ldots, \bar{y}_n)$ is not p-dominated, since no other production choice of the firm j gives exactly the same relative price system $\bar{p}$.

It should also be noticed that p-dominated is different from inefficient. When a firm moves to a more efficient production plan the price system will usually change. Therefore, a more efficient production plan does not have to p-dominate.

We now have:

Proposition 1 *Assume that the production sets Y_j, $j = 1, \ldots n$, are compact. Let p be an arbitrary price selection, and let $(\bar{y}_1, \ldots, \bar{y}_n)$*

$$\in \prod_{j=1}^{n} Y_j \quad \text{be arbitrary production plans for the firms, which are not } p\text{-}$$

dominated and which give positive profits. Then there exists a normalization rule α such that $(\bar{y}_1, \ldots, \bar{y}_n)$ is a Cournot–Walras equilibrium associated with p and α.

Proof Let $(\bar{y}_1, \ldots, \bar{y}_n) \in \prod_{j=1}^{n} Y_j$ be arbitrary production plans for

the firms, which are not p-dominated; and let $\bar{p} = p(\bar{y}_1, \ldots, \bar{y}_n)$.

For each firm j we define

$$Q_j = \{q \in \Delta| \text{ there exists } y_j \in Y \text{ such that } p(\bar{y}_1, \ldots, y_j, \ldots,$$
$$\bar{y}_n) = q\},$$

and a continuous function $v_j : \Delta \to \mathbb{R}_{++}$, such that

$$v_j(q) \geq \sup\{q \cdot y_j \mid p(\bar{y}_1, \ldots, y_j, \ldots, \bar{y}_n) = q\} \text{ for all } q \in Q_j,$$

$$v_j(\bar{p}) = \bar{p} \cdot \bar{y}_j, \text{ and } v_j(q) \geq v_j(\bar{p}) > 0 \text{ for all } q \in \Delta$$

Indeed, since Y_j is compact we can define the function $h_j(\cdot): Q_j \to \mathbb{R}$ by $h_j(q) = \sup \{qy_j \mid p(\bar{y}_1, \ldots, y_j, \ldots, \bar{y}_n) = q\}$. Of course, $h_j(\cdot)$ does not have to be continuous. However, since the production plans $(\bar{y}_1, \ldots, \bar{y}_n)$ are not p-dominated, we have that for all $\varepsilon > 0$ there exists $\delta > 0$ such that $q \in Q_j$ and $\|\bar{p} - q\| < \delta$ imply $h_j(q) \leq \bar{p} \, \bar{y}_j + \varepsilon$.

By considering a sequence $(\varepsilon_n)_n$, $\varepsilon_n \to 0$, and the corresponding sequence $(\delta_n)_n$, where we choose $\delta_n \leq \frac{1}{n}$, we can, using that $h_j(\cdot)$ is bounded, construct a piecewise linear function $v_j(\cdot)$ with the wanted properties.

We now choose an arbitrary continuous function $\beta: \Delta \to \mathbb{R}_{++}$, which has a unique maximum in $\bar{p}$, and define the continuous function α: $\Delta \to \mathbb{R}_+^{\ell}$ by

$$\alpha(q) = \frac{\beta(q)}{\prod\limits_{j=1}^{n} v_j(q)} \, q$$

The function α is the wanted normalization rule. Indeed α is continuous, and for any firm j and $y_j \in Y_j$

$$\pi_j^{\alpha}(\bar{y}_1, \ldots, y_j, \ldots, \bar{y}_n)$$

$$= \left[\frac{\beta(p(\bar{y}_1, \ldots, y_j, \ldots, \bar{y}_n))}{\prod\limits_{t=1}^{n} v_t(p(\bar{y}_1, \ldots, y_j, \ldots, \bar{y}_n))} \right] p(\bar{y}_1, \ldots, y_j, \ldots, \bar{y}_n) \cdot y_j \leq$$

$$\frac{\beta(p(\bar{y}_1, \ldots, y_j, \ldots, \bar{y}_n))}{\prod\limits_{\substack{t=1 \\ t \neq j}}^{n} v_t(p(\bar{y}_1, \ldots, y_j, \ldots, \bar{y}_n))} \leq \frac{\beta(\bar{p})}{\prod\limits_{\substack{t=1 \\ t \neq j}}^{n} v_t(\bar{p})}$$

However, letting $y_j = \bar{y}_j$ we get

$$\pi_j^\alpha(\bar{y}_1, \ldots, \bar{y}_j, \ldots, \bar{y}_n) = \frac{\beta(\bar{p})}{\prod_{\substack{t=1 \\ t \neq j}}^n v_t(\bar{p})}$$

Therefore $(\bar{y}_1, \ldots, \bar{y}_n)$ is a Cournot–Walras equilibrium associated with p and α.   QED

This proposition shows that when firms take into account that their choice of production plan influences the price system, profit maximization becomes arbitrary. The conclusions are in complete contrast to the conclusions in an economy with perfect competition. We also remark that if we had allowed the price normalization to depend on the production choices of the firms, all production plans $(\bar{y}_1, \ldots, \bar{y}_n)$, which give positive profits, can be obtained as Cournot–Walras equilibria.

1.3.2. Choice of Normalization Rule and Existence of Equilibrium

Since we have the indeterminacy result above, the question whether a Cournot–Walras equilibrium associated with a price selection and some price normalization exists is uninteresting. Indeed consider the price selection p and any production plans $(\bar{y}_1, \ldots, \bar{y}_n)$ which are not p-dominated. Since $(\bar{y}_1, \ldots, \bar{y}_n)$ can be obtained as a Cournot–Walras equilibrium with respect to p and some normalization rule, there of course exist Cournot–Walras equilibria with respect to some normalization rule. However, we shall see that the existence of a Cournot–Walras equilibrium associated with a fixed normalization rule depends crucially on the choice of normalization rule.

If p is a continuous price selection and α is an arbitrary normalization rule, there will, of course (under suitable compactness assumptions), always exist a Cournot–Walras equilibrium in mixed strategies with respect to p and α. In a mixed strategy equilibrium we allow the firms to choose probability measures on the production set. However, for some normalization rules there will exist Cournot–Walras equilibria (in pure strategies) and for others only equilibria in mixed strategies. Roberts and Sonnenschein (1977) give examples where the last is the case. In the light of the indeterminacy result above this is not surprising. Of course, the profit function associated with p and a normalization rule α does not have to be quasiconcave, a property which (in general) is needed in order to ensure existence of a Nash equilibrium. However, it could very well be that there does not exist a continu-

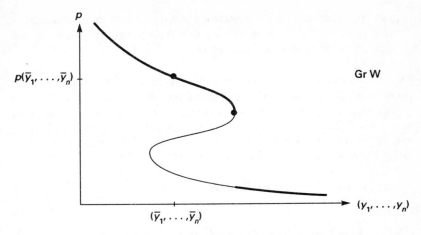

W does not have a continuous selection. There will be three
admissible price selections. One of the admissible price selections is
indicated in the figure.

Figure 1.2

ous price selection from W. Indeed, if we could ensure that for all
choices of production plans for the firms there was a unique relative
equilibrium price system in the corresponding exchange economy, then
W itself would be a continuous price selection. But, as was noticed
earlier, this will be true only in very special examples. If for some
choices of production plans there is more than one relative equilibrium
price system, there will generally not exist a continuous price selection. Therefore, the question arises: What happens if a continuous price
selection does not exist?

In order to restrict the number of discontinuity points for price selections let us define an *admissible price selection from W* as a price selection
p, which avoids discontinuities: i.e. only in points $(y_1, \ldots, y_n)$, where
there does not exist a continuous extension of p to a neighbourhood of
$(y_1, \ldots, y_n)$, is p allowed to have a discontinuity. See Figure 1.2.

In Dierker and Grodal (1986) an example is given, where:

1. there exists a normalization rule $\bar{\alpha}$ such that for all admissible price
   selections p there exists a Cournot–Walras equilibrium associated
   with p and $\bar{\alpha}$ (even the same for all the admissible price selections);

2. there exists a normalization rule $\bar{\alpha}$, such that for all admissible
   price selections p there is no Cournot–Walras equilibrium associated
   with p and $\bar{\alpha}$;

3. for all admissible price selections p there exists a normalization rule α, such that there is no Cournot–Walras equilibrium in mixed strategies associated with p and α.

Of course, property 3 depends crucially on the fact that in the example there is no continuous price selection from W. The example clearly demonstrates that it is not only the equilibrium production plans which depend on the normalization rule used. Also the question of the existence of an equilibrium for a fixed normalization rule depends crucially on the normalization rule.

1.3.3. Limits of Cournot–Walras Equilibria

The limits of Cournot–Walras equilibria, when all firms become arbitrarily small relative to the entire economy, have been analyzed thoroughly by Roberts (1980). He considers the sequence of economies which is generated when the original economy is replicated r times, $r \to +\infty$, and looks at the corresponding sequences of average production plans for each type of firm $j = 1, \ldots, n$. Roberts characterizes the set of limits of Cournot–Walras equilibria, and especially links this set to the set of Walras equilibria in the original economy.

Roberts works with a fixed normalization rule for the price systems. We shall show the normalization may affect the limit. We do this by giving a robust example of an even, strongly regular, economy where this is the case.

A Walras equilibrium in the economy is said to be a regular Walras equilibrium if the Jacobian matrix of the excess demand function is regular (has rank $\ell - 1$) at the equilibrium price system. In our (imagined) pure exchange economies we can also distinguish between regular and singular equilibria. Regular equilibria are equilibria where the Jacobian matrix of the excess demand function in the pure exchange economy is regular at the equilibrium price system. Singular equilibria are equilibria where the Jacobian matrix is singular. It should be noticed that whether equilibria are regular or singular depend only on relative prices, i.e. it is independent of the normalization rule. Also as we remarked in Section 1.2, a Walras equilibrium is especially an equilibrium of the corresponding (imagined) pure exchange economy.

We shall say an economy is *strongly regular* if all Walras equilibria are regular, and moreover are regular equilibria in the corresponding pure exchange economies (see Roberts, 1980).

In order to study the limits of Cournot–Walras equilibria we first remark that any limit of a sequence of Cournot–Walras equilibria associated with a price selection and a normalization rule will be an equilibrium in the pure exchange economy corresponding to the limit productions plans (see Roberts, 1980, theorem 1).

Roberts moreover shows that the points which are limits of Cournot –Walras equilibria for some price selection, and which are also regular equilibria of the corresponding pure exchange economies, are exactly the set of Walras equilibria (see Roberts, 1980, theorem 2 and theorem 3). Hence the set consisting of the limits of Cournot–Walras equilibria which are regular equilibria in the pure exchange economies, is independent of the normalization rule. This follows since the set of Walras equilibria depends on relative prices only.

However, Roberts also shows (1980 theorem 4) that there might be limits of Cournot–Walras equilibria which are not Walras equilibria. It is these limits of Cournot–Walras equilibria which depend on the normalization rule.

Proposition 2 *There exist non-pathological strongly regular economies in which the set of limits of Cournot–Walras equilibria associated with a price selection and a normalization rule depends on the normalization rule which is followed.*

Proof Consider exactly the same example as the one which is used to prove theorem 4 in Roberts (1980). If we change the normalization rule such that profit for a firm is higher in a neighbourhood of C' than in the neighbourhood of C, then (C, y) will no longer be a limit of a sequence of Cournot–Walras equilibria.   QED

The basic reason for Proposition 2 is simple. Consider a price selection as in Figure 1.3, and assume that there is only one type of firm. Assume $\bar{p}$ is an equilibrium price system for the pure exchange economy defined by the average production plan $\bar{y}$. In the neighbourhood of $\bar{y}$ each of the firms will have market power independently of how large the economy is. Therefore their behaviour is influenced not only by the relative price system but also by the absolute prices. Indeed, if we normalize the price system such that the profits for the relative price systems on the upper fold are essentially higher than on the lower fold, then we can get $\bar{y}$ to be a limit point of Cournot–Walras equilibria. If, on the other hand, we normalize prices such that profits on the lower fold are essentially higher than above, then $\bar{y}$ will not be a limit point of Cournot–Walras equilibria.

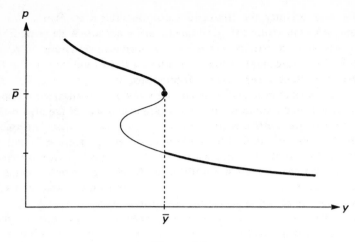

Figure 1.3

The proposition shows that it is not only in a fixed finite economy that the Cournot–Walras equilibria depends on the normalization rule. This may be the case even when the economy is replicated such that all firms become arbitrarily small relative to the entire economy.

1.3.4   Is Profit Maximization in the Interest of the Shareholders? The Case of a Single Owner

We shall in this part consider a firm which has a single owner, i.e. there exists one consumer for whom the share in the firm is one. We shall moreover assume that for some reason (e.g. an extended economic theory where not only the relative prices but also the absolute prices are determined) there is a normalization rule α for the price systems, $\alpha\colon \Delta \to \mathbb{R}^{\ell}_{+}$.

In the case of pure competition this one owner will maximize his utility, as a consumer, if and only if the firm chooses a production plan which maximizes profits with respect to the normalization rule α. Repeating from Section 1.2, since the firm cannot influence prices and since the owner takes the same price system as given, a production plan $y_j \in Y_j$ will maximize profits with respect to the normalization rule α, if and only if y_j is the best choice of production plan, when the owner maximizes his utility function.

Now let us look at imperfect competition. Since there is only one owner of the firm, the firm has a natural objective, namely to maximize the utility of the owner.

One way to interpret this criterion is that the firm should choose a production plan so that the utility of the owner when he trades at the Walrasian market is maximized, i.e. the firm should choose a production plan to maximize the indirect utility of the owner.

Of course, there are other interpretations. The owner can, for example, take into account that the firm he owns can produce commodities and deliver them directly to him. Compare Gabszewicz and Michel (1992). Also, since the firm, and thereby the owner, has information on W, the owner can behave strategically on the market in the pure exchange economy. However, allowing these possibilities, it becomes very important how the owner constrains himself as a consumer in the pure exchange economy. The situation can easily arise where the only equilibrium is a Walras equilibrium in the original economy or where, again, any production plan can be obtained as part of an equilibrium. We shall therefore restrict ourselves to the case where the objective of the firm, the owner, is to maximize the indirect utility. That is, if consumer i is the owner of firm j, firm j will choose a production plan $y_j \in Y_j$ such as to maximize

$$v_i(p(\bar{y}_1, \ldots, y_j, \ldots, \bar{y}_n), \, p(\bar{y}_1, \ldots, y_j, \ldots, \bar{y}_n) \cdot (y_j + \omega_i))$$

where $v_i \colon \mathbb{R}_+^\ell \backslash \{0\} \times \mathbb{R} \to \mathbb{R}$ is the indirect utility function of consumer i.

Since the indirect utility function is homogeneous of degree zero, this objective of the firm will be independent of the normalization rule α. Thus in an economy where all firms are owned by a single consumer and where all firms maximize the utility of the owner, the equilibria will depend only on the price selection and *not* on the choice of normalization rule. The choice of normalization rule does not have any real effect.

We want to stress that the reason for considering these *Utility-Cournot –Walras equilibria* associated with a price selection p is *not* the desire to include some new variables for the firms – 'psychic incomes' etc. – but simply that profit functions are arbitrary, unless profits are related to the price system with which the shareholders are confronted.

Since Utility-Cournot–Walras equilibria associated with a price selection p depends on relative prices only, the question whether such an equilibrium exists is well defined. However, as the indirect utility function of the owner of a firm is not necessarily a quasiconcave function of the production plan of the firm, there need not exist an equilibrium in pure strategies. Furthermore, since there need not exist a continuous price selection p from the Walrasian correspondence W, examples can be given in which there does not exist a Utility-Cournot–Walras equilibrium in mixed strategies. See Dierker and Grodal (1986).

It should be clear that Cournot–Walras equilibria and Utility-Cournot –Walras equilibria are different. Only if the normalization rule α is related in a very special way to the utility functions of the owners of the firms will a Cournot–Walras equilibrium associated with p and α be a Utility-Cournot–Walras equilibrium associated with p. Of course, our indeterminacy result shows that any Utility-Cournot–Walras equilibrium associated with a price selection p can be obtained as a Cournot –Walras equilibrium associated with p and an appropriate chosen normalization rule $\bar{\alpha}$. This follows, since a Utility-Cournot–Walras equilibrium with respect to p cannot be p-dominated. However, for the arbitrary, but fixed, normalization rule α the equilibrium condition of a firm j in the two types of equilibria is, of course, very different.

Let us now consider the two different objectives of firm j: profit maximization with respect to the price function p^α, and maximization of the indirect utility function given p and hence p^α.

Since the firm j takes the production plans of the other firms as given we can in the expression for the price selection omit the other firms' production plans. Also since we consider a fixed firm j we shall also omit the index j.

Now if the firm chooses a production plan to maximize profits associated with p^α, it solves the following maximization problem:

$$\max_{y \in Y} p^\alpha(y) \cdot y \qquad (1.1)$$

and if the firm maximizes the utility of the owner, it solves the following maximization problem:

$$\max_{y \in Y} v(p(y), p(y) \cdot (y + \omega)) \qquad (1.2)$$

where v is the indirect utility function of the owner. Of course, the problem (1.2) does not change if we substitute p^α for p (i.e. we change the normalization rule). In the following we shall for convenience assume $\omega = 0$.

Now consider a solution $\bar{y}$ to (1.1), and let $\bar{p} = p(\bar{y})$ and $\bar{\pi}^\alpha = \alpha(\bar{p}) \cdot \bar{y}$. Looking at the first-order condition to (1.2) we see that only in the exceptional case where

$$D_y p^\alpha(\bar{y}) D_p v(\alpha(\bar{p}), \bar{\pi}^\alpha) = 0 \qquad (1.3)$$

can we have that the solution $\bar{y}$ to (1.1) is also a solution to (1.2). Of course, (1.3) especially is satisfied if the firm cannot influence the prices, i.e. if $D_y p^\alpha(\bar{y}) = 0$.

By Roy's identity we see that the condition (1.3) is identical to

$$D_y p^\alpha(\bar{y}) \, \xi(\bar{p}, \bar{p} \cdot \bar{y}) = 0$$

where ξ is the demand function of the owner. In the case $\alpha(p) = p$ for all p (i.e. prices are normalized such that $\sum_{h=1}^{\ell} p_h = 1$) and rank $D_y p = \ell - 1$, this amounts to $\xi(\bar{p}, \bar{p} \cdot \bar{y}) = (\bar{p} \cdot \bar{y}, \ldots, \bar{p} \cdot \bar{y})$. That is, the owner must in the profit-maximizing equilibrium $\bar{y}$ consume equal amounts of all the commodities, or else he will be able to find another production plan which gives him higher utility. This is intuitively clear; since the first-order change in profit is zero the owner wants to change the price system in such a way that the price of the commodity of which he consumes the most decreases, and the price of the commodity of which he consumes the least increased correspondingly. Only in the case where the owner, when the firm maximizes profits, consumes the same amount of all commodities does he not want to change the production plan.

The remarks above show that when there is a single owner of a firm and the firm influences prices *à la* Cournot, the firm should not maximize profit, but instead maximize the utility of the owner.

1.3.5 Profit Maximization? A Single Firm with Many Shareholders

When there are many shareholders of the firm there is no natural objective function for the firm. This is the case even if all shareholders have the same homogeneous utility function but differ in the shares they have in the firm or differ in their initial resources. If the shareholders have the same utility function and the same property rights, then, of course, we can use the common indirect utility function as in the last section.

When we are not in this extreme case, we might try to resolve the problem by letting the firm choose a production plan which is Pareto optimal according to the preferences of the shareholders; or to get a less arbitrary production plan one might model a game among the shareholders for determining the production plan.

However, it is also clear that there *are* examples where the firm (imagines that it) influences the price system in a special way, and where all shareholders agree to a special objective function for the firm. It might even be the case that the firm can choose an objective function, which is to maximize profits with respect to a firm and shareholder specific normalization rule. Consider, for example, the case where production plans of the firm only involve the commodities $L_0 \subset \{1, \ldots, \ell\}$ and shareholders only consume and own commodities $L_1 \subset \{1, \ldots, \ell\}$ where $L_0 \cap L_1 = \emptyset$, *and* the *relative* prices of the consumed commodities L_1 are *independent* of the production plan of the firm. In this case, of course, the firm can choose any of the commodities in L_1 as numeraire, and all shareholders will unanimously agree to this objective function.

A special case where these assumptions are satisfied is when all shareholders in the firm own and consume only one specific commodity h, which the firm does not produce. In this case maximizing profit, choosing commodity h as numeraire, is identical to maximizing the indirect utility function of each shareholder. Another example is where the firm produces a commodity which the shareholders do not own and consume, and where the choice of production plan does not influence the relative prices of the commodities that are different from the one the firm produces. In this case the firm can choose any of the commodities which they do not produce as numeraire. The Island model of Hart (1985) is an example of a special structure where the above conditions are approximately satisfied.

1.3.6. Profit Maximization? The Case of Many Firms

It might look innocuous to make assumptions like those in Section 1.3.5, and therefore to use profit maximization with respect to a firm-specific normalization rule as the objective for the firm. However, such vague assumptions are extremely unrealistic as soon as they are made not only for a single firm but for all firms which influence prices *à la* Cournot. The assumptions contain statements about how the equilibrium price systems in a pure exchange economy change as a consequence of changes in initial resources of the consumers. We know, however, very little about this sort of comparative statics. Assume, for example, that there are $\ell - 1$ firms and that each of the first $\ell - 1$ commodities are produced by exactly one firm using the commodity ℓ as input.

The assumption that the choice of production plan of firm j does not influence the relative prices of the other firms' products amounts to saying that the relative price system has the form: $(p_1(y_1), \ldots, p_{\ell-1}(y_{\ell-1}), 1)$; and this is, of course, not justified by our theory of price formation in pure exchange economies.

1.4 CONCLUSION

The results in this Chapter are rather negative. We have shown that profit maximization is an arbitrary objective of a firm when imperfect competition prevails in the economy. We have used a model of imperfect competition *à la* Cournot; however, one should emphasize that the arbitrariness of profit maximization is generally true also in models with competition *à la* Bertrand. The results show that there is a need to study in more detail the interaction between the firms, the shareholders, and the markets. The objective of a firm must be derived from the economic structure of the model and must be independent of the arbitrarily chosen normalization of prices. If a firm has an objective function which is related to the preferences of its shareholders, one might also obtain that markets in shares of firms will be active in equilibrium. My conclusion is that until we have a better understanding of how the objectives of firms are determined, one should directly, as part of the description of a firm, state an objective function which depends on relative prices only. One should not rely on results which are obtained only by assuming that firms maximize profits with respect to an arbitrary and not justified normalization rule.

In partial equilibrium models with imperfect competition, one also needs to exercise a corresponding modesty. Since the models cannot be derived from a well-determined general equilibrium model by fixing some variables, one has to be careful when using profit maximization as the objective of firms. However, it is clear that some partial equilibrium models with imperfect competition are so special that profit maximization with respect to a firm-specific normalization rule is justified. However, the normalization rule should be given special attention in these models also, and should be justified by the economic structure of the model.

Note

1. The author thanks Beth Allen for comments on an earlier version of this paper, a version which was written when the author attended BoWo 1992, University of Bonn. The author acknowledges financial support by Deutsche Forschungsgemeinschaft, Sonderforschungsbereich 303, Gottfried-Wilhelm-Leibniss-Förderpreis, and Danish Social Science Research Council.

References

Böhm, V. (1990) 'General Equilibrium with Profit Maximizing Oligopolists', Universität Mannheim, DP 41.

Debreu, G. (1970) 'Economies with a Finite Set of Equilibria', *Econometrica*, vol. 38, pp. 387–92.

Debreu, G. (1982) 'Existence of Competitive Equilibrium', in K. Arrow and M. Intrilligator (eds), *Handbook of Mathematical Economics*, vol. 2. 669–730.

Dierker, H. and B. Grodal (1986) 'Non-Existence of Cournot – Walras Equilibrium in a General Equilibrium Model with Two Oligopolists', in W. Hildenbrand and A. Mas-Colell (eds), *Contributions to Mathematical Economics* (New York: North Holland) pp. 167–85.

Gabszewicz, J. and J.P. Vial (1972) 'Oligopoly "à la Cournot" in a General Equilibrium Analysis', *Journal of Economic Theory*, vol. 4, pp. 381–400.

Gabszewicz, J.J. and P. Michel (1992) 'Oligopoly Equilibria in Exchange Economies', CORE DP.

Grodal, B. (1984) 'Profit Maximizing Behaviour in General Equilibrium Models with Imperfect Competition' (in Danish), *Economic Essays no. 28* (Copenhagen: Akademisk Forlag) pp. 79–89.

Hart, O. (1985) 'Imperfect Competition in General Equilibrium: An Overview of Recent Work', in K. Arrow and S. Honkapohja (eds), *Frontier of Economics* (Oxford: Basil Blackwell).

Roberts, J. and H. Sonnenschein (1977) 'On the Foundations of the Theory of Monopolistic Competition', *Econometrica*, vol. 45, pp. 101–13.

Roberts, K. (1980) 'The Limit Points of Monopolistic Competition', *Journal of Economic Theory* (symposium issue) vol. 22, pp. 256–79.

Part II

Rationality

2 Suppose Everybody Behaved Like That?[1]

Ken Binmore
UNIVERSITY COLLEGE LONDON

> What if a man could save himself from the present danger of
> death by treachery? If reason should recommend that, it would
> recommend it to all men.
>
> (Benedict de Spinoza)

2.1 THE PRISONERS' DILEMMA

My mother, like most mothers, was fond of the question: Suppose
everybody behaved liked that? Her logic was the same as Spinoza's
(1674) in the quotation from his *Tractatus Politicus* that heads this
chapter. Since things would be bad for everybody if everybody behaved selfishly, selfishness must therefore be irrational. Rousseau (1762)
argues similarly in his *Inequality of Man* when telling the famous stag-
hunt tale.[2] However, Kant (1785) is the most famous pedlar of the
fallacy. As his categorical imperative puts it: Act only on the maxim
that you would at the same time will to be a universal law.

In modern times, proponents of the fallacy have seized upon the
Prisoners' Dilemma as the arena for debate. Such toy games always
come with a little story. The story for the Prisoners' Dilemma is set in
Chicago. The District Attorney knows that Adam and Eve are gang-
sters who are guilty of a major crime but is unable to convict them
without a confession from one or the other. He orders their arrest and
separately offers each the following deal: 'If you confess and your
accomplice fails to confess, then you go free. If you fail to confess
but your accomplice confesses, then you will be convicted and sen-
tenced to the maximum term in jail. If you both confess, then you will
both be convicted but the maximum sentence will not be imposed. If
neither confesses, then you will be framed on a minor tax evasion
charge for which a conviction is certain.'

25

The chief purpose of such stories is to serve as a reminder about who gets what payoff. Figure 2.1(a) shows the general form of the Prisoners' Dilemma. Adam's payoffs are placed in the southwest corner of each cell and Eve's in the northeast corner. For the entries x, y and z in the payoff table of Figure 2.1(a) to correspond to the story of the Prisoners' Dilemma, we need that $x > y > z > 0$. Confessing is labelled *hawk*, and holding out is labelled *dove*. These strategy choices are usually dramatized by imagining that Adam and Eve have discussed the game before playing it and exchanged promises not to use *hawk*. After such promises have been made, the two pure strategies need to be interpreted as *play-dove-and-keep-your-promise* and *play-hawk-and-break-your-promise*.

In most examples, we shall work with the special case of the Prisoner' Dilemma shown in Figure 2.1(b). The payoffs in this special case can be remembered with a less elaborate story than that usually given. Each player chooses *dove* or *hawk* quite independently. Choosing *dove* results in a payment of $2 to the opponent. Choosing *hawk* results in a payment of $1 to oneself.[3]

Game-theorists do not claim to be able to give an exhaustive list of what the criteria for a rational choice should be in all games. But they do not think an exhaustive list is necessary to analyze the Prisoners' Dilemma successfully. For this purpose, all that is needed is the weakest possible criterion for rational behaviour in a game. This criterion forbids the use of a *strongly dominated* strategy. For example, *hawk* strongly dominates *dove* in the Prisoners' Dilemma of Figure 2.1(b), because a player who uses *hawk* will get 3 rather than 2 when the opponent uses *dove*, and 1 rather than 0 when the opponent uses *hawk*. Thus *hawk* is strictly better than *dove* whatever the opponent does.

The conclusion that (*hawk, hawk*) is the solution of the Prisoners' Dilemma seems paradoxical to many authors because (*hawk, hawk*) is not a Pareto-efficient outcome of the Prisoners' Dilemma. The perceived paradox is embodied in the question: If you're so smart, why ain't you rich? Suppose, for example, that Adam and Eve play in the Prisoners' Dilemma as game-theory books recommend and hence end up with $1 each. Next door, Ichabod and Olive throw out their game-theory books and end up with $2 each. As a consequence, Ichabod and Olive end up richer than Adam and Eve. So what makes Adam and Eve so smart? A game-theorist will reply that they have made the best of the opportunities that life has offered them while Ichabod and Olive have not. In particular, if Adam had been lucky enough to be playing Olive, he would have come away with $3 instead of the $2

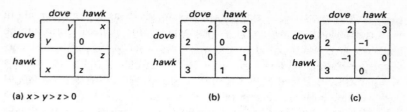

Figure 2.1 Prisoners' Dilemmas

that Ichabod obtained. If Ichabod had been unlucky enough to be playing Eve, he would have come away with nothing at all instead of the $1 that Adam obtained.

But such analyses cut no ice with those who argue that cooperation in the Prisoners' Dilemma is rational. Like the circle-squarers who harry mathematicians, such folk will doubtless always be with us. Their fundamental error is to see some version of the Prisoners' Dilemma as *the* paradigm for the human coordination problem. Since humans do indeed cooperate, the circle-squarers of social science then think it necessary to invent reasons why cooperation is rational in the Prisoners' Dilemma. They are thereby led into two errors. They model the human coordination problem with the wrong game and then confirm their prejudices by offering a wrong analysis of this wrong game.

Game theorists think it absurd to argue that the Prisoners' Dilemma summarizes the human coordination problem. If it did, *Homo sapiens* would not have evolved as a social animal. We believe it more realistic to think of the human coordination problem in terms of selecting an equilibrium in games that have many equilibria – like the indefinitely repeated Prisoners' Dilemma. However, this chapter is not about what game-theorists think is right, but what they believe to be wrong. It is a compendium of the various fallacies and paradoxes that have grown up around the Prisoners' Dilemma. I found it fun to write and perhaps those who are already converted will find it fun to read. I am less hopeful of reaching the unconverted, but someone has to try.

2.2 DEFECTION IS TAUTOLOGICALLY RATIONAL

This section seeks to explain why the assertion that defection is rational in the Prisoners' Dilemma is essentially a tautology, provided that the payoffs in the game are suitably interpreted.

Modern utility theory does not take the notion of utility as a primitive. It is regarded as a fallacy to argue that a person prefers *a* to *b* because the utility of *a* exceeds the utility of *b*. On the contrary, the analyst constructs a utility function *u* to have the property $u(a) \leq u(b)$ because he already knows that $a \prec b$. In particular, a player's payoffs in a game are deduced from his preferences over its possible outcomes.

For example, in the version of the Prisoners' Dilemma given in Figure 2.1(b), Adam's payoff for the outcome (*dove, dove*) is 1 and his pay-off for the outcome (*hawk, dove*) is 3. However, these payoffs are not primitives of the problem. Somewhere in the background is Adam's preference relation $\prec_A$. This is known to satisfy

$$(dove, \ dove) \prec_A (hawk, \ dove), \tag{2.1}$$

and hence the model-builder chooses to assign a payoff to (*dove, dove*) that is less than the payoff he assigns to (*hawk, dove*).

In the revealed preference theory developed by Sen (1973) and others, not even preferences are taken as primitives. Instead, choice behaviour becomes the primitive. One observes some of the choices that a player makes and then argues that he is making choices as though he were equipped with a preference relation.

From a revealed preference perspective, the preference (2.1) is deduced from the prior information that if Adam knew he had to choose between only (*dove, dove*) and (*hawk, dove*) then he actually would choose (*hawk, dove*). Similarly, the preference

$$(dove, \ hawk) \prec_A (hawk, \ hawk) \tag{2.2}$$

is deduced from the prior information that if Adam knew he had to choose between only (*dove, hawk*) and (*hawk, hawk*) then he actually would choose (*hawk, hawk*).

There may also be other prior information about Adam's choice behaviour, but the data that are important in predicting his behaviour in the Prisoners' Dilemma are the two facts that have been considered so far – namely: Adam chooses *hawk* both when he knows that Eve will choose *dove* and when he knows that she will not choose *dove*.

However, the problem in game theory is that one usually does not know what the opponent is going to do. A new assumption is therefore necessary to get any further. This is a very weak version of Savage's (1951) sure-thing principle. Consider three informational situations that differ only in what is known about some proposition *P*. In the first situation, Adam knows that *P* is true. In the second, he knows that *P* is false. In the third, he has doubts about whether *P* is true or false. It is given that Adam chooses *a* over *b* in both the first and the second situations. It therefore seems reasonable to argue that the truth or falsehood of *P* is irrelevant to which of *a* and *b* he chooses, and hence he will choose *a* over *b* in the third situation also. This is what our sure-thing principle says. In brief, if Adam chooses *a* over *b* both when he knows *P* is true and when he knows *P* is false, then he will choose *a* over *b* even when he is not fully informed about *P*.

In order to apply this sure-thing principle to the Prisoners' Dilemma, take *P* to be the proposition that Eve chooses *dove*. Take *a* to be Adam's pure strategy *hawk*, and take *b* to be his pure stategy *dove*. Since Adam will choose *hawk* both when he knows that Eve is choosing *dove* and when he knows she is not choosing *dove*, the sure-thing principle says that he must choose *hawk* whatever his thoughts might be about her prospective choice.

If it is accepted that the definition of rationality includes adherence to the sure-thing principle, then the preceding argument shows it to be a tautology that a rational player will necessarily choose *hawk* in the Prisoners' Dilemma. Unfortunately, this observation does not upset circle-squarers since they are in the habit of using the word 'tautological' in a pejorative sense to mean 'without substance'. However, for the rest of us, perhaps this section's strict analysis of the Prisoners' Dilemma using the theory of revealed preference will serve as a point of reference from which to survey the fallacies to come.

2.3   GAMES THAT ARE NOT THE PRISONERS' DILEMMA

Figure 2.2 shows some games that are not the Prisoners' Dilemma. Figure 2.2(a) shows the game that results after the players have exchanged unbreakable promises to play *dove*. Figure 2.2(b) is a game that models a situation in which the players have exchanged promises to play *dove,* but the promises are not unbreakable. However, each player is assumed to suffer a disutility from breaking a promise. It may be, for example, that breaking a promise causes each player some mental distress as a result of their childhood conditioning. This disutility is represented in Figure 2.2(b) by the number *x*. The interesting case occurs when $x > 1$.

Figure 2.2(c) shows a game in which each player sympathizes with

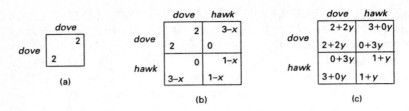

Figure 2.2 Games that are not the Prisoners' Dilemma

the other. They are 'members, one of another' to a sufficient degree that each shares in the opponent's joys and sorrows. This faculty for sympathetic identification is represented in Figure 2.2(c) by adding to each player's payoff a fraction y of the opponent's payoffs.[4] The interesting case occurs when $y > \frac{1}{2}$.

All three of these games admit (*dove*, *dove*) as a Nash equilibrium. For this reason, an analysis of one of these three games, or some similar game, is sometimes offered as an analysis of the Prisoners' Dilemma. However, game theorists see little point in such a ploy. It is true that the Prisoners' Dilemma does not properly represent the issues that human beings face in organizing the cooperative ventures that really matter in holding human societies together. However, if one shares the view that the Prisoners' Dilemma is not the right game to be studying, why not simply say so? Nothing would seem to be gained by defending whatever position one may hold by offering a wrong analysis of the wrong game. On the contrary, one obscures the question that really matters – namely, what is the right game? This same error will be apparent in the more sophisticated substitutes for the Prisoners' Dilemma considered next.

2.4   TRANSPARENT DISPOSITION FALLACIES

In a game-theoretic context, people speak of players 'having a disposition' to behave in a certain way, when they plan to assume that players can make commitments beyond those built into the rules of the game. Dispositions are 'transparent' if a player's opponents are necessarily aware of the commitments he or she makes. I do not think it necessary to repeat the arguments that are usually given when introducing the notion of a subgame-perfect equilibrium, to explain why game-theorists think one should not take for granted that people can make unbreakable commitments that bind their future behaviour. As

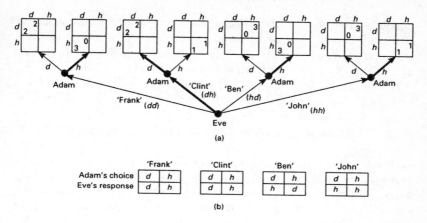

Figure 2.3 Choosing a transparent disposition

with the defence of strong domination given in Section 2.2, the principle of backwards induction can be made into a tautology if the payoffs are suitably defined. Game-theorists therefore argue against introducing the assumption that the players can make commitments, transparent or otherwise, into the *analysis* of a game. They do not thereby deny that the notion of a commitment is meaningful. They merely insist that, in modelling a situation as a game, any capacity for making commitments be built into the rules of the game. In justifying his model, the analyst is then forced to discipline himself by explaining the mechanism that enforces the commitments he postulates to be possible. However, no such self-discipline is practised by the authors of the tales that follow.

2.4.1 'Metagames'

Nigel Howard (1971) offers a variety of games as substitutes for the Prisoners' Dilemma. He refers to the substitute games as 'metagames'. The metagame studied in this section is what he calls the 1-2 metagame based on the Prisoners' Dilemma of Figure 2.2(b). This is usually explained using the metagame's payoff matrix given in Figure 2.4. However, I plan to attempt a simpler exposition based on the extensive-form game shown in Figure 2.3(a).

The extensive form of Figure 2.3(a) shows Eve making the first move in the role of player II. She chooses what Gauthier (1986, p. 170) calls a disposition but which I shall call a persona. The four possible personas from which Eve may choose are 'Frank', 'Clint,' 'Ben' and 'John'. It may be helpful in remembering their respective characters to think of their names as familiarized forms of St Francis of Assissi, Clint Eastwood, Benito Mussolini and Genghis Khan.

If Eve assumes the 'Frank' persona, then she will play *dove* in the Prisoners' Dilemma whatever action Adam may choose. If Eve assumes the 'John' persona, then she will play *hawk* whatever Adam does. The character played by Clint Eastwood in the spaghetti westerns is the basis for the 'Clint' persona. In the evolutionary literature, such a persona is said to be a 'retaliator'. If Eve assumes the 'Clint' persona, she will play *dove* if Adam plays *dove*, but she will play *hawk* if Adam plays *hawk*. Finally, Benito Mussolini is offered as the classic bully. If Eve assumes the 'Ben' persona, then she will play *hawk* if Adam plays *dove*, and *dove* if Adam plays *hawk*. Figure 2.3(b) summarizes the properties of the four personas available to Eve.

The next move in the game of Figure 2.3(a) is Adam's. When he makes this move, he knows the persona chosen by Eve. Gauthier (1986, p. 173) would say that Eve's choice of a disposition is transparent to Adam. Thus, for example, when Adam chooses between *dove* and *hawk* after Eve has chosen the persona 'Ben', he knows that he will get a payoff of 0 from the use of *dove* (because Eve will then play *hawk*), and a payoff of 3 from the use of *hawk* (because Eve will then play *dove*). His optimal choice under these circumstances is therefore to choose *hawk*, and the line representing this choice in Figure 2.3(a) has therefore been doubled. After doubling the lines representing the optimal choices at Adam's other decision nodes, the principle of backwards induction explained in Section 2.2 calls for us next to consider Eve's choice of persona. If Adam behaves rationally, Eve will get 0 from choosing 'Frank', 2 from choosing 'Clint', 0 from choosing 'Ben', and 1 from choosing 'John'. Her optimal choice is therefore 'Clint', and so the line representing this choice has been doubled in Figure 2.3(a).

The subgame-perfect equilibrium shown in Figure 2.3(a) by doubling suitable lines requires Eve to make the strategy choice 'Clint', and for Adam to make the strategy choice *hdhh*. Before explaining how Adam's pure strategies are labelled, it should be noted that he has a very large number of pure strategies. Recall that a pure strategy must specify what he should do under all contingencies that might arise in the game. Adam therefore has $16 = 2 \times 2 \times 2 \times 2$ pure strategies, because he has two possible choices at each of four decision nodes. The pure strategy labelled *hdhh* means that he should play *hawk* if Eve chooses 'Frank', *dove* if Eve chooses 'Clint', *hawk* if Eve chooses 'Ben', and *hawk* if Eve chooses 'John'. For similar reasons, Eve's pure strategy 'Clint' has been labelled *dh* in Figure 2.4, which is the strategic form of the 1-2 metagame whose extensive form is shown in Figure 2.3(a).

Notice that (*hdhh, dh*) is only one of three Nash equilibria starred in Figure 2.4. However, the other Nash equilibria may be rejected because they are not subgame-perfect. One may also note that Adam's pure strategy *hdhh* weakly dominates all its rivals.

If Adam and Eve use the unique subgame-perfect equilibrium of the 1-2 metagame, Eve will choose 'Clint', Adam will choose *dove*, and the result will be that they cooperate in the Prisoners' Dilemma. It is simple enough to observe that the 1-2 metagame is not the Prisoners' Dilemma, and so the fact that rational cooperation is possible in the 1-2 metagame does not imply that rational cooperation is possible in the Prisoners' Dilemma. However, I want to try to explain precisely why one cannot sensibly substitute the 1-2 metagame for the Prisoners' Dilemma.

In the first place, the extensive form of Figure 2.3(a) takes for granted that Eve can make commitments. It is assumed that she can make a commitment to any of the four personas 'Frank', 'Clint', 'Ben' and 'John'. To see why a commitment is involved, suppose that Eve chooses 'Clint' and then Adam chooses *dove*. The 'Clint' persona is then supposed to respond to Adam's playing *dove* by playing *dove* in return. But Eve will not wish to act as the 'Clint' persona requires after she learns that Adam is to play *dove,* because, as always in the Prisoners' Dilemma, the play of *dove* yields a lower payoff than the play of *hawk*. If she continues to act as the 'Clint' persona demands, it must therefore be because she has made a commitment to do so.

But, for the analysis of the 1-2 metagame to be relevant to the Prisoners' Dilemma, it is not enough that Eve be allowed to make commitments. She must also be able to convince Adam that she has indeed made a commitment. Her resolution must be naked for all the world to see. Not only this, but somehow Adam's intended play in the Prisoners' Dilemma must also be transparent. Otherwise Eve would not be able to choose a persona whose choice of action in the Prisoners' Dilemma depends on the choice of action made by the opponent.

Frank (1988) is the place to look if seeking reasons why such constructs as the 1-2 metagame are worthy of study. He argues that we

	dd		dh		hd		hh	
dddd		2		2		3		3
	2		2		0		0	
dddh		2		2		3		1
	2		2		0		1	
ddhd		2		2		0		3
	2		2		3		0	
ddhh		2	*	2		0		1
	2		2		3		1	
dhdd		2	*	2		3		3
	2		2		0		0	
dhdh		2		1		3		1
	2		1		0		1	
dhhd		2		1		0		3
	2		1		3		0	
dhhh		2		1		0		1
	2		1		3		1	
hddd		0		1		3		3
	3		1		0		0	
hddh		0		2		3		1
	3		2		0		1	
hdhd		0		2		0		3
	3		2		3		0	
hdhh		0	*	2		0		1
	3		2		3		1	
hhdd		0		1		3		3
	3		1		0		0	
hhdh		0		1		3		1
	3		1		0		1	
hhhd		0		1		0		3
	3		1		3		0	
hhhh		0		1		0	*	1
	3		1		3		1	

Figure 2.4 The payoff matrix for the 1–2 metagame based on the
Prisoners' Dilemma

have the power to train ourselves to adopt certain dispositions. What
is more, such dispositions will be transparent because Nature has so
wired us up that it is hard to conceal our emotions from others. Unfortunately, she seems to have left some wires loose in the characters
who sell me shoddy used cars or who take my money at the poker

table. However, this is not the place to discuss why I think Frank goes astray in arguing that social norms suitable for small-town living might also survive in big cities. It is enough to observe that even if it were possible to agree wholeheartedly with Frank, it would still be false that an analysis of the 1-2 metagame is an analysis of the Prisoners' Dilemma.

2.4.2 Constrained Maximization

Gauthier's (1986, p. 157) theory of 'constrained maximization' can be seen as a symmetrized version of the Metagame Fallacy of Section 2.4.1. He distinguishes a straightforward maximizer from a constrained maximizer, and argues that it is 'rational' to adopt the latter disposition. In the language of that section, Gauthier argues that the 'Clint' persona is more rational than the 'John' persona. Gauthier understands that it is necessary for the choice of persona to be properly advertised, but finesses this difficulty by writing:

> Since our argument is to be applied to ideally rational persons, we may simply add another idealizing assumption, and take persons to be *transparent*. Each is then directly aware of the disposition of his fellows, and so is aware whether he is interacting with straightforward maximizers or constrained maximizers. Deception is impossible. (Gauthier, 1986, p. 157)

He later notes that transparency can be replaced by translucency, by which he means that a player need not be sure of identifying an opponent's disposition for the argument to hold. It is enough if the opponent's disposition can be identified with a sufficiently high probability.

As observed in the previous section, game-theorists do not believe that it is acceptable to assume that we can commit ourselves to a disposition and then successfully advertise our commitment to those around us. Unless one wishes to follow Gauthier in arguing that transparency should be taken to be one of the attributes of an ideally rational person, there seems nothing to add to this earlier discussion. Rather than explaining again why Gauthier's 'constrained maximization' is a non-starter as a rationality principle, I shall therefore defend Gauthier against the charge that his model is incoherent.

The difficulty is that, in a symmetrized version of the Metagame Fallacy, Adam and Eve must choose their personas *simultaneously*. But each persona's choice of action in the Prisoners' Dilemma is

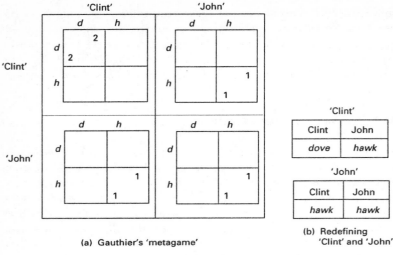

(a) Gauthier's 'metagame'

(b) Redefining 'Clint' and 'John'

Figure 2.5   Gauthier's metagame

contingent on the choice of the other. What I do therefore depends on what the other guy does. But this in turn depends on what I do. It therefore seems that we are trapped in a self-reference problem. However, self-references are not intrinsically paradoxical. For example, this sentence is self-referential without being paradoxical.

John Howard (1988)[5] considers a computer that has access to the printout of the programme of an opposing computer. Using an ingenious device proposed by Quine, such a computer can be programmed to play *dove* in the Prisoners' Dilemma if and only if its opponent has the same program as itself. The programme consists of a sequence of commands equivalent to the following algorithm:

> Play *dove* if and only if the opponent's instructions take the form X"X", where X is the material in quotes that follows this sentence. 'Play *dove* if and only if the opponent's instructions take the form X"X", where X is the material in quotes that follows this sentence.'

This observation makes it possible to redefine the personas 'Clint' and 'John' as shown in Figure 2.5(b). Gauthier's[6] 'metagame' is then the game of Figure 2.5(a). The game has two Nash equilibria, ('Clint', 'Clint') and ('John', 'John'). All standard equilibrium selection arguments favour the choice of the Pareto-dominant equilibrium ('Clint', 'Clint'). If the Prisoners' Dilemma were Gauthier's 'metagame', it would therefore indeed be true that cooperation was rational in the Prisoners' Dilemma!

2.5   THE SYMMETRY FALLACY

As was remarked in Section 2.1, Spinoza, Rousseau and Kant are among the more fancied runners in the moral philosophy race who have fallen at the fence raised by the question: Suppose everybody behaved like that? However, their arguments are so intertwined with other considerations that it is hard to pin down precisely where it is that they go wrong. However, Rapoport (1966) gives their argument in the following very straightforward form:[7]

> because of the symmetry of the game, rationality must prescribe the *same choice to both*. But if both choose the same, then (2,2) is clearly better than (1,1). Therefore I should choose *dove*.

Hofstadter (1983) seems to have come to the same conclusion independently when he gave the Symmetry Fallacy its biggest boost by endorsing it in the *Scientific American* of 1983. The words in which he expresses the fallacy are very Kantian:

> rational thinkers understand that a valid argument must be *universally* compelling, otherwise it is simply not a valid argument. If you grant this then you are 90 per cent of the way. All you need ask now is: Since we are all going to submit the same [strategy], which would be the more logical?

Let me repeat the argument. Since the Prisoners' Dilemma is symmetric, it seems reasonable to argue that rationality will necessarily lead Adam and Eve to make the same choice. If both choose *hawk*, each will get a payoff of 1. If both choose *dove*, each will get a payoff of 2. Which is the better? The answer to this question seems obvious. Since 2 is more than 1, rationality apparently requires that both players act 'unselfishly' by playing *dove*.

Some clearing of the air is necessary before the fallacy can be pinpointed. Various assumptions are hidden in the argument. Some of these assumptions happen to be valid in the special case of the Prisoners' Dilemma, but there is one crucial implicit assumption that is simply false.

In the first place, it is not true that rationality *necessarily* requires symmetric behaviour from the players in a symmetric game.[8] However, nobody would wish to deny that rationality does happen to require symmetric behaviour in the special case of the Prisoners' Dilemma.

The second difficulty arises from the question: Which is the better? This question is not necessarily meaningful when applied to several players jointly. It assumes that they share some 'common good'. However, the question does make sense when attention is confined to the set S consisting only of the two outcomes (*dove*, *dove*) and (*hawk*, *hawk*) on the main diagonal of the Prisoners' Dilemma's payoff matrix of Figure 2.2(b). Adam and Eve are unanimous in preferring (*dove*, *dove*) to (*hawk*, *hawk*). Their individual preferences are therefore identical on the set S, and hence can be said to define a 'common preference' on S.

But now we come to the crucial hidden assumption. The argument we are studying 'deduces' that rational players will choose (*dove*, *dove*) from the observation that Adam and Eve are agreed in preferring (*dove*, *dove*) to (*hawk*, *hawk*). But this argument neglects an elementary principle of rational decision theory. This principle calls for the set of feasible outcomes to be identified before seeking to decide what is optimal.

Nothing in the argument under study entitles us to the conclusion that everything in the set $S = \{(dove, dove), (hawk, hawk)\}$ is feasible. Even if one is willing to grant that it is impossible that an asymmetric outcome could pass whatever test of rationality is being applied, one is still only entitled to deduce that the set R of feasible outcomes is a subset of S. If one wishes to argue that $R = S$, it is necessary to say something about what test of rationality is being applied in order to justify such an extra step.

Game-theorists are only too willing to explain what test of rationality they are applying to get the final outcome on to the main diagonal S of the payoff matrix. It is the criterion: Never use a strongly dominated strategy. This test leads to a set R that contains only the single outcome (*hawk*, *hawk*).

Proponents of the Symmetry Fallacy are unwilling to say what test of rationality they are employing to get the outcome on to the main diagonal. They are therefore unable to tell us why their proposed second appeal to rationality in selecting (*dove*, *dove*) from S is consistent with their first appeal in selecting S from the set of all possible outcomes of the Prisoners' Dilemma. However, the rationality cow is like other cows. It can be milked only so often before it runs dry. In this particular case, it can be milked only once.

2.6 THE PARADOX OF THE TWINS

The general shape of the argument involved in Nozick's (1969) Paradox of the Twins is already familiar. In the Prisoners' Dilemma of Figure 2.2(b), Adam argues that Eve is his twin and hence: She will do whatever I do. So if I play *hawk*, we will both play *hawk*. If I play *dove*, we will both play *dove*. Since I prefer a payoff of 2 to a payoff of 1, I should therefore play *dove*. Eve is assumed to argue in precisely the same way, with the conclusion that Adam and Eve cooperate in the one-shot Prisoners' Dilemma.

This argument is not fallacious. After all, Eve might be Adam's reflection in a mirror. Adam would then be playing a simple one-person game rather than the Prisoners' Dilemma. The argument only becomes fallacious when attempts are made to prove that a rational Eve must be Adam's twin in the very strong sense required by the paradox. In one such argument, Adam supposedly reasons as follows:

> I am rational. So anything I decide to do will necessarily be rational. Eve is also rational and hence will aways make the same decision as I make when placed in identical circumstances. Therefore, she will do whatever I do in the Prisoners' Dilemma.

The error lies in the implicit assumption that an action is rational because it is chosen by a rational person. But to argue like this is to invert the causal chain. An action is not rational because it is chosen by a rational person. On the contrary, a person is said to be rational because he only chooses rational actions.

One can dismiss the Paradox of the Twins as a curiosity like the story of Buridan's Ass. Just as the ass would indeed starve if it were placed symmetrically between two bales of hay with no way to break the symmetry, so Adam would be right to choose *dove* in the one-player game in which Eve has no choice but to mimic whatever action Adam takes. But just as the predicament of Buridan's ass is too unlikely to be worth taking seriously, so is the hypothesis that Eve is so much Adam's twin that she can be relied upon to duplicate each passing whim or fancy that may enter his head.

However, my own view is that it is a mistake to dismiss the Paradox of the Twins so lightly. My guess is that it raises philosophical issues about the nature of the self that will one day be important in whatever theory of rational equilibrium selection finally emerges from the mess in which the foundations of game theory are currently floundering. When, for example, is it legitimate to appeal to the 'Harsanyi Doctrine' to argue that two specimens of *Homo economicus* with precisely the same history of experience will necessarily have precisely the same thoughts in their heads? And if Adam's thoughts precisely mirror Eve's under certain circumstances, how can she be said to be exercising 'free will'? In the draft of the book from which this paper is extracted, I write at great length on these subjects, but here I think it best to touch on such deep questions only to the extent that is necessary in the following discussion of Newcomb's Paradox.

2.7 NEWCOMB'S PARADOX

The Newcomb problem was introduced to the world by Nozick (1969), and immediately won the hearts of philosophers the world over. Levi (1982) captured the general spirit of the enthusiasm that reigned at the time by writing a paper on Newcombmania. Nowadays, the enthusiasm is more muted, but Newcombmania remains a flourishing cottage industry. My own opinion is that this industry is largely wasted, since Newcomb's Paradox makes assumptions about timing, predictability and free choice that cannot hold simultaneously. Like Bertrand Russell's barber, who shaves every man in a town who does not shave himself, there is therefore no such thing as a Newcomb problem.

Nevertheless, various models based on Newcomb's story are considered in this section. In each case, one of the three basic assumptions of the story has to be weakened in order to construct something coherent. As a consequence, none of the models studied will satisfy a determined Newcombmaniac. To those with maniacal tendencies, I can only say that I am doing my best to provide satisfaction – but there is just no way of realizing a contradiction!

Although Newcomb is said to have formulated the problem that bears his name while thinking about the Prisoners' Dilemma, it does not have the appearance of being a game-theoretic puzzle. It is posed in the form of a one-person decision problem. Two boxes may have money inside. Adam is free to take either the first box or both boxes. If he cares only for money, which choice should he make? This seems an easy problem. If *dove* represents taking only the first box and *hawk* represents taking both boxes, then Adam should choose *hawk* because this choice always results in his getting at least as much money as *dove*. Nozick (1969) abuses the terminology of Section 2.2. by saying that *hawk* therefore 'dominates' *dove*.

However, there is a catch – as there usually is when it seems that a free lunch is on offer. Moreover, this catch is a veritable Catch 22. It is certain that there is one dollar bill in the second box. The first box may contain nothing or it may contain two dollar bills. The decision about whether there should be money in the first box was made yesterday by Eve. She knows Adam very well. Indeed, she is what Brams (1983) calls a 'superior being'. She knows Adam so well that she is always able to make a perfect prediction of what he will do in all circumstances. Like Adam, she has two choices, *dove* and *hawk*. Her dovelike choice is to put two dollar bills in the first box. Her hawkish choice is to put nothing in the first box. For reasons best known to herself, she plays *dove* if and only if she predicts that Adam will choose *dove*. She plays *hawk* if and only if she predicts that Adam will choose *hawk*. Adam's choice of *hawk* would now seem to yield only one dollar bill whereas *dove* yields two dollar bills. But how can it be right for Adam to choose *dove* when we have already seen that this choice is 'dominated' by *hawk*?

Nozick (1969) tells us that Newcomb's Paradox exposes a conflict between 'domination' and the 'maximization of expected utility'. Nozick contemplates this supposed conflict between 'two principles of choice' with disinterested equanimity. He tells us that about 50 per cent of his correspondents are sure that domination is right and the other 50 per cent are sure that maximizing expected utility is right. However, if Nozick had really uncovered a conflict between the principles as they are understood in game theory, then the fall of the temple of the Philistines would be as nothing compared with the consequences that would follow for game-theorists and their works. If game theory makes any sense at all, there cannot be a contradiction between domination and expected utility maximization. A game-theorist must therefore be forgiven for looking elsewhere for the source of the contradiction.

2.7.1 Bad Timing

When game-theorists apply the principle of domination, they usually first begin by writing down a strategic form for the game in question. Before this can be done, one needs to identify the players' pure strategies. If there is any doubt about what the pure strategies are, it is necessary to take one step further back and to construct a preliminary extensive form for the game in all its detail. In studying the Prisoners' Dilemma, we have grown accustomed to treating *dove* and *hawk* as representing pure strategies. It therefore seems natural in Newcomb's story to continue to do the same. But is it right to think of *dove* and *hawk* as being strategies in Newcomb's problem? The answer depends on what we think appropriate as an extensive form for the Newcomb problem.

The first model to be considered retains Newcomb's assumptions on predictability and free choice, but abandons his assumptions about the physical timing of moves.

What does it mean to say that Eve is a superior being? It is important to understand that this does not simply mean that she will correctly predict what Adam actually does. Eve does not need to be superior to pull off this trick. Two rational players using a Nash equilibrium each correctly predict what the other will actually do, without any need to attribute superior intellect or knowledge to either. To be a superior being, Eve must be modelled as being an accurate predictor of Adam's behaviour in all relevant possible worlds – not just in the world that is actually realized. For example, it may be that Adam will actually choose *dove*. If so, then Eve must actually predict that he will choose *dove*. But it must also be true that if Adam had chosen *hawk* instead, then Eve would have predicted that he would choose *hawk*.

This strong definition of a superior being seems entirely coherent to me if taken on its own. If you share my belief that computer analogies are useful, you can imagine that Eve knows all the code of Adam's operating programme together with the data on which it operates. She can therefore always run his programme with his data on her machine to predict what he will do.[9] Of course, she will then need to be a more complex entity than Adam, but this is entirely consistent with her status as a superior being.

To construct a model that takes such a story about computer programmes literally is to use a hammer to smash a walnut. Much simpler models are adequate.[10] Indeed, a game-theorist will be content to follow Brams (1983) in modelling the hypothesis that Eve is a superior being with the extensive form of Figure 2.6(a). In this little game, the first move is assigned to Adam, who chooses between *dove* and *hawk*. Eve then observes his choice. In the manner of a political columnist, she then predicts his choice only *after* seeing what he does. This guarantees that she can make correct predictions if she so chooses. The doubled lines in Figure 2.6(a) show the choices attributed to the players. Since the Newcomb story does not explain Eve's choices, no payoffs for her are included in the diagram. She 'just does what she does'. Given her planned behaviour, Adam optimizes by playing *dove*. But the story is that *hawk* 'dominates' *dove*. How then can Adam maximize his expected utility by playing *dove*?

The answer is simple. Figure 2.6(e) shows a putative 2 × 2 strategic form for the extensive form of Figure 2.6(a). If this were the correct strategic form, then it would indeed be true that *hawk* dominates *dove*. But it is wrong to assign only two pure strategies to Eve. In Figure 2.6(a), she has two nodes at which she must specify what she would do if that node were reached. At each of these two nodes, she has two alternatives from which to choose. She therefore has 2 × 2 = 4 pure strategies in all. The correct strategic form is therefore the 2 × 4 payoff table shown in Figure 2.6(d). In the style of Section 2.3, Eve's four pure strategies are denoted by *dd*, *dh*, *hd*, and *hh*. For example, when Eve 'just does what she does', she uses *dh*. This strategy requires her to select *dove* if Adam chooses *dove*, and *hawk* if he chooses *hawk*. Notice that *hawk* does not dominate *dove* for Adam in Figure 2.6((d). Indeed, if Adam knows that Eve will use the strategy *dh* attributed to her by Newcomb's story, then the strategic form shows that he gets $2 from playing *dove* and only $1 from playing *hawk*. No conflict between 'domination' and 'expected utility maximization' therefore arises in this model.

What of the claim that the model of Figure 2.6(a) allows Adam to choose freely? I mean nothing fancy by this. Consider, for example, what would happen if we were to augment a formal model of a game by including a full account of Adam's thought processes and all the influences under which he acts. His apparent freedom would then disappear. Indeed, it is precisely to remove a rational player's apparent freedom to move where he will that game-theorists analyze games. After a game-theorist has determined what is rational in a game, a rational player can no longer be said to be free to choose.[11] If he were to make an irrational move, then he would not be rational. However, before we have specified what Adam's thought processes will be in a game, it makes perfectly good sense for us to say that he is free to make any move allowed by the rules. In particular, Adam is free to choose between *dove* and *hawk* in Figure 2.6(a) as long as we leave the interior of his head unmodelled. He is free to choose, because the manner in which he will choose has been left open.

2.7.2 No Superior Being

Figure 2.6(e) is the wrong strategic form for Brams's model of Figure 2.6(a), but it is the right strategic form for the extensive form obtained from Figure 2.6(a) by inserting an information set as shown in Figure 2.6(b). Notice that Figure 2.6(e) is also the strategic form for the

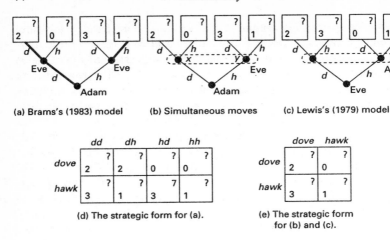

Figure 2.6 'Domination' in the Newcomb Paradox?

extensive form of Figure 2.6(c), in which Eve moves first and Adam moves second. This may seem paradoxical until one realizes that the physical timing of the moves in these games is irrelevant. It is no help for me to know that my opponent has made her decision already if I have no way of knowing what her decision is.

David Lewis (1979) claims that the Prisoners' Dilemma is really two Newcomb problems placed back-to-back. Newcomb presumably followed a similar line of reasoning when his musings on the Prisoners' Dilemma led him to formulate the Newcomb Paradox in the first place. Implicit in this view is the belief that the Newcomb problem can be usefully modelled as the game of Figure 2.6(c). If one agrees that Figure 2.6(c) is a legitimate extensive form for the Newcomb problem, then its correct strategic form is Figure 2.6(e). One must then accept Lewis's conclusion that the solution to the Newcomb problem is for Adam to take both boxes, because *hawk* strongly dominates *dove* in Figure 2.6(e). Indeed, Adam's payoffs in the strategic form of Figure 2.6(e) are the same as his payoffs in the Prisoners' Dilemma first introduced in Figure 2.1(b). Moreover, if suitable payoffs are assigned to Eve, then Figure 2.6(e) becomes identical with the Prisoners' Dilemma of Figure 2.1(b). If these same payoffs are inserted in Figure 2.6(b), this also becomes a Newcomb problem, but with Adam replacing Eve as the person who makes a prediction. We then have two Newcomb problems with a common strategic form. This common strategic form is the Prisoners' Dilemma.

After presenting his argument that the Prisoners' Dilemma is nothing other than a version of Newcomb's problem, Lewis writes: '*quod erat demonstrandum*'. Given that anything can be deduced from a contradiction, I guess that he is entitled to this flourish. However, we ought to register that Lewis's use of Figure 2.6(c) as a model of the Newcomb problem honours only Newcomb's timing and free-choice assumptions. The model meets the predictability requirement only partially. It is true that if Adam and Eve optimize in Figure 2.6(c) by using *hawk*, then each will actually predict the choice of the other successfully, because (*hawk, hawk*) is a Nash equilibrium. But this does not seem to me to capture the spirit of what Newcomb intends. Eve should be modelled so that she would predict Adam's choice, even if he were not to choose as he actually will choose. That is to say, Eve should be superior to Adam. One can then no longer easily sustain the hypothesis that the Prisoners' Dilemma consists of two Newcomb problems placed back-to-back. How can Adam and Eve each be superior to the other? Equivalently, how can Adam and Eve each simultaneously be the first to move in a model like Figure 2.6(a)?

2.7.3 No Free Choice

Brams's (1983) model for the Newcomb problem honours predictability and free choice. Lewis's (1979) model honours timing and free choice. However, I suspect that more is to be learned by looking at models that take up the third possibility. In these models, timing and predictability are honoured, but not free choice. More precisely, Adam's thinking processes will be modelled, albeit exceedingly abstractly, using Aumann's (1987) framework – within which Nature determines a player's state of mind, after which the player 'just does what he does'. Since we are already modelling Eve as someone who 'just does what she does', the games to be considered will therefore be *without players* as game-theorists usually understand the term. This last point will be emphasized in what follows by removing the options that Eve has hitherto been offered in models of the Newcomb problem. These options were included only to explain why some authors think that Newcomb's Paradox is relevant to the Prisoners' Dilemma. But now that this point has been covered, we might as well simplify and treat Eve as nothing more than a stimulus-response machine. Since she is a superior being she will be a more complicated stimulus-response machine than Adam, but the models are too abstract for this complexity to be explicitly represented.

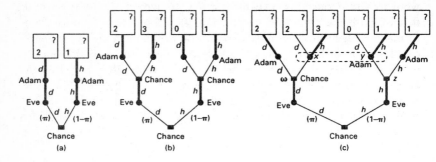

Figure 2.7 No free choice?

The first move in the no-player game of Figure 2.7(a) is a chance move. Nature decides at this move whether *dove* or *hawk* will be realized. The probability that Nature will choose *dove* is taken to be π. The probability that she will choose *hawk* is therefore $1 - \pi$. The chance move at which Nature chooses between *dove* and *hawk* replaces Adam's choice between the same alternatives in the previous models. The chance move determines Adam's state of mind, after which he 'just does what he does'. All the influences that determine Adam's choice are therefore separated into two classes: the class in which he is led to play *dove*, and the class in which he is led to play *hawk*.

The next event in the game is Eve's prediction of Adam's choice. To say that she is a perfect predictor is to say that she knows enough about Adam's circumstances and the way in which his mind works for us to be sure she will never predict his action wrongly. We must therefore carefully avoid drawing an information set that includes her two decisions nodes. Without an information set, we are saying that Eve knows everything that she needs to know in order to predict perfectly when she makes a prediction. Neither Adam nor Eve are modelled as being free to choose in Figure 2.7(a). Both are stimulus-response machines that simply repeat whatever signal Nature transmits to them. In particular, the final event of the game, in which Adam makes his choice between *dove* and *hawk*, is entirely predetermined by what has gone before.

A game-theoretic analysis of a game with no players is intellectually undemanding. We just sit back and admire the view. Adam will play *dove* with probability π, and *hawk* with probability $1 - \pi$. We may, of course, reasonably ask what determines these probabilities, but we must go outside the model in seeking an answer. For example, if Adam were free to choose his own disposition, he would choose a persona that would make π as close to 1 as possible. However, allowing Adam to make such a choice simply reduces the problem to a more complicated version of Brams's model of Figure 2.6(a). It is more interesting to consider an explanation that attributes the value of π to evolutionary forces. A meme inside Adam's head that leads to a large value of π will have more chance of being replicated to other heads than a meme that leads to a small value of π. The evolutionary pressures are therefore in favour of those Adams who play *dove* rather than those who play *hawk*.

2.7.4 Superior Guessing

Newcombmaniacs will dislike Figure 2.7(a) because of its uncompromising rejection of free choice. But free choice must be rejected. Adam cannot be allowed to choose *hawk* after nature has selected *dove*. To do so would be to deny the premiss that Eve knows everything necessary to make a perfect prediction of what Adam will do. Newcombmaniacs will hasten to explain that the paradox does not depend on Eve making a perfect prediction. It may be, for example, that Adam's experience of Eve's prowess at prediction leads him to the conclusion that she is only right some of the time. That is, she is only a superior guesser rather than a perfect predictor. Perhaps Eve guesses correctly with probability p when Adam chooses *dove*, and with probability q when he chooses *hawk*. To retain the conclusion of the original Newcomb story that Adam should continue to make the supposedly 'dominated' choice of *dove* in this new framework, we shall insist that

$$2p + 0(1 - p) \geq 1q + 3(1 - q)$$

This inequality is satisfied, for example, if $p + q \geq \frac{3}{2}$.

Figure 2.7(b) adapts the model Figure 2.7(a) to the new situation. The chance moves that follow Eve's prediction make it impossible for her to get things right all the time. Nevertheless, things are pretty much as the Figure 2.7(a), provided that the probabilities p and q are sufficiently large. In spite of the fact that Eve now only guesses at what he will do, Adam still cannot be allowed free choice. If he were allowed to choose freely, he might choose to play *hawk* all the time after Nature has signalled *dove*, and *dove* all the time after Nature has signalled *hawk*. This would deny the premiss that Eve is a superior guesser, since she would then be wrong all the time. Of course, it may seem to Eve that Adam is exercising free choice, since she is unable to predict exactly what he will do. Adam himself will perhaps also believe that he is exercising free choice, since he is unlikely to be equipped with any model at all of the events in his own mind that we have so crudely modelled with three chance moves. However, we analysts looking down from on high to observe the fall of the smallest sparrow, can see that each player 'just does what he does'.

Although I do not think that the way Newcombmaniacs model Eve as a superior guesser advances matters at all, I agree that removing the perfect prediction requirement from Newcomb's story does allow us to construct a model in which all of Newcomb's assumptions are satisfied simultaneously. Such a model is shown in Figure 2.7(c). Notice that Nature now sometimes leaves Adam free to choose – that is to say, the model does not tie down every aspect of his behaviour. We must therefore leave open the precise probabilities with which Eve is to guess correctly. However, since we shall still require that $p + q \geq \frac{3}{2}$, it is necessary that the probabilities with which Adam is offered the opportunity to choose freely are small. Notice that an information set has been drawn to include both the nodes x and y. This indicates that Adam does not know what Eve has predicted when he finds himself free to choose. More important, the exclusion of the nodes w and z from this information set shows that Adam *knows* when he is free to choose. One might say that it is the very realization that he has a choice to make that frees him from slavishly using whatever behaviour happens to verify Eve's prediction.

An analysis of Figure 2.7(c) is very simple. A game-theorist will recommend that Adam should play *hawk* when he is free to choose, because *hawk* strongly dominates *dove* in this game. If we finish modelling Adam's thought processes by assuming that he will take a game-theorist's advice whenever he finds himself free to choose, then the result will be as indicated by the doubled lines in Figure 2.7(c). This may not seem so different from our analysis of Figure 2.7(b), given that Adam's probability of having a free choice is assumed to be low. However, the difference in the two analyses becomes important when one considers the evolutionary implications. Evolutionary considerations based on Figure 2.7(b) will drive the system towards a population of Adams who all play *dove* – just as in Figure 2.7(a). But the same is not necessarily true in Figure 2.7(c). Deviant memes that insidiously suggest to their hosts that they are 'free to choose' in certain circumstances will have an evolutionary advantage. They will therefore tend to become more numerous in the population. Such a trend will destabilize the story that goes with the Newcomb problem. That is to say, if the assumptions of the Newcomb problem ever did hold, evolution would eventually sweep them away. Indeed, this is presumably why the Newcomb story strikes people as being so far-fetched in the first place!

We have now considered a number of attempts to model the Newcomb problem. Conventional reasoning led us to different conclusions in different models. However, no hint of any conflict between 'two principles of choice' was uncovered. For such a conflict to arise, we would need to have been led to different conclusions by different principles in the same model. To sustain the impression that a conflict exists, it is necessary that the nature of the model being used is left ambiguous.

2.8   THE PARADOX OF THE SURPRISE TEST

The moral just drawn from our study of Newcomb's Paradox is the same as the moral for the whole chapter. In brief, getting your model right is half the battle. Indeed, for the paradoxes and fallacies considered in this chapter, getting your model right is essentially the whole battle.

To press this point home, I now include one last paradox – the Paradox of the Surprise Test. In modelling Newcomb's Paradox, we had to answer the question: What is a prediction? To this we now add the rider: What is a surprise? My mundane answer is that a person is surprised when he has made a prediction that turns out to be wrong.[12]

In the story of the surprise test, Eve is a teacher who tells her class that they are to be given a test one day next week, but the day on which the test is given will come as a surprise. Adam is a pupil who has learned the lesson of backwards induction. He therefore works backward through the days of the coming school week. If Eve has not set the test by the time school is over on Thursday, Adam reckons that Eve will then have no choice but to set the test on Friday – this being the last day of the school week. If the test were given on Friday, Adam would therefore not be surprised. So Adam deduces that Eve cannot plan to give the test on Friday. But this means that the test must be given on Monday, Tuesday, Wednesday or Thursday. Having reached this conclusion, Adam now applies his backwards induction argument again to eliminate Thursday as a possible day for the test.

Once Thursday has been eliminated, he is then in a position to eliminate Wednesday – and so on, until all the days of the week have been eliminated. He then sighs with relief and makes no attempt to study over the weekend. But then Eve takes him by surprise by setting the test first thing on Monday morning!

If sense is to be made of this battle of wits between Adam and Eve, a suitable model needs to be constructed. This model will be a game. The game is unwieldy with a five-day school week and so Figure 2.8(a) just shows what the game would be if the school week consisted only of Thursday and Friday. The payoffs have been chosen so that Adam gets $+1$ if he predicts the day on which the test takes place, and -1 if he fails to do so. Eve's payoffs reverse these rewards. Figure 2.8(b) shows the strategic form for the game. Notice that Thursday is a weakly dominating strategy for both players. Each player will therefore be doing as well as he or she possibly can if Adam predicts that the test will be on Thursday and Eve runs the test on Thursday.

This doesn't seem right. Surely Eve would do better to switch the test to Friday if Adam is going to predict that it will take place on Thursday? But it is not the analysis of the game that is wrong, but the game itself! To say that Adam's strategy in the game of Figure 2.8(a) is Thursday is to say something complicated. It means that Adam should predict Thursday on Thursday, but if this prediction proves to be wrong, then he should switch his prediction to Friday on Friday! This may seem crazy, but it isn't my fault. The story of the surprise test definitely allows Adam to revise his prediction on Friday in the light of what has happened previously in the week. Its logic would fall apart if one were to add the requirement that none of Adam's previous predictions must have been falsified. But, like marks in a shell game, we never thought to consider what Adam might have been predicting earlier in the week when we considered what he would predict if Friday were reached! What is going on is very simple. Adam will never be surprised by having a prediction falsified if he is always allowed to predict that today is the day of the test. Eve was therefore mistaken in announcing that he will be surprised when she springs her test on him. If we insist on making her assertion an assumption, we therefore create a contradiction. But anything whatever can be deduced from a contradiction – including the conclusion that Adam will be surprised when the test is given on the first day of the week.

Figure 2.8(c) shows a strategic form for the story of the surprise test that accords much more closely with what we mean when we talk about people being surprised when their predictions fail to be realized.

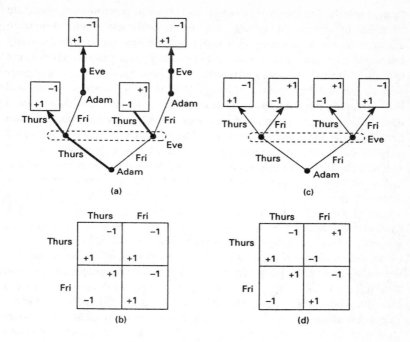

Figure 2.8 The surprise test

It is a simultaneous-move game in which Adam and Eve each choose either Thursday or Friday in ignorance of the choice of the other. However, if Adam chooses Thursday, he cannot change his mind if Thursday passes without a test. If he predicts Thursday, and Thursday passes without a test, then he will be surprised when Thursday comes to an end that his prediction is wrong. He might not be able to sustain his sense of astonishment overnight until Friday, but that is beside the point. To analyze Figure 2.8(c) is easy. The game has a unique Nash equilibrium in which Adam and Eve each use the mixed strategy that selects Thursday or Friday with equal probabilities. When this Nash equilibrium is used, Adam is surprised with probability $\frac{1}{2}$.

2.9 THE TIT-FOR-TAT HYPE

So far this chapter has been concerned with the fallacies and paradoxes that surround the one-shot Prisoners' Dilemma. However, now we turn to the infinitely repeated Prisoners' Dilemma, which has its own halo of mistakes and misapprehensions. In the infinitely repeated Prisoners' Dilemma, Adam and Eve keep playing the one-shot Prisoners' Dilemma over and over again. When making analytical statements, I shall use limit-of-the-mean payoffs to assess how well each player does in the repeated game.[13] One may think of this case as representing a limiting approximation to the game in which the one-shot Prisoners' Dilemma is repeated indefinitely often with a very small probability p that each repetition is the last. To retain comparability with some of the literature, the version of the one-shot Prisoners' Dilemma that will be repeated is that given in Figure 2.1(c) (instead of the version of Figure 2.1(b) with which we have been working up to now.)

The strategy Tit-for-Tat for the infinitely repeated Prisoners' Dilemma requires a player to begin by playing *dove*, and then to copy the action last made by the opponent at all subsequent stages of the game. If both players use Tit-for-Tat, the result will therefore be that *dove* always gets played. Figure 2.9(a) is a diagrammatic representation of Tit-for-Tat. The circles represent two possible 'states of mind'. The letters inside the circles show the action to be taken in each state. The sourceless arrow points to the circle representing the initial state. Since this contains the letter D, Tit-for-Tat begins by playing *dove*. Two arrows point away from the circle representing the initial state. One is labelled D and the other H. These arrows indicate the state to which a player using Tit-for-Tat should move after observing his opponent's reply to his use of *dove*. Notice that if the opponent ever 'cheats' by responding to *dove* by playing *hawk*, then a player using Tit-for-Tat moves to a 'punishment state' in which he plays *hawk*, and continues to do so until the opponent indicates his 'repentance' by playing *dove*. The existence of this punishment state ensures that it is a Nash equilibrium for both Adam and Eve to use Tit-for-Tat in the infinitely repeated Prisoners' Dilemma. Neither player has an incentive to deviate from Tit-for-Tat because such a deviation will be punished by the opponent.

Axelrod (1984) made the strategy Tit-for-Tat famous. Among other things, his book attributes the success of Tit-for-Tat in his computer tournament to its being both forgiving and nice. A 'nice' strategy is one that is never the first to defect. Figure 2.9(b) shows a 'nasty' strategy Tat-for-Tit first considered by Abreu and Rubinstein (1988). Figure 2.9(c)–(f) show some other strategies for the infinitely repeated Prisoners' Dilemma. The Grim strategy gets its name because it dif-

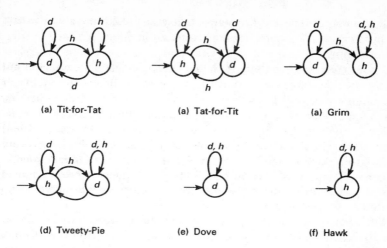

Figure 2.9 Strategies for the infinitely repeated Prisoners' Dilemma

fers from Tit-for-Tat in being utterly unforgiving. Nothing the opponent can do will serve to persuade Grim to leave its punishment state once it has been triggered. (No significance should be attached to the names given to the other strategies of Figure 2.9.) Notice that (*hawk, hawk*), (Tit-for-Tat, Tit-for-Tat), (Tat-for-Tit, Tat-for-Tit) and (Grim, Grim) are all Nash equilibria for infinitely repeated Prisoners' Dilemma when p is sufficiently close to 0.

Although the infinitely repeated Prisoners' Dilemma has infinitely many symmetric Nash equilibra, the literature focuses almost entirely on the equilibrium in which Adam and Eve both use Tit-for-Tat.[14] As Coll and Hirschleifer (1991) point out, this tunnel vision is accompanied by a stack of misapprehensions about what is and is not true of Nash equilibria in the infinitely repeated Prisoners' Dilemma. For example, Maynard Smith (1982, p. 202) offers a 'proof' that Tit-for-Tat is evolutionarily stable.[15] This is typical of a widespread belief that evolution will inevitably lead to the selection of Tit-for-Tat in the infinitely repeated Prisoners' Dilemma. Those who disdain evolutionary arguments are equally prone to error when defending Tit-for-Tat. The misapprehension under which they often labour is that (Tit-for-Tat, Tit-for-Tat) is not only a Nash equilibrium, but also a subgame-perfect equilibrium for the infinitely repeated Prisoners' Dilemma. Others make broader claims. Poundstone (1988, p. 245) tells us that:

It is a contention of game theory that you should never be the first to defect in a Prisoners' Dilemma situation.[16]

To set the record straight, it should be noted that Tit-for-Tat is not evolutionarily stable. In fact, no strategy is evolutionarily stable in the infinitely repeated Prisoners' Dilemma.[17] Nor is it true that the operation of evolution will necessarily lead to the selection of Tit-for-Tat. It is not even true that Tit-for-Tat was selected in Axelrod's (1984) simulated evolutionary process. It is not true that two Tit-for-Tats are a subgame-perfect equilibrium for the infinitely repeated Prisoners' Dilemma.[18] And it is very definitely false that game-theorists contend that a player should never be the first to defect in the infinitely repeated Prisoners' Dilemma.

Why have these myths grown up around Tit-for-Tat? Axelrod is partly to blame for writing his book so persuasively. However, I think the real reason is that Tit-for-Tat strikes such a chord of recognition in people's hearts that they cease to think critically about the arguments offered in its favour. Although we are all brought up as little deontologists, we all know deep down inside that it is reciprocity that really keeps society going. When we are offered this under-the-counter insight in the shape of a simple formula, we therefore seize upon it with relief. But some caution is advisable. Are not the reasons that make Tit-for-Tat intuitively attractive pretty much the same as those that led us to find the 'Clint' persona of Section 2.3 so appealing at first sight? Both endorse the highly practical principle that one should do-unto-others-as-they-do-unto-you.

Unlike the arguments for the 'Clint' persona based on players' choosing to have a transparent disposition, the arguments in favour of Tit-for-Tat do not call for out-of-equilibrium behaviour. The difficulty with Tit-for-Tat as a paradigm for rational behaviour in the infinitely repeated Prisoners' Dilemma is that it is only one of a very large number of equilibrium strategies. So why pick on Tit-for-Tat rather than one of its many rivals?

Tit-for-Tat owes its prominence to its success in a computer tournament reported in Axelrod's (1984) book. In this tournament, various individuals submitted computerized strategies for the repeated Prisoners' Dilemma. These were then matched against each other in pairs in order to determine which of the submitted strategies would do best. In a small pilot experiment with 14 entries, the most successful strategy was Tit-for-Tat, submitted by Anatol Rapoport.[19] This conclusion was advertised as a preliminary to the main experiment in which there was a field of 63 entries. Again Tit-for-Tat was the most successful strategy.

Axelrod reasoned that if he were to run further trials, then relatively unsuccessful strategies would be submitted less often. He therefore simulated further experiments artificially on a computer using an evolutionary process.[20] After simulating 1000 generations, he found that Tit-for-Tat was still the most successful strategy.

Nachbar (1989) offers a critical analysis of Axelrod's procedures.[21] He points out that Axelrod's evolutionary process cannot converge on anything that is not a symmetric Nash equilibrium of the 63 × 63 analog of the strategic form of Figure 2.5(b) that would be obtained by replacing its pure strategies by the 63 entrants in Axelrod's main experiment. In fact, after 1000 generations, Axelrod's evolutionary process comes very close to a mixed-strategy Nash equilibrium of the 63 × 63 game. That is to say, the fractions of the population using various strategies after 1000 generations approximate the probabilities with which these strategies are used in one of the Nash equilibria of the 63 × 63 game. In this mixed-strategy Nash equilibrium, Tit-for-Tat is used with a higher probability than any other pure strategy. However, there are other pure strategies that get used with probabilities that are only slightly smaller, and a whole stack of lesser pure strategies that get used with probabilities that are too large to be neglected. It is therefore not really true that Tit-for-Tat 'won' Axelrod's competition. The strategy that actually 'won' is a mixed strategy that calls for Tit-for-Tat to be used less than 15 per cent of the time.

In the preceding discussion, it is taken for granted that all 63 strategies in Axelrod's simulated evolutionary process get used equally often in the first generation. But one need not assume that the 63 submitted strategies are distributed evenly over the original population. Different strategies might be used by different fractions of the original population. Axelrod tried running his simulation with six different original strategy distributions. He found that Tit-for-Tat was the most numerous strategy after 1000 generations in five of these six cases. Actually, one can ensure convergence on *any* of the large number of Nash equilibria of the 63 × 63 game by choosing the original strategy distribution suitably. In repeating Axelrod's simulations, but using random initial strategy distributions, Linster (1990) finds that Tit-for-Tat is the most numerous strategy after 1000 generations only about 26 per cent of the time.

Perhaps it now begins to become clear that the 'success' of Tit-for-Tat in Axelrod's tournament is as much due to the nature of the initial population of strategies with which it had to compete as to its own intrinsic merits. Linster presses this point home by repeating Axelrod's procedure for the case in which the original population is no longer the 63 strategies studied by Axelrod, but consists instead of the 26 strategies that can be represented as in Figure 2.9 using no more than two circles to represent 'states of mind'. The most notable feature of Linster's simulation is the success, not of Tit-for-Tat, but of the unforgiving Grim strategy of Figure 2.9(c). Starting from random initial strategy distributions, it captures more than half of the population on average after 1000 generations.[22]

The lesson to be learned from this discussion is that one ought to be very cautious indeed before allowing oneself to be persuaded to accept general conclusions extrapolated from computer simulations. One always needs to ask how things would have changed if the circumstances under which the computer simulation was conducted had been different. If there is no evidence that similar data would have been generated under different circumstances, then one is not entitled to generalize any conclusions that the data available may suggest.

In respect of Axelrod's tournament, one may respond that Axelrod supports the conclusions suggested by his data theoretically. However, the theoretical arguments offered in defence of Tit-for-Tat can also be used to defend other strategies. For example, Tat-for-Tit of Figure 2.9(b) is also an equilibrium strategy for the infinitely repeated Prisoners' Dilemma that has just as simple a structure as Tit-for-Tat. But Tat-for-Tit is 'nasty' in that it begins by playing *hawk*. There is much that can be said in favour of a strategy like Tat-for-Tit. Its opening use of *hawk* may be interpreted as a signal of the type required in the Transparent Disposition Fallacies for the one-shot Prisoners' Dilemma. A player who uses *hawk* as a signal can be seen as advertising that he is the kind of tough guy that nobody would be wise to push around. If the signal is reciprocated, a player may then conclude that he has been paired with a like-minded player with whom it makes sense to cooperate on an equal basis. The anecdotes that Axelrod (1984, p. 73) tells about live-and-let-live arrangements between British and German units in the trenches during the First World War are at least as supportive of the real-life use of such a 'nasty' strategy as they are of the use of a 'nice' strategy like Tit-for-Tat.

What is more, Tat-for-Tit enjoys some evolutionary advantages over Tit-for-Tat if one believes that simplifying mutations should be regarded as more likely than complicating mutations. Imagine a population in which only the Tat-for-Tit replicator is originally present, but in which Tat-for-Tit is subject to continual mutation into the simpler replicators Dove and Hawk. Both these replicators will be at a disadvantage in a population in which the predominant replicator is Tat-for-Tit. Any foothold they establish in the population will therefore survive only because it is continually replenished by new mutations. However, the same is not true if the story is retold with Tit-for-Tat replacing Tat-for-Tit. The reason is that the replicator Tit-for-Tat cannot distinguish between an opponent who is hosting a copy of itself, and an opponent who is hosting Dove. Thus a population of all Tit-for-Tats is vulnerable to invasion by a simplifying mutation of itself. Indeed, if Hawk mutants did not occasionally appear on the scene and so keep the expansion of Doves in check, the latter would eventually displace the original Tit-for-Tat population altogether.[23]

I am not attempting to invent a new mythology for the infinitely repeated Prisoners' Dilemma in which the role of Tit-for-Tat is usurped by Tat-for-Tit. It is true that a population of all Tat-for-Tits is less vulnerable to invasion by simplifying mutations than a population of all Tit-for-Tats, but it is also true that Tat-for-Tits must be expected to have a harder time getting themselves established in a hostile environment. For example, in Linster's (1990) evolutionary simulation that uses all 26 one-state and two-state strategies as the original population, the fraction of the population controlled by 'nasty' strategies after 1000 generations is less than 0.0000000001.[24]

However, one should pause before generalizing too readily from either Axelrod's (1987) original study or from Linster's later study. Both proceed from an original population from which many possibilities have been excluded for no very good reason. A better guide is perhaps provided by the much more extensive simulation run by Probst (1992), who follows Axelrod (1987) in using Holland's 'genetic algorithm' to widen the class of available strategies from which natural selection can make a choice.[25] This study confirms that naive reciprocators like Tit-for-Tat do well in the short run, but casts doubt on their long-run viability. In Probst's study, the naive reciprocators that are so successful at the outset are eventually displaced by nasty machines like Tat-for-Tit which only cooperate after a suitable strength-signalling message has been exchanged.[26]

The truth is that the evolutionary considerations are complicated. The evidence does seem to support the hypothesis that evolutionary pressures will tend to select equilibria for the infinitely repeated Prisoners' Dilemma in which the players cooperate in the long run. (For some theoretical arguments that point in this direction, see Fudenberg and Maskin, 1990, or Binmore and Samuelson, 1990.) However, there are an infinite number of different equilibria that result in Adam and Eve eventually playing *dove* all the time in the infinitely repeated Prisoners' Dilemma. One cannot say anything definitive about precisely which of these evolution will select, because this will depend on accidents of history. However, the evidence from simulations does strongly suggest that it is unlikely that a pure equilibrium will get selected. One must anticipate the selection of a mixed Nash equilibrium. When such an equilibrium is realized, many different rules of behaviour for the infinitely repeated Prisoners' Dilemma will survive together in a symbiotic relationship. However, as all married folk know, to be part of a symbiotic relationship does not imply that pure harmony reigns. Neither the workings of enlightened self-interest nor the blind forces of evolution offer us any guarantees about the removal of 'nasty' strategies. On the contrary, nastiness is something with which a rational society must somehow learn to live.

2.10 CONCLUSION

One day, somebody will write a history of the myths and legends engendered by the Prisoners' Dilemma. Such a history will be a case study in how wishful thinking can triumph over plain common-sense – even when the thinkers are very clever and the problem with which they are faced is very simple. It is a history that will bring some game-theorists to the edge of despair. However, I prefer to look on the bright side. After all, we must be doing something worthwhile if so many clever folk can get so hung up on so trivial a game as the Prisoners' Dilemma.

Notes

1. This paper is condensed from chapters 2 and 3 of a planned book, *Playing Fair: Game Theory and the Social Contract*.
2. I think that game-theorists give Rousseau more credit than is his due in treating his tale as an equilibrium selection problem for the so-called Stag-Hunt Game.
3. The payoffs are given in dollars to give a concrete feel to the discussion. However, as always in a game-theoretic discussion, it should be assumed that the players seek to maximize their expected payoff.
4. This is a primitive representation because it neglects the fact that Adam,

for example, should gain some pleasure from contemplating the fact that Eve gains from contemplating his pleasure. For something more sophisticated, see Bergstrom (1989).

5. Who is not to be confused with the Nigel Howard of Section 2.4.1.
6. Gauthier was by no means the first to formulate this game. It is a perennial in the literature. But, as far as I know, only Gauthier claims that an analysis of his 'metagame' is the same thing as a rational analysis of the Prisoners' Dilemma.
7. Actually, Rapoport considers the general form of the Prisoners' Dilemma. I have doctored the quotation that follows to suit the particular case of Figure 2.1(b).
8. All finite symmetric games have at least one symmetric Nash equilibrium if mixed strategies are allowed. But why should the players use a symmetric equilibrium if they both prefer an asymmetric Nash equilibrium?
9. Game-theorists sometimes airily dismiss Newcomb's Paradox on the grounds that it is impossible that Eve could be sure of predicting Adam's choice, because he could always make his decision depend on the fall of a coin. But this is not a very useful response. We can modify the Newcomb story so that Eve always chooses *hawk* unless Adam chooses *dove* for certain. For this reason, I shall stick with the conventional story and not allow Adam to mix his choices.
10. For example, one can see Eve as nothing other than an embodiment of the 'Clint' persona of Section 2.3. The Newcomb problem then becomes a simplified form of Nigel Howard's 1–2 metagame of Figure 2.4. (The simplification is that Eve's reasons for choosing the 'Clint' persona are left unexplained.) Section 2.3 concentrated on the difficulties that Eve would have in making a *commitment* to the 'Clint' persona. But here such difficulties are assumed away. Instead, the Newcomb problem focuses attention on a second difficulty that was mentioned only in passing in Section 2.3. To operate the 'Clint' persona, Adam's intentions must be transparent to Eve. She must be able to predict his intentions perfectly. My guess is that part of the reason that stories involving the 'Clint' persona are popular, is that expressing this requirement in terms of such personas disguises the fact that the perfect prediction hypothesis is equivalent to Adam's moving *first* and Eve's moving *second* – as in Figure 2.6(a).
11. Except in the uninteresting sense that there are no physical barriers to his using one move rather than another.
12. A less crude definition will generate a more sophisticated paradox. However, I believe the definition proposed here is what is usually intended.
13. Each player's payoff is then taken to be the limit as $n \to \infty$ of his mean payoff over the first n repetitions of the one-shot Prisoners' Dilemma. Players are then interested only in what happens in the long run.
14. Indeed, the transaction-costs literature seems to know nothing of the theory of repeated games beyond the phrase 'tit-for-tat'. This is used to label any situation in which the author wishes to argue that a cooperative outcome can be sustained by the understanding that anyone who deviates will be punished in the future.
15. Maynard Smith attributes the proof of Axelrod. Axelrod (1984) actually

proves that Tit-for-Tat is what he calls 'collectively stable'. This just means that a pair of Tit-for-Tats is a Nash equilibrium. It is not true, as Axelrod (p. 217) asserts, that collective stability and evolutionarily stability are equivalent in the infinitely repeated Prisoners' Dilemma when attention is restricted to 'nice' strategies.

16. It is commonplace that commentators fail to appreciate the importance of distinguishing between the one-shot Prisoners' Dilemma and its infinitely repeated cousins.

17. A population whose members all play Tit-for-Tat is not evolutionarily stable because a mutant bridgehead of *doves* will not be extinguished. In general, no strategy in a game can be evolutionarily stable if its use by the whole population results in certain parts of the game tree never being reached.

18. Although, since I believe that evolutionary considerations are what is important in this context, I do not attach much significance to this fact.

19. In this pilot, the entrants were told that the Prisoners' Dilemma would be repeated precisely 200 times. Such a *finitely* repeated Prisoners' Dilemma has a unique subgame-perfect equilibrium in which both Adam and Eve plan to play *hawk* under all eventualities. There are also many Nash equilibria, but all of these result in *hawk* always actually being played. Axelrod abandoned the finitely repeated Prisoners' Dilemma for his main experiment and used instead a version of the infinitely repeated Prisoners' Dilemma in which each repetition was the last with probability $p = 0.00346$.

20. In this process, the fraction of the participants using a particular strategy in one generation is taken to be proportional to the product of the fraction using that strategy in the previous generation and the payoff it was accorded in the previous generation. Axelrod made no provision for mutation in his evolutionary simulation. No strategies beyond the original 63 were therefore allowed to enter the fray. He signals this by speaking of *ecological* success rather than *evolutionary* success.

21. Nachbar (1989) concentrates on the fact that Axelrod's evolutionary simulation was really based on the *finitely* repeated Prisoners' Dilemma rather than the infinitely repeated Prisoners' Dilemma that he advertised. In the infinitely repeated version, the number of times the Prisoners' Dilemma gets repeated is a random variable. For his main experiment, Axelrod accordingly sampled five game lengths (63, 77, 151, 156 and 308) from the appropriate exponential distribution, thereby creating five finitely repeated Prisoners' Dilemmas of varying lengths. Each strategy played each of these five repeated games against every other strategy. This is a legitimate method of implementing the requirement that the number of repetitions be indefinite. It is true that Axelrod knew the number of repetitions, but what matters is that the participants did not. However, Axelrod used the *same* game lengths in each generation of his simulated evolutionary process. This is not strictly legitimate because, although the participants did not know the chosen lengths at the first trial, everyone would eventually find out what they were after observing a sufficiently long sequence of trials. To dramatize the reason that this might conceivably matter, consider what would have happened if *all* pure strategies for the

308-times repeated Prisoners' Dilemma had been submitted. (One needs a large imagination to envisage this possibility, since the number N of such strategies is 2 raised to the power $\frac{1}{3}(4^{308}-1)$.) Axelrod would then have had to consider an $N \times N$ game instead of a 63 × 63 game. As in the 63 × 63 cases, his evolutionary process cannot converge on anything but a Nash equilibrium of the $N \times N$ game. But, in all such equilibria, only *hawk* ever gets played. Fortunately, it turns out that this line of criticism is academic. Linster (1990) has repeated the Axelrod calculations using the infinitely repeated Prisoners' Dilemma in each generation. This produces different results from those reported by Axelrod, but the differences are too slight to affect Axelrod's qualitative conclusions.

22. This is in stark contrast to the fate of Grim in Axelrod's tournament. This was submitted by James Friedman and hence referred to by Axelrod as 'Friedman'. Of all the 'nice' strategies in Axelrod's tournament, 'Friedman' did worst.

23. For a simple model, adapt the standard replicator dynamics so that there is a small probability ε that a child of a player hosting Tit-for-Tat is a mutant Dove or Hawk. If these mutations are equally likely and other mutations cannot occur, it is trivial to show that the dynamics admit a rest point in which Tit-for-Tat controls $\frac{1}{3}$ of the population, Dove controls $\frac{2}{3} - \delta$ and Hawk controls δ, where $\delta = 6\varepsilon/(1 + 6\varepsilon)$.

24. On the other hand, Grim's fraction is 0.575, Tit-for-Tat gets 0.163, and even Dove manages 0.007.

25. He allows finite automata with up to 25 states and considers time horizons of up to 10 000 generations.

26. This cooperative regime does not persist unperturbed. It is punctuated by rare and transient plunges into non-cooperative turmoil, after which nice machines briefly dominate again while the system finds its way back to the standard cooperative regime.

References

Abreu, D. and H. Rubinstein (1988) 'The Structure of Nash Equilibrium in Repeated Games with Finite Automata', *Econometrica*, vol. 56, pp. 1259–82.

Aumann, R. (1987) 'Correlated Equilibrium as an Expression of Bayesian Rationality', *Econometrica*, vol. 55, pp. 1–18.

Axelrod, R. (1984) *The Evolution of Cooperation* (New York: Basic Books).

Axelrod, R. (1987) 'The Evolution of Strategies in the Iterated Prisoners' Dilemma', in L. Davis (ed.), *Genetic Algorithms and Simulated Annealing* (Los Altos, Calif.: Morgan Kaufmann).

Bergstrom, T. (1989) 'Love and Spaghetti, the Opportunity Cost of Virtue', *Journal of Economic Perspectives*, vol. 3, pp. 165–73.

Binmore, K.G. and L. Samuelson (1990) 'Evolutionary Stability in Repeated Games Played by Finite Automata', forthcoming in *Journal of Economic Theory*.

Brams, S. (1983) *Superior Beings* (New York: Springer-Verlag).

Coll, J. and J. Hirshleifer (1991) 'The Limits of Reciprocity', *Rationality and Society*, vol. 3, pp. 35–64.

Frank, R. (1988) *Passions within Reason* (New York: Norton).

Fudenberg, D. and E. Maskin (1990) 'Evolution and Cooperation in Noisy Repeated Games', *American Economic Review*, vol. 80, pp. 274–9.

Gauthier, D. (1986) *Morals by Agreement* Oxford: Clarendon Press).

Hofstadter, D. (1983) 'Metamagical Themes', *Scientific American*, vol. 248, no. 6, pp. 14–20.

Howard, J. (1988) 'Cooperation in the Prisoners' Dilemma', *Theory and Decision*, vol. 24, pp. 203–13.

Howard, Nigel (1971) *Paradoxes of Rationality: Theory of Metagames and Political Behavior* (Cambridge, Mass.: MIT Press).

Kant, I. (1785) *Groundwork of the Metaphysic of Morals*, translated and analyzed by H. Paton (1964) (New York: Harper Torchbooks).

Levi, I. (1982) 'A Note on Newcombmania', *Journal of Philosophy*, vol. 79, pp. 337–42.

Lewis, D. (1979) 'Prisoners' Dilemma as a Newcomb Problem', *Philosophy and Public Affairs*, vol. 8, pp. 235–40.

Linster, B. (1990) 'Essays on Cooperation and Competition', PhD thesis, University of Michigan.

Maynard Smith, J. (1982) *Evolution and the Theory of Games* (Cambridge: Cambridge University Press).

Nachbar, J. (1989) 'The Evolution of Cooperation Revisted', Working Paper, Rand Cooperation.

Nozick, R. (1969) 'Newcomb's Problem and Two Principles of Choice', in N. Rescher (ed.), *Essays in Honor of Carl G. Hempel* (Dordrecht, Netherlands: Reidel).

Poundstone, W. (1988) *Labyrinths of Reason* (New York: Doubleday).

Probst, D. (1992) 'Evolution in the Repeated Prisoners' Dilemma', Working Paper (in preparation), University of Bonn.

Rapoport, A. (1966) *Two-Person Game Theory* (Ann Arbor, Michigan: University of Michigan Press).

Rousseau, J.-J. (1762) 'The Social Contract', in G. Cole (ed.) (1913), *Rousseau's Social Contract and Discourses*, pp. 5–123 (London: J.M. Dent).

Savage, L. (1951) *The Foundations of Statistics* (New York: Wiley).

Sen, A. (1973) 'Behaviour and the Concept of Preference', *Economica*, vol. 40, pp. 241–59.

Spinoza, B. De (first published 1674) *Tractatus politicus*, translated by R. Elwes (1909) in *Chief Works of Benedict de Spinoza, Volume I* (London: Bell).

3 Aggregation, Learning and Rationality

Jean-Michel Grandmont

CENTRE D'ÉTUDES PROSPECTIVES D'ÉCONOMIE MATHÉMATIQUE
APPLIQUÉE À LA PLANIFICATION, PARIS

3.1 INTRODUCTION

The assumption that individual economic units behave 'rationally' is widely used in many areas of economic theorizing, be it in micro-economics or macroeconomics. The purpose of this chapter is to review briefly a few recent studies that tend to challenge two aspects of this assumption.

The first issue concerns the pervasive idea that economic theory should start from 'first principles' and portray individual economic units (in particular, households) as maximizing a well-defined objective function. But it has been known for a while that this approach involves severe difficulties: if the distribution of individual characteristics is arbitrary, aggregation of optimizing households yields almost anything, hence nothing, at the macroeconomic level. In fact, postulates about individual rationality have to be used in practice jointly with additional, and often crucial, assumptions in order to get any meaningful result. For instance, some macro-economists make the extremely naive assumption that society as a whole behaves as a single optimizing individual. Theorists of imperfect competition or industrial organization often rely upon convenient but rather arbitrary assumptions about aggregate demand, such as concave revenue functions or even linear demand schedules. The problem with such auxiliary assumptions is that they do not appear to be grounded upon sound theorizing.

The first section of the paper reviews a few recent theoretical advances, suggesting that aggregation over a large heterogeneous population might provide a solution to these problems. The key point seems to be that heterogeneity tends to make aggregate expenditures more independent of relative prices. In a context of market equilibrium, this fact has strong implications for the prevalence of the weak axioms of revealed preference and of gross substitutability, and for the uniqueness and stability of a Walrasian exchange equilibrium. In (partial equilibrium) models of imperfect competition, demand heterogeneity leads to concave revenue functions and, for instance, to a unique Cournot oligopoly equilibrium. One of the most intriguing features of the new approach is that, while it is compatible with the standard postulate that individual households are indeed optimizing, it relies essentially upon distributional assumptions about heterogeneity and imposes very few 'rationality' requirements on individual behaviour. As heterogeneity of individual characteristics appears to be a plausible hypothesis, the new approach accordingly suggests that, in contrast with currently accepted views, attention in economic theory might advantagenously be shifted away from individual optimization and focussed more upon analysing the consequences of heterogeneous macroeconomic distributions.

The second part of the paper questions the 'rational expectations' hypothesis that is so widely used in dynamic economic models (and, for that matter, in game theory) or, specifically, the hypothesis that an individual's expectations about the future are correct at any moment, given current information. A frequently heard defence of the hypothesis is that it should be the asymptotic outcome of a dynamic process in which individuals learn about the laws of motion of their environment. The second section therefore also briefly reviews recent studies suggesting that taking learning into account often generates dynamic local instability. These studies suggest further that the dynamics, with learning, may be decidedly nonlinear and generate complex trajectories, and moreover that mistakes in forecasting may never vanish, even in the 'long run'.

3.2 AGGREGATION AND RATIONALITY

It is well known that standard economic theory (i.e. assuming individual optimizing behaviour) does not generate many restrictions on aggregate market phenomena. The nagging result here is Sonnenschein's (1973, 1974) indeterminacy theorem as refined by McFadden, Mantel, Mas-Colell, Richter, Debreu and others (survey by Shafer and Sonnenschein, 1982): if the distribution of microeconomic characteristics in the system is arbitrary, individual optimizing behaviour does not place any restrictions on excess demand in a competitive market, with any given set of prices, other than homogeneity and Walras's law. Indeterminacy of this sort is clearly bound to be a pervasive phenomenon. In particular, it should not be confined to models of competition.

Underlying this result is the assumption that the distribution of microeconomic characteristics is arbitrary. The diagnosis accordingly hints at a possible way out that has been known for some time, namely to build our theories upon plausible restrictions on the distribution of individual characteristics. In particular, it has often been observed that there is apparently significant behavioural heterogeneity among economic agents, and it has been accordingly suggested that taking into account such heterogeneity might be useful in this area.

There has been some progress in research on this front in recent times. Hildenbrand (1983) took a decisive step by showing that heterogeneity of the income distribution may make macroeconomic income effects negligible in multimarket consumer demand analysis, to leave us with 'nice' aggregate substitution effects only – specifically, the Jacobian matrix of the price derivatives of market demand becomes negative quasi-definite for every price system (see also Grandmont, 1987). Another important idea was due to Jerison (1982, 1984, 1992) who showed that, roughly speaking, increasing dispersion of household Engels curves as income rises leads to the weak axiom of revealed preference in the aggregate, when the distribution of income is fixed. By marrying the two lines of argument, variants of the above increasing dispersion hypothesis were also shown to imply negative quasi-definiteness of the Jacobian matrix of the price derivatives of market demand, and have been confronted with empirical data with rather convincing results (Härdle, Hildenbrand and Jerison, 1991; Hildenbrand, 1989, 1992). While this approach is an outstanding methodological achievement, it applies essentially to the case in which incomes or expenditures are independent of prices, and it is apparently difficult to extend it beyond this restrictive situation. When specialized to a market for a single good or service, it yields only a downward-sloping demand schedule, which still falls short of what is needed in the study of models of imperfect competition.

Another approach, complementary to that of Hildenbrand and Jerison, has recently been fairly successful. It seeks to introduce plausible heterogeneities in other dimensions of individual characteristics, namely in consumers' demand schedules. This line of attack has its roots in, and generalizes, the notion of household equivalence scales which has been much used in applied demand analysis (Prais and Houthakker,

1955; Barten, 1964; Jorgenson and Slesnick, 1987). Dispersion of such demand schedules was introduced in general competitive equilibrium analysis some time ago by Mas-Colell and Neuefind (1977) and by Dierker, Dierker and Trockel (1984). A particular case was considered under the name of 'replicas' in Jerison (1982 and 1984). It has also been used by H. Dierker (1989) and E. Dierker (1989) to inquire whether demand heterogeneity might help in ensuring existence of equilibrium in imperfect competition models.

The recent discovery has been that demand heterogeneity of this sort makes aggregate expenditures more independent of prices. In multimarket consumer demand analysis, with incomes or expenditures independent of prices, this yields an aggregate Jacobian matrix of price derivatives with a negative dominant diagonal for a large set of prices. Moreover, in a competitive general equilibrium context, in which incomes *are* dependent on prices, this fact has important consequences for the prevalence, in the aggregate, of the weak axiom of revealed preferences, of gross substitutability, and also for the uniqueness and stability of the Walrasian exchange equilibrium (Grandmont, 1922a). When specialized to a market for a single commodity, the approach implies that a relatively large heterogeneity in individual demand behaviours yields an aggregate demand that is not only downward sloping, but with an elasticity that is not too far from minus 1. Demand heterogeneity of this sort makes easier the study of imperfect competition. In particular, it implies a unique Cournot oligopoly equilibrium (Grandmont, 1992b).

An important feature of the approach is that while it is compatible with the hypothesis that individual households optimize it is in fact much more general, since it relies upon very few 'rationality' requirements for microeconomic behaviour. The approach accordingly suggests that attention in economic theory might fruitfully be redirected away from the study of individual optimization toward the analysis of macroeconomic distributions of individual characteristics.

The whole analysis rests upon the estimation of bounds for the price elasticities of aggregate demand that depend explicitly upon specific measures of heterogeneity. The derivation of these bounds is quite simple and we will present it in some detail here. We shall then explain heuristically how, on the basis of these bounds, heterogeneity generates strong macroeconomic regularities in general competitive exchange equilibrium and in models of imperfect competition.

3.2.1 Equivalence Scales

We consider an economic system in which ℓ goods or services are exchanged. A commodity bundle is then described by a vector x of $\mathbb{R}^\ell$. To focus ideas, we concentrate on households' consumption behaviour. A demand function will be a *continuous vector valued function* $x(p,b) \geqq 0$. It represents the commodity bundle demanded when the price system is p in $\text{Int}\mathbb{R}_+^\ell$ and the household's income is $b > 0$. We shall assume throughout that Walras's law holds (i.e. $p \cdot x(p,b) \equiv b$). At this stage, we do *not* assume homogeneity of degree 0 of demand with respect to (p,w), as many intermediary results do not require this property.

The core of the approach is that whenever a household having the demand function $x(p,b)$ is present in the population there is a continuum of individuals who have the same demand function, up to a rescaling of the units of measurement of each commodity h by a factor $\beta_h > 0$. To see what should be the form of the 'rescaled' demand function, consider a *fictitious* operation in which the unit of measurement of each commodity h is divided by β_h. If the price vector in the fictitious units is p, the price vector in the actual units is given by

$$(\beta_1 p_1, \ldots, \beta_\ell p_\ell) = \beta \otimes p$$

Thus demand, expressed in the fictitious units, is $\beta \otimes x(\beta \otimes p, b) = [\beta_1 x_1(\beta \otimes p, b), \ldots, \beta_\ell x_\ell(\beta \otimes p, b)]$. By definition, the rescaled demand function corresponding to the vector β, *expressed in the actual unit system* (which is in fact fixed throughout!) is equal to the above expression, that is to $\beta \otimes x(\beta \otimes p, b)$. In the sequel, it will be much more convenient to work with the rescaling parameters $\alpha_h = \text{Log}\beta_h$, which can take any positive or negative value. With the convention $e^\alpha = e^{\alpha_1}, \ldots, e^{\alpha_\ell})$, *the rescaled demand function is thus given by* $e^\alpha \otimes x(e^\alpha \otimes p, b)$.

It should be noted that although we did not (and shall not) require that demand functions be the outcome of utility maximization, rescaling operations are quite compatible with that requirement. If, for instance, the original demand function $x(p,b)$ is obtained by maximizing the utility function $u(x)$ under the budget constraint $p \cdot x = b$, then the rescaled demand function maximizes the rescaled utility function $u(e^{-\alpha} \otimes x)$ under the budget constraint

$$p \cdot x = (e^\alpha \otimes p) \cdot (e^{-\alpha} \otimes x) = b$$

3.2.2 Market Demand

Whenever a household present in the population has the demand function $x(p,b)$, there is a continuum of individuals who have the rescaled demand function $e^{\alpha}\otimes x(e^{\alpha}\otimes p,b)$. These individuals are indexed by the vector α of rescaling parameters and they are assumed to be distributed according to the density function $f(\alpha)$. Aggregating demands over this subpopulation yields the *conditional market demand*

$$X(p,b) = \int e^{\alpha}\otimes x(e^{\alpha}\otimes p,b)\, f(\alpha)\, d\alpha$$

We are now in a framework in which we can speak meaningfully of the 'heterogeneity' of this subpopulation by looking at the dispersion of the density $f(\alpha)$. We shall see that a large dispersion implies a well-behaved conditional market demand, even if individual demands are not well behaved.

Our strategy is to show that conditional market expenditures $p_h X_h(p,b)$ have continuous first derivatives and to estimate bounds for these derivatives that depend explicitly on the dispersion of the density $f(\alpha)$. For this purpose, it is convenient to introduce the notation $w_h(p,b) = p_h x_h(p,b)$. Then it follows from the definition of conditional market demand that conditional market expenditures are given by

$$p_h X_h(p,b) = \int w_h(e^{\alpha}\otimes p,b)\, f(\alpha)\, d\alpha$$

If we use the shorthand notation $\mathrm{Log}p = (\mathrm{Log}p_1,\ldots,\mathrm{Log}p_\ell)$, and make the change of variable $r = \alpha + \mathrm{Log}p$, we obtain

$$p_h X_h(p,b) = \int w_h(e^r,b)\, f(r - \mathrm{Log}p)\, dr \qquad (3.1)$$

It is clear from this expression that if we assume that *the density $f(\alpha)$ is continuously differentiable and its partial derivatives are uniformally integrable* $\left(\text{i.e. } \int \left|\dfrac{\partial f}{\partial \alpha_k}(\alpha)\right|\, d\alpha \leqq m_k\right)$ then conditional market expenditure is also continuously differentiable. Taking partial derivatives of (3.1) with respect to $\mathrm{Log}p_k$ and reverting to the original vector of variables $\alpha = r - \mathrm{Log}p$, yields, then,

$$\frac{\partial[p_h X_h(p,b)]}{\partial \mathrm{Log}p_k} = -\int w_h(e^{\alpha}\otimes p,b)\, \frac{\partial f}{\partial \alpha_k}(\alpha)\, d\alpha \qquad (3.2)$$

It is now easy to find bounds for the price derivatives of market expenditure. Since the absolute value of the right-hand side of (3.2) is bounded above by bm_k, we obtain

$$\left| \frac{\partial [p_h X_h(p,b)]}{\partial \mathrm{Log}\, p_k} \right| \; \leqq \; bm_k \tag{3.3}$$

It should be noted that these bounds are valid for all densities $f(\alpha)$, even if they are rather concentrated. The coefficients m_k appearing in (3.3) measure in some sense the dispersion of the density. If they are small, the distribution of the rescaling parameters α should be spread out. In that case, the inequalities (3.3) tell us that conditional market expenditures do not vary much with prices. This is the simple but important fact around which the whole analysis is built.

A nice feature of the inequalities (3.3) is that they are *additive*, in the sense that if we put together two subpopulations satisfying these inequalities, then the mixture will also satisfy them. Specifically, consider a set of 'types' a in some set A (we assume that A is a separable metric space). To each type a corresponds a demand function $x_a(p,b)$ and an income level $b_a > 0$ (we assume for the moment that income is independent of prices, but this assumption will be relaxed later). The population is distributed over types according to the probability distribution μ. For each type a present in the population (i.e. in the support of μ), there is a continuum of individuals who have the same demand up to a vector α of rescaling parameters, and these individuals are assumed to be distributed according to the conditional density $f(\alpha \,|\, a)$. Then for each type present in the population, *conditional market demand* is defined as before by

$$X_a(p,b) = \int e^{\alpha} \otimes x_a(e^{\alpha} \otimes p,b)\, f(\alpha \,|\, a)\, d\alpha \tag{3.4}$$

while *total market demand* is obtained by aggregating over types

$$X(p) = \int_A X_a(p,b_a)\, \mu(da) \tag{3.5}$$

(We assume here enough regularity for all these integrals to be well defined.) The important point is that, if the conditional densities $f(\alpha \,|\, a)$ have uniformly integrable partial derivatives with $\int \left| \frac{\partial f}{\partial \alpha_k}(\alpha \,|\, a) \right| d\alpha \leqq m_k$, for every type a in the support of μ, each *conditional* market demand satisfies the inequalities (3.3), with $b = b_a$. Then, if per capita total income is finite (i.e. $\bar{b} = \int b_a\, \mu(d_a) < +\infty$), *total* market demand will also satisfy them, by integration over all types; that is

$$\left| \frac{\partial[p_h X_h(p)]}{\partial \mathrm{Log}\, p_k} \right| \leqq \bar{b}\, m_k \tag{3.6}$$

We should therefore expect total market demand to be well behaved when there is significant heterogeneity in the system (i.e. when the conditional densities $f(\alpha\,|\,a)$ are spread out) since, according to the inequalities (3.6), total market expenditures become relatively independent of prices when the coefficients m_k are small. In order to make the argument tight, however, we have to ensure that total market demand does not vanish when heterogeneity grows. To this end, we suppose that aggregate budget shares are uniformly bounded away from 0, or more precisely that *there exist* $\gamma_h > 0$ *such that* $\gamma_h\, \bar{b} \leqq p_h X_h(p)$ *for all* p and all h. This assumption, together with (3.4), yields immediately

$$\left| \frac{\partial \mathrm{Log}\, X_h(p)}{\partial \mathrm{Log}\, p_k} + \delta_{hk} \right| \leqq \bar{b}\, m_k/p_h X_h(p) \leqq m_k/\gamma_h \tag{3.7}$$

where δ_{hk} is the Kronecker symbol (i.e. δ_{hk} is equal to 1 when $h = k$ and to 0 otherwise). These evaluations of market demand price elasticities show that when heterogeneity grows (if the coefficients m_k become small), other things being equal, the consumption sector behaves very well, since aggregate demand price elasticities become asymptotically close to those arising from the maximization of a Cobb–Douglas utility function. One has, of course, to be careful about the *ceteris paribus* clause and make sure that the parameters γ_h appearing in (3.7) are actually independent of the coefficients of heterogeneity m_k. One simple way to guarantee this outcome is to assume that the conditional densities $f(\alpha\,|\,a)$ are actually independent of the type a, and that when aggregating the demands $x_a(p, b_a)$ over all types, one indeed gets

$$\gamma_h \bar{b} \leqq p_h \int_A x_{ah}(p, b_a)\, \mu(da)$$

for all prices and all commodities h. The results we review here are all derived under this simplifying assumption of independence. But it should be emphasized that any other specification ensuring that aggregate budget shares are uniformly bounded below by $\gamma_h > 0$, independently of the coefficients of heterogeneity m_h, generates exactly the same picture.

Inequalities (3.7) imply that *the Jacobian matrix of total market demand price derivatives has a negative dominant diagonal on a set of prices that is large when, other things being equal, the coefficients of heterogeneity m_k are small.* To see this point, note first that from (3.7), total market demand for commodity h is a decreasing function of its own price when $m_h < \gamma_h$. In that case, (3.7) implies

$$\frac{1}{X_h(p)} \left| \frac{\partial X_h}{\partial p_h}(p) \right| \gtreqqless (\gamma_h - m_h)/(p_h \, \gamma_h)$$

while for $k \neq h$

$$\frac{1}{X_h(p)} \left| \frac{\partial X_h}{\partial p_k}(p) \right| \lesseqqgtr m_k/(p_k \, \gamma_h)$$

Then it follows that the Jacobian matrix $\dfrac{dX}{dp}(p)$ has a negative dominant diagonal (i.e. $\left| \dfrac{\partial p_h}{\partial p_h}(p) \right| > \sum_{k \neq h} \left| \dfrac{\partial X_h}{\partial p_k}(p) \right|$ on the set of prices defined by the inequalities $\sum_k (m_k/p_k) < \gamma_h/p_h$) for every commodity h. As stated above, this set of prices is large when, other things being equal, the densities $f(\alpha \mid a)$ are spread out, i.e. when the coefficients m_k are small.

3.2.3 Competitive Exchange Equilibrium

The methods we have presented above yield striking results when applied to a general exchange equilibrium. To be specific, let us assume now that a type a defines not only a demand function $x_a(p,b)$, but also an endowment of goods ω_a in $\mathrm{Int}\mathbb{R}_+^\ell$. For each type a present in the population, conditional market demand $x_a(p,b)$ is given by (3.4) as before. But income is now price dependent since it is equal to the value $p \cdot \omega_a$ of the endowment. *Conditional market excess demand* is thus equal to $Z_a(p) = X_a(p,p \cdot \omega_a) - \omega_a$, while *total market excess demand* is obtained by aggregation over all types

$$Z(p) = \int_A Z_a(p) \, \mu(da)$$

(we suppose here that per capita total endowment, i.e. $\bar{\omega} = \int_A \omega_a \mu(da)$, is finite). An *exchange equilibrium* is accordingly a price vector p^* such that total excess demand vanishes on each market (i.e. $Z(p^*) = 0$).

It turns out that demand heterogeneity, or more precisely conditional densities $f(\alpha|a)$ that are relatively spread out, has important consequences for the uniqueness and stability of equilibrium in a simple exchange economy of this sort. The method of analysis is, here as before, to evaluate bounds for price derivatives that depend explicitly on the degree of heterogeneity in the system (i.e. on the coefficients m_k). The method is applied here to the *excess* demands $Z_a(p)$, so these price derivatives involve not only the price derivatives of conditional market demand $X_a(p,b)$, but (since income is equal to $p\cdot\omega_a$) the income derivatives of X_a also. One has therefore to suppose here the elementary demand functions $x_a(p,b)$ to be homogeneous of degree 0 in prices and income, in order to keep aggregate income effects under control. Then application of the same type of argument as led to the inequalities (3.6) or (3.7) yields that total excess demand has a *gross substitutability* property (i.e. $\dfrac{\partial Z_h}{\partial p_k}(p) > 0$ for $h \neq k$) on a set of prices that is large when the degree of heterogeneity in the system is significant (i.e. when the coefficients m_k are relatively small), other things being equal. This implies *uniqueness* of the equilibrium price vector p^* (up to multiplication by a scalar). One gets in addition that the *weak axiom of revealed preferences* holds in the aggregate, i.e. $p^*\cdot Z(p) > 0$, as between the equilibrium price system p^* and any other price vector p that is not collinear to p^*. Finally, these results imply that the unique equilibrium price vector is *stable* in any standard tâtonnement process, its basin of attraction being large and filling eventually the entire price space when the degree of heterogeneity grows, i.e. when the coefficients m_k become small (for a precise analysis, see Grandmont, 1992a).

3.2.4 Cournot Oligopoly Equilibrium

Demand heterogeneity has important consequences for the study of Cournot oligopoly equilibrium as well (Grandmont, 1992b). To see this, let us specialize our previous formulation of market demand to a partial equilibrium analysis of what happens for a single commodity h, the conditions prevailing on other markets being fixed. The evaluation (3.7) of market demand's own price elasticity then reads

$$\left| \frac{\partial \text{Log} X_h(p)}{\partial \text{Log} p_h} + 1 \right| \leq m_h/\gamma_h \tag{3.8}$$

Thus we are sure that market demand is downward sloping whenever $m_h < \gamma_h$. This is not enough, however, if we wish to study Cournot competition among firms in that market. Indeed, the properties of market demand usually needed in configurations of this sort, such as concave revenue functions, require also that the second own price derivative of the market demand function be 'well behaved'. The important point about the approach presented here is *that heterogeneity allows us to keep under control not only the first price derivatives of market demand, but higher order price derivatives also*. This is most apparent if we go back to identity (3.1), which was the starting point of the whole analysis. This identity expresses conditional market expenditure, when we aggregate over 'rescaled' demand functions distributed according to the density $f(\alpha)$. Now, if we assume that the density function is twice continuously differentiable and that its second partial derivative with respect to α_h is uniformly integrable, with $\int |\frac{\partial^2 f}{\partial \alpha_h^2}(\alpha)| \, d\alpha \leqq m_h$, then the *same* argument that led to (3.3) shows, by differenciating (3.1) twice with respect to $\mathrm{Log}p_h$,

$$\left| \frac{\partial^2 [p_h X_h(p,b)]}{(\partial \mathrm{Log} p_h)^2} \right| \leqq b \, m_h$$

This inequality is also here additive (i.e. it is preserved when aggregating demand over different types). Thus the equivalent of (3.6) for the second derivative of total market demand becomes

$$\left| \frac{\partial^2 [p_h X_h(p)]}{(\partial \mathrm{Log} p_h)^2} \right| \leqq \bar{b} \, m_h \tag{3.9}$$

It should be intuitively clear that the inequalities (3.6), (3.7) and (3.9) are bound to give pretty good control of the first *and* second own price derivatives of market demand for commodity h when the degree of heterogeneity grows. In fact, when the coefficients m_h are small, other things being equal, market demand and its first and second price derivatives all behave approximately like a unit-elastic demand. It can be shown that this is sufficient to guarantee concave revenue functions, and even a unique Cournot oligopoly equilibrium, when firms (with constant marginal costs) compete in quantities in the market under consideration (Grandmont, 1992b).

This brief review strongly suggests that equivalence scales give us very powerful tools to study aggregation over heterogenous economic agents. An important feature of the analysis is that *heterogeneity alone* is capable of generating striking macroeconomic regularities, even when individual economic units are not necessarily 'rational' in the traditional sense (i.e. they do not maximize a well-defined objective function). This outcome is to be contrasted with the fact that in traditional economic theory the assumption of individual optimization generated very few macroeconomic predictions, owing to aggregation problems, as exemplified by Sonnenschein's indeterminacy theorem. The studies reviewed here suggest accordingly that attention might fruitfully be redirected away from individual optimization towards the analysis of the consequences of heterogeneous macroeconomic distributions. It remains to be seen whether this approach can be as successful as it has been in the research reviewed here, in analyzing aggregation over productive units, temporary equilibrium, other models of imperfect competition or even welfare issues.

3.3 LEARNING: ARE RATIONAL EXPECTATIONS UNSTABLE?

An essential feature of economic models is that expectations matter. Individual expectations about the future influence current decisions, hence observed market outcomes. On the other hand, observations about market outcomes determine individual expectations. In the absence of firmly established empirical facts about actual individual forecasting behaviour, quite a few economic theorists have chosen to impose in their models some kind of consistency between expectations and realized market outcomes, on the grounds that arbitrary assumptions about expectations would permit explanation of almost everything – and thus nothing. A common modelling strategy is indeed to postulate 'rational' expectations (i.e. that an individual's expectations about the future are correct at any moment, given current information).

A frequently heard defence of this hypothesis is that it should be the asymptotic outcome of a dynamic process in which individuals learn about the laws of motion of their environment. It is by no means clear, however, that taking learning into account should lead to convergence to a dynamic state where the 'rational' expectations hypothesis is satisfied. Economic 'reality' is not independent of how individual players conceive it. Changing beliefs about the economic system modify the laws of motion of that system.

This section of the chapter is devoted to a brief review of recent studies suggesting that, indeed, taking learning into account often generates dynamic local instability (Champsaur, 1983; Benassy and Blad,

1989; Grandmont and Laroque, 1991; Grandmont, 1990). Such a conclusion seem to agree with (admittedly casual) empirical observations. The economic time series that display most volatility are those for which it appears that expectations are important in shaping current decisions; investment in capital equipment, inventories, durable goods, financial and stock markets. As we shall see, imposing 'rational' expectations should lead to the exactly opposite experience: under the 'rational expectations' hypothesis the more their expectations matter, the more stable should be the market (in the absence of exogenous shocks to the 'fundamentals'). In contrast, the studies reviewed below suggest that local dynamic instability induced by learning is most likely to occur in markets where expectations matter significantly. They further suggest that in such markets the dynamics (with learning) may be highly nonlinear and generate complex trajectories, and moreover that forecasting mistakes may never vanish, even in the 'long run'.[1]

3.3.1 Smooth Forecasting Rules

To illustrate the point most simply, we consider a deterministic formulation (no random shocks) in which the state of the system in period t is described by a single real number x_t. The state at t is determined by the decisions made by traders in the past, which we summarize by the immediately preceding state x_{t-1}, and by the traders' forecast about the future x^e_{t+1}, through the temporary equilibrium relation

$$T(x_{t-1}, x_t, x^e_{t+1}) = 0 \tag{3.10}$$

We assume that there is a large number of traders, each of whom has a negligible influence on the market as a whole, so strategic considerations are also negligible. In (3.10), x^e_{t+1} should be interpreted as an *average* forecast (each individual's forecast being weighted by its relative influence on the dynamic evolution). The state variable can be viewed, say, as a price and (3.10) as a market clearing condition. The analysis will be local (i.e. near a steady state defined by $T(\bar{x}, \bar{x}, \bar{x})$ = 0). We shall assume throughout that T is smooth and denote by b_0, b_1 and a the partial derivatives of T with respect to x_t, x_{t-1} and x^e_{t+1}, evaluated at the stationary state. The parameter a, which measures the local influence of expectations in the market under consideration, is of course assumed to be different from 0, otherwise the issues we wish to analyze would disappear.

The other ingredient of the model is a specification of how forecasts are made. The traders' mental processes may be quite sophisticated: they may have 'models' of the world depending upon a number of unknown parameters, re-estimate these parameters at each date by using past data and use these estimates to forecast the future. It turns out that, for the purpose of the present analysis, we do not have to specify in great detail the traders' mental processes. In *all* cases, forecasts will depend on, and only on, past data. To simplify matters, we assume that the average forecast is a time-independent function of a finite (but possibly very large) array of past states[2]

$$x_{t+1}^e = \psi(x_t, x_{t-1}, \ldots, x_{t-L}) \tag{3.11}$$

We shall assume throughout that when presented with a long constant sequence of states equal to $\bar{x}$, then $x_{t+1}^e = \bar{x}$. We postulate (in this subsection) that learning is sufficiently regular for the forecasting rule ψ to be smooth, and we shall denote by $c_0, \ldots, c_L$ its partial derivatives with respect to $x_t, \ldots, x_{t-L}$, evaluated again at the steady state.

The dynamics with learning that will be actually observed is defined by putting (3.10) and (3.11) together

$$T(x_{t-1}, x_t, \psi(x_t, x_{t-1}, \ldots, x_{t-L})) = 0 \tag{3.12}$$

Clearly $x_t = \bar{x}$ is a stationary solution of (3.12). If we assume that the partial derivative of (3.12) with respect to x_t at the steady state differs from 0 (i.e. $b_0 + ac_0 \neq 0$) the actual dynamics with learning is well defined near the stationary solution $x_t = \bar{x}$. The issue is to analyze its stability.

The usual procedure to evaluate local stability is to linearize the equation near the steady state, look at the corresponding characteristic polynomial and see whether the resulting eigenvalues are stable (have modulus less than 1) or not. It is intuitively clear that all the information we need to proceed here is in fact embodied in the local behaviour of (3.10) and (3.11). Indeed, (3.12) is obtained by 'coupling' the dynamic systems (3.10) and (3.11) – in which the forecast x_{t+1}^e would be replaced by the actual state x_{t+1} in such a way that the variable x_{t+1} actually disappears. Stability or instability of the actual dynamics with learning will accordingly be a consequence of the interaction of the local eigenvalues of (3.10) and (3.11).

The local eigenvalues of (3.10) are the two roots of the characteristic polynomial obtained by replacing x^e_{t+1} by x_{t+1} and linearizing near the steady state

$$Q_T(z) \equiv b_0 + b_1 z + a z^2 = 0 \tag{3.13}$$

The corresponding local eigenvalues λ_1, λ_2 summarize the local behaviour of the economic system *under the assumption of perfect foresight*. One notes that, as stated earlier, this hypothesis leads to the counterfactual conclusion that the more their expectations matter (the larger the coefficient a given b_0 and b_1), the smaller the modulus of the two perfect foresight roots λ_1, λ_2, and thus the more stable the local dynamics of the system should be.

The same procedure applied to the forecasting rule yields the polynomial

$$Q_\psi(z) \equiv z^{L+1} - \sum_0^L c_j z^{L-j} = 0 \tag{3.14}$$

Since the characteristic polynomial is obtained by linearizing (3.11), the corresponding $L+1$ roots $\mu_1, \ldots, \mu_{L+1}$ (the local eigenvalues of the forecasting rule) describe the set of regularities (i.e. the trends and frequencies) that traders are on average able to filter out of current and past deviations Δx_t, $\Delta x_{t-1}, \ldots, \Delta x_{t-L}$ from the stationary state. If they extrapolate constant sequences ($\psi(x,x, \ldots, x) \equiv x$ near $\bar{x}$), then $\mu = 1$ is solution of 3.14). If they extrapolate sequences that oscillate between two values ($\psi(x,y,x,y, \ldots) \equiv y$ near $\bar{x}$), then $\mu = 1$ and $\mu = -1$ are solutions of (3.14). If traders are able to recognize and willing to extrapolate the specific trend r from past deviations, then $\mu = r$ is a solution of (3.14). More generally, the fact that $\mu = re^{i\theta}$ is a local eigenvalue of the forecasting rule means that people are able to recognize the trend r and the frequency associated with θ in past deviations from the stationary state. Of course, a smooth forecasting rule essentially acts locally as a linear filter and can extract only a finite set of regularities from a finite amount of data. When the memory L is large, and if the traders are relatively sophisticated, one should expect the set of local eigenvalues $\mu_1, \ldots, \mu_{L+1}$ of the forecasting rule to be somewhat spread out in the complex plane. It turns out that this configuration leads to local instability of the actual learning dynamics, especially when expectations matter significantly (i.e. when the coefficient a is large).

Specifically, let $\mu_1^* < \mu_2^*$ be the smallest and largest *real* local eigenvalues of the forecasting rule. Consider the situation where the

Rationality

two perfect foresight roots λ_1, λ_2 are either both complex or where, if they are real, they belong to the open interval (μ_1^*, μ_2^*). Then it is easy to show that the characteristic polynomial associated to the actual learning dynamics (3.12) has a real root ρ that lies outside the interval $[\mu_1^*, \mu_2^*]$. If we make the mild assumption that people are willing to extrapolate long sequences that oscillate between two arbitrary values x and y near the steady state, then as noted earlier, $\mu = 1$ and $\mu = -1$ are local eigenvalues of the forecasting rule. In that case $\mu_1^* \leqq -1$ and $\mu_2^* \geqq 1$, and the actual learning dynamics is bound to be locally unstable. This configuration, and thus local instability, is most likely to occur when expectations matter significantly (i.e. when the coefficient a measuring the local influence of forecasts on the evaluation of the system is relatively large), for then the modulus of the two perfect foresight roots λ_1, λ_2 is small.

3.3.2 Discontinuous Forecasting Rules

A smooth forecasting rule (locally, essentially a linear filter) can only extract a finite set of trends and of frequencies from a finite sequence of past deviations from the steady state. It is not difficult to think of learning rules (e.g. through least squares regressions on such past deviations) that would recognize and extrapolate *any* real trend present in past data. Of course, one is then bound to lose smoothness, and even continuity, of the associated forecasting rule. But do the previous instability results carry over to such learning processes? We are going to show that this is indeed the case.

To simplify we set $\bar{x} = 0$ (thus x_t stands now for a *deviation* from the steady state) and linearize (3.10)

$$b_1 x_{t-1} + b_0 x_t + a x_{t+1}^e = 0 \qquad (3.15)$$

with $a \neq 0$ (expectations matter) and $b_0 \neq 0$ so that we can actually solve (3.15) for the current state x_t. As for expectations, let us assume that people believe that the law of motion of the system is

$$x_n = \beta x_{n-1} + \varepsilon_n \qquad \text{or} \qquad x_n = (\beta + \varepsilon_n) x_{n-1} \qquad (3.16)$$

where β is an unknown coefficient and ε_n is white noise. Forecasts are generated as follows. At the outset of period t, traders form an estimate of the unknown coefficient β by looking at past states

$$\beta_t = g(x_{t-1}, \ldots, x_{t-L}) \tag{3.17}$$

and they formulate a forecast by iterating twice the relation (3.16)

$$x_{t+1}^e = \beta_t^2 x_{t-1}. \tag{3.18}$$

The relations (3.17) and (3.18) together define a forecasting rule $x_{t+1}^e = \psi(x_{t-1}, \ldots, x_{t-L})$ exactly as before. One possible interpretation of this learning procedure is that people know where the steady state lies, but try to improve their performances by forecasting growth rates. We may, however, lose continuity if we wish, as here, that people should be able to filter a continuum of trends out of past deviations from the steady state. For instance, if people estimate the models (3.16) through least squares, they will get

$$\beta_t = \frac{x_{t-1} x_{t-2} + \ldots + x_{t-L+1} x_{t-L}}{x_{t-2}^2 + \ldots + x_{t-L}^2}$$

or

$$\beta_t = \frac{1}{L-1} \left[\frac{x_{t-1}}{x_{t-2}} + \ldots + \frac{x_{t-L+1}}{x_{t-L}} \right]$$

which are only defined out of the steady state and, in fact, are highly discontinuous there. The nice feature of the above least squares learning schemes is that the estimates β_t are averages of past ratios x_{t-j+1}/x_{t-j}. As a result, the forecasting rule generated by (3.17) and (3.18) has the property that for every real number r,

$$\psi(r^{L-1} x, \ldots, rx, x) \equiv r^{L+1} x$$

People can extract any real trend from past deviations from the stationary state, or, in other words, any real number is a 'local eigenvalue' of the forecasting rule. The price to pay for this nice feature is the loss of continuity.

The actual learning dynamics is obtained, as before, by putting together (3.15) with the forecasting rule defined by (3.17) and (3.18), which yields

$$x_t = -b_0^{-1}[b_1 + a \beta_t^2] x_{t-1} \equiv \Omega(\beta_t) x_{t-1} \tag{3.19}$$
$$\beta_t \text{ given by (3.17)}$$

The relation (3.17) defining the actual learning dynamics involves a map Ω (introduced in the literature on the subject by Marcet and Sargent, 1989) that has a remarkably simple interpretation. Indeed it describes the link that exists between the *beliefs* people have at the outset of period t about the dynamics of the growth rates x_n/x_{n-1}, as summarized by the estimate β_t, and the *actual* ratio x_t/x_{t-1} that will be observed in that period. It is easy to verify that the fixed points of Ω coincide with the perfect foresight roots λ_1, λ_2 when these are real, and that Ω has no fixed points when λ_1, λ_2 are complex (the equation $\Omega(\beta) = \beta$ is in fact identical to (3.14) with $z = \beta$).

The smallest and largest real eigenvalues of the forecasting rule are $-\infty$ and $+\infty$ whenever the estimate (3.17) is an average of past ratios x_{t-j+1}/x_{t-j}, $j = 2, \ldots, L$. By analogy with the smooth case discussed earlier, we should expect that the actual learning dynamics is locally unstable in the present case as well, and this for *all* configurations of the two perfect foresight roots λ_1 and λ_2. It can be shown that this conjecture is indeed true under quite general conditions (Grandmont and Laroque, 1991). When the perfect foresight roots λ_1, λ_2 are complex, local instability occurs for all initial conditions. Suppose now that they are real, with $|\lambda_1| < |\lambda_2|$. Then local instability occurs for an open set of initial conditions, i.e. when the initial ratios x_{t-1}/x_{t-2}, etc. . . . all have the same sign as λ_2 and a modulus larger than $|\lambda_2|$. Were the forecasting rule smooth, local unstability for an open set of initial conditions would imply instability for almost every departure from the steady state. This may not be true here as the forecasting rule is discontinuous. If the map Ω is contracting at the perfect foresight root of smallest modulus (i.e. $|\Omega'(\lambda_1)| < 1$) and if that root is stable (i.e. $|\lambda_1| < 1$) then one will get local stability whenever all initial growth rates x_{t-1}/x_{t-2}, etc. . . . are close enough to λ_1. Of course, if $|\Omega'(\lambda_1)| > 1$, the phenomenon disappears. Be that as it may, the size of the open set for which local instability occurs becomes larger as the coefficient a measuring the relative influence of expectations goes up (the modulus of the two perfect foresight roots goes down). Thus we reach the same qualitative conclusion as in the smooth case: *the more expectations matter, the more probable becomes learning-induced local instability*, and *the more volatile market outcomes should be*.

To illustrate these points, we consider the particular situation where the estimate β_t is x_{t-1}/x_{t-2}. One then gets even sharper results that can be illustrated with simple diagrams. In view of (3.19) the actual dynamics with learning in this case is described by the recurrence equation $x_t/x_{t-1} = \Omega(x_{t-1}/x_{t-2})$. The curve representing Ω (a parabola) is

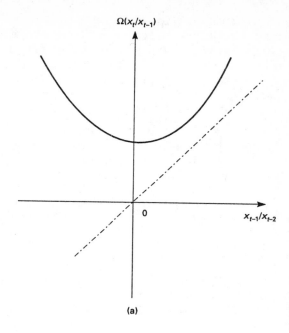

(a)

Figure 3.1

pictured in Figures 3.1(a) and 3.1(b) in the case where the sum of the two perfect foresight roots (i.e. $\lambda_1 + \lambda_2 = -b_0/a$) is positive (the reader can verify that we get identical results in the opposite case, with the asymptotic branches of the parabola going down). The two roots λ_1, λ_2 are complex in Figure 3.1(a), and we get local instability for all initial conditions. The two perfect foresight roots are real in Figure 3.1(b). There local instability occurs whenever the modulus of the initial ratio x_{t-1}/x_{t-2} exceeds $|\lambda_2|$. The ratios x_t/x_{t-1} converge to λ_1 whenever $|x_{t-1}/x_{t-2}| < \lambda_1$, and we get local stability if $|\lambda_1| < 1$. The size of the region for which we get instability grows as $|\lambda_2|$ goes down (i.e. when the coefficient a measuring the influence of expectations becomes large).

The foregoing analysis suggests strongly that learning is most likely to generate local instability in markets where expectations matter significantly. Another interesting feature is that although the world may be simple and close to linear (see (3.10) or (3.15)), the mental processes employed by economic agents when trying to learn the laws of motion of the system may be highly nonlinear. Then these nonlinearities

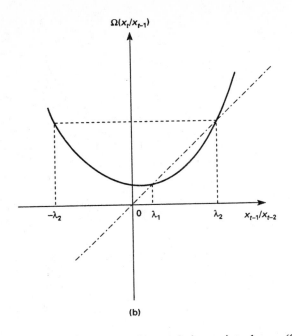

(b)

will also show up in the actual observed dynamics: here, (3.19) involves the map Ω which describes a parabola. That feature suggests that the actual learning dynamics may generate not only local instability but also quite complex, even chaotic, non-explosive expectations-driven fluctuations. The point is illustrated in Figure 3.2, in the simple case where the estimate β_t is equal to x_{t-1}/x_{t-2}. There, the map Ω is expanding at both perfect foresight roots. The actual ratios x_t/x_{t-1} cannot converge to either of them but they may follow chaotic trajectories that are trapped in some invariant interval $[-c,c]$.[3]

All this opens promising, and largely unexplored, avenues in business cycle theory. Although the 'fundamentals' of the economic system may display only small nonlinearities and may not vary much over time, the traders' learning schemes are presumably highly nonlinear and this may lead to complicated expectations-driven non-explosive fluctuations along which forecasting mistakes may never vanish, even in the 'long run'. This cannot, however, be the end of the story. For such a situation to be robust, of course, we should require some degree of consistency between the actual dynamics and private beliefs, so that traders have no incentive to change their views about how the world works. We might envisage, for instance, a situation in which

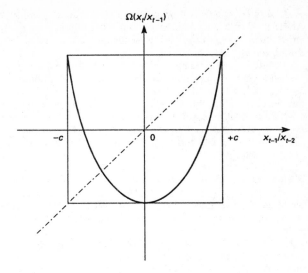

Figure 3.2

traders attribute their forecasting mistakes to 'noise', although the observed dynamics are actually deterministic but chaotic, as in Figure
3.2. As already indicated, this is largely unknown territory and should
be the subject of further research.

Notes

1. In the sequel, we follow the presentation of Grandmont and Laroque (1991).
2. Expectations may also depend on past forecasts, so as to allow people to
   learn from their past mistakes by comparing past forecasts with actual
   realizations. The results would be qualitatively the same (Grandmont, 1990).
3. Examples of cycles and chaos generated by learning have been provided
   for instance by Hommes (1991 and 1992) and Negroni (1992).

References

Barnett, W., B. Cornet, C. d'Aspremont, J. Gabszewicz and A. Mas-Colell
(eds) (1991) *Equilibrium Theory and Applications* (Cambridge: Cambridge
University Press).

Barten, A.P. (1964) 'Family Composition, Prices and Expenditure Patterns', in P. Hart, G. Mills and J.K. Whitaker (eds), *Econometric Analysis for National Economic Planning*, 16th Symposium of the Colson Society (London: Butterworth).

Benassy, J.P. and M. Blad (1989) 'On Learning and Rational Expectations in an Overlapping Generations Model', *Journal of Economic Dynamics and Control*, vol. 13, pp. 379–400.

Champsaur, P. (1983) 'On the Stability of Rational Expectations Equilibria', CORE DP 8324, Catholic University of Louvain, Belgium. French version in *Cahiers du Séminaire d'Econométrie*, vol. 26 (1984), pp. 47–65.

Dierker, E. (1989) 'Competition for Customers', Discussion Paper A-244, University of Bonn.

Dierker, E., H. Dierker and W Trockel (1984) 'Price-Dispersed Preferences and C^1 Mean Demand', *Journal of Mathematical Economics*, vol. 13. pp. 11–42.

Dierker, H. (1989) 'Existence of Nash Equilibrium in Pure Strategies in an Oligopoly with Price Setting Firms', Discussion Paper No. 8902, University of Vienna.

Grandmont, J.M. (1987) 'Distributions of Preferences and the Law of Demand', *Econometrica* vol. 55, pp. 155–61.

Grandmont, J.M. (1990) 'Expectations Formation and Stability of the Economic System', Presidential address, Econometric Society World Congress, Barcelona, forthcoming.

Grandmont, J.M. (1992a) 'Transformations of the Commodity Space, Behavioral Heterogeneity and the Aggregation Problem', *Journal of Economic Theory*, vol. 57, pp. 1–35.

Grandmont, J.M. (1992b) 'Behavioral Heterogeneity and Cournot Oligopoly Equilibrium', mimeo, CEPREMAP, Paris.

Grandmont, J.M. and G. Laroque (1991) 'Economic Dynamics with Learning: Some Instability Examples', in W. Barnett, B. Cornet, C. d'Aspremont, J. Gabszewics and A. Mas-Collel (eds), *Equilibrium Theory and Applications* (Cambridge: Cambridge University Press).

Härdle, W., W. Hildenbrand and M. Jerison (1991) 'Empirical Evidence on the Law of Demand', *Econometrica*, vol. 49, pp. 1525–49.

Hildenbrand, W. (1983) 'On the Law of Demand', *Econometrica*, vol. 51, pp. 997–1019.

Hildenbrand, W. (1989) 'Facts and Ideas in Economic Theory', *European Economic Review*, vol. 33, pp. 251–76.

Hildenbrand, W. (1992) 'Market Demand: Theory and Empirical Evidence', Discussion Paper No. A359, University of Bonn.

Hommes, C. (1991) 'Adaptive Learning and Roads to Chaos', *Economic Letters*, vol. 36, pp. 127–32.

Hommes, C. (1992) 'Adaptive Expectations and Nonlinear Cobweb Models: Stable Cycles, Chaos and Bifurcations', PhD Dissertation, University of Gröningen.

Jerison, M. (1982) 'The Representative Consumer and the Weak Axiom when the Distribution of Income is Fixed', Working Paper 150, SUNY, Albany.

Jerison, M. (1984) 'Aggregation and Pairwise Aggregation of Demand when the Distribution of Income is Fixed', *Journal of Economic Theory*, vol. 33, pp. 1–31.

Jerison, M. (1992) 'Optimal Income Distribution and the Nonrepresentative Representative Consumer', Working Paper, SUNY, Albany.

Jorgenson, J. and D. Slesnick (1987) 'Aggregate Consumer Behavior and Households Equivalence Scales', *Journal of Business, Economics and Statistics*, vol. 5, pp. 219–32.

Marcet, A. and T. Sargent (1989) 'Convergence of Least Squares Learning Mechanisms in Self-Referential Linear Stochastic Models', *Journal of Economic Theory*, vol. 48, pp. 337–68.

Mas-Colell, A. and W. Neuefind (1977) 'Some Generic Properties of Aggregate Excess Demand and an Application', *Econometrica*, vol. 45, pp. 591–9.

Negroni, G. (1992) 'Chaotic Temporary Equilibrium Dynamics in Overlapping Generations Models', Working Paper, Universita Cattolica del Sacro Cuoro, Milan.

Prais, S.J. and H.S. Houthakker (1955, 1971) *The Analysis of Family Budgets* (Cambridge: Cambridge University Press, 1st and 2nd edns).

Shafer, W. and H. Sonnenschein (1982) 'Market Demand and Excess Demand Functions', in K. Arrow and M. Intriligator (eds), *Handbook of Mathematical Economics*, Vol. II (New York: North Holland).

Sonnenschein, H. (1973) 'Do Walras' Identity and Continuity Characterize the Class of Community Excess Demand Functions?' *Journal of Economic Theory*, vol. 6, pp. 345–54.

Sonnenschein, H. (1974) 'Market Excess Demand Functions', *Econometrica*, vol. 40, pp. 549–63.

Discussion

Alan Kirman

GREQAM, EHESS, AT UNIVERSITY OF AIX – MARSEILLE III

In this chapter Grandmont addresses two of the central issues of modern economic theory. Both of these are essential in determining whether the sort of microeconomic and macroeconomic models that are widely used in the economic literature have anything useful to say in the analysis and understanding of real economic phenomena.

The first question posed can be summarized as saying that since virtually no restrictions on aggregate economic behaviour are imposed by the standard assumptions of individual rationality of what use is such a theory? In particular, although the existence of market equilibria can be guaranteed under very weak assumptions nothing can be said about the uniqueness or stability of such equilibria. Without uniqueness, comparative statics exercises make no sense; without stability, the value of the equilibrium notion itself is put into question. The 'invisible hand' story becomes vacuous.

Grandmont's contribution to a solution of this dilemma is to propose an elegant example of how heterogeneity of agents' characteristics may restore the important properties I have just mentioned.

In so doing he is working directly in a very long tradition. In particular, it should be mentioned that Cournot (1838) himself pointed out how aggregate demand might be 'smoothed' by the heterogeneity of individuals' demand behaviour and it was this idea that was developed and finalized much later by Trockel (1984) and Dierker et al. (1984) and in the other work cited by Grandmont. Houthakker (1955) made similar observations about the generation of smooth aggregate production functions from underlying individual fixed coefficients technologies.

The first observation that I have is that the point of the Grandmont exercise it to impose restrictions on the *distribution* of agents' characteristics and to obtain aggregate results by so doing. However, any economist familiar with modern macroeconomics might ask why he insists on heterogeneity. After all, the 'representative individual' model is a widely used and familiar approach. Would it not be a solution to restrict the distribution of characteristics so that agents were essentially the same? Indeed one could evoke an early result of Balasko (1975) in which he shows that if an economy is 'sufficiently near' a Pareto optimum at the outset, equilibrium will be unique and stable. Since, in an exchange economy for example, if all individuals are identical, the economy's initial allocation is a Pareto optimum, such a result might seem to imply that having sufficiently similar agents in an economy would generate a unique and stable equilibrium. Unfortunately this does not work. Indeed Kirman and Koch (1986) have shown that in an economy in which agents are as close to being identical[1] as one might wish, the Debreu–Mantel–Sonnenschein result still holds. Here, by 'close to identical' I mean that all agents have the *same preferences* and that their shares of total income can be as close to being equal as one wants.

Given this it seems natural to turn to heterogeneity. The essence of Grandmont's example is to show that the sort of heterogeneity he imposes makes expenditures on various goods, at the aggregate level, independent of prices. Thus we move towards a situation in which the aggregate economy behaves like an individual maximizing a Cobb–Douglas utility function.

The basic idea is to take a fixed finite number of preferences and then to generate individuals with preference distributed around each of these basic relations. This is done by distorting the commodity space through a particular transformation, defining the original preference relation in the distorted space and then removing the distortion. This generates a new relation in the original space.

I have two remarks about this.

Firstly, although Grandmont's particular example is beautifully tractable, any one of a whole class of transformations would also do the same job. However, other transformations which might seem equally plausible will not do so.

Secondly, this is a very particular sort of heterogeneity. Nothing is said about what would happen if we simply added more but different agents, in some general way, to the original set. Indeed it is perfectly possible to add agents who, by any reasonable criteria, are more and more heterogeneous without removing either multiplicity or instability of the equilibria in each of the economies thus generated.

My conclusion on this first question is that Grandmont has provided a valuable and important step in the direction of showing how micro heterogeneity may lead to macroeconomic regularity. His theoretical contribution complements nicely the recent more empirically oriented work on increasing dispersion of expenditures by Härdle *et al.* (1991) and Hildenbrand (1992). However, we are as yet far from showing that heterogeneity *necessarily* helps.

The second question addressed by Grandmont is in the framework of dynamic economic models in which individuals make forecasts about what will happen. These forecasts influence their decisions and hence, in turn, influence the variables about which they make forecasts. Several related problems arise. If agents learn in such a situation will their expectations become rational? Will trajectories along which agents have perfect foresight be stable? Will forecasting mistakes be eliminated in the course of learning?

The first problem has been addressed in the past by Bray (1982) and many others since, with success in a very limited context. The last problems are those tackled by Grandmont. He shows that, for a general class of smooth learning rules, if the weight of people's forecasts in determining the evolution of the system is large, local instability will occur. Although the assumptions made by Grandmont are not entirely innocent, he adds another brick to the edifice of results where learning about something which is strongly affected by the results of learning may produce instability (see, e.g., Blume and Easley, 1992).

Grandmont also shows how this sort of result carries over to widely used but no longer continuous forecasting rules, such as least squares for example. It seems to me that two avenues are relevant here. Firstly, there is the fixity of the learning rule itself. Should one also not learn how to learn? Grandmont makes a remark in this direction but it seems that there is something to be done here. Secondly, the role of the length of memory in learning stability is known to be important and results are not in general the same if the agent is allowed to accumulate more and more data as opposed to using a fixed finite set of past observations.

In sum, then, Grandmont has provided us with two very useful observations: the first more optimistic about the restoration of aggregate regularity in the standard general equilibrium model if agents are heterogeneous, and the second more pessimistic about the destabilising aggregate impact of learning, if that learning has an impact on the outcome which the agents are trying to learn about.

Note

1. One might wish to discuss whether the notion of closeness used here is more appropriate than that used by Balasko. It seems to me that the result cited above is more in the spirit of using distributional restrictions to look for aggregate results, and is thus in line with the approach adopted by Hildenbrand (1983) and developed by Grandmont in this chapter.

References

Balasko, Y. (1975) 'Some Results on Uniqueness and on Stability of Equilibrium in General Equilibrium Theory', *Journal of Mathematical Economics*, vol. 2, pp. 95–118.

Blume, L. And D. Easley (1995) 'What Has the Learning Literature Taught Us?', in *Rationality and Learning in Economics* (A.P. Kirman and M. Salmon, eds) (Oxford: Basil Blackwell).

Bray, M.M. (1982) 'Learning, Estimation and the Stability of Rational Expectations', *Journal of Economic Theory*, vol. 26, pp. 318–39.

Cournot, A. (1838) *Recherches sur les Principes Mathématiques de la Théorie des Richesses* (Paris: Librairie des Sciences Politiques et Sociales, M. Rivière & cie).

Dierker, E., H. Dierker and W. Trockel (1984) 'Price-Dispensed Preferences and C^1 Mean Demand', *Journal of Mathematical Economics*, vol. 13, pp. 11–42.

Härdle, W., W. Hildenbrand and M. Jerison (1991) 'Empirical Evidence on the Law of Demand', *Econometrica*, vol. 59, pp. 1525–49.

Hildenbrand, W. (1983) 'On the Law of Demand', *Econometrica*, vol. 51, pp. 997–1019.

Hildenbrand, W. (1992) 'Market Demand: Theory and Empirical Evidence', Discussion Paper no. A-359, University of Bonn.

Houthakker, A.S. (1955) 'The Pareto Distribution and the Cobb–Douglas Production Function in Activity Analysis', *Review of Economic Studies*, vol. XXIII, pp. 27–31.

Kirman, A. and K. Koch (1986) 'Market Excess Demand Functions: Identical Preferences and Collinear Endowments', *Review of Economic Studies*, vol. 53, no. 3, pp. 457–63.

Trockel, W. (1984) *Market Demand: An Analysis of Large Economies with Non-Convex Preferences* (Berlin: Springer-Verlag).

4 Evolution and Rationality: Some Recent Game-Theoretic Results[1]

Abhijit Banerjee
HARVARD UNIVERSITY

and

Jörgen W. Weibull
STOCKHOLM SCHOOL OF ECONOMICS

4.1 INTRODUCTION

A large part of economics, and economic theory in particular, relies on such solution concepts as Nash equilibrium and its refinements. Unfortunately, it is difficult to provide a solid theoretical or empirical justification for Nash equilibrium behaviour. 'Rationality', or even 'common knowledge of rationality', is not enough to generate such behaviour. Among other things, one also needs to assume that the players coordinate their beliefs about each other's actions (Armbruster and Boege, 1979; Johansen, 1982; Bernheim, 1984; Pearce, 1984; Bernheim, 1986; Binmore, 1987; Aumann, 1987; Tan and Werlang, 1988; Aumann and Brandenburger, 1991). Moreover, in games with a dynamic structure, the very notion of rationality becomes problematic, and common knowledge of rationality may even lead to logical contradictions (Rosenthal, 1981; Binmore, 1987; Bicchieri, 1989; Basu, 1988, 1990).

A completely different approach is to leave the epistemology of rationality aside and instead ask whether or not economic agents, and human decision-makers in general, behave *as if* they met the stringent rationality and coordination conditions inherent in Nash equilibrium and other non-cooperative solution concepts. One process which may justify this 'as if' approach is 'natural' selection.[2] More precisely, one may ask whether evolutionary selection among more or less boundedly 'rational' behaviours in strategic interaction situations leads to (aggregate and/or long-run) Nash equilibrium behaviour. One can then think of 'players' as 'hosts' of a variety of 'competing behaviours' – including potentially 'rational' behaviours – and ask which of these behaviours survive in an evolutionary selection process (Binmore, 1988). If the behaviours selected by evolutionary processes result in a Nash equilibrium outcome, then one can claim that whether or not players are genuinely 'rational' and 'coordinate their beliefs', in the long run they will behave as if they did indeed meet the underlying rationalistic assumptions (see Selten, 1991b, for a discussion of some relevant paradigms).

The most promising methodology for such an evolutionary justification of Nash equilibrium play is provided by recent advances in evolutionary game theory, a paradigm pioneered by the British biologist John Maynard Smith. This paradigm has been developed along two lines, one static approach using evolutionary stability as its key concept (Maynard Smith and Price, 1973; Maynard Smith, 1974, 1982), and one dynamic approach based on explicit Darwinian (or Malthusian) selection of behaviours. In the dynamic approach, one imagines pairwise and randomly matched interactions in a large population of individuals (Taylor and Jonker, 1978; Hofbauer *et al.*, 1979; Zeeman, 1980, 1981; Schuster *et al.*, 1981a; Schuster and Sigmund, 1983; Bomze, 1986; Hofbauer and Sigmund, 1988). The players are confined to a limited menu of behaviours, namely those corresponding to always playing the same pure strategies in the two-player game in question. Hence, one may think of the players as being 'programmed' to always play a certain (more or less involved) strategy when encountering another individual. In the biologists' models, payoffs represent reproductive fitness, usually measured as (expected) number of offspring, and the offspring inherits its (single) parent's behaviour. Hence, the growth rate of a population share of individuals programmed to a certain behaviour is proportional to its payoff in the current population composition. Using a term coined by the British socio-biologist Richard Dawkins, this reproductive selection dynamics is usually called the *replicator* dynamics.[3] The focus of the biologists' analysis is on population states which are attractors in this dynamics, such states being the natural candidates for long-run aggregate population behaviour.

The relevance of this literature for the social sciences in general, and economics in particular, is limited in several ways. First, in economics, the payoffs in a game do not usually represent reproductive fitness, but rather firms' profits or households' utility. Moreover, in most such applications, the selection mechanism is not biological but the aggregate result of more or less conscious choices made by the individuals. Accordingly, economists have generalized some of the analysis to fairly wide classes of selection dynamics containing the replicator dynamics as well as a variety of more or less rational individual adjustment processes (Nachbar, 1990; Friedman, 1991; Kandori *et al.*, 1991; Samuelson and Zhang, 1992; Swinkels, 1992). A related limitation in the standard set-up of evolutionary game theory is its focus on behaviours which are not conditioned on any information that a player may have, such as the current aggregate population behaviour or the type of the opponent player. One way to relax this restriction is to let players over time revise their choice of strategy in the light of the current population state (Banerjee and Weibull, 1991; Dekel and Scotchmer, 1992). An alternative way is to expand the menu of behaviours available at each moment (Robson, 1990; Banerjee and Weibull, 1991; Stahl, 1992; Banerjee and Weibull, 1992). There is also no *a priori* reason why, in all relevant situations, all the players should be modelled as coming from the same population. Indeed, a number of papers treat interactions between distinct populations occupying different player roles in the game in question (Schuster *et al.*, 1981b; Schuster and Sigmund, 1985; Hofbauer and Sigmund, 1988; Friedman, 1991; Ritzberger and Vogelsberger, 1991; Samuelson and Zhang, 1992; Swinkels, 1992).

The present chapter discusses a number of papers on explicitly dynamic models of evolutionary selection of behaviours in games. This literature is currently growing fast and is closely related to at least three strands in economic theory, none of which is discussed here. The obviously most closely related of these strands is the important literature on the static criterion of evolutionary stability.[4] The two other omitted fields are learning models and models in which decision-makers are represented as automata.[5] Moreover, we are aware that we have not even covered all current and important contributions to explicitly dynamic evolutionary analyses. In particular, we do not discuss multi-population dynamics. We feel that many important aspects of the relationship between rationality and evolution – the focus of the present chapter – come out already in symmetric two-person games. For the same reason, we only briefly touch upon explicitly stochastic dynamic models.

The material is organized as follows. Basic notation and elements of non-cooperative game theory are given in Section 4.2. The explicitly dynamic version of standard evolutionary game theory, in particular its implications for 'rational' and 'coordinated' behaviour, is discussed in Section 4.3. Section 4.4 discusses some extensions to a fairly wide class of dynamics of relevance for models of boundedly rational individuals who revise their strategy choice over time. Section 4.5 discusses some models of evolutionary selection among more general boundedly rational behaviours. Our main conclusions are summarized in Section 4.6.

4.2 NOTATION AND PRELIMINARIES

The analysis in the present chapter is restricted to finite and symmetric two-player games in normal form. Let $I = \{1,2, \ldots ,k\}$ be the set of *pure* strategies. Accordingly, a *mixed* strategy is a point x on the unit simplex $\Delta = \{x \in \mathbb{R}^k_+ : \Sigma_i x_i = 1\}$ in k-dimensional Euclidean space. The *support* of a mixed strategy $x \in \Delta$ is the subset $C(x) = \{i \in I : x_i > 0\}$ of pure strategies which are assigned positive probabilities. A strategy x is called *interior* (or *completely mixed*) if $C(x) = I$.

Let a_{ij} be the *payoff* of strategy $i \in I$ when played against strategy $j \in I$, and let A be the associated $k \times k$ payoff matrix. Accordingly, the (expected) payoff of a mixed strategy x, when played against a mixed strategy, y, is $u(x,y) = x \cdot Ay = \Sigma_{ij} x_i a_{ij} y_j$. The payoff function $u:\Delta^2 \to \mathbb{R}$ is clearly bi-linear, and the payoff of a pure strategy $i \in I$, when played against a mixed strategy y, is $u(e^i,y)$, where e^i is the i'th unit vector in $\mathbb{R}^k$, etc. We will frequently identify a pure strategy $i \in I$ with its mixed-strategy counterpart $e^i \in \Delta$.

A pure strategy, $i \in I$ is *weakly dominated* if there exists a strategy $x \in \Delta$ which never earns a lower payoff and sometimes earns a higher payoff (i.e., $u(x,y) \geq u(e^i,y)$ $\forall y \in \Delta$, with strict inequality for some y). A pure strategy $i \in I$ is *strictly dominated* if there exists a strategy $x \in \Delta$ which always earns a higher payoff (i.e., $u(x,y) > u(e^i,y)$ $\forall y \in \Delta$). A *best reply* to a strategy $y \in \Delta$ is a strategy $x \in \Delta$ such that $u(x,y) \geq u(x',y)$ $\forall x' \in \Delta$. For each $y \in \Delta$, let $\beta(y) \subset \Delta$ be its set of best replies. A *Nash equilibrium* is a pair (x,y) of mutually best replies, a Nash equilibrium is *strict* if each strategy is the unique best reply to the other, and a Nash equilibrium (x,y) is *symmetric* if $x = y$. By Kakutani's Fixed Point Theorem, every finite and symmetric game has at least one symmetric Nash equilibrium.

One solution concept which is weaker than Nash equilibrium is iterative strict dominance. A pure strategy $i \in I$ is said to be *iteratively strictly undominated* if it is not strictly dominated in the original game G, nor in the game G' obtained from G by removal of all strictly dominated strategies, nor in the game G'' obtained from G' by removal of all strategies which are strictly dominated in G', etc. A related, but different, solution concept is rationalizability. A pure strategy $i \in I$ is *never a best reply* if there exists no mixed strategy $y \in \Delta$ against which $i \in I$ is a best reply, and $i \in I$ is *rationalizable* (Bernheim, 1984; Pearce, 1984) if it is not a 'never best reply' in the original game G, nor in the game G' obtained from G by removal of all 'never best replies', nor in the game G'' obtained from G' by removal of all 'never best replies', etc. Each of these two methods of iterated elimination of pure strategies stops in a finite number of steps. Pearce (1984) has shown that while the two remaining sets may differ in games with more than two players, they coincide in all two-player games.[6] Hence, in the present setting, a strategy $i \in I$ is rationalizable if and only if it is iteratively undominated.

4.3 NASH EQUILIBRIUM AS THE RESULT OF BIOLOGICAL ADAPTATION

In the basic dynamic setting of evolutionary game theory, one imagines pairwise and randomly matched interactions in a large population of individuals, each interaction taking the form of play of a symmetric and finite two-player game. As in Section 4.2, let I denote the strategy set, A the payoff matrix, and $u: \Delta^2 \to \mathbb{R}$ the associated payoff function. Interactions take place continuously over time; the current *aggregate behaviour* of the population, or its *state*, is a vector $x = (x_1, \ldots x_k) \in \Delta$, where each component x_i is the population share currently using strategy $i \in I$. Accordingly, it is immaterial for a player whether he plays against a player using a mixed strategy $x \in \Delta$ or against a randomly drawn individual from a population of pure-strategy players in state $x \in \Delta$. In both cases, the (expected) payoff of a pure strategy $i \in I$ is $u(e^i, x)$. In the population setting, the *average payoff* in the population is simply $u(x,x) = \Sigma x_i u(e^i, x)$. In the biologists' models, payoffs represent 'fitness', which is usually taken to be the (expected) number of offspring, and each offspring inherits its (single) parent's strategy, so (implicitly presuming the law of large numbers) the *replicator dynamics* in continuous time is

$$\dot{x}_i = u(e^i - x, x) \cdot x_i \qquad [\forall i \in I, \ \forall x \in \Delta] \tag{4.1}$$

with dots for time derivatives.[7]

In other words, the growth rate $\dot{x}_i / x_i$ of each sub-population $i \in I$

equals the difference between its current payoff and the current population average. Evidently, a sub-population whose strategy $i \in I$ is a best reply to the current aggregate behaviour $i \in \Delta$ has the highest growth rate in this dynamics, but also other sub-populations may grow, namely those who use strategies which do better than average.

In the special case $k=2$, i.e. a (symmetric) 2×2 game, it is easily established that this implies convergence to some (symmetric) Nash equilibrium, from any interior initial state. More exactly, if initially all strategies in the game are used by some individuals, i.e. $x(0)$ is interior, then the state $x(t)$ converges over time to some state $x^* \in \Delta$ such that (x^*, x^*) constitutes a Nash equilibrium (Hofbauer and Sigmund, 1988). (In certain cases, the limit state x^* depends on the initial state $x(0)$.) Hence, the evolutionary approach lends strong support to the Nash equilibrium paradigm in such low-dimensional settings.

Unfortunately, for general symmetric $k \times k$ games the connection between evolutionary dynamics and Nash equilibrium is somewhat less tight. The problem is that the evolutionary selection process in higher-dimensional spaces need not converge. However, just as in the 2×2 case any population state which is (Lyapunov) stable in the replicator dynamics corresponds to a symmetric Nash equilibrium, and a strategy which is in Nash equilibrium with itself is stationary in this dynamics.[8] In other words, if evolutionary selection induces no movement in the composition of the population's aggregate behaviour, and that behaviour is dynamically robust with respect to small perturbations, then it is compatible with the stringent rationality and coordination hypotheses in the rationalistic justification of Nash equilibrium behaviour:

Proposition A (Bomze, 1986) If the population state x is (Lyapunov) stable in the replicator dynamics (4.1), then (x,x) is a Nash equilibrium. If (x,x) is a Nash equilibrium, then x is stationary in the replicator dynamics.

The intuition behind these claims is fairly straightforward. The second claim is simplest to see. For if (x,x) is a Nash equilibrium, and hence $x \in \Delta$ is a best reply to itself, then all pure strategies in its support $C(x)$ earn the same (maximal) payoff, which also is the average payoff, since strategies not in $C(x)$ are absent from the population. Thus each sub-population is either extinct or earns the average payoff, establishing $\dot{x} = 0$ in (4.1). The intuition for the stability claim is that if (x,x) is not a Nash equilibrium, and hence x is not a best reply to itself, then there exists some pure strategy i which earns more against

x than some pure strategy j in the support of x. Hence, along all solution paths of (4.1) in a neighbourhood of x, sub-population j decreases towards zero over time, implying that the population state leaves the neighbourhood (since by hypothesis $j \in C(x)$, and hence $x_j > 0$). Consequently, x then is not stable. In fact, by similar arguments one can show that, just as in the 2×2 case, if the population state converges from an initial state in which all strategies are used, then the limiting state has to be Nash equilibrium behaviour:[9]

Proposition B (Nachbar, 1990)   If an interior dynamic path in the replicator dynamics (4.1) converges to some $x \in \Delta$, then (x,x) is a Nash equilibrium.

This simple observation implies that every strictly dominated strategy is wiped out from the population, granted all strategies are represented in the initial population and that the induced dynamic path converges. But what if aggregate behaviour does not converge? It turns out that all strictly dominated strategies are nevertheless wiped out. In fact, as shown by Samuelson and Zhang (1992), only strategies which are rationalizable can survive evolutionary selection, given that all pure strategies are initially present in the population.[10]

Proposition C (Samuelson and Zhang, 1992)   If a pure strategy is not rationalizable, then its population share converges to zero along any interior dynamic path in the replicator dynamics (4.1).

Consequently, even if the evolutionary selection process fails to converge, in the long run virtually no individual will behave irrationally in the sense of playing strategies which are never best replies, nor will they play strategies which are never best replies when others avoid strategies which are never best replies, etc. In fact, since all non-rationalizable strategies are wiped out in the long run, all players eventually behave almost as if rationality (in the sense of best-reply behaviour) were common knowledge. What is missing from the kind of behaviour presumed in Nash equilibrium play is the coordination of beliefs.[11]

However, the intuition for this result is not so straightforward. Indeed, by way of a cleverly construed counter-example, Dekel and Scotchmer (1992) show that the result is *not* valid in the standard discrete-time version of the replicator dynamics,

$$x_i(t + 1) = \frac{u[e^i, x(t)]}{u[x(t), x(t)]} \cdot x_i(t) \qquad (4.2)$$

In this version, each generation lives for one period, and all individuals reproduce simultaneously. If an individual using strategy $i \in I$ has $u[e^i, x(t)]$ offspring when the population state is $x(t)$, and all offspring inherit their 'parent's' strategy, then (4.2) results.[12] It turns out that a strategy which is strictly dominated by a mixed strategy, but not by any pure strategy, may, along non-convergent solution paths to (4.2), periodically do sufficiently well to avoid extinction.

The example in Dekel and Scotchmer (1992) is the special case $\alpha = 0.35$ and $\beta = 0.1$ of the following extension of the so-called 'Rock–Scissors–Paper' game:

$$A = \begin{bmatrix} 1 & 2+\alpha & 0 & \beta \\ 0 & 1 & 2+\alpha & \beta \\ 2+\alpha & 0 & 1 & \beta \\ 1+\beta & 1+\beta & 1+\beta & 0 \end{bmatrix}$$

It is easily verified that the fourth strategy is strictly dominated by the unique Nash equilibrium strategy $m = (\frac{1}{3}, \frac{1}{3}, \frac{1}{3}, 0) \in \Delta$ if $\alpha > 3\beta > 0$, a condition met by Dekel and Scotchmer's numerical example. Moreover, one can show that near the boundary face $x_4 = 0$ of the unit simple Δ (i.e., in states where only a small fraction of the population uses the dominated strategy 4) this sub-population grows whenever aggregate behaviour $x \in \Delta$ is at some distance from m. In fact, when $\alpha < 4\beta$, as in Dekel and Scotchmer's example, x_4 grows outside a circular disk as shown in Figure 4.1.[13] Hence, if along a dynamic path near this face the population state drifts along the edges, then the population share x_4 grows. In the continuous-time replicator dynamics (4.1) this does not happen; for the system converges towards m from any initial state on (the relative interior of) that face. However, in the discrete time dynamics (4.2), the system diverges on the face $x_4 = 0$ towards the three edges of that face. Dekel and Scotchmer (1992) prove that $x_4(t)$ converges to zero in the dynamics (4.2) if and only if initially all three undominated strategies appear in identical shares.

However, the discrete-time version (4.2) does not seem entirely compelling for general evolutionary analyses since it assumes that the whole population reproduces at the same time. As a first approximation, it appears more natural to assume that agents reproduce continuously,

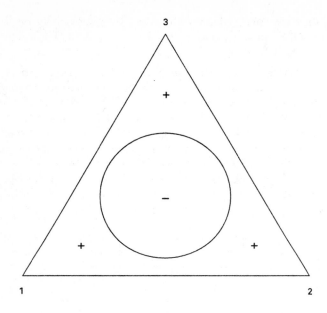

Figure 4.1

or else discretely but in smaller batches, at a more or less uniform rate over time. Indeed, Cabrales and Sobel (1992) show that if one uses discrete time but lets only a small fraction, λ, of the whole population reproduce each time, then the discrete-time dynamics differs from (4.2) and in fact becomes more and more similar to the continuous-time dynamics as λ decreases. In this fashion, they establish the validity of Proposition C also for discrete-time versions of the replicator dynamics with λ sufficiently small. As a result, the anomaly raised by Dekel and Scotchmer is not too damaging to the qualitative results discussed above.

In the current formulation, the population share of each strategy changes in a deterministic way. A more general formulation would allow for a stochastic evolution of the population shares. A pioneering contribution in this vein is Foster and Young (1990), who add white noise to the (continuous-time) replicator dynamics (4.1). In this fashion they obtain an ergodic stochastic process with a unique limiting distribution. (Hence, unlike the deterministic replicator dynamics, its long-run behaviour is independent of its initial state.) In this framework, and using powerful analytical techniques due to Freidlin and Wentzell

(1984), they are able to derive interesting limiting results for the case when the white-noise term is reduced towards zero, for a number of numerical examples.[14]

4.4 NASH EQUILIBRIUM AS THE RESULT OF BOUNDEDLY RATIONAL ADAPTATION

In applications to economics and other social sciences, payoffs usually represent utility or profits, and, moreover, one is interested in the dynamics of cognitive and social adaptation processes, such as learning or imitation of successful behaviour, rather than in biological reproduction as such.[15] Hence, we now ask whether the results for the replicator dynamics carry over to such dynamics. In fact, economists have recently studied properties of certain classes of evolutionary dynamics which are intended to be wide enough to contain a variety of plausible social evolutionary processes. All of these dynamics are, in one way or another, monotone with respect to payoff differences between current strategies (Nachbar, 1990; Friedman, 1991; Samuelson and Zhang, 1992; Swinkels, 1992).

Here, we formalize one particular such class, namely dynamics with the property that if some pure strategy earns more than another, then the first sub-population grows at a higher rate than the second. Clearly the replicator dynamics belongs to this class, but note the new interpretations that such a generalization admits; one may now think in terms of infinitely lived, boundedly rational individuals who consciously choose their strategy, or, more precisely, revise their choice of strategy over time. The dynamics will simply represent the aggregate effect of the rules for revising strategies that individuals use.[16] A wide range of dynamics is admissible under this specification, including arbitrarily fast revisions towards the current best replies.[17]

Formally, the class of dynamics under consideration, to be called *monotone*, is given by

$$\dot{x}_i = \varphi_i(x) \cdot x_i \qquad [\forall i \in I, \ \forall x \in \Delta] \tag{4.3}$$

for some Lipschitz continuous function $\varphi : \Delta \to \mathbb{R}^k$ satisfying the *orthogonality* condition $x \cdot \varphi(x) = 0$ at all states $x \in \Delta$, and the *monotonicity* condition $\varphi_i(x) \gtreqless \varphi_j(x)$ if $u(e^i, x) \gtreqless u(e^j, x)$, conditions clearly met by the replicator dynamics.[18] The orthogonality condition is necessary and sufficient to leave the unit simplex Δ invariant.

It is easily verified that in the special case of (symmetric) 2×2 games the qualititative properties of the replicator dynamics are shared by all monotone dynamics (Weibull, 1992). Hence, irrespective of how close the dynamic adjustment is to instant best-reply behaviour, aggregate behaviour always converges to Nash equilibrium in these low-dimensional settings.

Moreover, it is not difficult to show that, even for arbitrary (symmetric) $k \times k$ games, many properties of the replicator dynamics are valid for any monotone dynamics. In particular, Propositions A and B generalize directly:

Proposition A′ (Friedman, 1991) If the population state x is (Lyapunov) stable in some monotone dynamics (4.3), then (x,x) is a Nash equilibrium. If (x,x) is a Nash equilibrium, then x is stationary in any monotone dynamics (4.3).[19]

Proposition B′ (Nachbar, 1990) If an interior dynamic path in a monotone dynamics (4.3) converges to some state x, then (x,x) is a Nash equilibrium.

The more subtle Proposition C does not appear to be fully generalizable to the present class of dynamics; instead of asserting the extinction of all strategies which are strictly (iteratively) dominated by some pure *or mixed* strategy, Samuelson and Zhang only assert, for monotone dynamics, the extinction of all strategies which are strictly (iteratively) dominated by some *pure* strategy:

Proposition C′ (Samuelson and Zhang, 1992) If a pure strategy is (iteratively) strictly dominated by a pure strategy, then its population share converges to zero along any interior dynamic path in any monotone dynamics (3).[20]

The stochastic version of monotone dynamics (4.3) requires that if one strategy performs better than another, the share of the former is likely to grow faster than that of the latter. A model along these lines is offered by Kandori, Mailath and Rob (1991), who consider stochastic evolution under monotone dynamics in a class of 2×2 coordination games. In contrast to Foster and Young (1990), who add a stochastic term to the continuous-time replicator dynamics (4.1), Kandori, Mailath and Rob assume deterministic monotone adjustment towards the more profitable strategy, and introduce the stochastic element by assuming that the population is finite, time is discrete, and each player has a positive (i.i.d) probability of switching, or 'mutating', to the other strategy. Given these assumptions, the evolution of each individual's strategy is governed by an irreducible Markov chain, and therefore each individual's play will converge to the same ergodic distribution over the two strategies. Furthermore, Kandori, Mailath and Rob show that as the (exogenous) mutation probability tends to zero, the probability that in the ergodic limiting distribution the individual will play the risk-dominant strategy, goes to 1. Hence, not only does this approach, just as the deterministic monotone dynamics approach, lend support for Nash equilibrium; in simple games the stochastic approach even selects among Nash equilibria which, taken individually, are stable in the corresponding deterministic monotone dynamics.[21]

4.5 MORE GENERAL BOUNDEDLY RATIONAL BEHAVIOURS

The results discussed in the preceding section suggest that the close connection between evolution and Nash equilibrium that was obtained under the replicator dynamics extends to a wide range of adaptive dynamics.[22] Nevertheless, this can only be among the very first steps in studying the long-run evolution of boundedly rational behaviours. In the present section, we try to identify important limitations of the model of bounded rationality underlying the evolutionary models discussed above, and we investigate some of the consequences of generalizing that model.

The only element of the *history* of play that goes into the above models of strategy adaptation is the current payoff. In reality, individuals use their memory, and the success of different strategies over (at least part of) the past count in their decision-making. A variety of models of behavioural adaptation based on the history of play is supplied by the learning literature, a research field falling outside the scope of this chapter. However, an interesting environment for evolutionary selection over history-contingent behaviours arises when interacting individuals use differing learning or search rules. These rules may be more or less *ad hoc*; some may use Bayesian updating etc. Within the context of a stochastic asset market with this flavour, Blume and Easley (1991) find that the link between evolutionary selection and rationality is weak. Although their analysis is quite interesting, its setting falls outside the scope of the present chapter. Another element of the history that appears often to be significant in social adaptation is the pattern of choice made by others. People may, for example, be prone to choose strategies that others are using, or, phrased differently, adopt prevalent behaviours. Weibull (1992) suggests that if players can sample other players' current payoffs and move from less to more profitable strategies on the basis of such sampling, then the resulting selections dynamics is monotone, and hence the results of the previous section apply.

Another important aspect which is not captured in the monotone adaptive dynamics discussed in the previous section is that, in the real world, people are to some extent *forward looking*. There are really two independent issues here. First, in the standard evolutionary models discussed in the previous sections, individuals are myopic in the sense of only paying attention to current payoffs. In models with a finite number of (long-lived) individuals, it may not always be optimal to choose the myopically best strategy. By choosing some other strategy, a player may influence other players' future behaviour to his advantage. Second, in choosing their strategies, agents (in finite or infinite populations) may want to anticipate the future behaviour of others. After all, they know that as they themselves change strategy, everybody else is also changing theirs, so that what is currently a good strategy may not be quite so good by the time it gets played. This kind of anticipatory behaviour is beyond the scope of the models outlined above (see Selten, 1991a). On the other hand, continuous-time monotone dynamics does permit strategy adaptation arbitrarily close to the instantaneous adoption of a best reply (IABR henceforth). It may be argued that as one approaches IABR, the individuals' strategy choices may not be very different from those which incorporate a forward-looking element. (For, after all, the limit case of IABR is one in which agents perfectly anticipate what the others will choose.) However, this is not true; as each individual's play approaches IABR, the whole population may change strategies faster and faster. As a result, even though everybody is only a little late in responding to what the others are doing, they may be way off in strategy space.

Lack of anticipatory behaviour is one aspect of the broader issue that standard evolutionary models are based on a very mechanical model of boundedly rational play. Bounded rationality should not be equated with using a mechanical rule to move towards a strategy that is currently doing well. Boundedly rational players *think*, albeit imperfectly. The imperfection in their thinking can take many forms and there is no *a priori* reason why some of these are more appropriate for evolutionary analysis than others. Therefore, the right way to do evolutionary analysis appears to be to allow for the widest possible variety of boundedly rational behaviours.

The paper which comes closest to this project is Stahl (1992), who, in an otherwise standard set-up of evolutionary game theory, introduces a hierarchy of increasingly sophisticated players whom he calls *smart*$_n$ players, for $n = 0,1,2,\ldots$.[23] The usual pre-programmed players in evolutionary game theory are called smart$_0$, and, for $n>0$, a smart$_n$ player is one who knows the current aggregate behaviour of all players at all lower smartness levels. This limits the possible beliefs of a smart$_n$ player about what his potential opponents could be playing, and he plays a (pure) strategy which is optimal under some belief satisfying this restriction.[24] The total population, within which the usual random matchings takes place, is decomposed into n^* smartness categories, and the distribution across strategies within each such category n can be represented as a point x^n on the (usual) unit simplex Δ, for $n = 0,1,2,\ldots,n^*$.

If the share of the total population in smartness category n is λ_n, the aggregate population behaviour is the convex combination $p = \Sigma\lambda_n x^n$, again a point on the unit simplex Δ. Stahl uses a version of the discrete-time replicator dynamics (4.2) which induces dynamic paths close to those of the continuous-time version (4.1) (cf. discussion of Dekel and Scotchmer, 1992, and Cabrales and Sobel, 1992 in Section 4.3 above). In Stahl's setting, this selection dynamics specifies the growth rates of each of the $k\cdot(n^* + 1)$ population shares.

Despite this much more general environment, Stahl is able to show that the counterparts to Propositions B and C hold. He also shows that, whether or not the process converges, the sub-population of smart$_0$ players will never be wiped out, granted, of course, that initially all types of player are present. Intuitively, the smart$_0$ players survive despite the presence of more rational players because some of them happen to be programmed to the 'right' strategies, and hence these earn the same payoff in a stationary state as smarter players. Put in the author's words: 'being right is just as good as being smart'. However, one should remember that in general the aggregate population behaviour changes over time. Therefore, smarter players, who can adjust their play to their environment, will often be in a better position than smart$_0$ players who always play the same strategy, and, consequently, the survival of smart$_0$ players is non-trivial:

Proposition D (Stahl, 1992)   If an interior path in the discrete-time replicator dynamics converges to some $p \in \Delta$, then (p,p) is a Nash equilibrium. The population shares of smart$_0$ players playing non-rationalizable strategies converge to zero along any interior dynamic path. Moreover, for an interior path in the dynamics, the limit superior of the population share $\lambda_0(t)$ of smart$_0$ players is positive.

In sum: as long as the evolutionary process in Stahl's setting converges, the long-run outcome remains a Nash equilibrium. In this sense, the 'as if' justification of Nash equilibrium generalizes beyond the standard environment of evolutionary game theory. On the other hand, whether the process will converge and what its long-run behaviour will be like if it does not converge, does depend on the composition of the population in terms of levels of rationality. The result concerning the survival of smart$_0$ players is important because it says that if the initial population contains smart$_0$ players, the long-run population will also contain smart$_0$ players and therefore (as long as the process does not converge) the presence of smart$_0$ players may have a real effect on the long-run behaviour of the system. In other words, one cannot simply ignore the actual levels of rationality of the players in the game, as the proponents of the 'as if' methodology would suggest we do.

Another generalization of the basic evolutionary environment, different from the ones considered by Stahl (1992), is introduced in Banerjee and Weibull (1991). We define the set of types to be some finite set $T = \{1,2,\ldots,r\}$, and consider any (symmetric) two-player game with pure strategy set $I = \{1,2,\ldots,k\}$. One can then think of a possible *behaviour* as a map from T to I, i.e., a map b which for each type $\tau \in T$ of opponent prescribes a strategy $i \in I$. Denote the set of all behaviours $\mathcal{B}$. A *player-cell* then is an element of the product set $T \times \mathcal{B}$, i.e., each player in cell (τ,b) is himself of type $\tau \in T$ and uses strategy $b(\tau') \in I$ when meeting a player of type $\tau' \in T$.

In this terminology, the standard environment of evolutionary game theory is the special case of k types, i.e., $T = I$, and every player of type $i \in T$ is constrained to the constant behaviour $b(j) = i \ \forall j \in T$. Banerjee and Weibull (1991) corresponds to the somewhat less special case of $k + 1$ types, i.e., $T = I \cup \{k + 1\}$, each of the k first types being constrained to constant behaviours, just as in the standard setting of evolutionary game theory, and the $k + 1$'st type being constrained to the best-reply mapping.[25] More specifically, we there study the replicator dynamics (4.1) in an environment with k types of smart$_0$ players, one for each pure strategy $i \in I$, and one additional type, $k + 1$, who plays a best response against each of the other types, and some rationalizable strategy (or strategies) against its own type. Let α denote the payoff that players of the *optimizing* type $k + 1$ obtain when meeting each other.

In this mixed set-up, and in the correspondingly augmented continuous-time replicator dynamics (4.1), we provide sufficient conditions for $smart_0$ players to persist, or vanish, in the longer run. Let $I^+ \subset I$ be the (possibly empty) subset of pure strategies which earn more than α when meeting their best replies, and let $I^- \subset I$ be the (possibly empty) subset of strategies which earn less than α when meeting their best replies. One may refer to strategies in I^+ as *aggressive* and those in I^- as *yielding*. It is intuitively clear that if the game has some aggressive strategy, then the stationary state in which all players are of the optimizing type $k + 1$ is unstable in the replicator dynamics. For suppose there are virtually only such players around. Then these obtain a lower payoff than the few aggressive $smart_0$ players who are present, since the latter meet virtually only optimizing players. Conversely, all yielding $smart_0$ players vanish in the long run:

Proposition E (Banerjee and Weibull, 1991)   Consider any interior path in the replicator dynamics (4.1) for k types of $smart_0$ players and one optimizing type, $k + 1$. If $I^+ \neq \phi$, the share of optimizing players does not converge to 1 over time. For each $i \in I^-$, the population share x_i of players of type i converges to zero.

An immediate consequence of this result is that if the game lacks aggressive strategies, which for example is the case with every constant-sum game which has no symmetric Nash equilibrium in pure strategies, then only optimizing players survive in the long run, along any interior dynamic path. In constrast, if a game has some aggressive strategy (such as the 'hawk' strategy in the famous Hawk–Dove game), then some aggressive $smart_0$ players may survive in the long run, along with optimizing players.

Moreover, in striking contrast with the results for the replicator dynamics in the standard setting of evolutionary game theory, (Lyapunov) stable states in environments containing optimizing players need not correspond to Nash equilibrium behaviour at all (cf. Proposition A). In fact, even *asymptotically* stable states may involve the playing of a strictly dominated strategy.[26] This disturbing phenomenon arises in the following dominance-solvable game:

$$A = \begin{bmatrix} 3 & 1 & 6 \\ 0 & 0 & 4 \\ 1 & 2 & 5 \end{bmatrix}$$

Here strategy 2 is strictly dominated by strategy 1 (and by strategy 3), and, once strategy 2 has been deleted, strategy 1 strictly dominates strategy 3. In the absence of $smart_0$ players, the outcome would hence be the standard non-cooperative solution that all optimizing players use the unique rationalizable strategy 1. Likewise, if only $smart_0$ players were present in the population, as in the standard setting of evolutionary game theory, the long-run dynamic outcome would, once again, be that only strategy 1 would be used (Proposition C). But the presence of both types of player allows for an asymptotically stable outcome in which all three strategies are used.

To see how this is possible, first note that the strictly dominated strategy 2 is the unique aggressive strategy of the game, and strategy 3 is its unique yielding strategy. By Proposition E, the share x_4 of optimizing players will not converge to 1, and the share x_3 of players of type 3 will converge to zero. Figure 4.2 shows the qualitative properties of the replicator dynamics near the face $x_3 = 0$ of the unit simplex. The diagram shows one basin of attraction for a continuum of stationary states, all of which contain a mix of $smart_0$ players of type 1 and optimizing players. In these (Lyapunov) stable states, all players use the unique rationalizable strategy 1. However, one also sees a basin of attraction for an asymptotically stable state in which 2/3 of the players are optimizers and 1/3 are $smart_0$ of the aggressive type 2. In this stationary state, the latter type of player of course uses strategy 2, since by definition they have no choice, and the optimizing players use the uniqe rationalizable strategy 1 against each other and the iteratively dominated strategy 3 against the aggressive players – the latter strategy being the best reply to the strictly dominated strategy 2. As a result, the aggregate population behaviour is the completely mixed strategy $m = (4,3,2)/9$. The reason why $smart_0$ players of type 1 are selected against in a neighbourhood of this state is that they perform worse than the optimizing players in states with aggressive (type 2) players present.

Robson (1990) enriches the standard set-up of evolutionary game theory in a similar way. In his model, players may be of (a few different) types; some players can distinguish the type of their opponent and condition their behaviour accordingly. He shows that this richer set-up enables evolutionary selection for the Pareto-efficient Nash equi-

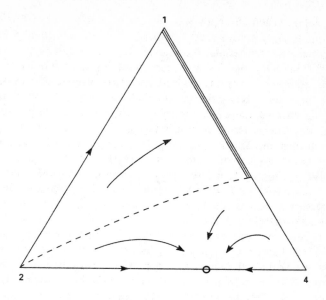

Figure 4.2

librium in simple coordination games (just as the model of Kandori, Mailath and Rob, 1991, would predict), and that it also enables temporary cooperation in the Prisoners' Dilemma game. However, he does not allow for all possible behaviours, and hence, as he notes, cooperation in the Prisoners' Dilemma may break down if some players of the 'cooperative type' in fact play the dominant strategy.

Both these models (Robson, 1990; Banerjee and Weibull, 1991) contain restrictions on the set of behaviours. As the above example shows, such restrictions can lead to outcomes which are sharply at odds with Nash equilibrium. In principle, one should allow for all possible behaviours (i.e. the full set $\mathcal{B}$) when testing whether or not evolution in such richer behavioural frameworks can lead away from the Nash paradigm (Banerjee and Weibull, 1992).

4.6 CONCLUSIONS

In broad outlines, the current stage of research in the field of game-theoretic approaches to evolution and rationality provides some support for the rationalistic approach of non-cooperative game theory.

One conclusion which appears to be fairly robust is that if aggregate behaviour is (Lyapunov) stable with respect to evolutionary dynamic forces, then it corresponds to some Nash equilibrium of the underlying game. In this sense, evolutionary selection makes individuals behave as if they obeyed the stringent rationality and coordination requirements underlying the rationalistic approach to Nash equilibrium. Likewise, if the evolutionary selection process converges, then its limiting state (even if it is not stable) again corresponds to some Nash equilibrium. There is nothing inherent in the evolutionary process, however, which guarantees its convergence. If the process does not converge, aggregate behaviour is nevertheless rational, in the sense of not being strictly (iteratively) dominated. Thus, when evolutionary convergence is lost, so is the coordination but not the rationality of the induced aggregate behaviour.

Moreover, the above qualitative results remain valid even if the biological reproduction dynamics is replaced by some boundedly rational process of individual behaviour adaptation, and irrespective of how close the adaptive behaviour is to instant switching to optimal strategies. However, the possibility remains open, in games with more than two pure strategies, that fewer trajectories are convergent as adaptive behaviour approaches instant switching to optimal strategies. Using somewhat metaphorical language, let us imagine that we identify the form of 'rational and coordinated' behaviour, represented by some Nash equilibrium in a given game, by a 'point of full rationality', p, in some 'rationality space'. It is then possible that there is a neighbourhood of this point outside which long-run aggregate behaviour conforms to the Nash equilibrium but inside which it does not, except at the point p itself. If this is the case, the Nash equilibrium paradigm is problematic, representing only an isolated 'ideal point' in 'rationality space'. It is clearly important for the validity of both the rationalistic and the standard evolutionary approach to determine whether this is the case. More generally, it is an interesting research task to understand whether the introduction of more sophisticated players might make the evolutionary process less likely to converge.

The qualitative results mentioned above all concern individuals who are constrained to particularly simple behaviours in the game played. Judging from some recent research, evolutionary selection in richer behaviour spaces – containing more or less boundedley rational, information-conditioned behaviours – even when convergent, need not result in Nash equilibrium behaviour. However, it still remains an open question whether results which are negative in this sense are robust with respect to expansions of the space of behaviours. Maybe we will see some 'rationalistic' equilibrium behaviour result from evolutionary selection processes in sufficiently rich behaviour spaces (Banerjee and Weibull, 1992).

There is also the further issue of whether we are justified in rationalizing Nash equilibrium play in terms of arguments which refer only to the long-run outcomes. After all, the long run could be very long indeed. In terms of interpreting the above results, it would hence be extremely useful if environments and adaptation rules could be identified for which the convergence to Nash equilibrium is relatively rapid/slow.

Finally, a specific lacuna in the literature can be located: there is a serious shortage of explicit selection mechanisms with plausible and general boundedly rational micro foundations. Also, it seems desirable to complement the current standard framework of pairwise interactions towards multi-player interactions (see references mentioned in the introduction) and towards more market-like settings. Viewing this whole enterprise as bridge-building between evolutionary (biological) and rationalistic (economic) approaches, one could say that while most current research builds from the biology end of the bridge, borrowing much of the general setting and technical machinery from there, we now need more work on its economics end, using the settings of standard economic institutions.

Notes

1. This paper was presented at the Tenth World Congress of the International Economic Association, Moscow, 24–28 August 1992. We are grateful for comments from Ken Binmore, Jonas Björnerstedt, Jean-Michel Grandmont, Peter Norman, Roy Radner, Susan Scotchmer, Johan Stennek and Karl Wärneryd, as well as from the participants in seminars at the Institute for International Economic Studies, Stockholm University, and at the C.V. Starr Center for Applied Economics, New York University.

   Banerjee gratefully acknowledges the hospitality of the Institute for International Economic Studies at Stockholm University. Weibull gratefully acknowledges financial support from the Industrial Institute for Economic and Social Research, Stockholm, Sweden, and from the Jan Wallander Research Foundation.
2. For pioneering suggestions in this direction, in the context of competitive markets, see Alchian (1950), Friedman (1953) and Winter (1964, 1971).

3. Dawkins used the term 'replicator' for entities which can get copied and which are such that (a) their properties can affect their probability of being copied, and (b) the line of descent copies is potentially unlimited.

4. Every evolutionary stable strategy $x \in \Delta$ is asymptotically stable (see footnote 26) in the replicator dynamics (Hofbauer *et al.*, 1979), so the connection between the static and dynamic approaches is fairly tight.

5. Unfortunately, a discussion of connections between these three research paradigms falls outside the scope of the present chapter. Two relevant papers are Blume and Easley (1991), for a connection between learning behaviours and evolution, and Binmore and Samuelson (1992), for the connection between automata and evolution.

6. A strictly dominated strategy is never a best reply, and hence the set of rationalizable strategies is always a subset of the set of strategies surviving the iterated elimination of strictly dominated strategies.

7. This system of ordinary differential equations is polynomial. Hence, it has a unique solution through every initial state $x(0) \in \Delta$. Moreover, it leaves the unit simplex Δ invariant, $x(0) \in \Delta \Rightarrow x(t) \in \Delta \ \forall t \geq 0$, and the system (4.1) is unaffected by affine transformations of payoffs, modulo a change of time scale. For an analysis of the validity of the implicit use of the law of large numbers, see Boylan (1992).

8. A state is called *stationary* if, starting in x, the system remains at x. A state $x \in \Delta$ is said to be *(Lyapunov) stable*, if there for every neighbourhood $V \subset \Delta$ of x exists some neighbourhood $U \subset \Delta$ of x such that, starting in U, $x(t)$ never leaves V; see e.g. Hirsch and Smale (1974).

9. If the initial state $x(0)$ is interior, then so are all future states $x(t)$. In other words, the interior of the unit simplex Δ is invariant in the replicator dynamics (4.1), and so one may unambiguously speak about interior (solution) *paths*.

10. Samuelson and Zhang establish this for interactions between two populations, implying the present claim as a corollary. For a direct proof, see Weibull (1992).

11. Even in certain non-convergent cases Nash equilibrium does appear; Schuster *et al.* (1981a) show that if a game has a unique interior Nash equilibrium $p \in \Delta$, then p is also the time average of every periodic dynamic path in Δ (whenever such exist).

12. Unlike the continuous-time version of the replicator dynamics, (4.2) requires all payoffs to be positive. With this restriction, the dynamics (4.2) leaves the unit simplex, as well as its interior, invariant. However, while the continuous-time version (4.1) is invariant under affine transformations of payoffs, (4.2) is not. Indeed, addition of a positive constant γ to all payoffs in (4.2) does affect its solution paths in Δ (Hofbauer and Sigmund, 1998).

13. Near the face $x_4 = 0$, $\dot{x}_4 > 0$ iff $x_1^2 + x_2^2 + x_3^2 > 1 - 2\beta/\alpha$; see Weibull (1992) for details.

14. See Fudenberg and Harris (1992) for an alternative stochastic specification.

15. An exception being evolutionary theories for the formation of preferences such as altruism etc.

16. To this date, only very special and simplistic social evolutionary adaptation mechanisms have been studied (Friedman, 1991). In this respect,

the learning literature is more advanced than the evolutionary literature; see discussion is Section 4.5.

17. Note that the limiting case of individuals who instantly switch to the best replies in general does not induce a well-defined dynamics in continuous time, since the best-reply correspondence need not be lower hemicontinuous, and hence not always permit a continuous selection; see Gilboa and Matsui (1991) for an approach to this issue.

18. The latter property is called *relative monotonicity* in Nachbar (1990), *order compatibility* (of predynamics) in Friedman (1991), and *monotonicity* in Samuelson and Zhang (1992).

19. Friedman (1991) makes the slightly weaker claim (for a wider class of dynamics) that *asymptotic* stability implied Nash equilibrium play; see his proposition 3.3. A simple proof of the present claim is given in Weibull (1992).

20. Samuelson and Zhang (1992) in fact show that the statement in Proposition C′ is valid for two-population dynamics implying Proposition C′ as a corollary. They also show, again for two-population dynamics, that the slightly stronger statement in Proposition C is valid for a subclass of monotone dynamics which they call *aggregate monotone*. Nachbar (1990) established Proposition C′ in the special case of games in which only one strategy survives the iterated elimination of pure strategies which are strictly dominated by other pure strategies.

21. See Kandori and Rob (1992) for an extension to $k \times k$ games. See Nöldeke and Samuelson (1992) for a model of stochastic evolutionary dynamics in a class of sequential-move games in extensive form.

22. Actually, the extension is not quite complete since the stronger Proposition C holds only for aggregate monotone dynamics; see Samuelson and Zhang (1992). It is still not clear whether there are reasonable social adaptation procedures which are monotone but not aggregate monotone; see Friedman (1991) and Swinkels (1992) for discussions of wide classes of adaptation dynamics.

23. Also Blume and Easley (1991) analyze evolutionary selection of more or less sophisticated behaviours, but do this in the context of a stochastic asset market rather than for pairwise game playing.

24. In order to specify selections within best reply sets, all players of smartness $n \geq 1$ are assumed to have some lexicographic preference over strategies.

25. In a similar spirit, Dekel and Scotchmer (1992, example 2) introduce players who play best responses to last period's population state. Banerjee and Weibull (1991) also study the case of players who play best responses to the current state, in continuous time.

26. A state $p \in \Delta$ is called *asymptotically stable* if there is a neighbourhood $U \subset \Delta$ of p such that solution paths in U approach x as $t \to \infty$; see e.g. Hirsch and Smale (1974).

References

Alchian, A. (1950) 'Uncertainty, Evolution and Economic Theory', *Journal of Political Economy*, vol. 58, pp. 211–22.

Armbruster, W. and W. Boege (1979) 'Bayesian Game Theory', in O. Moeschlin and D. Pallaschke (eds.), *Game Theory and Related Topics* (Amsterdam North-Holland).

Aumann, R. (1987) 'Correlated Equilibrium as an Expression of Bayesian Rationality', *Econometrica*, vol. 55, pp. 1–18.

Aumann, R. and A. Brandenburger (1991) 'Epistemic Conditions for Nash Equilibrium', Hebrew University and Harvard Business School.

Banerjee, A. and J.W. Weibull (1991) 'Evolutionary Selection and Rational Behaviour', forthcoming in A. Kirman and M. Salmon (eds), *Rationality and Learning in Economics* (Oxford: Blackwell).

Banerjee, A. and J.W. Weibull (1992) 'Evolution of Behaviours Contingent upon Opponents' Identities', work in progress.

Basu, K. (1988) 'Strategic Irrationality in Extensive Games', *Mathematical Social Sciences*, vol. 15, pp. 247–60.

Basu, K. (1990) 'On the Non-Existence of a Rationality Definition for Extensive Games', *International Journal of Game Theory*, vol. 19, pp. 33–44.

Bernheim, D. (1984) 'Rationalizable Strategic Behavior', *Econometrica*, vol. 52, pp. 1007–28.

Bernheim, D. (1986) 'Axiomatic Characterizations of Rational Choice in Strategic Environments', *Scandinavian Journal of Economics*, vol. 88, pp. 473–88.

Bicchieri, C. (1989) 'Self-Refuting Theories of Strategic Interaction: A Paradox of Common Knowledge', *Erkenntnis*, vol. 30, pp. 69–85.

Binmore, K. (1987) 'Modelling Rational Players: Part I', *Economics and Philosophy*', vol. 3, pp. 179–214.

Binmore, K. (1988) 'Modelling Rational Players: Part II', '*Economics and Philosophy*', vol. 4, pp. 9–55.

Binmore, K. and L. Samuelson (1992) 'Evolutionary Stability in Repeated Games Played by Finite Automata', *Journal of Economic Theory*, vol. 57, pp. 278–305.

Blume, L. and D. Easley (1991) 'Economic Natural Selection and Adaptive Behavior', mimeo, Dept. of Economics, Cornell University, forthcoming in A. Kirman and M. Salmon (eds), *Rationality and Learning in Economics* (Oxford: Blackwell).

Bomze, I.M. (1986) 'Non-Cooperative Two-Person Games in Biology: A Classification', *International Journal of Game Theory*, vol. 15, pp. 31–57.

Boylan, R. (1992) 'Laws of Large Numbers for Dynamical Systems with Randomly Matched Individuals', *Journal of Economic Theory*, vol. 57, pp. 473–504.

Cabrales, A. and J. Sobel (1992) 'On the Limit Points of Discrete Selection Dynamics', *Journal of Economic Theory*, vol. 57, pp. 407–19.

Canning, D. (1989) 'Convergence to Equilibrium in a Sequence of Games with Learning', LSE Discussion Paper TE/89/190.

Dekel, E. and S. Scotchmer (1992) 'On the Evolution of Optimizing Behavior', *Journal of Economic Theory*', vol. 57, pp. 392–406.

Foster, D. and P. Young (1990) 'Stochastic Evolutionary Game Dynamics', *Theoretical Population Biology*, vol. 38, pp. 219–32.

Freidlin, M. and A. Wentzell (1984) *Random Perturbations of Dynamical Systems* (New York: Springer Verlag).

Friedman, D. (1991) 'Evolutionary Games in Economics', *Econometrica*, vol. 59, pp. 637–66.

Friedman, M. (1953) 'The Methodology of Positive Economics', in M. Friedman, *Essays in Positive Economics* (Chicago: University of Chicago Press).

Fudenberg, D. and C. Harris (1992) 'Evolutionary Dynamics with Aggregate Shocks', *Journal of Economic Theory*, vol. 57, 420–41.

Gilboa, I. and A. Matsui (1991) 'Social Stability and Equilibrium', *Econometrica*, vol. 59, pp. 859–67.

Hirsch, M. and S. Smale (1974) *Differential Equations, Dynamical Systems, and Linear Algebra* (San Diego: Academic Press).

Hofbauer, J. and K. Sigmund (1988) *The Theory of Evolution and Dynamical Systems*, London Mathematical Society Students Texts, vol. 7, (Cambridge: Cambridge University Press).

Hofbauer, J., P. Schuster and K. Sigmund (1979) 'A Note on Evolutionary Stable Strategies and Game Dynamics', *Journal of Theoretical Biology*, vol. 81, pp. 609–12.

Johansen, L. (1982) 'The Status of the Nash Type of Noncooperative Equilibrium in Economic Theory', *Scandinavian Journal of Economics*' vol. 84, pp. 421–41.

Kandori, M. and R. Rob (1992) 'Evolution of Equilibria in the Long Run: A General Theory and Applications', University of Pennsylvania, CARESS Working Paper 92–06R.

Kandori M., G. Mailath and R. Rob (1991) 'Learning, Mutation and Long Run Equilibria in Games', mimeo, University of Pennsylvania.

Maynard Smith, J. (1974) 'The Theory of Games and the Evolution of Animal Conflicts', *Journal of Theoretical Biology*, vol. 47, pp. 209–21.

Maynard Smith, J. (1982) *Evolution and the Theory of Games* (Cambridge: Cambridge University Press).

Maynard Smith, J. and G.R. Price (1973) 'The Logic of Animal Conflict', *Nature*, vol. 246, pp. 15–18.

Nachbar, J. (1990) '"Evolutionary" Selection Dynamics in Games: Convergence and Limit Properties', *International Journal of Game Theory*, vol. 91, pp. 59–89.

Nöldeke, G. and L. Samuelson (1992) 'The Evolutionary Foundations of Backward and Forward Induction', Mimeo, University of Bonn and University of Wisconsin.

Pearce, D. (1984) 'Rationalizable Strategic Behavior and the Problem of Perfection', *Econometrica*, vol. 52, pp. 1029–50.

Ritzberger, K. and K. Vogelsberger (1991) 'The Nash Field', Mimeo, Institute for Advanced Studies, Vienna.

Robson, A.J. (1990) 'Efficiency in Evolutionary Games: Darwin, Nash and the Secret Handshake', *Journal of Theoretical Biology*, vol. 144, pp. 379–96.

Rosenthal, R. (1981) 'Games of Perfect Information, Predatory Pricing and the Chain-Store Paradox', *Journal of Economic Theory*, vol. 25, pp. 92–100.

Samuelson, L. (1991) 'Does Evolution Eliminate Dominated Strategies?', Mimeo, University of Wisconsin.

Samuelson, L. and J. Zhang (1992) 'Evolutionary Stability in Asymmetric Games', *Journal of Economic Theory*, vol. 57, pp. 363–91.

Schuster, P. and K. Sigmund (1983) 'Replicator Dynamics', *Journal of Theoretical Biology*, vol. 100, pp. 533–8.

Schuster, P. and K. Sigmund (1985) 'Towards a Dynamics of Social Behaviour: Strategic and Genetic Models for the Evolution of Animal Conflicts', *Journal of Social Biological Structure*, vol. 8, pp. 255–77.

Schuster, P., K. Sigmund, J. Hofbauer and R. Wolff (1981a) 'Selfregulation of Behaviour in Animal Societies I: Symmetric Contests', *Biological Cybernetics*, vol. 40, pp. 1–8.

Schuster, P., K. Sigmund, J. Hofbauer and R. Wolff (1981b) 'Selfregulation of Behaviour in Animal Societies II: Games Between Two Populations Without Selfinteraction', *Biological Cybernetics*, vol. 40, pp. 9–15.

Selten, R. (1991a) 'Anticipatory Learning in Two-Person Games', in R. Selten (ed.), *Game Equilibrium Models I* (Berlin: Springer Verlag).

Selten, R. (1991b) 'Evolution, Learning and Economic Behavior', *Games and Economic Behavior*, vol. 3, pp. 3–24.

Stahl, D. (1992) 'Evolution of Smart$_n$ Players', Mimeo, University of Texas.

Swinkels, J. (1992) 'Adjustment Dynamics and Rational Play in Games', mimeo, Stanford University.

Tan, T. and S.R. Werlang (1988) 'The Bayesian Foundations of Solution Concepts of Games', *Journal of Economic Theory*, vol. 45, pp. 370–91.

Taylor, P. and L. Jonker (1978) 'Evolutionary Stable Strategies and Game Dynamics', *Mathematical Biosciences*, vol. 40, pp. 145–56.

Weibull, J.W. (1992) 'An Introduction to Evolutionary Game Theory', Mimeo, Department of Economics, Stockholm University.

Winter, S. (1964) 'Economic "Natural" Selection and the Theory of the Firm', *Yale Economics Essays*, vol. 4, pp. 225–72.

Winter, S. (1971) 'Satisficing, Selection, and the Innovating Remnant', *Quarterly Journal of Economics*, vol. 85, pp. 237–61.

Zeeman, E.C. (1980) *Population Dynamics from Game Theory*, Lecture Notes in Mathematics 819 (Berlin: Springer Verlag).

Zeeman, E.C. (1981) 'Dynamics of the Evolution of Animal Conflicts', *Journal of Theoretical Biology*, vol. 89, pp. 249–70.

Discussion

Ken Binmore
UNIVERSITY COLLEGE LONDON

In this excellent survey, the authors begin by drawing attention to the inadequacies of traditional attempts to provide a foundation for the theory of games using the principle that it should be 'common knowledge that the players are perfectly rational'. I am very much in sympathy with their view that such an eductive approach needs to be replaced or supplemented by evolutive models in which the process by which equilibrium is reached is not abstracted away.

Although I share the authors' view that the way forward lies in the study of evolutive models, I am less hopeful that it will prove possible to obtain genuinely worthwhile theorems that apply simultaneously to most of the equilibrating processes in which economists should take an interest. Those quoted in the chapter, for example, apply to deterministic processes in continuous time. However, processes in discrete time, or processes with some noise built in, can have sharply different behaviour. For example, Dekel and Scotchmer (1992), as Banerjee and Weibull note, examine a version of the discrete replicator dynamics in which a strictly dominated strategy does not disappear in the long run.

To evaluate the significance of such examples, it seems to me necessary for us to think harder about the derivation of the evolutionary dynamics we choose to study. It is a minor scandal, for example, that the standard textbooks offer so little motivation for the orthodox replicator equation in continuous time. Nor can we afford to neglect the fact that there are serious interpretative problems about the 'correct' replicator equation in discrete time (Hofbauer and Sygmund, 1988). Nor yet can we afford to think of biological fitness as a straightforward analogue of a von Neumann and Morgenstern payoff. Fitness *levels* can matter, especially in noisy models. Moreover, Banerjee and Weibull are surely right in drawing our attention to the fact that socio-economic processes need not share the properties of biological processes. But does it follow that biological fitness should be replaced by a firm's profit or a consumer's utility? After all, biologists might more naturally measure payoffs in grammes of food or square metres of territory. Perhaps we should follow their lead in tailoring our concept of a payoff to the socio-economic process that we want to study.

My own excitement about the current flurry of papers in evolutionary game theory differs from that of Bannerjee and Weibull. I agree that the extent to which evolutionary proccesses can be anticipated to generate rational behaviour is a fascinating topic, but I also have hopes that the study of noisy evolutionary processes will lead to progress on the problem of equilibrium selection that eductive theory finds so intractable. Space does not allow me to do more than refer to the work of Foster and Young (1990), Young (1992), Kandori, Mailath and Rob (1991), Samuelson (1991) and Canning (1990), who all follow the first-named authors in applying the ideas of Freidlin and Wentzell (1984) to game theory. This work is in its early stages and can be criticized on various grounds. For example, the result of Kandori, Mailath and Rob, that a best-response dynamic with random mutation will select the risk-dominant equilibrium in the Stag-Hunt Game with probability one in the long run, can be criticized on the grounds that it depends on k simultaneous mutations being less likely than l simultaneous mutations when $k > l$. But such considerations can only matter in the very long run if l is large! However, such interpretative difficulties are only teething troubles. The noise that allows an equilibrium to be selected does not have to derive from rare mutations. The current papers only study this case for mathematical simplicity. My guess is that future work will be equally successful in selecting equilibrium with much more interesting evolutionary models. But first we shall need to sharpen up our mathematical technique.

References

Canning, D. (1990) 'Social Equilibrium', Working Paper, Pembroke College, Cambridge.

Dekel, E. and S. Scotchmer (1992) 'On the Evolution of Optimizing Behavior', forthcoming in *Journal of Economic Theory*.

Foster, D. and H. Young (1990) 'Stochastic Evolutionary Game Dynamics', *Theoretical Population Biology*, vol. 38, pp. 219–322.

Freidlin, M. and A. Wentzell (1984) *Random Perturbations of Dynamical Systems* (New York: Springer-Verlag).

Hofbauer, J. and K. Sigmund (1988) *The Theory of Evolution and Dynamical Systems*, London Mathematical Society Student Texts 7 (Cambridge: Cambridge University Press).

Kandori, M., G. Mailath and R. Rob (1991) 'Learning, Mutation and Long Run Equilibria in Games', Working Paper, University of Pennsylvania.

Samuelson, L. (1991) 'How to Tremble if You Must', Working Paper, University of Wisconsin.

Young, H. (1992) 'The Evolution of Conventions', Working Paper, University of Maryland.

Part III

Game Theory, General Equilibrium, and Information

5 Implementation in Iteratively Undominated Strategies

Dilip Abreu[1]
PRINCETON UNIVERSITY

5.1 PRELIMINARY REMARKS

This chapter surveys some joint work of Hitoshi Matsushima and the author on the topic of the title. It is in no way intended as an overview of the large literature on implementation theory.[2] Indeed, discussion of related work is primarily meant to provide a context for our own contribution.

Typically, economic analysis and game theory take as given the basic strategic elements of the environment within which agents interact (e.g. oligopoly theory). Implementation theory is noteworthy in that its exclusive concern is with *designing* strategic environments, taking as given only agents' preferences and information.

The abstract framework for the theory is as follows. One starts with a principal or planner, a group of agents and a collection of alternatives. Agents have preferences over alternatives and the principal would like to select a particular alternative as a function of his agents' preferences. The principal's desired choices are expressed as a *social choice function* mapping from possible preference profiles for agents to the set of alternatives. The implementation problem derives from the assumption that the principal is ignorant of agents' actual preferences. The objective of the theory is to identify the kinds of social choice functions for which the planner can devise mechanisms which induce self-interested agents to, in effect, reveal their true preferences, and conversely it is concerned with with characterizing the social choice functions which different mechanisms generate.

A *game form* or *mechanism* is any scheme which makes the alternative chosen depend on players' choice of messages from some specified set of messages. The principal problem is to design a game form whose equilibrium outcome(s) *coincides* with the social choice function for all profiles of individual preferences (within the domain of the social choice function). Notice that it is required that not merely one but *all* solutions obtained from the solution concept in question be consistent with the social choice function. A variety of solution concepts have been explored in the literature including dominant strategy and iterative dominance based solutions, Nash equilibrium and refinements of Nash equilibrium.

In terms of an alternative terminology which is perhaps more familiar, implementation theory is concerned with principal–*multiple* agent problems with *hidden information*. A huge variety of such problems have been recognized to be interesting theoretically and are clearly important in practice. These include:

− Classical public goods problems
− Design of auctions
− Designing contracts between a principal (government, firm) and a set of suppliers with, say, unknown costs
− Designing constitutions and voting procedures
− Incomplete contract design.

The first general result in implementation theory (and possibly the deepest and most beautiful) is the famous Gibbard–Satterthwaite theorem.

Gibbard–Satterthwaite Theorem (Gibbard, 1973; Satterwaite, 1975) *Suppose there are at least three alternatives. Then any social choice function which is defined for all possible strict preference profiles, and whose range contains at least three elements, is implementable in dominant strategies if and only if it is dictatorial.*

In order to obtain positive results one needs to adopt an alternative (weaker) solution concept or place restrictions on the domain of allowable preferences, or both. These avenues have been explored in subsequent work and indeed are both relevant to the approach Matsushima and I have taken.

Two distinct literatures are particularly central in providing a backdrop for our work.

One begins with the seminal paper by Maskin (1977) on *Nash* implementation. Maskin showed that a condition termed *monotonicity* essentially characterizes the class of Nash implementable social choice functions (scf's) in complete information environments with three or more players. It turns out that an even *wider* class of scf's are implementable using *refinements* of Nash equilibrium. For the same environments (at least three players, complete information) Moore and Repullo (1988) show, roughly speaking, that any social choice function is implementable in subgame perfect equilibrium (see also Abreu and Sen, 1990), and Palfrey and Srivastava (1991) show that any scf is implementable in undominated Nash equilibrium. A serious drawback of this literature is that the proofs rely on mechanisms which have somewhat non-standard features from the point of view of conventional game theory. These include 'integer games' in which players can announce any non-negative integer. See Jackson (1992) for a systematic critique.

Specifically, unwanted equilibria are eliminated by triggering integer games which themselves have no equilibrium. When such games are triggered the player who announces the highest integer can in effect choose his most preferred alternative. If there is conflict amongst players regarding what the best alternative is, such an integer game will not have an equilibrium since any integer announcement is permitted (no conflicting players would wish to assign positive probability to a losing integer). The spirit of these constructions is illustrated in the example below, which may be embedded in a standard implementation framework.

Example 1

There are two players, $i = 1, 2$, each of whom has strategy sets $M_i = \{0,1,2,\ldots\}$. They receive payoffs $g(m_1, m_2) \in \mathbb{R}^2$ where

$$g(m^1, m^2) = \begin{cases} (0,0) & \text{if either } m_1 \text{ or } m_2 = 0 \\ (2,1) & \text{if } m_1 > m_2 \, 0 \\ (1,2) & \text{if } m_2 > m_1 > 0 \\ (1.5,1.5) & \text{if } m_1 = m_2 > 0 \end{cases}$$

This game has a unique Nash equilibrium $m_1^* = m_2^* = 0$ so that the outcome $(0, 0)$ is, so to speak, 'implemented in Nash equilibrium'. Is this a sensible prediction? I would, with Jackson (1992), contend that it is not. There is a fundamental tension here between the solution concept and the structure of the strategic problem to which it is being applied. The unboundedness of the strategy sets (actually non-compactness, in that we could also use $M_i = [0, 1)$ in the example above) strongly suggests that there is something fishy going on, and this suspicion is confirmed by the example. An alternative device that has been employed in this literature are 'modulo games'.[3] While these games are finite, they lead to unwanted *mixed* strategy equilibria so that the implementation is in *pure* strategy Nash equilibrium. The arbitrary exclusion of mixed strategies is especially disturbing in the implementation context in that the entire objective of the theory is to take account of *all* equilibrium behaviour. In fact mixed strategies arise very naturally in the modulo constructions and cannot be eliminated by any refinement of Nash equilibrium that has been seriously proposed. Again, an illustrative example (which could be embedded in the standard implementation framework) makes the point.

Example 2

Two players with strategy sets $M_i = \{0,1,2\}$. The outcomes are given by

		|	m_2	
		0	1	2
	0	0,0	0,0	0,0
m_1	1	0,0	2,1	1,2
	2	0,0	1,2	2,1

Now $m_1^* = m_2^* = 0$ is the only *pure* strategy Nash equilibrium. However, can we with confidence claim to have implemented the outcome (0,0) when players may quite plausibly use their strategies $m_i = 1,2$ in playing (for instance) a mixed-strategy Nash equilibrium?

The second strand of the literature begins which a remarkable contribution by Farquharson (1957) on implementation in 'sophisticated equilibrium'. The most visible contributor to this tradition is Moulin (1979, 1980, 1981, 1983, etc.). This literature has considered implementation in iteratively (weakly) undominated strategies. The focus has been on examples of particular social choice functions and on appealing and simple mechanisms rather than on general characterizations. The presumption in this literature is that only a restricted class of social choice functions is implementable in iteratively undominated strategies.

In comparison with the latter literature our results provide general characterizations which are very permissive. Consequently, within our framework our characterizations are complete. Furthermore, this literature concentrates on the complete information case whereas our results extend to Bayesian environments. As compared with the Nash and Bayesian–Nash implementation literature, our results are obtained using finite mechanisms and encompass mixed strategies. The theoretical difficulties alluded to above are therefore evaded.

At this point it is useful to set down some notation:

Agents	$i \in \{1, 2, \ldots, n\}$
Alternatives	$a \in A$
Agent i's preference (index)	$\psi_i \in \Psi_i$
Agent i's utility function	$u_i: A \times \Psi_i \to \mathbb{R}$
Profiles of preferences	$\psi \in \Omega \subseteq \underset{i}{X} \Psi_i$
Social choice function	$x: \Omega \to A$

A game-form or mechanism is denoted $G = ((M_i)_i, g)$ where M_i is a message set for each agent i and $g: \underset{i}{X} M_i \to A$ is the outcome function. For a given social choice function x the implementation problem is solved relative to a solution concept E if for some game form G, $E(G, \psi) = x(\psi)$ for all $\psi \in \Omega$.

The first key element of our approach is to view the social choice function as a mapping to *lotteries* over alternatives. That is, $x: \Omega \to A$ where A is interpreted to be the set of (simple) lotteries over some set of pure alternatives Γ. For $a \in A$ let $a(\tau)$ denote the probability of the pure alternative τ. In this lottery setting we have a natural way to talk about the distance between lotteries and between social choice functions. Specifically,

Definition 1 The lotteries $a, b \in A$ are ϵ-close if $\sum_\tau |a(\tau) - b(\tau)| \leq \epsilon$.

Definition 2 A social choice funtion x is ϵ-close to a social choice function y if the lotteries $x(\psi)$ and $y(\psi)$ are $y(\psi)$ are ϵ-close for all $\psi \in \Omega$.

We say that a social choice function is *exactly* implementable if it is implementable in the ordinary sense. The definition of virtual implementation can now be given.

Definition 3 A social choice function x is *virtually* implementable if for all $\epsilon > 0$ there exists an scf y which is ϵ-close to x and also *exactly* implementable.

If a social choice function is virtually implementable, then a planner's goals can be attained up to any desired level of accuracy; the expected utility of agents can be made arbitrarily close to the utility they would receive in the original social choice function. The concept of virtual implementation was introduced independently by Matsushima (1988) and Abreu and Sen (1990).

5.2   COMPLETE INFORMATION

In this section I make the complete information assumption that every agent knows his own preferences as well as those of all other agents. This special case has received and continues to receive a tremendous amount of attention in the literature. In addition, we assume that:

- for all i, Ψ_i is finite;
- players have von Neumann–Morgenstern preferences over lotteries;
- players are never indifferent over *all* lotteries and distinct utility indices correspond to distinct preference orderings over lotteries;
- *small* (of order ϵ) fines can be imposed on players. (This is a simplifying assumption. It is *sufficient* for the assumption we use in the formal proof.)

Theorem 1 (Abreu and Matsushima, 1992a)   *Suppose there are three or more agents. Then any social choice function is virtually implementable in iteratively undominated strategies.*

Remarks

- Our mechanisms involve the iterative elimination of *strictly* dominated strategies. This elimination leads to a *unique* iteratively undominated profile. The latter is a unique Nash equilibrium, which is consequently both pure and strict.
- Our mechanisms are *finite*, hence compact. They do not entail integer constructions and unbounded message sets. Unlike the 'modulo' constructions which have also been widely used in the equilibrium implementation literature, our mechanisms do take account of *mixed* strategies.
- In summary, our result is permissive, is obtained using a 'well-behaved' (in particular, finite) mechanism, and employs a solution concept which is theoretically more compelling than Nash equilibrium.

– In comparing Theorem 1 with the Gibbard–Satterthwaite theorem observe that the solution concept is weaker *and* we have domain restrictions on individual preferences over A, the space of *lotteries*. In particular, the usual von Neumann–Morgenstern assumptions imply that preferences have a linear structure.

The proof of the theorem relies on the following basic (and straightforward) lemma.

Lemma For all i there exists $f_i: \Psi_i \to A$ s.t.

$$u_i(f_i(\psi_i),\psi_i) > u_i\,(f_i(\psi_i'),\psi_i) \qquad \text{for all } \psi_i' \in \Psi_i\backslash\{\psi_i\}$$

That is, player i's best lottery *in the set* $\{f_i(\theta_i)|\theta_i \in \Psi_i\}$ is unique and *varies* with ψ_i.

The lemma follows from the assumptions of non-universal indifference and the assumption that distinct utility indices correspond to distinct preferences over lotteries. We now sketch a proof of the theorem. The proof is constructive and uses the mechanism specified below.

Mechanism

$$M_i = \Psi_i \times \underbrace{\Omega \ldots \times \Omega}_{K \text{ times}} = M_i^0 \times M_i^1 \times \ldots \times M_i^K$$

where K is an integer yet to be specified. Each player's *message* consists of $(K + 1)$ simultaneous *announcements*. The first announcement is of his own preference index ψ_i, and each of the remaining announcements is of the entire preference *profile*.

Notation: $m^k \equiv (m_i^k, \ldots, m_n^k) \in M^k$

Let x be the scf to be implemented. The outcome function g is defined as:

$$g(m) = \frac{\epsilon}{n} \sum_{i=1}^{n} f_i(m_i^0) + \frac{1 - \epsilon}{k} \sum_{h=1}^{k} \rho(m^h) \text{ "+" small fines yet to be}$$

specified

where
$$\rho(m^h) = \begin{cases} x(\psi) & \text{if at least } (n\text{-}1) \text{ players} \\ & j \text{ announce } m_j^h = \psi \\ b & \text{otherwise} \end{cases}$$

and b is an arbitrary, constant lottery. Note that ρ is well defined only if $n \geq 3$.

Our mechanism may be well understood by means of the following analogy suggested to us by Faruk Gul. The idea is to think of a lottery as being a field of unit size and of different outcomes of the lottery as being different crops. To visualize the specific outcome function we use, think of each player as having an individual plot of size ϵ/n. The remainder of the field is divided into K equal strips. Recall from the lemma the functions f_i. A player's zero-th announcement 'dictatorially' determines the crop $f_i(m_i^0)$ which will be planted on the player's own plot. Let the loss in utility from having the 'wrong' crop planted on one's own plot be equivalent to a fine of strictly more than \$2. Note that these fines are of order ϵ. Assume that K is large enough such that the loss from having one's worst crop planted as opposed to one's best (in the (finite) range of x), on any one strip, is less than \$1 (Figure 5.1)

The crop planted on the h-th strip is determined by all players' h-th announcements. If all players make the same announcement ψ the crop planted is $x(\psi)$. If a single player deviates from an otherwise unanimous announcement ψ the outcome is still $x(\psi)$ but the deviating player is fined \$$\frac{1}{K}$ (note that we are here using the assumption of at least three players). In all other cases, the outcome is some arbitrary crop (lottery) $b \in A$.

Let $\psi = (\psi_i, \ldots, \psi_n)$ be the true profile. Notice that if all players i announce $m_i^* = (\psi_i, \psi, \ldots, \psi)$ then the crop planted $x(\psi)$ will be the right crop on almost $((1-\epsilon)$ of) the entire field.

In addition to the penalties above (which do not depend on the zero-th announcements) we assume that each player has an additional 'dollar' available for fines. Whether or not this \$1 fine is levied depends on whether or not players' subsequent announcements $m_i^h \in \Omega$ equal the *profile* of zero-th announcements. The precise rule used is critical and will be specified presently.

First note that irrespective of the rule specified, since the latter fine is at most \$1, the first round of removal of dominated strategies will eliminate any message m_i for which $m_i^0 \neq \psi_i$ (the true profile). Such an m_i is dominated *strictly* by the strategy $\bar{m}_i$ which differs from m_i only in that $m_i^{-0} = \psi_i$. Thus the first round of iterative elimination guarantees truth-telling in the zero-th announcement. This conclusion is one of the two key elements of our proof.

Subsequent announcements may now be compared with the true profile

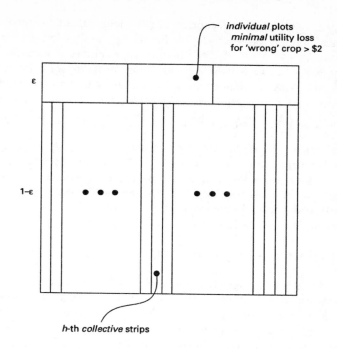

Figure 5.1 Outcome $\rho(m_1^h, \ldots, m_n^h)$. K chosen large enough such that *maximal* utility gain from changing crop on a collective strip is less than $1.

of the zero-th announcements. The second step in our argument involves using the $1 punishment available to induce each player to announce the true preference profile in *all* his remaining K announcements. The difficulty here is that the $1 fine is only larger than the potential gain from lying on any *one* strip. The way around this difficulty is extremely simple. The punishment is invoked sequentially; in particular, *misreporting by a player i with respect to his h-th announcement* $(m_i^h \neq m^0)$ *is only punished if all players reported all 'previous' announcements* $m_j^1, \ldots, m_j^{h-1}$ *truthfully.* This rule provides the appropriate incentives.

Consider $h = 1$ and player. Consider a strategy for other players in which $m_i^h \neq m^0 = \psi$ for some $j \neq 1$. (Recall that the first round of iterative removal yields $m^0 \neq \psi$, the true profile.) The fines for misreporting will only be levied with respect to the first announcement and player 1 is better off reporting $m_1^1 = \psi$ (*irrespective* of what announcements he will make later), since that $1 fine is large relative to any utility gain the first announcement might yield. On the other hand, consider a strategy for other players for which the first announcement is truthful; $m_j^1 = \psi$ for all $j \neq 1$. In this case, player 1 is better off reporting $m_1^1 = \psi$, *even if he expects to be fined for subsequent announcements*. This is because an individual deviation from an otherwise unanimous first announcement does not change the crop planted on the first strip but instead results in an *additional fine* of $\frac{1}{K}$ dollars.

Thus the second round of iterative removal yields $m_1^1 = \psi$ for all i.

This argument inducts to iteratively yield truthful reporting by all players of own preferences in the zero-th announcement and of the entire preference profile in all subsequent announcements, as the only iteratively undominated strategy profile.

Let us review the basic elements of the argument:

- Randomization allows us to 'chop up' the problem into little pieces.
- A *small* fine is *large* relative to any *little piece* of the original problem.
- The rules for fines were designed so that the small fine loomed large iteratively over each little incentive problem without ever being invoked, and hence exhausted. In a sense, the construction creates an endogenous free-rider problem with respect to who will be the 'first to deviate'.

5.3   INCOMPLETE INFORMATION

I turn now to general incomplete information environments with *two* or more players. The assumption that agents are incompletely informed about the preferences of others seems eminently reasonable and there has been much interest in *Bayesian Nash implementation* in the last decade. As noted earlier, the survey by Palfrey (1992) is a useful guide to contributions in this area. We note that like the Nash and Nash refinements literature on complete information, the Bayesian Nash implementation literature is flawed by its reliance on 'integer' games.

The essential logic of our approach extends very naturally to the Bayesian setting. I first specify the environment and then provide an intuitive argument for a rather special case. The relevant reference is Abreu and Matsushima (1992c).

The Setting

S_i	finite set of types or signals of individual i.
$P_i(s_{-i}/s_i)$	posterior distribution of i.
$S = \underset{i}{\times} S_i$	set of 'states' or signal-profiles.
scf	$x: S \to A$.

A basic condition in Bayesian environments is the *self-selection* condition: *The scf x satisfies self-selection if for all i and $s_i \in S_i$*

$$\sum_{s_{-i}} u_i\left(x(s_i,s_{-i}),s\right) p_i(s_{-i}|s_i) \geq \sum_{s_{-i}} u_i\left(x(s_i',s_{-i}),s\right) p_i(s_{-i}|s_i)$$

for all $s_i' \neq s_i$.

Self-selection is equivalent to the requirement that truth-telling be a Bayesian equilibrium in a direct revelation mechanism, and it is a (straightforward) *necessary* condition for implementation under any solution concept.

We also derive a new necessary condition which we term *measurability*. This condition requires that the social choice function be measurable with respect to a particular *partition* of each player's signal space. This condition is necessary for implementation in iteratively undominated strategies and for Bayesian Nash implementation *also*. The measurability condition is not immediate and its derivation somewhat involved. I will not go into any details here but the interested reader may consult the reference below.

Theorem 2 (Abreu and Matsushima 1992c) *A social choice function is virtually implementable in iteratively undominated strategies if and only if it satisfies self-selection and the measurability condition.*

Notice that this result provides a unified treatment of the complete and incomplete information cases and the two, and three-or-more player cases.

– With complete information the measurability condition is trivial, in the sense that it is satisfied by *any* scf.
– With complete information and three or more players the self-selection condition is trivial.

Hence Theorem 1 is a corollary of Theorem 2.

- With complete information and two players self-selection is not trivially satisfied. It is equivalent to a condition termed the *intersection
property*. The latter condition requires that for any pair of profiles
(ψ_1, ψ_2), $(\psi_1', \psi_2') \in \Omega$, the set of lotteries which are weakly worse
than $x(\psi_1', \psi_2')$ for player 1 with preferences ψ_1' has a non-empty intersection with the set of lotteries which are weakly worse than
$x(\psi_1, \psi_2)$ for players 2 with preferences ψ_2.

Corollary   Under complete information and two players, a social choice
function is virtually implementable in iteratively undominated strategies if and only if the scf satisfies the intersection property.

The intersection property is only one of a rather complex set of necessary and sufficient conditions obtained by Dutta and Sen (1991) and
Moore and Repullo (1990) for *exact* two-person *Nash* implementation.

Proof of Theorem 2   We sketch the incomplete information proof
for a special case in which an argument very similar to the complete
information one may be used.
    The special case is defined by:

1. *private values*: Player i's preferences over lotteries depend only on
   her own type. Since u_i is independent of s_{-i}, we simply write $u_i(a, s_i)$
   instead of $u_i(a, s_i, s_{-i})$.
2. that for every $i \in N$, and $s_i \in S_i$, there exist $a, a' \in A$ such that $u_i(a, s_i)$
   $> u_i(a', s_i)$.
   That is, for each type of player i, we exclude the possibility of
   universal indifference across lotteries.
3. that distinct types of player i have distinct orderings over lotteries.

(Assumption 2 is not innocuous. In particular it excludes the complete information case. A player's signal represents what she *knows*,
and in the complete information setting this is the *entire* profile of
players' preferences. Hence two distinct signals for player i may represent
differences in *other* players' preference orderings and *not her own*.)
    The preceding assumptions imply that for every $i \in N$ there exists a
function $f_i : S_i \to A$ such that for every $s_i \in S_i$ and every $s_i' \in S_i \setminus \{s_i\}$,

$$u_i(f_i(s_i), s_i) > u_i(f_i(s_i'), s_i)$$

This straightforward result corresponds to the Lemma in the complete information case, and may be proved analogously. We may think of f_i as a social choice function which is independent of s_{-i}. It gives player i's 'dictatorial' choice within the set $\{a : a = f_i(s_i)$ for some $s_i \in S_i\}$. By construction this choice *varies* with s_i.

We now construct a mechanism as follows. Every player i makes $(K + 1)$ simultaneous announcements, each of which is of her *own* signal: $M_i = M_i^0 \times M_i^1 \times \ldots \times M_i^k = S_i \times \ldots \times S_i$. Recall that S_i is finite so that this construction will yield a *finite* mechanism. Denote

$$m_i = (m_i^0, \ldots m_i^k) \in M_i, \; m_i^h \in M_i^h.$$
$$m = (m^0, \ldots m^k) \in M, \; m^h = (m_i^h)_{i \in N} \in M^h = \times_{i \in N} M_i^h$$

Given a social choice function x, for any profile of player messages m, the lottery chosen is

$$g(m) = \frac{\epsilon}{n} \sum_{i \in N} f_i(m_i^0) + \frac{1 - \epsilon}{K} \sum_{h=1} x(m^h)$$

where ϵ is strictly positive.

Assume for simplicity that x satisfies *strict* self-selection (and not simply self-selection).

In the above mechanism, player i's zero-th announcement affects the outcome with probability $\frac{\epsilon}{n}$. With this probability the outcome is $f_i(m_i^0)$, and this lottery depends *only* on player i's zero-th announcement. On the other hand, player i's h-th announcement ($h \geq 1$) affects the outcome with probability $\frac{1 - \epsilon}{K}$ via the term $x(m_i^h, m_i^h)$ which *does* depend on other players' h-th announcements.

In addition to this lottery players receive small *fines* according to the following rules. The first deviant from her own zero-th announcement is fined η. That is, player i is fined $t_i : M \to R$ where

$t_i(m) = \eta$	if player i is the first deviant. i.e., for some h, $m_i^h \neq m_i^0$ and $m^{h'} = m^0$ for all $h' < h$.
$t_i(m) = 0$	otherwise.

Agent i's *total* utility is simply defined to be $u_i(g(m), s_i) - t_i(m)$. Choose η sufficiently small, such that for every $i \in N$,

$$\frac{\epsilon}{n} \{u_i(f_i(s_i),s_i) - u_i(f_i(s_i'),s_i)\} > \eta \text{ for all } s_i \in S_i \text{ and all } s_i' \in S_i \backslash \{s_i\}$$

Note that η is smaller than the 'direct' expected utility loss from a zero-th message $m_i^0 \neq s_i$.

Let σ be an iteratively undominated strategy profile. Recall that $\sigma_i:S_i \rightarrow M_i$. Denote strategies for players by

$$\sigma_i = (\sigma_i^0, \ldots, \sigma_i^K), \ \sigma_i^h:S_i \rightarrow M_i^h$$

$$\sigma = (\sigma^0, \ldots, \sigma^K), \ \sigma^h:S \rightarrow M^h$$

Since m_i^0 affects player i's utility only through f_i and t_i, it follows directly from the definition of η that if σ_i is iteratively undominated, then

$$\sigma_i^0(s_i) = s_i.$$

We will now show that if for every $i \in N$, *every* iteratively undominated strategy profile $\tilde{\sigma}_i$ and every $s_i \in S_i$, $\tilde{\sigma}_i^h(s_i) = s_i$ for all $h \in \{0, \ldots, k\}$, then

$$\sigma_i^{k+1}(s_i) = s_i \text{ for all } i \in N \text{ and all } s_i \in S_i$$

The above inductive step completes the argument: for any (small) $\epsilon > 0$, the mechanism yields a unique iteratively undominated profile σ with $\sigma_i^k(s_i) = s_i$ for all $s_i \in S_i$, all $i \in N$ and all $k = 0, \ldots, K$. The resultant outcome is

$$(1 - \epsilon) \, x(s) + \frac{\epsilon}{n} \sum_{i \in N} f_i(s_i)$$

and there are no fines.

For the inductive step to go through we must choose K sufficiently large, such that for every $i \in N$, every $s_i \in S_i$ and evey $s' \in S$,

$$\eta > \frac{1 - \epsilon}{K} \{u_i(x(s'/s_i),s_i) - u_i(x(s),s_i)\}$$

Then the fine η is larger than $\dfrac{1 - \epsilon}{K}$ times the maximal 'direct' utility gain from changing the outcome.

Suppose that $\sigma_i^{k+1}(s_i) \neq s_i$ for some $i \in N$ and some $s_i \in S_i$. Define $\bar{\sigma}_i$ such that

$\bar{\sigma}_i^h = \sigma_i^h$ for $h \neq k + 1$, $\bar{\sigma}_i^{k+1}(s_i') = \sigma_i^{k+1}(s_i')$ for all $s_i' \in S_i \backslash \{s_i\}$, and $\bar{\sigma}_i^{k+1}(s_i) = s_i$

Under the inductive hypothesis above if $\sigma_j^{k+1}(s_j) = s_j$ for all $j \in N \backslash \{i\}$ and all $s_j \in S_j$, then by strict self-selection $\bar{\sigma}_i$ yields higher payoff than σ_i even if player i will be the first to deviate given $(\bar{\sigma}_i, \sigma_{-i}^0)$. On the other hand, if for some $j \in N \backslash \{i\}$, $s_j(s_j) \neq s_j$ for all $s_j \in S_j$, then (by the choice of K above) $\bar{\sigma}_i$, by saving the fine η, yields higher payoff than σ_i. Thus $\bar{\sigma}_i$ dominates σ_i for player i of type s_i. In fact this argument is not complete in that *some* types of player j may announce $\sigma_j'(s_j) \neq s_j$, while others make truthful announcements. This extra subtlety is dealt with in Abreu and Matsushima (1992c).

5.4 EXACT IMPLEMENTATION

While virtual implementation of a social choice function yields players almost the same expected utility ex-ante as the original social choice function, ex-post the outcomes might be (with very small probability) substantially different. It is not clear to me that this should be a cause for concern; as welfare economists we are typically willing to accept expected utility as a welfare indicator without particular concern about the precise manner in which the expectation is achieved. At any rate, the theorem below serves to alleviate such concerns. From the technical perspective, the results suggest that the virtual perspective is more convenient than essential, whereas the lottery structure is key. In this section we show that if one is willing to replace 'iterative removal of *strictly* dominated strategies' by 'iterative removal of *weakly* dominated strategies' one gets an *exact* (as opposed to virtual) result.

Theorem 3 (Abreu and Matsushima, 1994) *Suppose complete information and three or more players. Then any scf x is exactly implementable via the iterative elimination of weakly dominated strategies.*

Remark: The main drawback of iterative weak removal compared to iterative strict removal is that, in general, different *orders of removal* of weakly dominated strategies lead to different iteratively undominated sets. A nice feature of our mechanisms is that they yield the same unique iteratively undominated profile *independently* of the order of removal.

The basic idea of the proof is similar to the argument in Section 5.2 and the intuitive account given there usefully supplements the verbal discussion below.

Each player i makes $(K+2)$ *simultaneous* announcements indexed $-1, 0, 1, \ldots, K$. The minus-one-th announcement is of his *own* utility index, the zero-th is of his *successor's* (player $i+1$'s) utility index, and all 'subsequent' announcements are of all players' (that is, an n-vector of) utility indices. That is, player i's message space is

$$M_i = \Psi_i \times \Psi_{i+1} \times \Omega \times \ldots \times \Omega = M_i^{-1} \times M_i^0 \times M_i^1 \times \ldots \times M_i^k$$

where Ω, a subset of $\underset{i \in N}{\times} \Psi_i$, is the set of possible utility indices.

Suppose that fines of \$7 are available where each dollar-unit should be thought of as being 'small'. The messages determine both the lottery chosen and the fines imposed on each player. For the moment ignore the latter.

For the purpose of this informal discussion we will consider the 'standard' process of iterative removal of weakly dominated strategies in which at every round *all* weakly dominated strategies in that round are removed. The full argument addressing the irrelevance of the *order* of removal is more subtle and relegated to the formal development.

By the lemma in Section 5.2, for every $i \in N$, there exists a function $f_i : \Psi_i \to A$ such that for every $\psi_i \in \Psi_i$,

$$u_i(f_i(\psi_i), \psi_i) > u_i(f_i(\psi_i'), \psi_i) \text{ for all } \psi_i' \in \Psi_i \backslash (\psi_i)$$

The function f_i may be thought of as a dictatorial social choice function for player i over the choice set $\{f_i(\psi_i) : \psi_i \in \Psi_i\}$.

Let $m = (m_1, \ldots, m_n)$, $m_i = (m_i^{-1}, m_i^0, m_i^1, \ldots, m_i^k)$ and $m^h = (m_1^h, \ldots, m_n^h)$. For any message profile m, the lottery chosen is

$$g(m) = \frac{e(m^0, \ldots, m^k)}{n} \sum_{i \in N} f_i(m_i^{-1}) + \frac{1 - e(m^0, \ldots, m^k)}{K} \sum_{h=1}^{k} \rho(m^h)$$

where the functions ρ will be defined later and we note for the moment that e has value either 0 or $\in > 0$.

The rules for fines we use are such that the fines to player i do not depend on m_i^{-1}. The latter only affects player i's utility through the term $f_i(m_i^{-1})$. Now suppose that the true profile is $\psi = (\psi_1, \ldots, \psi_n)$, and let m be an iteratively weakly undominated strategy profile. It follows immediately (modulo issues of order of removal) that $m_i^{-1} = \psi_i$

for all $i \in N$. *Each player's minus-one-th announcement is truthful.* Let us now introduce fines. Player i is fined \$4 if $m_i^0 \neq m_{i+1}^{-1}$. (The subscript '$i+1$' means '1'.) Player i's zero-th message also affects the function e (recall that the value of e is either 0 or ϵ) and possibly whether or not he receives an additional fine of \$2, as specified below. Since Ψ_i is finite (and u_i is bounded) we may choose ϵ small enough such that the utility impact of the former effect is strictly bounded above by \$1. Using the fact that for any iteratively weakly undominated profile $m_{i+1}^{-1} = \psi_{i+1}$, it follows that $m_i^0 = \psi_{i+1}$. Thus $(m_n^0, m_1^0, \ldots, m_{n-1}^0) = (\psi_1, \ldots, \psi_n)$, the true profile of utility indices. Let $\hat{m}^0 = (m_n^0, m_1^0, \ldots, m_{n-1}^0)$. It is time to define the function ρ: $\rho(m^h) = x(\theta)$ if $m_j^h = \theta$ for at least $(n-1)$ players j, and some arbitrary lottery b otherwise. Player i is fined \$2 if his h-th announcement is the *first* to differ from the n-tuple of zero-th announcements $\hat{m}^0$. In the event of ties all players who are first to deviate are fined \$2. Furthermore, if player i's h-th announcement differs from the otherwise unanimous h-th announcements of other players (that is, if $m_j^h = m_k^h$ for all j, $k \neq i$ and $m_i^h \neq m_j^h$), player i is fined \$$\frac{1}{K}$. There are no other fines.

Player i's announcement m_i^h ($h \geq 1$) affects his utility via fines he pays, and through the lottery received. The latter effect operates through the function e (we have already chosen ϵ to strictly bound this effect by \$1) and the term $\frac{\rho(m^h)}{K}$. Now we may choose K larger enough such that the last term has utility impact strictly less than \$1. Thus the \$2 fine exceeds other possible utility losses. It therefore follows that $m_i^1 = \hat{m}^0$. This needs some argument. Suppose $m_i^1 = \hat{m}^0$ and let $\bar{m}^i = (m_i^{-1}, m_i^0, \hat{m}^0, m_i^2, \ldots, m_i^K)$. Then against any strategy $\tilde{m}_{-i}$ such that $\tilde{m}_j^1 \neq \hat{m}^0$ for some $j \neq i$ the strategy $\bar{m}_i$ yields strictly higher utility since player i is then fined \$2 less. On the other hand, against any strategy $\tilde{m}_{-i}$ such that $\tilde{m}_j^1 \neq \hat{m}^0$ for all $j \neq i$, player i saves at least \$$\frac{1}{K}$ (the fine for being the lone deviant to an otherwise unanimous first announcement) even if he is fined \$2 for being the 'first' deviant 'later', without having any impact on the lottery: $\rho(m_i^1, \tilde{m}_{-i}^1) = \rho(\bar{m}_i^1, \tilde{m}_{-i}^1)$. Hence if m is iteratively undominated, $m_i^1 \neq \hat{m}^0$ for all $i \in N$. This argument inducts to yield $m_i^h = \hat{m}^0$ for all $i \in N$, all $h = 1, \ldots, K$. Thus there is a unique iteratively weakly undominated profile m. For this strategy profile each player receives zero fines; furthermore, $e(m^0, \ldots, m^K) = 0$ and $\rho(m^h) = x(\psi)$ for all $h = 1, \ldots, K$, so that the resultant lottery is $x(\psi)$ as required.

5.5 CONCLUSION

The work surveyed here provides permissive results for implementation in iteratively undominated strategies in a lottery setting. The basic structure of the mechanisms proposed turns out to adapt flexibly to complete and incomplete information environments and problems with two, and three or more players. The mechanisms are finite and take account of mixed strategies, thereby avoiding troubling theoretical difficulties which undermine the large literature on implementation in Nash equilibrium, refinements of Nash equilibrium and Bayesian-Nash equilibrium.[4] These difficulties were alluded to at some length earlier. In addition, the results are obtained for a more appealing, nonequilibrium based, solution concept.

At this stage it is probably fair to say that the substantial literature on implementation has led to a rather good understanding of the problem as traditionally formulated. On hand are a large set of possibility (and impossibility) results. Rather than being ends in themselves, the possibility results should be viewed as opening the door to the development of intuitively appealing mechanisms, which the canonical constructions employed to obtain broad characterizations were (quite appropriately) never meant to be. There is at this point a troubling gap between the delicacy (and permissiveness) of the theory and the typically rather crude mechanisms which can be discerned in practice. It is perhaps time to attempt to close this gap from both directions: by educating practice (which cannot be invariably relied upon to have evolved to the most ingenious and creative schemes); and by reformulating the theory to address such annoying considerations as repeated interaction, simplicity and transparency which are probably of the essence for successful application.

Notes

1. I am most grateful to Eric Maskin for delivering this lecture on my behalf in Moscow.
2. For excellent recent surveys of implementation in complete and incomplete information environments, see Moore (1992) and Palfrey (1992) respectively.
3. In addition to other messages, each player i announces an integer $z^i \in \{0,1,\ldots,n\}$ where n is the number of players. When such games are triggered the winner is player j where j is one plus the modulus of Σz^i with respect to n.

4. Our own work has not escaped criticism, most notably by Glazer and Rosenthal (1992). A spirited response is offered in Abreu and Matsushima (1992b). Rather than regurgitate the respective arguments, we refer readers to these short notes.

References

Abreu, D. and H. Matsushima (1992a) 'Virtual Implementation in Iteratively Undominated Strategies: Complete Information", *Econometrica*, vol. 60, pp. 993–1008.

Abreu, D. and H. Matsushima (1992b) 'A Response to Glazer and Rosenthal', *Econometrica*, vol. 60, pp. 1439–42.

Abreu, D. and H. Matsushima (1992c) 'Virtual Implementation in Iteratively Undominated Strategies: Incomplete Information', mimeo, Princeton University.

Abreu, D. and H. Matsushima (1994) 'Exact Implementation', *Journal of Economic Theory*, vol. 64.

Abreu, D. and A. Sen (1990) 'Subgame Perfect Implementation: A Necessary and Almost Sufficient Condition', *Journal of Economic Theory*, vol. 50, pp. 285–99.

Abreu, D. and A. Sen (1991) 'Virtual Implementation in Nash *Equilibrium*', Econometrica, vol. 59, pp. 997–1021.

Dutta, B. and A. Sen (1991) 'A Necessary and Sufficient Condition for Two-Person Nash Implementation', *Review of Economic Studies*, vol. 58, pp. 121–8.

Farquharson, R. (1957/1969) Theory of Voting (New Haven, Conn.: Yale University Press).

Gibbard, A. (1973) 'Manipulation of Voting Schemes: A General Result', *Econometrica*, vol. 41, pp. 587–602.

Glazer, J. and R. W. Rosenthal (1992) 'A Note on Abreu–Matsushima Mechanisms', *Econometrica*, vol. 60, pp. 1435–8.

Jackson, M. (1992) 'Implementation in Undominated Strategies: A Look at Bounded Mechanisms', *Review of Economic Studies*, vol. 59, 757–76.

Maskin, E. (1977) 'Nash Implementation and Welfare Optimality', mimeo, Massachusetts Institute of Technology.

Matsushima, H. (1988) 'A New Approach to the Implementation Problem', *Journal of Economic Theory*, vol. 45, pp. 128–44.

Moore, J. (1992) 'Implementation, Contracts and Renegotiation in Environments with Complete Information', in J-J. Laffont (ed.), *Advances in Economic Theory: Sixth World Congress*, Vol. 1 (Cambridge: Cambridge University Press) pp. 182–282.

Moore, J. and R. Repullo (1988) 'Subgame Perfect Implementation', *Econometrica*, vol. 46, pp. 1191–220.

Moore, J. and R. Repullo (1990) 'Nash Implementation: A Full Characterization', *Econometrica*, vol. 58, pp. 1083–99.

Moulin, H. (1979) 'Dominance-Solvable Voting Schemes', *Econometrica*, vol. 47, pp. 1337–51.

Moulin, H. (1980) 'Implementing Efficient, Anonymous and Neutral Social Choice Functions', *Journal of Mathematical Economics*, vol. 7, pp. 249–69.

Moulin, H. (1981) 'Prudence versus Sophistication in Voting Strategy', *Journal of Economic Theory*, vol. 24, pp. 398–412.

Moulin, H. (1983) *The Strategy of Social Choice* (Amsterdam: North-Holland Publishing Company).

Palfrey, T. (1992) 'Implementation in Bayesian Equilibrium: The Multiple Equilibrium Problem in Mechanism Design', in J-J. Laffont (ed.), *Advances in Economic Theory: Sixth World Congress*, Vol. 1 (Cambridge: Cambridge University Press) pp. 283–323.

Palfrey, T. and S. Srivastava (1991) 'Nash Implementation Using Undominated Strategies', *Econometrica*, vol. 59, pp. 479–501.

Satterthwaite, M. (1975) 'Strategy-Proofness and Arrow's Conditions: Existence and Correspondence Theorems for Voting Procedures and Social Welfare Functions', *Journal of Economic Theory*, vol. 10, pp. 187–217.

6 Mechanism Design with Incomplete Information

Sanjay Srivastava

CARNEGIE-MELLON UNIVERSITY

6.1 INTRODUCTION

A mechanism is the procedure through which actions of various individuals result in an outcome. Mechanism design theory studies the relationship between alternative procedures and the outcomes that result. This chapter describes some of the theoretical progress that has been made in the study of mechanism design when there is incomplete information about the preferences of the individuals. It is expository in nature and is not intended to be a survey.[1]

As an example of a mechanism, consider an auction. Suppose that you own a very nice painting, but your cash-flow situation has made you decide to sell it. How should you sell it? One way would be to auction it. The mechanism could be: let all interested parties make a bid for the painting; the highest bidder buys the painting at the price he bids. Here, the individual actions are the bids, and the outcome (which is a function of the actions) is the person who gets the painting and the price he pays. Incomplete information comes from the fact that the seller does not know how much the buyers are willing to pay for the painting.

An alternative mechanism for selling the painting is that you decide that it is worth P; you announce P, and sell the painting to the first person who agrees to pay you P. Here, the actions are your announcement of P and the response (yes or no) of the others and the timing of their responses. The outcome is the sale of the painting. Of course, the mechanism must also describe what happens if no one buys it at P.

The two different ways of selling the painting illustrate some critical aspects of the mechanism design problem. In the first auction, the bid of a potential buyer will clearly depend on his strategic assessment of what others are likely to bid. Therefore, we cannot determine the performance of a mechanism without some specification of how

141

people behave. By contrast, in the second auction, each buyer only has to think about whether he would be willing to pay P for the painting. Thus, the rules of the mechanism, which specify the possible actions of the participants and the consequences of those actions, will typically affect the strategic considerations which affect actions, and thus outcomes.

One question that can be posed, and which mechanism design theory can be used to answer, is: what is the best procedure for the seller of the painting to employ? Here, 'best' is naturally interpreted as raising the most cash for the seller. In another context, if a productive resource, such as a factory or an oil tract, is being auctioned, 'best' may mean selling it to the person(s) who can run it most efficiently.

As a second example, consider the bargaining problem which arises when a buyer and a seller meet. The seller has an object the buyer wants, and the buyer has money the seller wants. There is a minimum price the seller is willing to accept (t_s) and a maximum price the buyer is willing to pay (t_b). However, the buyer wants to pay as little as possible while the seller wants to obtain as much as possible for the object. Information is incomplete; neither the buyer nor the seller knows how the other values the object. There are many ways in which the exchange could proceed.

One is for each secretly to write down a price on a piece of paper, say p_b for the buyer, p_s for the seller. The pieces of paper are opened by a mediator, and trade is conducted as follows. If $p_b \geq p_s$, the buyer gets the object at the price p_b. Otherwise, there is no trade. A second way is for each to submit a price, and if $p_b \geq p_s$, to trade at the average price $(1/2)(p_s + p_b)$. This mechanism, which we will use repeatedly as an example, is called the 1/2 double auction. A third way, in the same circumstances, is to trade at the price quoted by the seller.

Similar questions can be posed in this case as with auctions. We could take the buyer's point of view and ask how the buyer can extract as much as possible from the seller. Similarly, we could take the seller's point of view. Alternatively, we could take an egalitarian point of view and ask if there is a mechanism whose outcome is that the surplus $(t_b - t_s)$ is divided equally between the buyer and the seller whenever it is positive. Or we could only require efficiency, i.e. try to construct a mechanism so that the good is exchanged whenever $t_b \geq t_s$.

After providing a basic model in Section 6.2, we will review in Section 6.3 developments which make it possible to analyze the types of questions posed above. These developments, which adopt a Bayesian-Nash point of view, will provide a precise way of characterizing the outcomes that can emerge from mechanisms. This is called *weak implementation*. In Section 6.4, we will see that the mechanisms constructed in Section 6.3 can have unintended outcomes. Consequently, we will characterize outcomes which can be implemented by mechanisms without any undesirable outcomes. This is called *full implementation*. In Section 6.5, we will discuss the impact of relaxing some of the assumptions of the model.

6.2   A BASIC MODEL

There are I people in the economy, and we refer to them as agents, indexed by $i = 1, \ldots, I$. There is a set B of alternatives, which we think of as the resources that have to be allocated. We will assume that B has a particular structure: $B = A \cup R^I$, where R is the real line. This is the particular case in which there is a transferable good, perhaps 'money', which can be allocated independently of the rest of the resources. In the sequel, we will take semantic liberty and call an element of A an alternative. A vector $r \in R^I$ will be called a transfer, while r^i, the i'th component of r, will be called the transfer to i.

For some of the applications of the model, it will be useful to allow random allocations. For example, in a first price auction, if two people submit the highest bid, then we might pick the winner randomly. In this case, we will write the set of possible alternatives as $P(A) \times R^I$, where $P(A)$ is the set of all probability distributions of A. For the model described below, randomization over transfers is not needed.

The source of uncertainty in the model will be the preferences of the agents over the elements of A. Following the Bayesian paradigm, we will model these by defining a set of possible 'types' for each agent.[2]

T^i will denote a (usually finite) set which completely describes agent i. This is called the set of *types* of agent i. An element $t_i \in T^i$ describes the preferences (*and* information) of agent i. The type t_i completely summarizes agent i in the sense that if we knew the constraints facing i and we knew t_i, we would know exactly what agent i would do.

Let $T = T^1 \times T^2 \times \ldots \times T^I$ denote the aggregate set of types, and let $t \in T$ denote a vector of types. We will generally write t = (t_i, t_{-i}), denoting the type of agent i and the types of all the other agents.

Given a type t_i, an alternative $a \in A$, and a real number r^i, the utility of agent i is given by $U^i(a, t_i) + r^i$, where r^i is a monetary transfer to agent i, and can be positive or negative.

We next define a mechanism. As stated in the introduction, a mechanism is the procedure through which individual actions result in an outcome. This is quite simple to model. We denote by a set M^i the set of actions available to agent i. Agent i's problem is to choose an element $m^i \in M^i$. Of course, to make a choice, the agent must understand the consequences of the choice. The consequence is the collective choice that results from the actions of all the agents, which is an element of $A \times R^I$. The function that specifies the relationship between actions and outcomes is called the outcome function.

Formally, a mechanism is a pair (M,g), where $M = M^1 \times M^2 \times \ldots \times M^I$ and g is a function $g: M \rightarrow A \times R^I$. M^i is called the message space of agent i, and g is the outcome function. We will write $g = (g_a, g_r)$ to denote the two component functions of g.

The actions of an individual are modelled by a *strategy*, which specifies a message for each type of agent. A strategy will actually be the essential object chosen by an agent.

Definition   A strategy for i is a function $\sigma^i: T^i \rightarrow M^i$.

A *strategy profile* is a vector of strategies, one for each agent. Given such a profile, we can use the outcome function to determine the alternatives which will be chosen if the agents play these strategies. If the vector of types is t, then agent i employs the action $\sigma^i(t_i)$, and the outcome is $g(\sigma(t))$.

Suppose for a moment that there are only two agents, and consider the problem facing agent 2 who is of type t_2, and who is trying to determine which action to take. If he chooses action m^2, then the outcome will be $g(m^1, m^2)$. Of course, agent 2 will generally not know m^1, since m^1 will be chosen by agent 1, and agent 1's choice of m^1 will generally depend on agent 1's type, which agent 2 does not know. How does agent 2 choose an action?

The Bayesian approach solves this problem by making two assumptions. First, it is assumed that agents have beliefs about the types of the other agents. The second is common knowledge of strategies.

The beliefs of an agent are modelled by a *probability distribution* over the set of types. Thus, $F^i(t_{-i})$ will denote the distribution over T^{-i} that is the belief of agent i. In general, F may depend on t_i as well. The importance of this distribution stems from the fact that it allows an agent to evaluate how a strategy will perform given some assumed strategies of the other players. Given a strategy profile $\sigma = (\sigma^1, \ldots, \sigma^I)$, the (interim) utility, or the expected payoff, of agent i at type t_i is given by

$$W^i(\sigma,t_i) = \int_{T^{-i}} \{U^i(g_a(\sigma(t),t_i) + g^i_r(\sigma(t))\} \, dF^i(t_{-i})$$

Of course, in order to pick a strategy, agent i must also have some expectations about the strategies which will be employed by the others. The Bayesian approach to mechanism design theory assumes as a part of the definition of equilibrium that the strategies which will be employed are common knowledge, which means that everyone knows the strategies to be played, everyone knows that others know this, and so on. In addition, the structure of the problem, which includes the set of possible types of all agents, the set of alternatives, and the beliefs of all agents are also assumed to be common knowledge. A Bayesian equilibrium to a mechanism is defined as follows.

Definition σ is a (pure strategy) *Bayesian equilibrium* if for all i and t_i,

$$W^i(\sigma,t_i) \geq W^i(\sigma^{-i},\alpha^i,t_i) \text{ for all } \alpha^i: T^i \to M^i$$

An equilibrium is a strategy profile so that the expected payoff to each agent at each type is greater than that from any other strategy, given the strategy choices of the other agents. Alternatively, each σ^i is a best response to the strategies being employed by the other agents. One way to motivate common knowledge of strategies is that if the structure of the problem is common knowledge, then every agent can in fact calculate the set of possible equilibrium strategies.

If σ is an equilibrium to (M,g), then $g(\sigma)$ is called a *Bayesian equilibrium outcome* to (M,g). Note that $g(\sigma)$ is a function from T into $A \times R^I$. This motivates the following definition.

Definition   An *allocation rule* is a function $x : T \to A \times R^I$.

Given an allocation rule x, we define the interim utility of i by

$$V^i(x,t_i) = \int \{U^i(x^i_a(t_{-i},t_i),t_i) + x^i_r(t_{-i},t_i)\} \, dF^i(t_{-i})$$

An equilibrium outcome of a mechanism, then, is an allocation rule. The mechanism design problem is to characterize which allocation rules are equilibrium outcomes to mechanisms. This is taken up in the next two sections.

Before proceeding to these characterizations, we first summarize some important simplifying assumptions that have been made, and also show how the bargaining problem discussed earlier fits into our model.

The main simplifying assumptions are:

— *type-independent alternative* set, because we have assumed that the set A does not depend on the vector of types. This excludes the possibility that a type also denotes the endowment of an agent.
— *transferable utility*, because we have assumed that the set of alternatives and the utility function have a separable component.
— *independent types*, because we have assumed that $F^i(t_{-i})$ does not depend on t_i. More generally, we could have assumed a distribution of the form $F^i(t_{-i}|t_i)$, which would be the case of *correlated types*. In this case, a type would also represent the beliefs of the agent.
— *private values*, because we have assumed that $U^i(a,t_i)$ does not depend on t_{-i}. Thus, the preferences of agent i are determined by i's own type only. More generally, we could assume $U^i(a,t)$, which would be the case of correlated values. For example, if the elements of A were alternative production processes and t_{-i} represented the information of the other agents about the productivity of these processes, then agent i's preferences over the alternatives could well depend on t_{-i}.

In the last section of the chapter, we will discuss the implications of relaxing some of these assumptions. While some of the results based on them extend easily to the general case, other important difficulties remain unresolved. Further, the nature of certain results also changes, as we will see.

To make some of the ideas concrete, consider again the bargaining problem. The seller has a valuation for the good, t_s, which is the minimum price he is willing to receive. The buyer has a valuation t_b, which is the maximum price he is willing to pay. Suppose that both t_s and t_b lie in the unit interval, and are uniformly distributed. The set of alternatives is $A \times R^2$, where $A = \{1,0\}$, the element 1 means the buyer gets the good, 0 means the seller keeps the good. The utility functions are

$$U^s(a,t_s) + r_s = (1 - a)t_s + r_s$$
$$U^b(a,t_b) + r_b = at_b + r_b$$

Thus, if the buyer gets the good, so $a = 1$, the buyer's payoff is $t_b + r_b$ and the seller's payoff is r_s. Of course, we also require that $r_b = -r_s$, so the payment received by the seller is that made by the buyer.

Suppose the mechanism being employed is the 1/2 double auction described in the introduction. In this mechanism, $M^b = M^s = R$, and $g_a(m^b, m^s) = 1$ if $m^b \geq m^s$ and 0 otherwise. In the former case, the payment made by the buyer is $g_r^b(m^b, m^s) = (1/2)(m^b + m^s)$, and the seller receives $g_r^s(m^b, m^s) = -g_r^b(m^b, m^s)$.

A strategy for the buyer is a function $\sigma^b(v_b)$, that for the seller is $\sigma^s(v_s)$. Then, it can be shown that the following strategies form a Bayesian equilibrium:[3]

$$\sigma^b(t_b) = (1/12) + (2/3)t_b$$

$$\sigma^s(t_s) = (1/4) + (2/3)t_s$$

The calculation is easily checked. For the buyer, suppose the seller plays σ^s. When the buyer is of type t_b, he has to choose a bid, say b. This bid will be chosen to

$$\text{maximize} \int_{\{\tau : b \geq \sigma^s(\tau)\}} [t_b - (1/2)[b + \sigma^s(\tau)]]d\tau$$

and it can be verified that the buyer should bid as described by σ^b. For the seller of type t_s, he would choose a price s to

$$\text{maximize} \int_{\{\tau : s \leq \sigma^b(\tau)\}} (1/2)[s + \sigma^s(\tau)]]d\tau + \int_{\{\tau : s > \sigma^b(\tau)\}} t_s \, d\tau$$

In terms of the allocation rule implemented by this equilibrium, the outcome has trade taking place if $t_b \geq (1/4)t_s$, and the payment made by the buyer is $(1/6) + (1/3)(t_b + t_s)$.

Other problems of interest that are covered by this model include auctions, public good provision and, with a slight reinterpretation, pure exchange economies.

To cast an auction into our framework,[4] we allow random allocations. Suppose a seller wishes to auction an object, and there are I buyers. Let t_i denote the value of the object to buyer i. Let a_0 denote the alternative 'the seller keeps the object', and a_j the alternative 'buyer j gets the object'. Then, $p(a_j, t)$ is the probability that j gets the object, and $r^j(t)$ is the payment made by buyer j.

In the case of public goods,[5] consider the simple problem of either building or not building a public good such as a bridge. Suppose the bridge costs C; let a_1 denote the alternative 'the bridge is built' and a_2 the alternative 'the bridge is not built'. The utility to agent i from having the bridge is $U^i(a_2, t_i)$, depending on the type of agent i. We interpret the transfers to be the taxes paid by the agents to finance the construction of the bridge.

In a pure exchange economy, A can be the set of feasible redistributions of an aggregate endowment, and we typically ignore the transfers. Thus, letting $w \in R_+^L$ denote the aggregate endowment, we have

$$A = \{ a \in R_1^{LI} : \sum_i a^i \leq w \}$$

as the set of feasible redistributions of the aggregate endowment. The utility function U^i can be assumed to have the usual properties such as continuity, concavity, etc. On a cautionary note, the arguments made in Section 6.4 will use transfers quite heavily, so the proofs do not apply directly to pure exchange economies. However, similar arguments can be constructed, and some of these are presented in Palfrey and Srivastava (1992).

6.3   THE REVELATION PRINCIPLE

Recall the main question we are trying to answer: which allocation rules can arise as Bayesian equilibrium outcomes to a mechanism? As a specific example, let us ask the following: in the bilateral bargaining problem, can we ensure that whenever $t_b \geq t_s$, the buyer gets the good, and the price paid by the buyer is a linear combination, say $kt_s + (1 - k)t_b$ with $0 \leq k \leq 1$, of the types of the two agents?

At first glance, this seems like a formidable problem. We know that this is not the outcome in the equilibrium we calculated in the 1/2 double action. Perhaps we should see if there are other equilibria to the mechanism. Or perhaps we should change the mechanism in some way. Upon reflection, it becomes clear that it is not feasible to search across mechanisms, calculating all the equilibria, to see if an equilibrium outcome to any one of them coincides with the desired allocation rule.

It turns out that the answer to the question is made possible by a powerful device known as the revelation principle.[6] Formally, it states:

If (M,g) is a mechanism and $x = g(\sigma)$ is a Bayesian equilibrium outcome of (M,g), then truth-telling is an equilibrium to the mechanism (T,h) where $T = T^1 \times \ldots T^I$, and $h(t) = x(t)$ for all t.

In the mechanism (T,h), truth-telling means that each agent reports his or her type honestly, and (T,h) is called an equivalent direct mechanism or the associated revelation mechanism since the truthful equilibrium results in the same allocation rule. Since $h = x$, sometimes x is itself called a mechanism, it being implicitly understood that the message spaces are the individual type sets.

The proof of the principle is actually quite simple. We illustrate it in some detail for the case of two agents in a finite setting.

Let

$$T^1 = \{t_1, \ldots, t_K\} = \text{set of types of agent 1}$$

$$M^1 = \{m_1, \ldots, m_N\} = \text{message space of agent 1}$$

$$T^2 = \{\tau_1, \ldots, \tau_K\} = \text{set of types of agent 2}$$

$$M^2 = \{n_1, \ldots, n_N\} = \text{message space of agent 2}$$

Let σ be an equilibrium to (M,g). Without loss of generality, assume that $\sigma^1(t_1) = m_1, \ldots, \sigma^1(t_K) = m_K$, and similarly for agent 2. Then, the situation is as depicted in Figure 6.1.

Now, note that we can eliminate the strategies not used by σ (labelled $K + 1$ to N for both agents) and σ is still an equilibrium to the remaining mechanism. Finally, we can re-label the messages and the outcome function to arrive at the revelation mechanism (Figure 6.2).

Truth-telling is clearly an equilibrium to the revelation mechanism. For example, if agent 1 does better by playing t_j when he is of type t_1, then he should have played m_j in the original mechanism instead of playing m_1.

As an example, let us return to the 1/2 double auction. In the original mechanism, the message space of both the buyer and the seller was the real line, and the outcome function was

$$g_a(m^b,m^s) = 1 \text{ and } g_r(m^b,m^s) = \{(1/2)(m^b + m^s),$$

$$- (1/2)(m^b,m^s)\} \text{ if } m^b \geq m^s$$

$$g_a(m^b,m^s) = 0 \text{ and } g_r(m^b,m^s) = \{0,0\} \text{ otherwise}$$

As calculated in the previous section, an equilibrium is for the buyer to bid

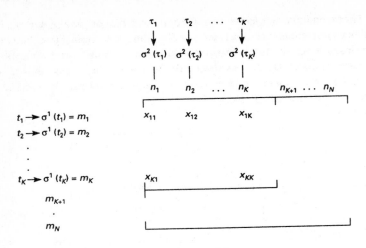

Figure 6.1

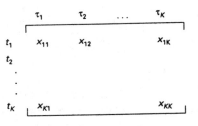

Figure 6.2

$$\sigma^b(t_b) = (1/12) + (2/3)t_b$$

and for the seller to ask

$$\sigma^s(t_s) = (1/4) + (2/3)t_s$$

The allocation rule that results from this equilibrium is $x_a(t) = 1$ if $t_b \geq (1/4) + t_s$, $x_r^s(t) = (1/6) + (1/3)(t_b + t_s)$, $x_r^b(t) = -x_r^s(t)$, where the subscripts on x indicate the allocation of the good and of the transfers.

The equivalent revelation mechanism would have both the buyer and the seller report their valuations, t_b and t_s, and would have the buyer receive the good if $t_b \geq (1/4) + t_s$ in which case the buyer would pay $(1/6) + (1/3)(t_b + t_s)$. It can be verified that truth-telling is an equilibrium to this revelation game. In fact, verifying this requires us to check exactly the same calculation as in the original case.

In this example, we calculated an equilibrium to the original mechanism and then constructed the revelation mechanism. The power of the revelation principle emerges when we do not have a mechanism but are interested in an allocation. To see this, let us return to the specific question posed at the beginning of this section. The allocation rule we proposed is:

$x_a(t) = 1$ if $t_b \geq t_s$, with the seller receiving $kt_s + (1 - k)t_b$ when the good is exchanged, $0 \leq k \leq 1$.

It turns out that there is no mechanism which has this outcome. In fact, there is no mechanism which ensures that the buyer always gets the object only when $t_b \geq t_s$ for any transfer rule we can think of. A proof of the general result is beyond the scope of this chapter, but we can easily use the revelation principle for the specific class of transfer rules where the payment by the buyer is a linear combination of the valuations of the two agents. All we need to check is whether each agent will respond truthfully if the other is telling the truth.

For the buyer, this involves checking if $b = t_b$ solves

$$\text{maximize} \int_{\{\tau:b \geq \tau\}} [t_b - k\tau - (1 - k)b]d\tau$$

The solution to this maximization problem is $b = t_b/(2 - k)$, so the buyer will bid truthfully if $k = 1$, i.e. the buyer pays the seller's price. For the seller, the problem is to choose s to

$$\text{maximize} \int_{\{\tau:s \leq \tau\}} [ks + (1 - k)\tau]d\tau + \int_{\{\tau:s > \tau\}} t_s \, d\tau$$

The solution is $s = (t_s + k)/(1 + k)$, so the seller will be truthful if $k = 0$, i.e. the seller pays the buyer's price. Taken together, we find there is no k such that both the seller and the buyer will be truthful.

The revelation principle allowed us to check quite easily whether the allocation rule we were interested in was implementable. All we did was to see if truth-telling by the buyer was a best response to truth-telling by the seller. More generally, an allocaton rule which satisfies this property is said to be *incentive compatible*.

For any $\tau_i \in T^i$, let

$$V^i(x,t_i,\tau_i) = \int_{T^{-i}} \{U^i(x_a(t_{-i},\tau_i),\ t_i) + x_r(t_{-i},\tau_i)\}\ dF^i(t_{-i})$$

denote the expected utility to agent i from the allocation rule x when i is of type t_i but pretends to be of type τ_i.

Definition   An allocation rule x is incentive compatible if for all i and $t_i \in T^i$, and for all $\tau_i \in T^i$,

$$V^i(x,t_i,t_i),\ \geq\ V^i(x,t_i,\tau_i)$$

In terms of the specific question posed at the beginning of this section, the allocation rule being considered was shown not to be incentive compatible.

The concept of incentive compatibility plays a central role in mechanism design theory.[7] It summarizes the restrictions imposed on attainable allocation rules by incompleteness of information, or, more precisely, by the requirement that the allocation rule be attained as an equilibrium outcome of some mechanism.

The fact that incomplete information imposes restrictions on attainable allocations means that we have to re-define what we mean by efficiency. Specifically, the allocation rule we tried to obtain earlier is certainly efficient from a classical point of view; it requires trade whenever there are gains from exchange. However, it is not attainable, as we have seen. Consequently, in defining efficiency, we must restrict ourselves to incentive compatible allocation rules.[8] It turns out there are several alternative ways of defining efficiency.[9] The one we will focus on is called *interim efficiency* (and sometimes *incentive efficiency*).

Definition   An allocation rule x is interim efficient if it is incentive compatible and there is no other incentive compatible rule, say y, such that $V^i(y,t_i) \geq V^i(x,t_i)$ for all i and t_i, and $V^i(y,t_i) > V^i(x,t_i)$ for some i and t_i.

The equilibrium outcome we analyzed in studying the 1/2 double auction is interim efficient.[10] Since that allocation rule does not always have trade occurring when there are gains from exchange, we see that there is a difference between interim efficiency and classical notions such as Pareto efficiency.

This completes our discussion of the revelation principle. In summary, the principle led to the concept of incentive compatibility, which is a restriction which must be imposed on allocation rules if they are to arise from a decentralized decision-making procedure or mechanism. This does not mean that the only relevant mechanisms are revelation mechanisms. As we will see in the next section, there are important reasons why we should consider broader classes of mechanisms.

6.4 FULL IMPLEMENTATION

The development of our argument so far has allowed us to characterize the set of feasible allocations when there is incomplete information, where incentive compatibility is added to the usual restrictions embodied in the set of alternatives. One problem that remains is the problem of designing a mechanism which has only nice or desirable outcomes. This is called the full implementation problem.

The importance of full implementation can be illustrated in the bargaining problem. It turns out that both the 1/2 double auction and the revelation mechanism associated with the efficient equilibrium discussed previously also have a large number of inefficient equilibria.

In the revelation mechanism associated with the equilibrium we computed, trade takes place if $t_b \geq (1/4) + t_s$, and the payment made by the buyer is $(1/6) + (1/3)(t_b + t_s)$.

Another equilibrium to the revelation mechanism is the following:

$$\sigma^b(t_b) = 1/2 \text{ if } t_b \geq 1/2 \ \sigma^b(t_b) = 0 \text{ otherwise}$$

$$\sigma^s(t_s) = 1/2 \text{ if } t_s \leq 1/2, \ \sigma^s(t_s) = 1 \text{ otherwise}$$

To check that this is equilibrium, note that the buyer should not bid below 1/2 if $t_b > 1/2$, since in that case the buyer simply loses some opportunities to trade. Furthermore, there is no incentive to bid above 1/2, since all that happens then is that the buyer pays more than 1/2 for the good when he could have obtained it for 1/2. A similar argument establishes that σ^s is a best response to σ^b.

The number 1/2 does not play any special role in the above; we can replace it by any $z \in (0, 1)$, and obtain a family of what have been called *single-price equilibria*.[11] In fact, in the 1/2 double auction (or more generally, in the k-double auction with $0 < k < 1$), there are even more equilibria. The single price equilibria can be extended to step-function equilibria (where the bids/asks remain constant over subintervals of the type space), and there is even a continuum of differentiable equilibria.[12]

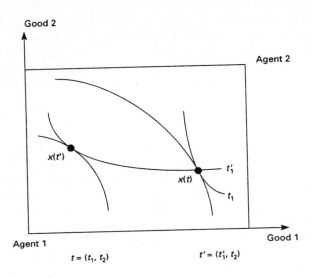

Figure 6.3
Source: Palfrey and Srivastava (1989).

A nice feature of the equilibrium described in the previous sections was that it led to an incentive efficient allocation rule. Unfortunately, most of the other equilibria are not efficient. Changing from the double auction to the revelation game does not eliminate the problem; the single price equilibrium outcomes also emerge from the revelation game.

This multiplicity problem is not confined to the double auction problem. It also arises with public goods and in pure exchange economies. A particularly simple example of the latter is shown in Figure 6.3 (taken from Palfrey and Srivastava, 1989). In the example, agent 1 has two types, agent 2 has only one. The desired allocation rule is denoted by x. The allocation rule has very nice efficiency properties. It is in fact efficient in the classical sense of Pareto efficiency, and is also incentive efficient. Unfortunately, a second equilibrium is for agent 1 always to claim to be of type t'_1, which is not so good for agent 2.

The existence of multiple equilibrium outcomes with undesirable properties poses an important challenge to mechanism design theory, since the ultimate aim of the theory is to describe how we might set up mechanisms to attain or implement desirable allocation rules. If these mechanisms also have undesirable equilibria, then we may not implement the desirable allocation rule.

A fully implementable allocation rule is one which is the unique equilibrium outcome of a mechanism, and much recent effort has been expended in characterizing such allocation rules. Of particular interest is whether efficient allocation rules can be fully implemented. In the model being considered here, there is a simple proof which shows that any interim efficient allocation rule can be fully implemented. This is not the case in more general settings, as we will discuss later.

The characterization of fully implementable rules is made difficult by the fact that revelation mechanisms will generally not be sufficient (as shown by the double auction example). However, the principle simplifies our search for a fully implementing mechanism since we can start with a revelation mechanism and attempt to add strategies to it to selectively eliminate unwanted equilibria.[13]

To start the study, then, let x be incentive compatible, and consider the set of all possible equilibrium startegies to the revelaton mechanism (T,x). For agent i, the entire set of strategies available is $\{\alpha^i : T^i \rightarrow T^i\}$. If α is not the identity, then we call it a 'deceptive' strategy or a 'deception', since it means that by using α^i, agent i is reporting $\alpha^i(t_i) \neq t_i$ for some $t_i \in T^i$.

If $\alpha = \{\alpha^1, \ldots, \alpha^I\}$ is an equilibrium to the revelation mechanism and one of the α^i is not the identity, then the outcome at t is no longer $x(t)$ but instead $x(\alpha(t)) \equiv x_\alpha(t)$. The problem arises when $x_\alpha(t) \neq x(t)$ for some t, in which case we have an undesired outcome to the mechanism.

Suppose we add a strategy to (T,x) by giving agent i an extra message, say m^i. Can we make sure that α is not an equilibrium? To do so, we must construct the outcome function so that when the other agents are using α, agent i deviates at some type, say t_i, and instead plays m^i. Let $y(t_{-i},m^i)$ denote the outcome function when agent i plays m^i. Then, we need there to exist t_i such that

$$V^i(y_\alpha,t_i) > V^i(x_\alpha,t_i)$$

On the other hand, we still want truth-telling to be an equilibrium. This means that y will have to satisfy the restriction

$$V^i(y,t_i) \leq V^i(x,t_i) \text{ for all } t_i$$

Definition x satisfies *Bayesian monotonicity* if for every collection of functions $\alpha = \{\alpha^1, \ldots, \alpha^I\}$ with $\alpha^i : T^i \rightarrow T^i$, $i = 1,2,\ldots, I$, if $x_\alpha \neq x$, then there exists an allocation rule y such that $V^i(y_\alpha,t_i) > V^i(x_\alpha,t_i)$ for some i and t_i and $V^i(x,t_i') \geq V^i(y,t_i')$ for all i and t_i', where $x_\alpha(t) = x(\alpha(t))$ and $y_\alpha(t) = y(\alpha(t))$ for all t.

We are frequently interested in implementing one out of a collection of allocations, such as the set of market equilibrium allocations. In this case, if F is a set of such allocations, the set F satisfies Bayesian monotonicity if every $x \in F$ satisfies it. In this case, to implement F, we require a mechanism such that every equilibrium outcome be an element of F and there exists at least one equilibrium outcome. A stronger requirement, that of full implementation, is that every element of F be an equilibrium outcome.

Bayesian monotonicity is a necessary condition for full implementation of x, as implied by the discussion leading to the definition, and incentive compatibility is also a necessary condition. These two conditions are generally not sufficient to implement an allocation rule. However, with tranferable utility, they are sufficient.[14] We present next a 'generic' sufficiency proof, which forms the basis of most of the proofs of sufficiency found in the literature.[15]

The 'Generic' Sufficiency Proof to Implement Allocation Rule x

Let $D^i = \{y \in X \mid$ there exists α which is an equilibrium to the revelation mechanism, and i and y are the agent and allocation rule which satisfy the requirements of Bayesian monotonicity$\}$.

Let b^i be an allocation where agent i receives a very large transfer, paid for by the other agents, and which agent i prefers at any t_i to any possible expected payoff from the revelation mechanism (T,x).

Let $M^i = T^i \times (D^i \cup \{0,1,2,\ldots,\})$

The outcome function is defined in Figure 6.4.

We argue that this mechanism fully implements F. First, note that 'truth-telling', which here corresponds to honest reports of type and a report of 0, is an equilibrium. This is because agent i, for example, can unilaterally change the outcome in only two ways: first by reporting $y \in D^i$, and second by lying about his type. Since x is incentive compatible, lying about his type does not pay. The restrictions on y imposed by Bayesian monotonicity imply that if everyone else is telling the truth, then reporting y does not pay either.

Second, there is no equilibrium outside the top left corner of the box in Figure 6.4. There are two reasons for this. First, say agent 2 is always reporting either y or an integer greater that 0, then by always reporting a larger integer, agent 1 can guarantee receiving b^1. If agent 2 is only sometimes reporting something other than 0, then agent 1

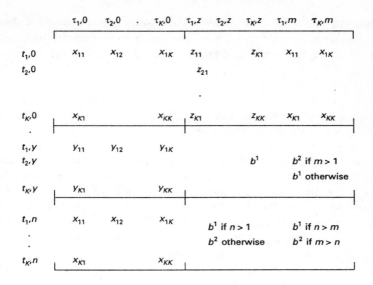

Figure 6.4

can again obtain b^1 when agent 2 does not report 0 by reporting a high enough integer.[16] In either case, by reporting an even higher number, agent 2 can now get b^2, and so on.[17]

Third, x is the unique equilibrium outcome. This is because if $\alpha = \{\alpha^i, 0\}$ is an equilibrium then Bayesian monotonicity implies that one of the agents should deviate and report y instead of 0.

Hence this mechanism fully implements x. Several aspects of the argument deserve mention. First, we used transferable utility to create the b^i. This is not essential; as long as there is some good over which there is conflict of interest among the agents, it is possible to construct outcomes which will serve this purpose. Second, we used a finite number of types. This again is not essential, though we would otherwise have to be a little more creative in constructing the b^i. Third, we ignored mixed strategies. This poses an important set of difficulties which we will discuss in the last section.

When x is interim efficient, we do not need such complications, and there is an easy way to show that x is essentially fully implementable given transferable utility and either transferable utility or a convexity type of condition on the feasible set. The reason for the qualifier 'essentially' is that we do not eliminate equilibria in which x_α gives exactly the same interim utility to every agent:

Definition   An allocation rule x is *essentially implementable* if there exists a mechanism (M,g), with at least one Bayesian equilibrium, such that for every Bayesian equilibrium, σ, for all i and t_i,

$$V^i(x,t_i) = W^i(\sigma,t_i)$$

Theorem (Palfrey and Srivastava, 1991)   Let x be interim efficient. Then x is essentially implementable.

Proof   The original proof of this result uses the ability to pick random allocations. The same argument can be applied if we assume instead:[18] for all i and t_i, for any $a_1, a_2 \in A$, and for any $0 \le p \le 1$, there exists a such that $U^i(a,t_i) = pU^i(a_1,t_i) + (1 - p)U^i(a_2,t_i)$.

Let x be interim efficient, with $V^i(x,t_i)$ being the expected payoff to i when i is of type t_i. Let α be another equilibrium to the direct mechanism which weakly implements x, and let

$$\delta^i(\alpha,t_i) = V^i(x,t_i) - W^i(\alpha,t_i)$$

Since there are a finite number of types, there are only finitely many (pure strategy) equilibria in the direct mechanism. Define

$$\eta = \min \{\delta^i(\alpha,t_i) : \delta^i(\alpha,t_i) > 0, i = 1, \ldots, I, t_i \in T^i, \text{ and } \alpha \text{ an}$$
equilibrium to the direct mechanism$\}$.

Given our assumption above, we define $\alpha(t_i)$ to be the element of A such that $\int U^i(x_a(t_{-i},t_i),t_i)dF^i(t_{-i}) = U^i(a(t_i),t_i)$.

Now, if there is an undesirable equilibrium outcome to the revelation mechanism, then we must have $\eta > 0$. To eliminate such an equilibrium, we expand the message space to allow agents to say that rather than play the mechanism, they would like simply to get the utility they would have got if everyone was being truthful. Thus, let

$$M^i = T^i \times [0,1]$$

If no one deviates by reporting a number in the second part of their message, the outcome is x:

$$g(m) = x(t) \text{ if } m^i = (t_i,0) \text{ for all } i$$

If exactly one agent, say i, says $\epsilon > 0$, the alternative chosen is $a(t_i)$ and i receives the transfer $\int x_r^i(t_{-i}, t_i) dF^i(t_{-i})$, and we can assume that this is paid equally by the other agents.

If many agents report a positive number, we can pick the one reporting the smallest number to play the same role as if he was the only one saying a positive number, and ties can be broken by some randomization device.[19]

The original allocation rule is an equilibrium outcome of the mechanism when everyone reports their types truthfully and no one ever reports a positive number. To see that this is still an equilibrium when the latter condition is not fulfilled, note that deviating to a positive number does not change an agent's expected utility by choice of $a(t_i)$. If agent i reports $t_i' \neq t_i$, then the payoff from this is exactly the same as if the agent reported t_i' in the revelation game; since x is incentive compatible, this cannot benefit agent i.

Now, consider any other equilibrium to the mechanism. We argue that it must give every agent at least the same utility as the truthful equilibrium. If not, then some agent should report a lower number[20] than any to be used by the other agents and obtain this utility. Thus every equilibrium outcome is at least as good as x. But it cannot be better than x since x is interim efficient. This concludes the proof.

An implication of this result is that if x is interim efficient, then the set of allocation rules defined by

$$F = \{x_\alpha : V^i(x_\alpha, t_i) = V^i(x, t_i)\}$$

must satisfy Bayesian monotonicity. The proof is trivial; if $V^i(x_\alpha, t_i) \neq V^i(x, t_i)$ for some i and t_i, we simply let $y = (a(t_i), r(t_i))$, where $r(t_i)$ is the vector of transfers used in the proof when exactly one agent reported a positive number.

With complete information, it is known that several important sets of allocation rules are fully implementable. In pure exchange economies, these include the (constrained) Walrasian correspondence, the Pareto correspondence, and the Lindahl correspondence. The extensions of these allocation rules to incomplete information are typically not fully implementable. It is known that allocation rules corresponding to rational expectations equilibria do not generally satisfy incentive compatibility. Even when they do, they are only known to be implementable in the special case when individual endowments are state independent. The results for Lindahl allocations are similar in nature. The main results for efficient allocations are those given in this section. These do not extend to the case of correlated types.

6.5   EXTENSIONS AND COMPLICATIONS

In this section, we briefly indicate some studies which contain extensions of the basic model studied in this chapter. We start with the basic assumptions of the model. The definitions of incentive compatibility and of Bayesian monotonicity are easily extended to correlated values and correlated types. However, the impact of these conditions can be quite different from the private values case. For example, with correlated types, a seller can expect to obtain the same revenues from an auction as if he knew the valuations of all the buyers (see Cremer and McLean, 1988). Correlated types also introduce some fundamental complications into the implementation problem, which are explored by Palfrey and Srivastava (1991), Jackson (1991), and Dutta and Sen (1992). Correlated values pose less of a problem; in fact, if the utility function is separable, i.e. takes the form $U^i(a,t_i) + \phi^i(a,t_{-i})$, then none of the results of Section 6.4 are affected in the model with transferable utility.

A second extension concerns the equilibrium concept. Different results obtain in full implementation theory if we change the solution concept. Two such concepts have been studied in the literature. One is undominated Bayesian equilibrium, which is a Bayesian equilibrium in which no agent uses a weakly dominated strategy. This concept leads to very powerful full implementation results if we do not restrict the class of mechanisms which can be employed (see Palfrey and Srivastava, 1989). One feature of the mechanism used in that study is that it uses an infinite chain of dominated strategies to eliminate unwanted equilibria. Such a mechanism has been called 'unbounded' by Jackson (1991), and boundedness is now considered a desirable property of a mechanism. The impact of restricting attention to bounded mechanisms with incomplete information has not been studied. However, with complete information, Jackson, Palfrey, and Srivastava (1992) show that boundedness does not significantly restrict the class of implementable allocations. A second concept is the iterated elimination of weakly dominated strategies studied by Abreu and Matsushima (1990). In a model with transferable utility, they show that the ability to use randomizations allows the virtual implementation of any incentive compatible allocation rule. (See Glazer and Rosenthal (1992) for a critique of their mechanism. This criticism is based on examples that show the existence of strategies that could be considered 'focal points' and which are eliminated, and on the fact that in the mechanism, many rounds of elimination of weakly dominated strategies are required.)

Another aspect of the full implementation literature which is not understood concerns mixed strategies. In our construction, we restricted attention to pure strategies. However, there may be mixed strategy equilibria which produce undesirable outcomes. It turns out that with transferable utility, mixed strategies are easily handled if we allow unbounded mechanisms (see Palfrey and Srivastava, 1991). The problem can also be solved if we do not require that agents always have best responses to any (mixed) strategy of the other agents. This last criterion, which is at least as desirable as boundedness, also affects the literature with complete information for both Nash implementation and for refinements of Nash equilibrium. The following question remains unsolved: what characterizes a fully implementable allocation rule where the implementing mechanism is bounded, every agent always has a best response to every strategy of the others, and mixed strategy equilibria do not lead to undesirable outcomes?

The last broad area we consider are the issues of communication and renegotiation. An implicit assumption of our model was that the only way agents could communicate was through the mechanism. What is the implication of assuming that agents can communicate in other ways? One possibility that emerges is that, even though the allocation that will emerge will depend on the messages reported to the mechanism, agents could coordinate on some of these messages by communicating 'outside' the mechanism. Myerson (1986) studies the effect of communication on the revelation principle, where it is shown how the principle extends to this case. Palfrey and Srivastava (1991) study the effect of communication on full implementation. They show that, under weaker assumptions than we have made, any interim efficient allocation rule can be fully implemented even if agents can communicate outside the mechanism.

Finally, another assumption in the analysis was that the agents did not have a choice about the mechanism employed. One way to interpret a mechanism is that a mechanism designer 'imposes' it. Another interpretation, which is more popular, is that the mechanism itself is the outcome of a negotiating process among the agents. In this case, agents naturally have the option of renegotiating the mechanism. In particular, one might expect agents to renegotiate the mechanism if the outcome is inefficient. Maskin and Tirole (1990) examine the effect of renegotiation in a model somewhat different from that examined here, and Palfrey and Srivastava (1992, ch. 5) study the effects of renegotiation on full implementation. Both these papers model the renegotiation process as a non-cooperative game played at the interim stage, i.e. when each agent knows his or her type, but when the original mechanism has not yet been played. Maskin and Tirole (1990) essentially show that interim efficient allocation rules are immune to renegotiation. Palfrey and Srivastava (1992, ch. 5) show that in the class of models studied in this paper, any interim efficient allocation rule is fully implementable even if agents can renegotiate the mechanism, and across a very wide class of renegotiation procedures.

Notes

1. A broad exposition of the theory is contained in Palfrey and Srivastava (1992).
2. Harsanyi (1967) is the classic reference on Bayesian games.
3. This equilibrium was first described by Chatterjee and Samuelson (1983).
4. See Myerson (1981).
5. See, for example, D'Aspremont and Gerard-Varet (1979).
6. This principle seems to have first appeared in Gibbard (1973), in the context of dominant strategy implementation. It was subsequently rediscovered in the Bayesian context, and can be found in Dasgupta, Hammond and Maskin (1979), Myerson (1979), and Harris and Townsend (1981).
7. See Myerson (1979) and Harris and Townsend (1981).
8. See Harris and Townsend (1981) and Holmstrom and Myerson (1983).
9. See Holmstrom and Myerson (1983).
10. See Myerson and Satterthwaite (1983).
11. See Leininger, Linhart and Radner (1989).
12. See Leininger, Linhart and Radner (1989) and Satterthwaite and Williams (1989).
13. This approach was first used by Maskin (1977) in the context of Nash implementation. The phrase 'selective elimination' is due to Mookherjee and Reichelstein (1990).
14. The first study of full implementation in Bayesian equilibrium was Postlewaite and Schmeidler (1986), who studied the problem when incentive compatibility was not a binding constraint. Their work was extended by Palfrey and Srivastava (1989a and b), who incorporated incentive compatibility into the problem and developed the Bayesian monotonicity condition. Their characterization was not complete in that the sufficiency argument required a stronger incentive compatibility condition. Jackson (1991) completed the characterization. The most recent general characterization, together with a discussion of some of the remaining difficulties, is given in Dutta and Sen (1992).

15. This proof, and the next one, covers both the two-agent and the multi-agent case. This is because we have assumed private values and independent types.

16. The second complication does not arise in complete information settings when attention is restricted to pure strategy equilibria.

17. I have chosen this proof to illustrate the nature of the sufficiency argument. It has the feature that most strategies are weakly dominated, so the mechanism is 'unbounded'. Bounded mechanisms will be discussed in the last section, where this proof will be used to illustrate the concept. Unboundedness here is trivially avoided: change the outcomes so that agent 1 gets $b_r^1 - \epsilon$ if $n = m - 1$, agent 2 gets $b_r^2 - \epsilon$ if $m = n - 1$, where ϵ is small enough so that $b_r^1 - \epsilon$ and $b_r^2 - \epsilon$ do not alter the nature of b^1 and b^2, where we recall that the subscript r denotes the transfer associated with an allocation rule.

18. This condition always holds in the private values, independent types model if we allow random allocations.

19. To eliminate boundedness problems, we can charge the winning agent η in case of a tie.

20. This relies on a finite number of types.

References

Abreu, D. and Matsushima H. (1990) 'Virtual Implementation in Iteratively Undominated Strategies: Incomplete Information', mimeo, Princeton University.

Chatterjee, K. and W. Samuelson (1983) 'Bargaining under Incomplete Information', *Operations Research*, vol. 31, pp. 835–51.

Cremer, J. and R. P. McLean (1988) 'Full Extraction of the Surplus in Bayesian and Dominant Strategy Auctions', *Econometrica*, vol. 56, pp. 1247–58.

Dasgupta, P., P. Hammond and E. Maskin (1979) 'The Implementation of Social Choice Rules: Some General Results on Incentive Compatibility', *Review of Economic Studies*, vol. 46, pp. 185–216.

D'Aspremont, C. and L. Gerard-Varet (1979) 'Incentives and Incomplete Information', *Journal of Public Economics*, vol. 11, pp. 25–45.

Dutta, B. and A. Sen (1992) 'Further Results on Bayesian Implementation', mimeo, Indian Statistical Institute.

Gibbard, A. (1973) 'Manipulation of Voting Schemes', *Econometrica*, vol. 41, pp. 587–601.

Glazer, J. and R. Rosenthal (1992) 'A Note on Abreu–Matsushima Mechanisms', forthcoming *Econometrica*.

Harris, M. and R. Townsend (1981) 'Resource Allocation with Asymmetric Information', *Econometrica*, vol. 49, pp. 33–64.

Harsanyi, J. (1967, 1968) 'Games of Incomplete Information Played by Bayesian Players', *Management Science*, vol. 14, pp. 159–82, 320–34, 486–502.

Holmstrom, B. and R. Myerson (1983) 'Efficient and Durable Decision Rules with Incomplete Information', *Econometrica*, vol. 51, pp. 1799–819.

Jackson, M. (1991) 'Bayesian Implementation', *Econometrica*, vol. 59, pp. 461–78.

Jackson, M., T. Palfrey and S. Srivastava (1992) 'Undominated Nash Implementation Using Bounded Mechanisms', mimeo, forthcoming in *Games and Economic Behavior.*

Leininger, W., P. Linhart and R. Radner (1989) 'Equilibria of the Sealed Bid Mechanism for Bargaining with Incomplete Information', *Journal of Economic Theory*, vol. 48, pp. 63–106.

Maskin, E. (1977) 'Nash Equilibrium and Welfare Optimality', mimeo.

Maskin, E. and J. Tirole (1990) 'The Principal Agent Problem with an Informed Principal', *Econometrica*, vol. 58, pp. 379–410.

Matthews, S. and A. Postlewaite (1989) 'Pre-Play Communication in Two-Person Sealed-Bid Double Auctions', *Journal of Economic Theory*, vol. 48, pp. 238–63.

Mookherjee, D. and S. Reichelstein (1990) 'Implementation Via Augmented Revelation Mechanisms', *Review of Economic Studies*, vol. 57, pp. 453–76.

Myerson, R. (1979) 'Incentive Compatibility and the Bargaining Problem', *Econometrica*, vol. 47, pp. 58–73.

Myerson, R. (1981) 'Optimal Auction Design', *Mathematics of Operations Research*, vol. 6, pp. 58–73.

Myerson, R. (1986) 'Multistage Games with Communication', *Econometrica*, vol. 54, pp. 323–58.

Myerson, R. and M. Satterthwaithe (1983) 'Efficient Mechanisms for Bilateral Trading', *Journal of Economic Theory*, vol. 29, pp. 265–81.

Palfrey, T. and S. Srivastava (1989a) 'Implementation with Incomplete Information in Exchange Economies', *Econometrica*, vol. 57, pp. 115–34.

Palfrey, T. and S. Srivastava (1989) 'Mechanism Design with Incomplete Information: A Solution to the Implementation Problem', *Journal of Political Economic*, vol. 97, pp. 668–91.

Palfrey, T. and S. Srivastava (1991) 'Efficient Trading Mechanisms with Preplay Communication', *Journal of Economic Theory*, vol. 55, pp. 17–40.

Palfrey, T. and S. Srivastava (1992) 'Bayesian Implementation, forthcoming (Reading, UK: Harwood Academic Publishers).

Postlewaite, A. and D. Schmeidler (1986) 'Implementation in Differential Information Economies', *Journal of Economic Theory*, vol. 39, pp. 14–33.

Radner, R. and A. Schotter (1989) 'The Sealed Bid Mechanism: An Experimental Study', *Journal of Economic Theory*, vol. 48, pp. 179–220.

Satterthwaite, M. and S. Williams (1989) 'Bilateral Trade with the Sealed Bid k-Double Auction: Existence and Efficiency', *Journal of Economic Theory*, vol. 48, pp. 107–33.

7 Issues and Results in General Equilibrium Theory

Beth Allen[1]

UNIVERSITY OF MINNESOTA AND FEDERAL RESERVE BANK OF MINNEAPOLIS

7.1 INTRODUCTION

My assignment here is very broad: to discuss general equilibrium theory. However, rather than attempting a general survey of this topic, I will focus selectively, with varying degrees of emphasis, on the current research areas that I consider most interesting and fruitful to pursue.

General equilibrium theory is the study of (at least) several markets that may interact. When more than one commodity is available, the price at which transactions occur for one good can affect traders' behaviour with respect to other commodities. Needless to say, perhaps, I use the by-now classic definition of a *commodity* as a good or service that is completely specified by physical description, location, and date of delivery, as well as by the set of states of the world in which it is delivered. Economists often use the term *general equilibrium* when they mean *competitive equilibrium*. The latter implies that each agent takes all prices (or more generally, the set of feasible actions) as given and incapable of influence by the agent's own behaviour in the economy. This obviously precludes most possibilities for strategic behaviour by such perfectly competitive economic agents.

7.2 THE CONCEPT OF COMPETITIVE EQUILIBRIUM

In most of my discussion, the actors or decision-makers in the model are consumers – individuals or households who begin with an initial endowment vector specifying the quantity of each commodity that they have available for consumption or sale. I also use the words *trader*, *agent*, and *player* for this concept, although admittedly the game-theoretic term *player* carries strategic connotations. I mention firms only when their presence is essential for my topic.

By definition, a *competitive equilibrium* consists of a price vector (specifying one price for each commodity) and an individual allocation vector (specifying a quantity of each commodity) for each consumer in the economy such that all markets clear (meaning that aggregate excess demand for each commodity is zero) and each agent's allocation is maximal with respect to the agent's preferences among the affordable consumption bundles defined by the equilibrium price vector.

To fix notation, let $I = \{1,\ldots,n\}$ be the set of consumers in an economy with ℓ commodities. Suppose that each trader $i \in I$ has consumption set $\mathbb{R}_+^\ell$, an initial endowment $e_i \in \mathbb{R}_+^\ell$, and a utility function $u_i : \mathbb{R}_+^\ell \to \mathbb{R}$ representing the trader's preferences $\leq_i$ (a complete preorder on $\mathbb{R}_+^\ell$). Then a *competitive equilibrium* is $(p^*,x_1^*,\ldots,x_n^*) \in \mathbb{R}_+^\ell \times \mathbb{R}_+^{\ell n}$ such that

1. $\displaystyle\sum_{i=1}^n x_i^* = \sum_{i=1}^n e_i$ and

2. for all $i \in I$, $x_i^* \in \arg\max \{u_i(x_i) \mid p \cdot x_i \leq p \cdot e_i\}$.

Note that the budget sets $\beta(p,e_i) = \{x_i \in \mathbb{R}_+^\ell \mid p \cdot x_i \leq p \cdot e_i\}$ are unchanged when all prices are multiplied by the same strictly positive scalar $[\beta(p,e_i) = \beta(\lambda p,e_i)$ for all $p \in \mathbb{R}_+^\ell$, all $e_i \in \mathbb{R}_+^\ell$, and all $\lambda \in \mathbb{R}_{++}]$. Therefore, whenever $(p^*,x_1^*,\ldots,x_n^*)$ is a competitive equilibrium for some economy, so is $(\lambda p^*,x_1^*,\ldots,x_n^*)$ for the same economy, for all $\lambda > 0$. In view of this, I can normalize prices to lie in the closed unit simplex $\bar{\Delta} = \{p \in \mathbb{R}_+^\ell \mid \sum_{j=1}^\ell p_j = 1\}$. A monotonicity assumption on preferences implies that aggregate excess demand $Z(p) = \displaystyle\sum_{i=1}^n \arg\max \{u_i(x_i) \mid p \cdot x_i \leq p \cdot e_i\} - \sum_{i=1}^n e_i$ satisfies Walras' Law $[p \cdot Z(p) = 0$ for any $p \in \Delta]$.

If the economy has uncountably many agents, endowments and allocations become measurable functions defined on the measure space of agents, the sum in part 1 of the definition of competitive equilibrium must be replaced by an integral, and exceptional null sets should be permitted in part 2 of the definition. If the set of commodities is not finite, then the commodity space and consumption sets should be carefully specified and endowed with more structure (for instance, a nice topology so that the commodity space becomes a well-behaved topological vector space) in an economically meaningful way; the definition of the infinite-dimensional space of prices must also be considered carefully. (For an early example of the huge literature on general equilibrium with infinitely many commodities, see Bewley, 1972). These considerations are unfortunately all beyond the scope of this chapter. Similarly, the important economic issues of public goods, externalities, uncertainty, and so forth, can be incorporated into the basic general equilibrium model, albeit perhaps at some cost in terms of either modelling assumptions or attractive results.

7.3 THE EXISTENCE OF EQUILIBRIA

Of course, just because I have defined a competitive equilibrium doesn't necessarily mean that one exists. Existence of equilibria is considered a basic consistency requirement for economic models; this is a result that must be demonstrated before an analysis of the properties of such equilibria is justified. Often, however, one encounters 'too many' rather than 'too few' equilibria; uniqueness should not be presumed. Nor should one confuse the concept of static equilibrium with any dynamic features. To say that an equilibrium exists is not to imply that it can be reached by some sensible economic process. An additional caveat is that equilibria can sometimes be so complicated ('too complex' in the sense of modern computer science, for instance) as to be impractical.

Nevertheless, despite these important qualifications, general equilibrium theory seems to be a modern success story in economics. The basic general equilibrium model and many of its important and interesting extensions have competitive equilibria; in fact, some nice classes of economies generally have only finitely many equilibria. A more technical paraphrase of this metatheorem states that if the data describing an economy are sufficiently smooth, then a generic (open and dense or residual) subset of an appropriately topologized space of such economies exhibits a finite (and odd) number of equilibria which depend smoothly on parameters in the generic set. An implication of this result is that these equilibria generally have good predictive properties; if our observations of the economy are subject to small errors, then the actual equilibria should lie quite close to the predicted ones and, similarly, economies in the small (non-generic) set on which this may fail can be approximated arbitrarily closely by economies that are well behaved in this sense. Restricted to the generic subset, the dependence on economies of the equilibrium correspondence is lower hemicontinuous. It is upper hemicontinuous everywhere.

Based on sensible microeconomic assumptions, one cannot easily obtain important restrictions on economy-wide excess demand beyond continuity or smoothness and these generic results on the number and dependence of equilibria on the underlying economic data. In fact, if preferences in an exchange economy are assumed only to be strictly convex, monotone continuous complete preorders, then if one has any function from strictly positive price vectors to the commodity space that satisfies four mild conditions, then, when restricted to any fixed set of prices bounded away from zero, the given function equals the aggregate excess demand of some pure exchange economy which can be taken to have no more consumers than commodities. Of course, this is also true for large economies. The four conditions are as follows: (i) continuity, (ii) Walras' Law, (iii) boundedness from below (that is, by $-\sum_{i=1}^{n} e_i$ if consumption sets are $\mathbb{R}_+^\ell$), and (iv) the boundary condition that along any sequence of price vectors converging to a point in the boundary of the price set (so that in the limit, the price of at least one commodity is zero), aggregate excess demands must be unbounded. The fact that aggregate excess demand is essentially unrestricted means that no reasonable microeconomic assumptions (note that homothetic preferences do not help) can lead to sharper results for general equilibrium in a pure exchange economy. Note, however, that aggregate excess demand cannot be replaced by aggregate demand in this result, nor can endowments be replaced by wealths. Moreover, one cannot necessarily find a finite pure exchange economy generating a given (continuous, for example) function as its excess demand on the entire price simplex. For a survey of this literature, see Shafer and Sonnenschein (1982).

These minimal restrictions permit a quite simple proof that a competitive equilibrium exists. Let $Z : \Delta \to \mathbb{R}^\ell$ be a continuous function which is bounded from below, satisfies Walras' Law [$p \cdot Z(p) = 0$ for all $p \in \Delta$], and satisfies the boundary condition that if $p_n \to p_0 \in \partial\Delta$, then $\|Z(p_n)\|$ is unbounded. (Note that $Z(p_0)$ need not be defined and that this assumption does not say that if a price goes to zero, then the excess demand for that commodity must become infinite.) Define a mapping $\Psi : \bar{\Delta} \to \bar{\Delta}$ by $\Psi(p) = \{\bar{q} \in \bar{\Delta} \mid \bar{q} \cdot Z(p) = \max_{q \in \Delta} q \cdot Z(p)\}$ if $p \in \Delta$ and $\Psi(p) = \{\bar{q} \in \bar{\Delta} \mid \bar{q} \cdot p = 0\}$ if $p \in \partial\Delta$. Then Ψ is a non-empty, convex-valued and upper hemicontinuous correspondence taking the non-empty compact convex subset $\bar{\Delta}$ of $\mathbb{R}^\ell$ into itself. By Kakutani's Fixed Point Theorem, Ψ has a fixed point $p^* \in \bar{\Delta}$ such that $p^* \in \Psi(p^*)$. Clearly, $p^* \notin \partial\Delta$, so that p^* maximizes the value of $Z(p^*)$. Since $0 = p^* \cdot Z(p^*) \geq p \cdot Z(p^*)$ for all $p \in \bar{\Delta}$, this means that, by an argument using Walras' Law, $Z(p^*) = 0$, so that the fixed point p^* is indeed a competitive equilibrium price vector. This sketch follows the proof that appears in the monograph by E. Dierker (1974).

7.4 THE PROPERTIES OF COMPETITIVE EQUILIBRIA

Beyond these issues of existence and multiplicity of equilibria, other standard results illustrate the attractive properties that competitive equilibria possess. The two fundamental theorems of welfare economics constitute the most classic instance. The first welfare theorem states that under very minimal assumptions, every competitive equilibrium allocation is Pareto optimal. This efficiency property means that no feasible alternative allocation can be found which makes all consumers at least as happy while making at least one person strictly happier according to the individual's own preference relations. The proof involves using prices to show that since the better allocation cannot lie in agents' budget sets (or else the traders would not have chosen the given competitive equilibrium allocation), it cannot be feasible in the aggregate. The second welfare theorem requires convexity to show that any Pareto optimal allocation can be achieved as a competitive equilibrium with a reallocation of initial endowments; its proof uses a separating hyperplane argument to find the appropriate competitive equilibrium prices.

Another early result states that every competitive equilibrium belongs to the core of the economy. (Its proof is essentially the same as that of the first welfare theorem, which can be restated to claim that the grand coalition cannot block a competitive equilibrium allocation.) The result also states that in an economy with a non-atomic continuum of traders, any core allocation is also a competitive equilibrium. Alternatively, the core shrinks as the economy grows larger and more competitive – until its limit equals the set of perfectly competitive allocations. Here the core of an economy equals the set of feasible allocations that cannot be blocked by any coalition, where to be *blocked* means that some non-empty set of traders can find an alternative allocation which is feasible for them using only their own resources and which is strictly preferred by all members of the coalition. When the core is non-empty, justifying any non-core allocation as an economic outcome is difficult. If utilities are fixed to represent preferences, then traders' utilities at core allocations equal their payoffs in the core of the game with non-transferable utility induced by the economy. A balancedness argument guarantees that the core of the game is non-empty or, alternatively, one can observe that competitive equilibrium allocations (which necessarily exist) belong to the core of the economy.

Similar asymptotic and limit results have been obtained to relate the concept of competitive equilibrium to other game-theoretic solution concepts from cooperative and non-cooperative game theory. For example, the value and the bargaining set have been examined, as have Nash–Cournot and Bertrand–Edgeworth equilibria. These convergence and equivalence results have come to be viewed as an economic standard for an acceptable strategic solution concept.

To complete this overview, I should remark that much research effort has been devoted to studying general equilibrium when the classic hypotheses fail. Competitive equilibrium has been extended, for example, to take account of the presence of uncertainty and asymmetric information, externalities, public goods, land, and incomplete markets. It has been examined with incomplete or non-transitive preferences, non-convex preferences, non-convex consumption sets (including indivisible goods), and infinitely many commodities. Of course, production can be incorporated into the economic model.

7.5   EXTENSIONS AND OPEN QUESTIONS

In the remainder of this chapter, I would like to discuss some of these extensions as well as certain classic properties in terms of current open research questions in general equilibrium theory. My comments strongly reflect my personal and perhaps idiosyncratic opinions. I do not devote equal time to all topics. Rather, I attempt to point out a number of interesting issues that deserve further research effort. In some cases, these topics are receiving or have recently received fruitful attention. Unfortunately, my treatment is less precise than I would prefer; I must deliberately give short and sketchy summaries in order to focus on a few topics about which I am most enthusiastic.

7.5.1 Oligopolistic Behaviour

What happens when economic agents do not take prices as given? Such deviations from perfectly competitive behaviour are usually attributed to firms, which are more likely to be large relative to the economy (or to the markets in which they transact) than households, although certain consumers can realistically exert market power. Oligopoly theory is often studied in a single-market context because the presence of several interrelated markets, and especially the failure of market-clearing prices to be unique, can cause additional difficulties.

In the Nash–Cournot model of quantity competition, the normalization of prices matters, players' best responses in the associated non-cooperative game need not be well defined, and the lack of a continuous (globally defined) selection from the market-clearing price correspondence can cause non-existence of oligopolistic equilibria. Even if existence is not problematic, upper hemicontinuity can fail at the limit perfectly competitive economy.

The alternative of price competition gives rise to a dilemma. Equilibrium may be insensitive to the number of agents (that is, two agents are enough for perfect competition in the classical Bertrand model, which seems intuitively implausible). Alternatively, mixed strategies must be used (which are somewhat sensitive to the demand-rationing rule, or the way in which consumers are assigned to firms). The definition of demand vectors when consumers face rationing in some commodities at various price realizations is difficult. This problem arises in the capacity-constrained Bertrand–Edgeworth model as well as for price competition with endogenous production decisions made by firms facing strictly increasing costs.

A further problem is that the results in our oligopoly models depend greatly on the precise specification of the associated non-cooperative games. Recent work has begun to develop a theory of the firm based on its internal organization and especially the possibilities and incentives for the transmission of information within the firm. For an introduction to this area, see the book by Milgrom and Roberts (1992).

7.5.2 Uncertainty and Information

Perhaps the most basic open question is how to define the appropriate economic equilibrium concept with asymmetric or endogenous information. Unfortunately, space constraints preclude discussion of this interesting and important topic.

7.5.3   Financial Markets and the Firm

In most developed market economies, production (and especially the necessary capital or fixed cost) is financed by a combination of equity (the firm sells portions of its returns, as well as control, in the form of stocks) and debt (the firm sells bonds or, effectively, takes loans from other economic agents). What is the appropriate goal for such firms? What objective function should (or do) they maximize when shareholders may have diverse tastes and different information? These questions are most interesting in the presence of uncertainty. Departures from perfect competition can interact with these issues, as well as lead to policy questions about insider information and programme trading. Seminal papers in this area include Grossman and Hart (1979), Hart (1979), Kihlstrom and Laffont (1982), and Mas-Colell (1983).

7.5.4   Endogenous Market Structure

Which markets arise? What innovations, differentiated products, and financial securities are available in markets? If an economy has both a planned sector and a market sector, what determines the assignment of particular goods and services to these groups? For instance, one suspects that perfect substitutes or extreme complements must fall into the same group. (Rationing left shoes is probably equivalent to rationing right shoes, so that they are effectively bundled.) Can one meaningfully propose a metric or topology on goods or a partial order (perhaps signifying intermediate goods in the production process) to explain what objects are traded on markets? Can this be a universal categorization, independent of history or purely political decisions? Can alternative assignments be evaluated in terms of welfare economics? Related literature includes Grodal and Vind (1992) and the huge volume of work on exogenously-given incomplete financial markets, as exemplified by Geanakoplos, Magill, Quinzii and Drèze (1990). Also see the references cited in Section 7.5.10 below and the exploration by Glomm and Lagunoff (1992) of property rights in general equilibrium models.

7.5.5   Price Formation

General equilibrium results indicate that equilibrium prices exist and that they lead to allocations exhibiting certain attractive properties. Yet we have little to say about how equilibrium prices arise. A game-theoretic attempt to answer this question in the context of a price-setting oligopoly model appears in Allen and Hellwig (1986a, 1986b).

7.5.6 Complexity Considerations

Competitive equilibrium is equivalent to a fixed point of some derived mapping. To compute or find all of these fixed points (or even one) requires much information about economic agents. The transmission of this information and its use in the requisite computations are costly (but becoming less so as data networks and computers improve). The process also demands much of individual economic agents.

7.5.7 The Structure of Equilibria

Open questions remain regarding the nature of critical economies and their equilibria. However, because these problems are quite technical, I do not attempt to discuss the specifics here.

7.5.8 Aggregation

The question whether restrictions on the distributions of agents' characteristics could lead to meaningful restrictions on aggregate relationships was initially posed by Debreu (1972). For many years thereafter, results were available on convexification by aggregation with respect to a non-atomic measure space of agents (by Liapounov's Theorem – in this case, the restriction simply consists of the lack of large agents and the result predates Debreu's suggestion by about a decade) and on the smoothing by aggregation over a suitably dispersed distribution of microeconomic characteristics (using sophisticated tools from differential topology).

The possibility of obtaining sharper results than merely that demand be a single-valued continuous or smooth function eluded investigators for many years, until Hildenbrand's (1983) seminal study. Roughly speaking, he showed that if (for almost every preference relation) the conditional income distribution has compact support and a density which is strictly positive at zero and (more importantly) everywhere non-increasing, then total demand is downward sloping. A key result of Jerison (1984) states that, for a fixed income distribution, increasing dispersion of individual Engel curves as income rises implies that aggregate demand satisfies the weak axiom of revealed preference. Hildenbrand and his collaborators have had success in testing his conclusion empirically (see Hildenbrand, 1994), despite the natural suspicion that the assumptions may not be satisfied in reality. Yet the significance of Hildenbrand's (1983) surprising result is less as a positive theorem than as an indication that strong and significant aggregation results are indeed possible.

More recently, Grandmont (1992) has shown that distributional assumptions on characteristics can suffice to guarantee that aggregate demand satisfies the weak axiom of revealed preference (or the gross substitutes property), so that competitive equilibria are unique. Individual demands are required to be homogeneous and to satisfy Walras' Law, but they need not be rationalizable as the result of a constrained maximization problem. A more important difference is that, in contrast to Hildenbrand's (1983) analysis, Grandmont (1992) permits price-dependent wealth; he examines excess demand rather than demand, so that his work falls more naturally into the basic general equilibrium framework. As he observes, the specification of an appropriate dispersion condition requires that the space of preferences be endowed with a linear structure (although the one used in earlier work (Grandmont, 1978) on intermediate preferences and voting does not suffice for this purpose). Instead, Grandmont uses Cobb–Douglas affine transformations of the commodity space.

Accordingly, write $x \geq_\alpha y$ if and only if $(e^{-\alpha_1}x_1, \ldots, e^{-\alpha_\ell}x_\ell) \geq (e^{-\alpha_1}y_1, \ldots, e^{-\alpha_\ell}y_\ell)$, where $\alpha \in \mathbb{R}^\ell$ is a parameter vector; if $u : \mathbb{R}_+^\ell \rightarrow \mathbb{R}$ represents $\geq$, then $u_\alpha(\cdot)\ \mathbb{R}_+^\ell \rightarrow \mathbb{R}$ defined by $u_\alpha(x) = u(e^{-\alpha_1}x_1, \ldots, e^{-\alpha_\ell}x_\ell)$ represents $\geq_\alpha$. The result roughly states that if the conditional density on α given each underlying parameter a (specifying a preference type and a wealth) is continuously differentiable (in a and α) and uniformly integrable with respect to α for each parameter a, then (in the presence of other technical conditions) aggregate demand is differentiable. More importantly, if the conditional densities are also sufficiently flat, then the α-transformed demands are close to Cobb-Douglas demands and their integral (with respect to a) is also well behaved in this sense. In summary, heterogeneity with respect to the Cobb-Douglas α-transform and the possibility of such a finite-dimensional representation (using the parameter a) yields downward-sloping demand. The technique is reminiscent of the smoothing by aggregation methodology developed by Dierker, Dierker, and Trockel (1984) and more recently used by H. Dierker (1989) to study the existence of non-cooperative pricing equilibria in an oligopoly model. (See also Grandmont's (1993) recent application to Cournot oligopoly.)

Before leaving this topic, I should mention the introduction of log-concavity (or, more generally, ρ-concavity) to study majority rule aggregation (Caplin and Nalebuff, 1991a) and, more to the point, to obtain oligopolistic equilibrium (Caplin and Nalebuff, 1991b, and E. Dierker, 1991).

7.5.9 Strategic Behaviour

Some recent literature at the interface of game theory and microeconomic theory takes a new approach to the fundamental issue of strategic behaviour by economic agents. Rather than merely providing analogues and extensions of classic equivalence and convergence theorems, this work focuses on different questions and therefore attempts to say much more about this important issue.

Part of this work stems from the literature on implementation, beginning with incentives considerations and, in particular, the introduction of incentive compatibility constraints. Later developments in the area have led to the study of mechanisms. Such a serious game-theoretic model has the advantages of rigorously specifying outcomes in non-equilibrium strategy configurations and of clearly delineating the effect of changes in the equilibrium concept.

Another strand of literature having this flavour is the study of strategic market games. Here, again, out-of-equilibrium situations are carefully formulated, although to date this work has emphasized Nash equilibrium. An additional concern is the nature of the trading process and whether the games analyzed are played (or could be played) in reality, although complexity is not explicitly studied.

More recent excitement centres on bridging the gap between cooperative and non-cooperative game theory, especially as applied to economics. By definition, cooperative games let players make binding agreements whereas non-cooperative games do not. Note that the explicit formation of coalitions is a separate issue and that non-cooperative games sometimes permit communication among players.

Following the Kalai, Postlewaite, and Roberts (1979) article on incentive compatible mechanisms leading to core outcomes, a series of papers has examined the (non-cooperative) bargaining foundations of cooperative solution concepts, beginning with Gul's (1989) article on the value. Lagunoff (1994), Okada (1991), and Perry and Reny (1992) have analyzed the core. The stories of Lagunoff (1994) and Okada (1991) are parallel, except that Okada (1991) takes the core with transferable utility, whereas Lagunoff (1994) models the non-transferable utility core; the sequencing of moves in the bargaining game really matters here. Finally, Hart and Mas-Colell (1996) provide a unified n-person non-cooperative bargaining foundation for cooperative game theory, obtaining weighted Shapley values in the transferable utility case, the Nash bargaining solution for the pure bargaining case, and the Maschler–Owen consistent value solution with non-transferable utility. In contrast to Gul (1989), Hart and Mas-Colell (1996) permit multilateral meetings of players. However, all of this research displays the well-known problem of bargaining theory: results are extremely sensitive to the precise specification of the game.

Zhao's (1992) hybrid solution takes a different approach to the mixing of cooperative and non-cooperative game theory. Zhao proposes a two-stage game in which one stage is cooperative and the other non-cooperative.

Yet a third approach to this topic is explicitly based on information. The key ideas here are to study games with partial commitment and to derive the class of allowable commitments from differential information considerations. For example, see Allen (1991a, 1991b, 1991c) and the references cited there for the case in which the information available to a coalition of asymmetrically informed agents is exogenously specified. This can be rendered endogenous through the use of incentive compatibility or mechanisms, so that the set of payoff vectors attainable by a coalition (in the derivation of the non-transferable utility cooperative game from an economic model) reflects either incentive compatibility constraint restrictions on underlying strategies or equilibrium outcomes of the mechanism (in which case, non-cooperative equilibria generate the cooperative game). For details, see Allen (1992a, 1992b, 1993) and Ichiishi and Idzik (1992).

Other recent themes involving strategic behaviour appear in the work of Greenberg (1990) on social standards of behaviour, Hart and Mas-Colell (1989) on potentials, and Lagunoff (1992) and Allen (1993) on endogenous mechanism selection.

7.5.10 Mixed Economies

Mathematical economists in Russia have analyzed general equilibrium models in which some goods are produced and sold in the market while others are subject to centralized planning by a government agency. The planned sector of such a mixed economy is essentially modelled as if it were subject to exogenously given price and/or quantity constraints. See the recent papers of Koshevoy (1991, 1992), Polterovich (1993), and Zak (1989).

7.6 DYNAMIC GENERAL EQUILIBRIUM THEORY

For competitive general equilibrium models with time structures, one would like to obtain existence results, welfare theorems, and a characterization of the further properties of equilibria. One begins by expanding the commodity space so that commodities are indexed by date of delivery as well as physical description and location (plus delivery event for contingent commodities under uncertainty). Goods at different dates may exhibit possibilities for intertemporal substitution or, in models with production, they may be saved and invested in future productive capacity; any level of depreciation – from perishable goods to those that never depreciate – may be allowed. Consumers' preferences may be assumed to be of particular forms, such as those representable by additively separable utilities. (See, for instance, Brown and Lewis, 1981, for a precise definition of myopic preferences.)

In intertemporal economies, several modelling issues must be faced. The choices involve finite versus infinite horizon models, discrete versus continuous time, and overlapping generations versus infinitely lived agents. These assumptions about the temporal structure sometimes greatly affect the results that one can obtain. Moreover, continuity can fail at the limit so that while certain models may seem to approximate a particular model, the qualitative nature of the conclusions need not be robust to such perturbations. A further choice concerns whether one envision time for stability analysis as real (with intermediate consumption along the time path) or artificial (with no consumption, so that one has a thought experiment). In other words, does one use a tâtonnement or non-tâtonnement process?

The next decisions to be made by a theorist addressing dynamic general equilibrium revolve around the nature of the equilibrium solution to be studied. Does one wish to require that equilibria be stationary or Markov? Should one impose complexity bounds or invoke considerations limiting the transmission of data or the computability of outcomes? If uncertainty is present, it should be modelled as a date-event tree or, more generally, an (increasing) filtration of sub-σ-fields defining the measurable events at each instant of time. Should expectations be assumed to be rational? What assumptions should be made about the learning process? The information that can be observed at each time by each economic agent must be specified, so that the conditioning operations are performed correctly in the decision-theoretic analysis.

Finally, dynamic general equilibrium theory can provide a framework for examining observed economic data; see the discussion of calibration methods by Cooley and Prescott (1994). Moreover, some policy conclusions can be drawn since many considerations (such as money, government spending, taxation, and investment) can be incorporated into these models. A good reference for these issues is the Stokey and Lucas (1989) book.

Note

1. Preparation of this paper was supported, in part, by the National Science Foundation, the Curtis Carlson Professorship in Economics at the University of Minnesota, and the Federal Reserve Bank of Minneapolis. The views expressed herein are those of the author and not necessarily those of the Federal Reserve Bank of Minneapolis or the Federal Reserve System.

References

Allen, Beth (1991a) 'Market Games with Asymmetric Information: The Value', Center for Analytic Research in Economics and the Social Sciences Working Paper no. 91-08, Department of Economics, University of Pennsylvania.

Allen, Beth (1991b) 'Market Games with Asymmetric Information and Non-transferable Utility: Representation Results and the Core', Center for Analytic Research in Economics and the Social Sciences Working Paper no. 91-09, Department of Economics, University of Pennsylvania.

Allen, Beth (1991c) 'Transferable Utility Market Games with Asymmetric Information: Representation Results and the Core', Center for Analytic Research in Economics and the Social Sciences Working Paper no. 91–16, Department of Economics, University of Pennsylvania.

Allen, Beth (1992a) 'Incentives in Market Games with Asymmetric Information: The Core', CORE Discussion Paper 9221, Center for Operations Research and Econometrics, Université Catholique de Louvain, Louvain-la-Neuve, Belgium.

Allen, Beth (1992b) 'Incentives in Market Games with Asymmetric Information: The Value', Center for Analytic Research in Economics and the Social Sciences Working Paper no. 92-11, Department of Economics, University of Pennsylvania.

Allen, Beth (1993) 'Supermechanisms', mimeo, Department of Economics, University of Minnesota.

Allen, Beth and Martin Hellwig (1986a) 'Bertrand-Edgeworth Oligopoly in Large Markets', *Review of Economic Studies*, vol. 53 (April) pp. 175–204.

Allen, Beth and Martin Hellwig (1986b) 'Price-Setting Firms and the Oligopolistic Foundations of Perfect Competition', *American Economic Review*, vol. 76 (May) pp. 387–92.

Bewley, Truman F. (1972) 'Existence of Equilibria in Economies with Infinitely Many Commodities', *Journal of Economic Theory*, vol. 4 (June) pp. 514–40.

Brown, Donald J. and Lucinda M. Lewis (1981) 'Myopic Economic Agents', *Econometrica*, vol. 49 (March) pp. 359–68.

Caplin, Andrew and Barry Nalebuff (1991a) 'Aggregation and Social Choice: A Mean Voter Theorem', *Econometrica*, vol. 59 (January) pp. 1–23.

Caplin, Andrew and Barry Nalebuff (1991b) 'Aggregation and Imperfect Competition: On the Existence of Equilibrium', *Econometrica*, vol. 59 (January) pp. 25–59.

Cooley, Thomas F. and Edward C. Prescott (1995) 'Economic Growth and Business Cycles', chapter 1 in Thomas F. Cooley (ed.), *Frontiers of Business Cycle Research* (Princeton, New Jersey: Princeton University Press) pp. 1–38.

Debreu, Gerard (1972) 'Smooth Preferences', *Econometrica*, vol. 40 (July) pp. 603–15.

Dierker, Egbert (1974) *Topological Methods in Walrasian Economics* (Berlin, Germany: Springer-Verlag).

Dierker, Egbert (1991) 'Competition for Customers', in William A. Barnett *et al.* (eds.), *Equilibrium Theory and Applications: Proceedings of the Sixth International Symposium in Economic Theory and Econometrics* (Cambridge, UK: Cambridge University Press), ch. 17, pp. 383–402.

Dierker, Egbert, Hildegard Dierker and Walter Trockel (1984) 'Price-Dispersed Preferences and C^1 Mean Demand', *Journal of Mathematical Economics*, vol. 13 (April) pp. 11–42.

Dierker, Hildegard (1989) 'Existence of Nash Equilibrium in Pure Strategies in an Oligopoly with Price Setting Firms', Discussion Paper no. 8902, University of Vienna.

Geanakoplos, J., M. Magill, M. Quinzii and J. Drèze (1990) 'Generic Inefficiency of Stock Market Equilibrium When Markets Are Incomplete', *Journal of Mathematical Economics*, vol. 19, pp. 113–51.

Glomm, Gerhard and Roger D. Lagunoff (1992) 'On the Social Stability of Coalitional Property Rights Regimes', *Social Choice and Welfare*, forthcoming.

Grandmont, Jean-Michel (1978) 'Intermediate Preferences and the Majority Rule', *Econometrica*, vol. 46 (March) pp. 317–30.

Grandmont, Jean-Michel (1992) 'Transformations of the Commodity Space, Behavioral Heterogeneity and the Aggregation Problem', *Journal of Economic Theory*, vol. 57 (June) pp. 1–35.

Grandmont, Jean-Michel (1993) 'Behavioral Heterogeneity and Cournot Oligopoly Equilibrium', CEPREMAP Discussion Paper 9305, Paris, France. Also Cowles Foundation Discussion Paper 1044, Yale University, New Haven, Connecticut.

Greenberg, Joseph (1990) *The Theory of Social Situations: An Alternative Game-Theoretic Approach* (Cambridge, UK: Cambridge University Press).

Grodal, Birgit and Karl Vind (1992) 'Equilibrium with Arbitrary Market Structure', mimeo, Department of Economics, University of Copenhagen.

Grossman, Sanford J. and Oliver D. Hart (1979) 'A Theory of Competitive Equilibrium in Stock Market Economies', *Econometrica*, vol. 47 (March) pp. 293–329.

Gul, Faruk (1989) 'Bargaining Foundations of Shapley Value', *Econometrica*, vol. 57 (January) pp. 81–95.

Hart, Oliver D. (1979) 'On Shareholder Unanimity in Large Stock Market Economies', *Econometrica*, vol. 47 (September) pp. 1057–83.

Hart, Sergiu and Andreu Mas-Colell (1989) 'Potential, Value, and Consistency', *Econometrica*, vol. 57 (May) pp. 589–614.

Hart, Sergiu and Andreu Mas-Colell (1996) 'Bargaining and Value', *Econometrica*, vol. 64, pp. 357–380.

Hildenbrand, Werner (1983) 'On the "Law of Demand"', *Econometrica*, vol. 51 (July) pp. 997–1019.

Hildenbrand, Werner (1994) *Market Demand: Theory and Empirical Evidence* (Princeton, New Jersey: Princeton University Press).

Ichiishi, Tatsuro and Adam Idzik (1992) 'Bayesian Cooperative Choice of Strategies', Department of Economics Working Paper 92–6, Ohio State University.

Jerison, Michael (1984) 'Aggregation and Pairwise Aggregation of Demand When the Distribution of Income Is Fixed', *Journal of Economic Theory*, vol. 33 (June) pp. 1–31.

Kalai, Ehud, Andrew Postlewaite and John Roberts (1979) 'A Group Incentive Compatible Mechanism Yielding Core Allocations', *Journal of Economic Theory*, vol. 20 (February) pp. 13–22.

Kihlstrom, Richard E. and Jean-Jacques Laffont (1982) 'A Competitive Entrepreneurial Model of a Stock Market', in John J. McCall (ed.), *The Economics of Information and Uncertainty* (Chicago: University of Chicago Press/ National Bureau of Economic Research).

Koshevoy, Gleb A. (1991) 'An Equilibrium Analysis of Mixed Economies', mimeo, CEMI, Russian Academy of Sciences, Moscow.

Koshevoy, Gleb A. (1992) 'Mixed Economies with Two Currencies', mimeo, CEMI, Russian Academy of Sciences, Moscow.

Lagunoff, Roger (1992) 'Fully Endogenous Mechanism Selection on Finite Outcome Sets', *Economic Theory*, vol. 2 (October) pp. 465–80.

Lagunoff, Roger D. (1994) 'A Simple Noncooperative Core Story', *Games and Economic Behavior*, vol. 7, pp. 54–61.

Mas-Colell, Andreu (1983) 'The Profit Motive in the Theory of Monopolistic Competition', mimeo, Department of Economics, Harvard University.

Milgrom, Paul R. and John Roberts (1992) *Economics, Organization and Management* (Englewood Cliffs, New Jersey: Prentice Hall).

Okada, Akira (1991) 'Noncooperative Bargaining and the Core of an n-Person Characteristic Function Game', Kyoto Institute of Economic Research Discussion Paper no. 336, University of Kyoto.

Perry, Motty and Philip J. Reny (1992) 'A Non-Cooperative View of Coalition Formation and the Core', Department of Economics Research Report 9203, University of Western Ontario.

Polterovich, Victor (1993) 'Rationing, Queues, and Black Markets', *Econometrica*, vol. 61 (January) pp. 1–28.

Shafer, Wayne and Hugo Sonnenschein (1982) 'Market Demand and Excess Demand Functions', in Kenneth J. Arrow and Michael D. Intriligator (eds.), *Handbook of Mathematical Economics*, Volume II (Amsterdam: North-Holland), pp. 671–93.

Stokey, Nancy L. and Robert E. Lucas, Jr., with Edward C. Prescott (1989) *Recursive Methods in Economic Dynamics* (Cambridge, Massachusetts: Harvard University Press).

Zak, F.L. (1989) 'Rationing and Market: The Structure and Stability of Equilibria in Makarov's Model', mimeo, CEMI, Russian Academy of Sciences, Moscow.

Zhao, Jingang (1992) 'The Hybrid Solutions of an N-Person Game', *Games and Economic Behavior*, vol. 4 (January) pp. 145–60.

8 The Determinacy of Equilibria 25 Years Later[1]

Andreu Mas-Colell
HARVARD UNIVERSITY

8.1 INTRODUCTION

The paper by G. Debreu, 'Economies with a Finite Set of Equilibria', appeared in *Econometrica* in 1970. As is commonly known, the paper has had since then a great impact on the style and the substance of economic theorizing. If I had been more energetic I would have verified this impact in the Index of Citations. Yet, whatever the latter says, it is bound to be a considerable underestimate of the impact. Often, the sign of the success of a paper is its being referred to only implicitly, without authors even being aware of the fact. In our case, for example, any user of the term 'generic' is indebted to Debreu's paper. At any rate, the research directly inspired by the paper is enormous. By now it includes, at least, two full-length systematic books (Balasko, 1988, and Mas-Colell, 1985).

As a personal note, I would like to add that the paper appeared at a time where it could mark a young researcher like myself most decisively. And it did. As a young mathematical economist in Minnesota I saw that gold had been discovered in California and I did not hesitate to join the rush (where I encountered not only Debreu but also Stephen Smale.)

I would say that the contributions of the 1970 paper were three, the first two of a methodological character and the last substantive:

(1) The paper shaped the basic conceptual apparatus for the analysis of the *determinacy* of equilibrium. To start with, it reinvigorated the traditional desideratum that the equilibrium of an economic model be determinate. But, more important, it gave a precise mathematical expression to the notion of a determinate equilibrium: local uniqueness and robustness (i.e. persistency). It also formulated the quest for determinacy as the desideratum that the property hold not for every but for 'almost every' economy. That is, exceptions are allowed in

182

rare cases which, by definition and common sense, we think of as pathological. This leads to the notion of a *generic* property, now of standard use in economics.

(2) The paper also proposed that differential topology, in general, and transversality theory, in particular, were the appropriate mathematical tools for the study of the determinacy problem. In spite of the nature of this contribution being more technical, it should be added that these techniques had all the right resonances for economists. Indeed, they can be viewed as the modern version of the counting equations and unknowns, a procedure most familiar to the economist of yore.

(3) Finally, the substantive contribution of the paper was the claim, and the proof, that the classical Walrasian model of the general equilibrium is generically determinate.

In the following pages I limit myself to presenting a few remarks on the two methodological aspects. On the substantive aspect I would say, however, that much as the theory has been clarified and extended (and the frontiers of its validity – narrower than it was first suspected – drawn), I do not believe we have got to the bottom of the matter. I think, for example, that we do not yet understand in a very deep way the contrast, as it concerns the determinacy property, between classical Walrasian theory and game theory.

Let me also note that although I am classifying the methodological innovations of Debreu's paper into two, the reality is that in that paper, as well as in the areas of mathematics that influenced it, the two aspects are intimately connected. So the current exercise definitely belongs to the conceptual splitting variety.

8.2 ON THE CONCEPT OF DETERMINACY

The new framework for the analysis of the determinacy problem has much enriched our box of tools; yet its practical use has revealed some conceptual puzzles. I comment on three of these.

The first has to do with the information content of the term 'local uniqueness'. For an economic model imbedded, mathematically speaking, in a finite dimensional world, and under natural compactness hypotheses, the notions of 'local uniqueness' and of 'finiteness of the number of equilibria' coincide. But in infinite dimensional models (and these have a significant presence in economics), this is typically not so. The question arises: which desideratum should we then privilege, local uniqueness or finiteness?. Intuitively speaking, the first seems more fundamental because it is at the base of comparative static analysis. But there is a problem: the notion of local uniqueness is topological and therefore it depends on the choice of topology. Thus, in an equilibrium model with infinitely many commodities it may depend on the topology on prices. Different natural choices may give different conclusions. Clearly, additional thinking is needed on what we should mean by local uniqueness in these situations and how the appropriate notion is connected with, or emerges from, the comparative-statics analytical needs. At any rate, as long as we are in a finite dimensional context the problem does not arise: there is a standard topology and the finiteness of the number of equilibria implies its local uniqueness.

The second comment has to do, also, with informational content. Suppose that we have the finiteness of the number of equilibria and its local uniqueness. We should still ask: how finite is finite?, or, how local is the local uniqueness? It is, obviously, not the same to have a few equilibria (say 3 or 5) as to have a few thousands. In fact, in the latter case a result on finiteness may be misleading: a great density of equilibria may be better modelled by a continuum than by the notion of a finite set. The conceptualization as a continuum, for example, opens the door to refinement since it allows one to distinguish sizes of continua by means of dimension.

The above is not an abstract issue. It arises in economics. The simplest example (which is trivial but not degenerated) may well be the following. Consider an economy with a number n of states of the world but no insurance possibilities whatsoever (i.e. there are no financial instruments allowing the transfer of wealth across states). For every state of the world the spot markets of these economies have three equilibria. Then, every assignment of spot equilibrium prices to states is an overall equilibrium price vector. The number of such vectors is 3^n, which is a large number if n is not very small! See Mas-Colell (1991) for further elaboration.

My third remark concerns the possibility of a conflict between the desiderata of local uniqueness/finiteness and of robustness, that is, of persistency under small perturbations of parameters.

The robustness desideratum is the expression of a judgment not to take seriously a theory in which predictions are fragile and may change drastically with small misspecifications of the model. However, situations have been encountered (not so much in equilibrium theory as in game theoretical models) where a given theory yields no locally unique equilibrium predictions (not even generically), yet the equilibrium set is robust, at least in the weak sense of upper hemicontinuity (and even generically). The research drive for predictibility as local uniqueness points then towards refinements programmes, that is, to bringing in new equilibrium considerations so as to size down the equilibrium set. We can often do so, but typically we lose along the way any sort of robustness we may have had. We succeed in predicting perhaps even a unique equilibrium, but at the cost that a perturbation of the basic data can easily make it vanish. A researcher committed to the robustness desideratum would then ask if it may not be more honest to predict the occurrence of a large set, but at least a persistent one. Wouldn't this be more convincing than the spurious, fragile precision accomplished by the refinement programme?.

I cannot offer an answer to this conflict, but there is a clear lesson from the discussion: If you are swayed by the judgement underlying the robustness desideratum then you should give up the logic of refinements. If local uniqueness is of the essence of what you are after, then you should give at least a thought to the possibility that the theory needs complete reconstruction from the bottom up.

8.3 ON THE USE OF TRANSVERSALITY METHODS

Thanks to Debreu's 1970 contribution, smoothness becomes once again an acceptable, even respectable, hypothesis in economics. Also, the Implicit Function Theorem and Sard's Theorem (the key technical tools of transversality theory) have become familiar instruments for economic theorists (the second, Sard's theorem, was completely absent from economics before that date).

I will make three comments on these technical aspects. Only the last has any significance.

(1) It is not easy to comprehend, from today's perspective, why differentiability methods became so unpopular in the period that spans from 1950 to 1970. In fact, we still have some remnants of this and one can ocasionally encounter resistance to smoothness hypotheses, or perhaps simply a lingering judgement that an environment of smoothness hypotheses carries with it a whole different order of restrictiveness than, say, an environment of continuous, or of Lipschitz, hypotheses. Yet the research on determinacy (local uniqueness, etc) shows, in my view very persuasively, that this is misguided. With smoothness hypotheses a simple and elegant theory emerges. Without them it is very difficult to prove anything. It is hard to resist the conclusion that from

the vantage of theory a differentiable world (properly interpreted for every model at hand: it may sometimes mean piecewise differentiable) is the world that fits the problem.

(2) In today's theoretical research the appeal to Sard's theorem has become routinized. But it is still technique-intensive. Establishing genericity results is usually hard work, sometimes very hard work. Yet, often, but not always, the result is quite predictable. One soon develops a feel for what is and what is not generic. But, of course, a 'feel' is not the same thing as a metatheorem. It would be nice indeed if there could be a shortcut!

(3) Finally, I will conclude with a historical curiosity or paradox. Debreu introduced into economics the methods of transversality theory, in general, and Sard's Theorem in particular, so as to establish that, generically, Walrasian equilibria are locally unique. However, the use of Sard's theorem is not required for this purpose. Since this is not widely known I would like to offer some explanation.[2]

Consider an exchange economy with L commodities and I consumers. We assume that each consumer has a utility function $u_i: \mathbb{R}^L_{++} \to \mathbb{R}_+$ which is smooth, strictly quasiconcave, strictly increasing, has no critical point, has all sets of the form $u_i^{-1}([\alpha, \infty))$ closed relative to $\mathbb{R}^L$, and gives rise to a differentiable demand function $\varphi_i(p, w_i)$. The description of an economy is completed by a vector $\omega = (\omega_{11}, \ldots, \omega_{L1}, \ldots, \omega_{1I} \ldots, \omega_{LI}) \in \mathbb{R}^{LI}_{++}$ of initial endowments for the different consumers. In what follows, utility functions are kept fixed and possible economies are indexed by ω. For every ω we then have an aggregate excess demand function $f(p; \omega) = \sum_{i=1}^{i=I} [\varphi_i(p, p \cdot \omega_i) - \omega_i]$; note for later reference that this function is well defined even if some components of initial endowments are negative; what is required is that $p \gg 0$ and $p \cdot \omega_i > 0$ for every i.

The economy represented by ω (from now on we will just say 'the economy ω') is called *regular* if every price equilibrium of this economy is regular, that is, if whenever $f(p; \omega) = 0$ we have that rank $D_p f(p; \omega) = L - 1$. By the Implicit Function theorem every regular equilibrium is locally isolated. A price equilibrium which is not regular is called *critical*. An economy which is not regular (that is, having at least one critical equilibrium) is called *critical*. We then have:

Theorem (Debreu, 1970):   The set of critical economies $C \subset \mathbb{R}^{LI}_{++}$ is null (i.e. it has LI-dimensional Lebesgue measure zero).

Proof: Note that it suffices to show that for every vector of total endowments $\bar{\omega} \in \mathbb{R}_{++}^L$ the set of critical economies $C_{\bar{\omega}} = \{\omega \in C \cap \mathbb{R}_{++}^{LI} : \sum_{i=1}^{i=I} \omega_i = \bar{\omega}\}$ is null in the $L(I\text{-}1)$ dimensional set $E = \{\omega \in \mathbb{R}_{++}^{LI} : \sum_{i=1}^{i=I} \omega_i = \bar{\omega}\}$, that is, it has $L(I\text{-}1)$ Lebesgue measure zero. Therefore from now on we fix the total endowments $\bar{\omega} \in \mathbb{R}_{++}^L$. The proof proceeds then in two steps. In the first, we construct a more convenient parameterization of the space of economies. In the second, the proof is established by means of an argument relying on polynomial functions. There is no appeal to Sard's Theorem.

Step 1

Denote then by U' the relative interior of the Pareto frontier in utility space, that is, $U' = \{ u \in \mathbb{R}_{++}^I : u = (u_1(x_1), \ldots, u_1(x_1))$ where $(x_1, \ldots, x_I)$ is some Pareto optimal allocation of the total endowments $\bar{\omega} \}$. It is well known that under the stated conditions on utility functions and total endowments, U' is a differentiable manifold of dimension $I-1$ (e.g. Mas-Colell, 1985, ch. 5). Normalizing by $p_L = 1$, to every $u \in U'$ we can associate a unique vector of supporting prices $p(u) \in \mathbb{R}_{++}^L$ and a unique Pareto optimal allocation $x(u) \in \mathbb{R}^{LI}$. Denote also $w_i(u) = p(u) \cdot x_i(u) > 0$. The maps $p(\cdot), x(\cdot)$, and $w_i(\cdot)$ are smooth.

Let ω' stand for a $(L-1)(I-1)$ vector of initial endowments which excludes the last good and the last consumer. The set of such vectors is $E' = \{\omega' \in \mathbb{R}_{++}^{(L-1)(I-1)} : \sum_{i=1}^{i=I} \omega'_{\ell i} < \bar{\omega}_\ell$ for $\ell = 1, \ldots, L-1\}$.

For every pair $(u, \omega') \in U' \times E'$ denote then by $\omega(u, \omega') \in \mathbb{R}^{LI}$ the vector where $\omega_{\ell i}(u, \omega') = \omega'_{\ell i}$ for $\ell < L$ and $i < I$, $\omega_{\ell I}(u, \omega') = \bar{\omega}_\ell - \sum_{i=1}^{i=L-1} \omega_{\ell i}$ for $\ell < L$, and $p(u) \cdot \omega_i(u, \omega') = w_i(u) > 0$ for every i. In words: for every consumer i the endowment $\omega_{Li}(u, \omega')$ of the last good is determined so that at the Pareto prices associated with u, $p(u)$, the consumer attains the corresponding level of wealth $w_i(u)$. The map $\omega(\cdot)$ is smooth.

Note that the dimensions of $U' \times E'$ is $I-1 + (L-1)(I-1) = L(I-1)$ and define:

$$C^* = \{(u, \omega') \in U' \times E' : \text{rank } D_p f(p(u); \omega(u, \omega')) < L - 1\}.$$

In Step 2 we show that $C^* \subset U' \times E'$ is null, that is, it has $L(I-1)$ Lebesgue measure zero. Let us assume for the moment that this is true.

We claim that $C_{\bar{\omega}} \subset \omega(C^*)$. Indeed, suppose that $f(p; \omega) = 0$, $\omega_{\ell i} > 0$ for every ℓ and i, and $\sum_{i=1}^{i=I} \omega_i = \bar{\omega}$. Then by the first welfare theorem if we let $u_i = u_i(\varphi^i(p, p \cdot \omega_i))$, for every i, and $\omega'_{\ell i} = \omega_{\ell i}$ for $\ell <$

$L-1$ and $i < I-1$, we have that $u = (u_1, \ldots, u_I) \in U'$, $\omega' = (\omega'_{11}, \ldots$
$\omega'_{L-1,1}, \ldots, \omega'_{1,I-1}, \ldots, \omega'_{L-1,I-1}) \in E'$, $\omega = \omega(u, \omega')$, and $p = p(u)$. Thus,
$D_p f(p; \omega) = D_p f(p(u); \omega(u, \omega'))$ and, therefore, if rank $Df(p; \omega) < L-1$
(which necessarily occurs for some p if $\omega \in C_{\bar{\omega}}$) it follows that rank
$D_p f(p(u); \omega(u, \omega')) < L - 1$ and so, that $(u, \omega') \in C^*$ and $\omega = \omega(u, \omega')$.
Hence $C_{\bar{\omega}} \subset \omega(C^*)$, as claimed.

Because $\omega(\cdot)$ is differentiable the $L(I-1)$ Lebesgue measure of
$\omega(C^*) \cap E$, hence of $C_{\bar{\omega}}$, must be zero.

Step 2

We now show that for every $u \in U'$ the set $C_u^* = \{\omega' : (u, \omega') \in C^*\}$
$\subset \mathbb{R}^{(L-1)(I-1)}$ is null, i.e. has $(L-1)(I-1)$ Lebesgue measure zero. Because dim $U' = I-1$, Fubini's Theorem implies that C^* has $L(I-1)$
Lebesgue measure zero, the desired conclusion.

From now on we fix a value of $u \in U'$. Define then a function g:
$\mathbb{R}^{(L-1)(I-1)} \rightarrow \mathbb{R}$ by letting $g(\omega')$ equal the the value of the determinant of the $L - 1 \times L - 1$ northwest submatrix of $D_p f(p(u); \omega(u, \omega'))$.
Of course, $C_u^* \subset g^{-1}(0)$. We shall show that $g^{-1}(0)$ is null.

Denote $p = p(u)$, $x_i = x_i(u)$, $w_i = w_i(u)$. Let also $x_i' = (x_{1i}, \ldots, x_{L-1,i})$
and $x' = (x_1', \ldots, x_I')$. Then for any $\omega' \in \mathbb{R}_{++}^{(L-1)(I-1)}$ and $\ell < L$ we
have

$$f_\ell(p(u), \omega(u, \omega')) = \sum_{i=1}^{i=I} [\varphi_{\ell i}(p, w_i) - \omega'_{\ell i}]$$

and so,

$$g(\omega') = \det [\sum_{i=1}^{i=I} (S_i(p, w_i) - (x_i' - \omega_i')^T c_i(p, w_i))]$$

where the $S_i(p, w_i)$ are $L-1 \times L-1$ substitution matrices, and the $c_i(p, w_i)$
are $L-1$ row vectors of wealth terms.

Observe that in the above expression neither the $S_i(p, w_i)$ matrices
nor the $c_i(p, w_i)$ vectors depend on ω'. Thus the expression tells us
that $g(\cdot)$ is a polynomial formula in ω'. Moreover, this polynomial is
not identically equal to zero. Indeed, $g(x') = \det [\sum_{i=1}^{i=I} S_i(p, w_i)] \neq 0$,
because the matrix $\sum_{i=1}^{i=I} S_i(p, w_i)$ is negative definite (in words: when
$\omega_i' = x_i'$ for every i there are no wealth effects terms and the substitution
terms aggregate nicely). But for a polynomial that is not identically
zero it is always true that $g^{-1}(0)$ is null. Hence, the conclusion. Q.E.D

To conclude, I will say that it is actually very good that Debreu did not proceed in the above manner. It is 'too clever'. It uses more of the economic structure than needed. If something is true for very general, almost purely mathematical, reasons then one should know that this is so. If, in addition, this becomes known to us by means of the use of a new and far-reaching technique, then it is not hard to conclude that by 'being clever' we would in fact be missing something and ending up poorer.

Notes

1. This is a lecture that I delivered at the University of Bonn on 4 July 1991 on the occasion of the seventieth anniversary of G. Debreu (the celebration was organized by W. Hildenbrand). Its content has a substantial overlap with the comments I delivered in Moscow at the Congress of the IAE.
2. The point to be made has also been made in the same way by Balasko (1992). Our research on this topic has been independent. I have arrived at this proof by the exploitation of a key polynomial trick in a manner similar to the one presented in Mas-Colell (1988) (in these lectures I appealed to the 'polynomial trick' used here to show that generically economies have a regular equilibrium). For a previous usage of the polynomial trick, see Mas-Colell (1973).

References

Balasko, Y. (1988) *Foundations of the Theory of General Equilibrium* (New York: Academic press).

Balasko, Y. (1992) 'The Set of Regular Equilibria', *Journal of Economic Theory*, vol. 58, no. 1, pp. 1–8.

Debreu, G (1970) 'Economies with a Finite Set of Equilibria', *Econometrica*, vol. 38, no. 3, pp. 387–92.

Mas-Colell, A (1973) 'Three Notes on Equilibrium Prices and the Equilibrium Price Correspondence in Pure Exchange Economies', Working Paper IP-182, May 1973, Center for Research in Management Science, University of California, Berkeley.

Mas-Colell, A (1985) *The Theory of General Economic Equilibrium: a Differentiable Approach* (New York: Cambridge University Press).

Mas-Colell, A (1988) 'Four Lectures on the Differentiable Approach to General Equilibrium Theory', in A.Ambrosetti, F.Gori and R.Lucchetti (eds), *Mathematical Economics*, Lecture Notes in Mathematics 1330 (New York: Springer-Verlag) pp. 19–43.

Mas-Colell, A (1991) 'Indeterminacy in Incomplete Market Economies', *Economic Theory*, vol. 1, no. 1, pp. 45–62.

9 On the Value of Information[1]

Christos H. Papadimitriou

UNIVERSITY OF CALIFORNIA, BERKELEY

9.1 INTRODUCTION

The student of economic theory and the theory of computation will find a surprising extent of common ground (despite the obvious differences in context, scope, emphasis, and style). For example, the study of massively parallel computation deals with the interaction of a large number of independent agents (Karp and Ramachandran, 1991), certainly an environment familiar in economic theory. In game theory, it has been useful to introduce concepts of computational complexity, sometimes as a means of capturing bounded rationality. (Ben-Porath, 1987; Neyman, 1985; Papadimitriou, 1992). In complexity theory, on the other hand, games and their complexity have been a most central paradigm (Chandra, Kozen and Stockmeyer, 1981).

This chapter deals with the following parallel between the two fields: capturing the economic value of information is a question of current interest in economic theory (Arrow, 1984) and cases in which differences in information result in tangible economic effect are sought and studied. In computer science, on the other hand, there is a very common and much-studied area in which lack of information results in performance degradation: distributed computation. For example, the amount of information exchange needed to carry out computational tasks in a distributed fashion has been studied extensively (Papadimitriou and Sipser, 1984). But it is in distributed decision-making where the effect is most pronounced. In this chapter I survey some recent results concerning distributed decision-making, in which the effect of information and communication is very tangible and significant.

9.2 DISTRIBUTED SCHEDULING

In Papadimitriou and Yannakakis (1991) the following simple problem of distributed scheduling was studied. There are three cooperating agents (common payoffs), and agent i knows the length of a task. Denoted by x_i; the x_i's are reals uniformly distributed in [0,1]. There are only two processors on which to execute the tasks.

A strategy for each player[2] is a mapping $f_i:[0,1] \mapsto \{1,2\}$, deciding for each value of the length x_i which of the two processors to schedule it. The common payoff for strategies (f_1, f_2, f_3), when the lengths are x_1, x_2, x_3, is

$$c(x_1, x_2, x_3; f_1(x_1), f_2(x_2), f_3(x_3)) = \text{prob}[\sum_{f_i(x_i)=j} x_i \leq 1, j = 1, 2]$$

That is, the agents win if no processor has tasks adding to more than one, and they lose otherwise. The payoff of the triple of strategies (f_1, f_2, f_3) is defined as $\hat{c}(f_1, f_2, f_3) = \mathcal{E}_{x_i} [c(x_1, x_2, x_3; f_1(x_1), f_2(x_2), f_3(x_3))]$.

In other words, each agent sees a value in [0,1] for the length x_i of the corresponding task, and chooses a processor; agent i has no information about $x_j, j \neq i$. The agents win if both processors can finish all tasks within the deadline of 1. The common payoff is the expected (over all task length combinations) of the probability of winning. What is the combination of strategies that maximizes $\hat{c}$?

Despite its simple statement, this seems to be a hard analytical problem. The obvious conjecture, namely that the optimum strategy is $f_1(x_1) = 1, f_2(x_2) = 1, f_3(x_3) = 2$, with $\hat{c} = .5$, turns out to be false (a counterexample is given below in Theorem 1.) The following is a perfectly credible conjecture, which is known to hold in all variants of the problem studied next:

The Simple Strategy Hypothesis There are optimum strategies that are simple, that is, all three f_i's are of the form

$$f_i(x_i) = \begin{cases} j_i, & \text{if } x_i \leq b_i, \\ 3 - j_i, & \text{otherwise} \end{cases}$$

for some appropriate bounds b_i, and choice of processor j_i.

Theorem 1 Under the Simple Strategy Hypothesis, the following is an optimum simple strategy; For all i, processor $j_i = 1$ and bound, $b_i = 1 - \frac{1}{\sqrt{7}}$. The outcome is $\frac{1}{6} + \frac{1}{\sqrt{7}} > 0.5$.

But studying this problem is only the beginning of an interesting story. Suppose now that the agents have more information than before. We may consider the situation in which agent i knows, besides x_i, one or both of the other x_j's. Let agent x_i know the values of all variables in set X_i, where we assume that $x_i \in X_i$. The quantity to be optimized now is

$$\hat{c}(f_1, f_2, f_3) = \varepsilon_{x_i}[c(x_1, x_2, x_3; f_1(X_1), f_2(X_2), f_3(X_3))].$$

The sets X_i can be captured as a directed graph with three nodes, like the ones shown in Figure 9.1. An arc from node i to node $j \neq i$ means that $x_i \in X_j$. We assume that always $i \in X_i$, and so we omit self-loops from our graphs. The directed graph can be thought of as the communication network that has to be in place for the information implied by the X_i's to be available. Notice that there is no assumption of transitivity here: that i knows x_j and j knows x_k does not necessarily imply that i knows x_k. We still want to find the strategies $f_i: [0,1]^{k_i} \mapsto \{1,2\}$ (where $k_i = |X_i|$) that maximizes $\hat{c}$. We have thus sixteen different problems, one for each of the sixteen possible non-isomorphic graphs with three nodes. Of these, we show eight in Figure 9.1, with the associated optimum payoffs. The remaining eight networks have one of the two networks on the bottom as a sub-network, and thus they have payoff 0.75 (the best possible):

Theorem 2 The optimum payoffs for all communication networks are as shown in Figure 9.1 (except possibly for the empty one at the top, whose optimal payoff is subject to the Simple Strategy Hypothesis).

Thus, we have understood the optimum strategies in all information regimes except for the simplest one! Before proceeding to an analysis of this result from the point of view of the economics of information, perhaps a commentary on the proof of Theorem 2 is in order. The network with only two arcs emanating from node 1 (second level from the top) has the following optimum strategy: Agent 1 always goes to processor 1 (it is easy to see that this is no loss of generality; if 1 moves around, he only confuses the other agents). The crucial observation is that, at optimality, agent 2 always goes to 2 (this takes some proving). Thus the optimum strategy for agent 3 is to go to processor 1, if $x_1 + x_3 \leq 1$ (remember, agent 3 knows x_3 and x_1), otherwise to go to processor 2 – hoping that $x_2 + x_3 \leq 1$. The payoff is $\frac{2}{3}$. But notice that the optimum strategy does not use the fact that x_2 knows

x_1. Therefore, it is the optimum strategy for the network with only one arc (same level)!

The hardest case is the one where one agent knows everything, and the other two have only their own information. This degenerates into a game between the two agents, since the first agent is known to play optimally and possess all information. Optimizing the strategies in this game turns out to be a hard exercise in nonlinear optimization (see Papadimitriou and Yannakakis, 1991, for more details). The optimum turns out to be $\frac{37}{54} > \frac{2}{3}$.

At the bottom of Figure 9.1 we have the network with two opposing arcs: the two agents achieve common knowledge about their mutual values, although they still do not know the length of the third task. But this knowledge turns out to be unnecessary: by symmetry we can assume that the third task goes to processor 1; the two agents with common knowledge go both to 2 if their sum is one or less; otherwise the smaller one goes to 1 and the larger to 2. It is hard to argue that they could have done better even if they had known the third length.

Figure 9.1 is conducive to speculation concerning the optimum way to distribute information in a distributed decision-making environment. Naturally, there is nothing clever that can be done about the first arc: wherever it is placed it has, by symmetry, the same effect. The effect of the second arc varies from case to case in a way that is as dramatic as it is instructive. Placing it in a way opposing to the first one, thus achieving common knowledge, is the best. Failing this, the next best thing is to place the second arc so that it forms a path of length two with the first one. This is rather surprising, since there is no easy physical interpretation of what is gained this way. Next, if the second arc is directed towards the same agent as the first, then global knowledge is achieved by one agent, and apparently this has advantages. Placing the second arc out of the same agent as the first adds nothing. One should always remember that these graphs and results pertain only to the simple scheduling problem being studied, and such conclusions as are in this paragraph have no more general scope.

We see next an interesting variant on this scheduling problem, analyzed by a very different technique.

9.3 THE REGRET RATIO

Research in the theory of computation is known to be prone and responsive to fashion and trend. A vastly popular theme of research in

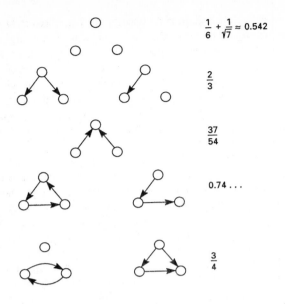

Figure 9.1 Communication networks and optimum payoffs

recent years has been that of regret analysis of algorithms under incomplete information. The general setting is attractively simple (and I
think in a way that an economist would appreciate).

We must make decisions under incomplete information. At each time
we have to make a decision y without knowing everything about the
world x. The cost incurred by decision y on world x is $c(x,y)$. We only
know a set W of possible worlds, and x could be any one of them.
How does one evaluate the quality of the decisions made? Traditionally, one should resort to some prior distribution for x, and adopt the
expectation $\varepsilon_x[c(x,y)|x \in W]$ as our measure. From the point of view
of the theory of computation and the kinds of problems it deals with,
this has several disadvantages. First, prior distributions are unknown
or hard to defend. More important, the expectation measure is not appropriate for most computational applications. When your software does
not work, it is little consolation that your data are only a statistically
insignificant exception. Many repeated runs on random data are not
the norm, and certain applications are subject to hard deadlines. Obviously, some kind of worst-case analysis is called for.

But what kind of worst-case analysis can we apply to this general
formulation of decision-making under uncertainty? Suppose that we

knew the world x. Then there is an optimal decision, call it $\hat{y}(x)$. However, in the absence of complete information about x, our algorithm A arrives at the imperfect decision $y_A(W)$. The worst-case ratio

$$\max_{x \in W} \frac{c(x, y_A(W))}{c(x, \hat{y}(x))} \tag{9.1}$$

is called the regret ratio of our algorithm.[3] Thus, we seek the algorithm A which minimizes the ratio in (9.1).

As I mentioned above, this is a tremendously popular topic among theoretical computer scientists. The first application of this approach was to problems in memory management (Sleator and Tarjan, 1985), and was followed by applications to other resource allocation problems (see Borodin, Irani, Raghavan and Schieber, 1991; Borodin, Linial and Saks, 1987; Copersmith, Doyle, Raghavan and Smir, 1990; Fiat, Rabani and Ravid, 1990; Grove, 1991; Karlin, Manasse, Rodolf and Sleator, 1993; Manasse, McGeoch and Sleator, 1987; Raghavan and Snir, 1989). The common denominator of these problems is the following. Requests must be serviced, and we must respond to requests without knowing future requests. But the precise way in which we respond (e.g., which server we send where) may affect tremendously the cost of servicing future requests. We seek an algorithm that will not fare too badly, when compared with an omniscient algorithm that knows all future requests. One of the good things to come out of this line of research is an apparently very deep mathematical problem, the k-Server Conjecture (see Fiat, Rabani and Ravid, 1990, for the latest on it).[4]

Another common theme is exploration (see Papadimitriou and Yannakakis, 1989; Baeza-Yates, Culbertson and Rawlins, 1993; Blum, Raghavan and Schieber, 1991; Deng, Kameda and Papadimitriou, 1991; Deng and Papadimitriou, 1991; Fiat, Foster, Karloff, Rabani, Ravid and Vishwanathan, 1991; Fiat, Rabani and Ravid, 1990; Klein, 1991). An unknown terrain must be explored or traversed in a way that is not too wasteful; and this kind of problem has the added attractive feature that information can be extracted by exploring interesting parts of the terrain. In fact, researchers working on these two problem areas (resource allocation and exploration) arrived at the regret ratio approach independently. There has also been regret ratio analysis of graph optimization problems. (Irani, 1990; Lovasz, Saks and Trotter; Vishwanathan, 1990) and of processor scheduling (Baruch, Koren, Mishta, Raghunathan, Rosier and Shasha, 1991; Feldman, Sgall and Teng, 1991; Schmoys, Wein and Williamson, 1991).

The game-theoretic nature of the problem has probably not escaped the astute reader. The algorithm plays a game against an adversary, who tries to embarrass the algorithm. The game-theoretic connection has been most helpful in this area. For example, it has been instrumental in understanding the power and limitations of randomization in on-line algorithms (Ben-David, Borodin, Karp, Tardos and Wigderson, 1990). Also, the complexity of finding the optimum regret ratio is best understood again via the associated game (Papadimitriou and Yannakakis, 1989).

The area that covers the regret analysis of algorithms usually goes by the name 'on-line algorithms'. The reason is that the missing information is always the future, and the algorithm must make decisions 'on-line', with no knowledge of the future. In a recent paper (Deng and Papadimitriou, 1992) we broke with this tradition, and used regret analysis to study problems in which the missing information is due to the distributed nature of the decision-making process.

One of the problems that we studied is a variant of the two-processor, three-agent scheduling problem of Papadimitriou and Yannakakis (1991) discussed in Section 9.2 above. We assume that the ith agent knows the lengths in X_i where $x_i, \in X_i$. This time we do not need to restrict the x_i's at all (except by non-negativity), and so no explicit deadline is given. Instead our cost is the makespan

$$c(x_1, x_2, x_3; f_1(X_1), f_2(X_2), f_3(X_3)) = \max\{\sum_{f(X_i)=1} x_i, \sum_{f(X_i)=2} x_i\}$$

We wish to find the f_i's which minimize the maximum ratio

$$\max_{x_1, x_2, x_3} \frac{c(x_1, x_2, x_3; f_1(X_1), f_2(X_2), f_3(X_3))}{\hat{c}(x_1, x_2, x_3)}$$

(compare with (9.1)). Here $\hat{c}(x_1, x_2, x_3)$ is the optimum complete-information cost: either the longest task, or the sum of the two shortest ones, whichever is bigger. It is easy to see that this ratio will be somewhere between 1 and 2; we wish to make it as small as possible.

Again we study from this point of view all possible X_i's (or, equivalently, all possible three-node communication networks).

Theorem 3 The minimum regret ratios for all communication networks are as shown in Figure 9.2.

For the proof, which for each of the sixteen cases ranges from trivial

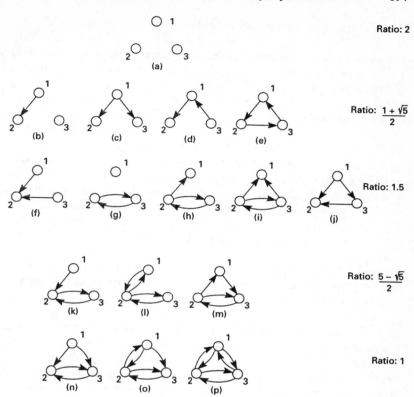

Figure 9.2 The optimum regret ratios

to quite challenging (for example, case (h)) (see Deng and Papadimitriou, 1992). This is a far more complex picture than Figure 9.1, and equally tempting for speculation. For example, it is instructive to compare the networks with three arcs: they are all over the performance spectrum.

Of course, one could analyze similarly all graphs with 4 nodes, then 5, etc. But I strongly recommend against continuing for too long: ominous forces of complexity are at work here:

Proposition Finding the best ratio for a communication network and number of processors is a NP-complete problem.

9.4   THREE RELATED PROBLEMS

We examine now three other problems of distributed decision-making under uncertainty that can be analyzed as in Section 9.3. For proofs see Deng and Papadimitriou (1992).

9.4.1   Load Balancing

To change the rules a little, assume that there are n agents and n processors, no communication, but each agent needs to schedule several tasks, each of arbitrary length. Once more, the objective to be minimized is the maximum makespan. This models the situation in which n cooperating processors wish to balance their loads by downloading tasks to each other, albeit in a single round of exchanges, and without previously exchanging load information.

Theorem 4   There is a deterministic algorithm that achieves a regret ratio of $2\sqrt{n}$. Furthermore, no deterministic algorithm can achieve a ratio better then $\sqrt{n}$.

Sketch of the lower bound: Suppose for a moment that each agent is assigned $\sqrt{n}$ equal tasks. By the 'pigeonhole principle', there is one processor, call it 0, that will be assigned at least $\sqrt{n}$ tasks. Consider the set S of agents that assign at least one task to 0; if there are more than $\sqrt{n}$ such processors, choose any $\sqrt{n}$ of them. Now, if all agents in S get $\sqrt{n}$ tasks and all others none, processor 0 will again get $\sqrt{n}$. But in this case the optimum makespan would be one (there is one task per processor on the average).

If randomized algorithms are allowed we can do much better (the algorithm is just a little more sophisticated than sending tasks to processors at random);

Theorem 5   There is a randomized algorithm that achieves a ratio of $\log n/\log \log n$.

Noga Alon (1992) has shown that the randomized algorithm in Theorem 5 is optimum.

9.4.2 On Two Problems by Witsenhausen and Arrow

'Witsenhausen's (1968) counterexample' is an important paradigm in distributed control theory, one that brings out the intricacies (and nonlinearities, and non-convexities) of distributed decision-making. We wish to design control function $\gamma(x)$ and $\delta(x + \gamma(x) + v)$, where x and v are random variables of known distribution, so as to minimize $(\gamma^2 + (\delta - x)^2)$. In other words, γ knows x, and wishes to communicate its value to another agent δ, in the presence of an additive 'noise' v. The objective function penalizes both errors of δ's estimation of x, and the usage of large signals by γ. It is known that the solution is NP – complete to calculate when the distributions of x and v are discrete and given (see Papadimitriou and Tsitsiklis, 1986). Competitive analysis helps reveal yet another aspect of the difficulty of this problem.

In general, suppose that we wish to minimize $f(y; S)$, where y is a partially observable variable and S is a strategy by the partially knowledgeable decision agents. In Witsenhausen's counter-example, y is the pair of variables x, v, and S the pair of decision functions (δ, γ). For a minimization problem, we are interested in obtaining a strategy S which minimizes the ratio $f(y; S)/f^*(y)$, where $f^*(y)$ is the cost of the solution when perfect information is available. When y has a known prior distribution, we wish to minimize the ratio $E[f(y; S)]/E[f^*(y)]$.

To model Witsenhausen's counterexample in this setting, let us assume that $v \leq \epsilon x$. Or, we can assume that v is a random variable which is iid to ϵx, for some constant $\epsilon > 0$. In both cases the following holds:

Theorem 6 There is no algorithm that achieves a bounded regret ratio in Witsenhausen's problem.

Sketch: Consider the problem facing the second agent. Let x to be in an interval between $(-\infty, \infty)$ and v is anywhere between $[-a, a]$. No matter what the first agent does, it could be that $v \in [-a, -a/2]$ and $v \in [a/2, a]$. If the first agent makes a decision $\gamma(x)$ deviating from x by at least $a/2$, then the objective function is at least $a^2/4$. Otherwise, no matter how the first agent codes its decision, the second agent cannot tell the difference between $v \in [-a, -a/2]$ and $v \in [a/2, a]$. Thus, the adversary can always force a decision deviating from γ by at least $a/2$ which forces the objective function to be at least $a^2/4$ again.

Kenneth Arrow (1987) proposed a similar problem, whose intention is to model group optimization. In this problem, we are also asked to design two control functions, γ for Agent 1 and δ for Agent 2. The objective function to minimize is $(\delta + \gamma - x)^2 + \delta^2 + \gamma^2$. The variable x follows normal distribution $N(0,1)$. Agent 1 observes the variable x by a deviation with normal distributed error, i.e., it observes a value y which follows a normal distribution $N(x, \sigma_1)$ and makes its decision on the value y. Agent 2 also observes the variable x by a normal distributed error $N(x, \sigma_2)$; it also observes the value of Agent 1's decision γ by a normal distributed error, i.e. $N(\gamma, \epsilon)$. All the random variables are independent. We can show:

Theorem 7   There is a bounded regret algorithm for Arrow's problem.

The contraposition of the two problems provided by Theorems 6 and 7 has only winners and no losers, as it has the effect intended by the researchers who proposed these problems: Witsenhausen's problem is indeed a nasty counterexample, while Arrow's model seems a plausible framework for team optimization.

9.5 FURTHER WORK

We cannot understand a complex area without trying our hand on a few examples first – and this is at best what was done in the work reviewed here. Using regret ratio analysis as a means for studying the value of information is in my opinion a very promising direction. We hope that studying more general problems of this sort will provide a better understanding of both the method and the issue. Several other domains, besides the scheduling and load balancing examples, come to mind: How best to share information in order to compute, say, Boolean functions? Or, suppose that the x_i's are cost and technology coefficients of some linear programme (the c_i's b_i's and the a_{ij}'s), while the decisions made correspond to the levels of the variables in the solution. Which sharing of coefficients – which 'organizational principle' – leads to the best results in this and similar situations? Some initial results along these lines have been recently obtained by the author and Mihalis Yannakakis (Papadimitriou and Yannakakis, 1993).

Notes

1. Many thanks to Kenneth Arrow for inviting me to speak at the Congress (and therefore to think about this area), and also for providing some inspiring criticism. I have had many helpful discussions with Yannis Ioannidis and Joel Sobel concerning these results and what they can mean to economists.

2. It is easy to see that mixed strategies are no advantage in this problem.

3. The established term within the theory of computation is 'competitive ratio', but using this term in addressing economists would be hopelessly misleading and confusing. Actually, the term 'regret ratio' is better. It follows a concept first considered by Leonard Savage (1954). Savage called regret (or 'loss') the *difference* of the actual and the perfect-information utilities; the disagreement between ratio and difference is a minor one, owing to modelling and context (they coincide for logarithmic utility, for example). I also like the term 'embarrassment quotient', because that's what it is: it is a measure of how embarrassed we are likely to be because of our lack of perfect information about the world.

4. The *k*-server conjecture was recently proved (within a factor of two) by Koutsoupias and Papadimitriou (1994).

References

Alon, N. (1992) Private communication.

Arrow, K (1984) *The Economics of Information* (Cambridge, Mass.: Harvard University Press).

Arrow, K. (1987) Personal communication.

Baeza-Yates, R.A., J.C. Culberson and G.J.E. Rawlins (forthcoming 1993) 'Searching in the Plane', *Information and Computation*.

Baruch, S., G. Koren, B. Mishra, A. Raghunathan, L. Rosier and D. Shasha (1991) 'On-Line Scheduling in the Presence of Overload', *Proceedings of the 32nd Annual Symposium on Foundations of Computer Science*, pp. 100–10.

Ben-David, S., A. Borodin, R. Karp, G. Tardos and A. Wigderson (1990) 'On the Power of Randomization in Online Algorithms', *Proceedings of the Association for Computing Machinery 22nd Annual Symposium on Theory of Computing*, pp. 379–86.

Ben-Porath, E. (1987) 'Repeated Games with Finite Automatons', preliminary paper presented at the Arrow Workshop, Stanford University.

Blum, A., P. Raghavan and B. Schieber (1991) 'Navigating in Unfamiliar Geometric Terrain', *Proceedings of the Association for Computing Machinery 23rd Annual Symposium on Theory of Computing*, pp. 494–504.

Borodin, A., N. Linial and M. Saks (1987) 'An Optimal On-Line Algorithm for Metrical Task Systems', *Proceedings of the Association for Computing Machinery 19th Annual Symposium on Theory of Computing*, pp. 373–82.

Borodin, A., S. Irani, P. Raghavan and B. Schieber (1991) 'Competitive Paging with Locality of Reference', *Proceedings of the Association for Com-*

puting Machinery 23rd Annual Symposium on Theory of Computing, pp. 249–59.

Chandra, A., D. Kozen and L.J. Stockmeyer (1981) 'Alternation', *Journal of the Association for Computing Machinery*.

Copersmith, D., P. Doyle, P. Raghavan and M. Snir, (1990) 'Random Walks on Weighted Graphs, and Application to On-line Algorithms', *Proceedings of the Association for Computing Machinery 22nd Annual Symposium on Theory of Computing*, pp. 369–78.

Deng, X. and S. Mahajan (1991) 'Infinite Games: Randomization, Computability and Applications to Online Problems', *Proceedings of the Association for Computing Machinery 23rd Annual Symposium on Theory of Computing*, pp. 289–98.

Deng, X. and C.H. Papadimitriou (1991) 'Exploring an Unknown Graph', *Proceedings of the IEEE Computer Society 31st Annual Symposium on Foundations of Computer Science*, pp. 355–61.

Deng, X. and C.H. Papadimitriou (1992) 'Competitive Distributed Decision-Making', *Proceedings of the 12th Congress of the International Federation of Information Processing Societies*, Madrid, Spain.

Deng, X., T. Kameda and C.H. Papadimitriou (1991) 'How to Learn an Unknown Environment', *Proceedings of the 32nd Annual Symposium on Foundations of Computer Science*, pp. 298–303.

Feldman, A., J. Sgall and S.H. Teng (1991) 'Dynamic Scheduling on Parallel Machines', *Proceedings of the 32nd Annual Symposium on Foundations of Computer Science*, pp. 111–20.

Fiat, A., Y. Rabani and Y. Ravid (1990) 'Competitive k-Server Algorithms' *Proceedings of the 31st Symposium on Foundations of Computer Science*, pp. 454–63.

Fiat, A., D.P. Foster, H. Karloff, Y. Rabani, Y. Ravid and S. Vishwanathan (1991) 'Competitive Algorithms for Layered Graph Traversal', *Proceedings of the IEEE Computer Society 32nd Annual Symposium on Foundations of Computer Science*, pp. 288–97.

Grove, E.F. (1991) 'The Harmonic Online k-Server Algorithm is Competitive', *Proceedings on the Association for Computing Machinery 23rd Annual Symposium on Theory of Computing*, pp. 260–6.

Irani, S. (1990) 'Coloring Inductive Graphs On-line', *Proceedings of the 31st Symposium on Foundations of Computer Science*, pp. 470–9.

Karlin, A.R., M.S. Manasse, L. Rudolph and D.D. Sleator (forthcoming 1993) 'Competitive Snoopy Caching', *Algorithmica*.

Karloff, H., Y. Rabani and Y. Ravid, Y. (1991) 'Lower Bounds for Randomized k-Server and Motion-Planning Algorithms', *Proceedings of the Association for Computing Machinery 23rd Annual Symposium on Theory of Computing*.

Karp, R.M. and Ramachandran (1991) 'Parallel Algorithms for Share Memory Machines', in J. van Leeuwen (ed.), *The Handbook of Theoretical Computer Science* (Massachusetts Institute of Technology Press).

Klein, R. (1991) 'Walking and Unknown Street with Bounded Detour', *Proceedings of the 32nd Annual Symposium on foundations of Computer Science*, pp. 304–13.

Koutsoupias, E. and C.H. Papadimitriou (1994) 'On the k-server Conjecture', *Proceedings of the 1994 Symposium on the Theory of Computing*.

Lovasz, L., M. Saks and W.A. Trotter 'An On-Line Graph Coloring Algorithm with Sublinear Performance Ratio', Bellcore Technical Memorandum ARH-O13014.

Manasse, M.S., L.A. McGeoch and D.D. Sleator (1987) 'Competitive Algorithms for On-Line Problems', *Association for Computing Machinery 20th Annual Symposium on Theory of Computing*, pp. 322–33.

Neyman, A. (1985) 'Bounded Complexity Justifies Cooperation in the Infinitely Repeated Prisoner's Dilemma', *Economics Letters*, vol. 19, pp. 227–9.

Papadimitriou, C.H. (1985) 'Games Against Nature', *Journal of Computer and Systems Science*, vol. 31, pp. 288–301.

Papadimitriou, C.H. (1992) 'On Players with a Bounded Number of States', *Games and Economic Behavior*, vol. 4, pp. 122–31.

Papadimitriou, C.H. and M. Sipser (1984) 'Communication Complexity', *Journal of Computer and Systems Science*, vol. 28, pp. 260–9.

Papadimitriou, C.H. and J. Tsitsiklis (1986) 'Intractable Problems in Control Theory', *SIAM Journal of Control and Optimization*, vol. 24, pp. 639–54.

Papadimitriou, C.H. and M. Yannakakis (1989) 'Shortest Paths Without a Map', *Proceedings of the 16th International Colloquium on Automata, Languages and Programming* (Springer), pp. 610–20. Also, special issue of *Theoretical Computer Science*, 1991.

Papadimitriou, C.H. and M. Yannakakis (1991) 'On the Value of Information in Distributed Decision-Making', *Proceedings of the Association for Computing Machinery 10th Symposium on Principles of Distributed Computing*, pp. 61–4.

Papadimitriou, C.H. and M. Yannakakis (1993) 'Linear Programming without the Matrix', *Proceedings of the Association for Computing Machinery 25th Annual Symposium on Theory of Computing*.

Raghavan, P. and M. Snir (1989) 'Memory vs Randomization in On-Line Algorithms', *Proceedings of the 16th International Colloquium on Automata, Languages and Programming* (Springer).

Savage, L.J. (1954) *The Foundations of Statistics* (Dover).

Shmoys, D.B., J. Wein and D.P. Williamson (1991) 'Scheduling Parallel Machines On-Line', *Proceedings of the 32nd Annual Symposium on foundations of Computer Science, p. 139.*

Sleator, D.D. and R.E. Tarjan (1985) 'Amortized Efficiency of List Update and Paging Rules', *Communications of the Association for Computing machinery*, vol. 28, no. 2, pp. 202–8.

Vishwanathan, S. (1990) 'Randomized On-Line Coloring of Graphs', *Proceedings of the the IEEE Computer Society 31st Symposium on Foundations of Computer Science*, pp. 464–9.

Witsenhausen, H.S. (1968) 'A Counterexample in Stochastic Optimum Control', *Society for Industrial and Applied Mathematics Journal of Control and Optimization*, vol. 6, pp. 138–47.

10 Theories of Optimal Capital Structure: A Managerial Discretion Perspective*

Oliver Hart[1]

HARVARD UNIVERSITY

10.1 INTRODUCTION

In the thirty or so years since the Modigliani–Miller theorem, scholars have worked to relax the theorem's assumptions in order to obtain a better understanding of the capital structure of firms.[2] This work has produced some important insights but has not yet delivered a fully coherent theory of optimal capital structure. For example, at present we do not understand very well the distinguishing features of debt and equity or why these claims, as opposed to the many instruments that could be chosen, are most frequently issued by firms. Given this state of affairs, existing explanations of the debt–equity ratio must be seen as still preliminary, as must efforts to use these explanations to understand global trends such as the large increases in leverage in the United States and United Kingdom during the 1980s.

In the first part of this chapter, I will argue that one reason progress on understanding capital structure has been limited is that relatively few analysts have adopted an explicit agency-theoretic or managerial discretion perspective. In particular, although the literature, starting with the work of Michael Jensen and William Meckling (1976), frequently refers to conflicts of interest, most of it does not emphasize the conflict of interest between a firm's management and its security holders. But I argue that this particular conflict of interest – that is, the idea that management is self-interested – is critical. In the absence of this conflict, optimal capital structure would look very different from what is observed in the world. In particular, firms would not issue senior or secured debt, whereas in fact a considerable amount of corporate debt has at least one of these features.[3] Thus, standard departures from the Modigliani–Miller framework that focus on the role of taxes, asymmetric information, or incomplete markets but ignore managerial self-interest are not sufficient to explain observed capital structure.

In the second part of the analysis I will discuss what has been learned from the relatively few studies that have explicitly adopted an agency-theoretic perspective. This body of work, although itself quite preliminary, can explain the use of senior or secured debt or both, as well as shed light on some observed patterns of capital structure, including a number of findings from studies that measure the response of security prices to important events that affect optimal capital structure ('event studies').

10.2 WHY AN AGENCY PERSPECTIVE IS CRITICAL

To fix ideas, it will be useful throughout the chapter to work with the following simple model, first laid out by Stewart Myers (1977).[4]

Consider a firm consisting of assets in place and new investment opportunities, and suppose that it exists at three given dates (Figure 10.1). At date 0 the firm's financial structure is chosen. At date 1 the assets in place yield a return of y_1 and a new investment opportunity costing i appears. At date 2 the assets in place yield a further return y_2 and the new investment opportunity – if it was taken at date 1 – yields r. At this date the firm is liquidated, receipts are allocated to security holders, and the world ends.

Suppose that the firm is run by a single manager.[5] This manager decides whether to take the new investment opportunity. The variables y_1, y_2, i, and r are typically uncertain at date 0 (however, with a probability distribution that is common knowledge). Assume for simplicity that the manager (and sometimes the market as well) learns the outcomes of y_1, y_2, i, and r at date 1: all uncertainty is resolved for the manager at this date. Finally, again for simplicity, assume an interest rate of zero.

I start with the case in which there are no taxes, the market is risk-neutral with regard to this firm's return (for example, because investors hold well-diversified portfolios), and the manager and the market have the same information at date 1 (as well as at date 0). Each of these assumptions will be relaxed in turn in what follows.

To consider what can be said about capital structure in the absence

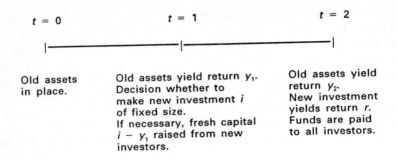

Figure 10.1 Investment decision

of a conflict of interest between the manager and security holders, I also make the following assumption:

— the manager is not self-interested, all decisions require the same amount of effort, and the manager is (in the absence of any incentive scheme) indifferent about whether the new investment opportunity is taken.

Finally, assume the manager's opportunity cost at date 0 is zero and that he has no initial wealth.

In this context the manager should invest if and only if the project has positive net present value ($r > i$). Moreover, it is very easy to implement this rule. Choose the firm's financial structure to be all equity at date 0, give the manager the authority to issue any new equity or any other claim needed to finance new investment, and provide the manager with a compensation package equal to a small fraction θ of the firm's date 2 liquidation receipts minus the amount received from any date 1 security issue plus any dividends paid at date 1. This makes the manager's payoff

$$\begin{cases} \theta\,(y_1 + y_2) & \text{if he does not invest} \\ \theta\,(y_1 + y_2 + r - i) & \text{if he invests} \end{cases} \tag{10.1}$$

It is easiest to understand this equation in three steps. First, if the manager does not invest, he may as well save the date 1 earnings y_1 (without interest), making the firm's date 2 liquidation receipts equal to $(y_1 + y_2)$; of these the manager obtains a fraction θ. Second, if the manager invests and $y_1 > i$, he will finance the investment out of retained earnings, save the amount $(y_1 - i)$ in a zero-interest-bearing account, and the firm's liquidation receipts will equal $(y_1 - i + y_2 + r)$. Third, if $y_1 < i$ and the manager invests, he issues new equity to the value of $(i - y_1)$, which implies that total date 2 profit net of the receipts from new equity at date 1 is $y_2 + r - (i - y_1) = y_1 + y_2 + r - i$.

Thus the equation represents the manager's payoff in all cases. Obviously a manager who maximizes his payoff will invest if and only if $r > i$, which is the efficient investment rule.[6]

Not only can the efficient outcome be achieved through an all-equity firm with a suitable compensation package for management, but any other initial capital structure may lead to inefficiency. Suppose, for example, that the firm's date 0 capital structure includes some senior debt that promises to pay an amount d at date 2, as well as equity; and suppose ownership of this debt is dispersed, so that renegotiation is hard to arrange. Then if the value of $y_1 + y_2$ (which, recall, is learned at date 1) turns out to be less than d, the manager may be unable to finance a new investment opportunity at date 1, even though it would be profitable. This is the consequence of a version of the well-known debt overhang problem, first pointed out by Stewart Myers (1977). If the firm can only issue claims at date 1 that are junior to the existing debt, then the most that can be reserved for new date 1 claimants out of date 1 and date 2 receipts is $y_1 + y_2 + r - d$. However, if d is large, $y_1 + y_2 + r - d$ can be less than i, even though $r > i$. In this case, it will be impossible to find security holders at date 1 who are prepared to put up the needed investment funds $(i - y_1)$, and a profitable investment opportunity will be missed.[7]

We now see how the conclusion that an all-equity firm is optimal changes if one allows for taxes, incomplete markets, or asymmetric information.

10.2.1 Taxes

To begin with, suppose that there are no profits at date 1 $(y_1 = 0)$. Assume that any profit at date 2, net of investment costs, is subject to the corporation tax t_c but that interest payments are tax deductible. Also, for simplicity, ignore personal income taxes.[8]

It is clear that there is now a role for debt financing. Suppose no new investment at date 1 is ever warranted $(r < i)$. Then the efficient outcome for the firm can be achieved by having debt in the initial capital structure with a promised repayment d at date 2 that exceeds the highest possible value of y_2. (Of course, this debt will sell at a discount given that the firm will almost always default at date 2.) Then *all* the firm's date 2 receipts are paid out to creditors, no corporation taxes are incurred, and the firm's initial date 0 value of debt plus equity is Ey_2, where E stands for expected value.[9] In contrast, an all-equity firm would have a date 0 value equal to $Ey_2 (1 - t_c)$, since it does have to pay corporation tax.

Now allow for profitable new investment projects ($r > i$). Because high levels of debt can cause debt overhang, one might think there would be an interesting trade-off between debt and equity; a firm with low debt would pay high taxes and a firm with high debt might be unable to finance profitable projects. However, this is not so. The debt overhang problem arises only with respect to *senior* debt. One strategy open to a firm is to issue only junior (or subordinated) debt at date 0; this debt contains a covenant stating that the firm has the option to issue debt senior to it later. Under these conditions, the debt overhang problem disappears: new claimants at date 1 can be offered up to the full amount $y_2 + r$ of the firm's date 2 receipts (through dilution of the date 0 junior debt) and, of course, this exceeds i whenever $r > i$. Thus profitable projects can be financed. Moreover, *only* profitable projects will be financed, given the incentive scheme corresponding to equation (10.1). In addition, the firm still pays no corporation tax because all its receipts are paid out to creditors. Hence the efficient outcome is achieved, and the firm's date 0 value is E max $(y_2 + r - i, y_2)$.[10]

The theory therefore now predicts that there should be firms with 100 per cent subordinated debt, something we do not observe (see note 3).

So far I have ignored the possibility of bankruptcy. But suppose the assumption that $y_1 = 0$ is dropped. If $y_1 > 0$, then if a firm wants to avoid paying corporation tax at date 1, it must have outstanding (short-term) debt that absorbs y_1 as interest. However, suppose a bad state of the world occurs, y_1 is low, and the promised interest payment $d_1 > y_1$. Under these conditions, a firm may have to default and may be forced into bankruptcy. Could the resulting bankruptcy costs limit the firm's desire to issue debt at date 0?

This is unlikely, given the working hypothesis that the manager is not self-interested. In view of this, why would the creditors not be prepared in advance to let the manager postpone any interest he cannot pay at date 1 until date 2 by letting him issue payment-in-kind (PIK) bonds?[11] Given the incentive scheme corresponding to equation (10.1), the manager has no incentive to postpone unless it is necessary. Thus if d_1 is chosen to be high, the manager will pay out any profit the firm makes at date 1 and avoid corporation taxes, but he will never need to default or go into bankruptcy if $y_1 < d_1$ because he can always postpone.

Of course, the Internal Revenue Service might view with suspicion a firm with huge levels of outstanding subordinated and postponable debt that mop up earnings in essentially the same way the equity is meant to.[12] In particular, the IRS might decide to treat the debt as if it were equity. The fear of this reaction may cause firms to issue less than 100 per cent debt in the first place and to issue some senior debt. Although it would no doubt be possible to develop a theory of capital structure based on fear of the reaction of the authorities, I do not know whether such a theory could explain the variations in capital structure observed across industries, countries, and over time. In any event, I am not aware of attempts to develop a theory along these lines.

10.2.2 Risk Aversion and Incomplete Markets

So far I have assumed that investors are risk-neutral. But what happens if they are not and if markets are incomplete?

Analysts often contend that firms issue debt because some investors are more risk-averse than others and, by issuing debt as well as equity, the firms can cater to the risk-averse. This argument implicitly supposes some market incompleteness, because, if a complete set of contingent security markets existed, investors could purchase the state-contingent securities they like without going through firms. However, even when markets are incomplete, firms should issue only junior or subordinated securities. That is, clientele effects cannot explain the existence of *senior* debt.

I develop the argument for a particular case of market incompleteness. Suppose that a firm is originally owned by N investors at date 0 with von Neumann–Morgenstern utility functions $U_1, \ldots U_N$ defined over date 2 wealth.[13] Assume that these investors invest only in this firm (an extreme form of market incompleteness) and cannot make any further capital contributions at date 1. The firm can, however, borrow and lend on the open market at date 1 at a riskless rate of interest of zero. The question I ask is: what kinds of securities should this firm issue?

Clearly it is Pareto optimal for the firm to invest at date 1 if and only if $r > i$ (recall that, as earlier, all the uncertainty is resolved at date 1).[14] This makes the firm's date 2 receipts (net of date 1 borrowing) equal to $R = \max(y_1 + y_2, y_1 + y_2 + r - i)$. These receipts should be allocated among the investors according to N sharing rules $s_1(\cdot)\ldots$ $s_N(\cdot)$, so as to solve:

Max $EU_1(s_1(R))$

S.T. $EU_i(s_i(R)) \geq \bar{U}_i$ for all $i = 2,\ldots.\, N$

$$\sum_{i=1}^{N} s_i(R) = R \text{ for all } R$$

where the expectation is taken with respect to the distribution of R, and $\bar{U}_i$ denotes the reservation expected utility level for each investor, $i > 1$.

This is a classic risk-sharing problem and the details of the solution need not concern us here (see Wilson, 1968). The important point is that there is a simple way to implement the optimum: give the manager the compensation package corresponding to equation (10.1). This ensures that he will invest if and only if $r > i$; issue N date 0 claims whose date 2 returns are defined by the functions $s_1,\ldots,s_N$; and give the manager the right to issue debt at date 1 that is senior to these claims. In other words, the N original claim-holders have rights to the firm's date 2 receipts, but only after senior date 1 creditors have been paid off (this reduces the date 2 receipts $y_2 + r$ to $y_1 + y_2 + r - i$ in the event that $y_1 < i$ and the manager needs to borrow $(i - y_1)$ at date 1).

Such a scheme achieves the best of both worlds. On the one hand it ensures that an efficient investment choice is made. On the other it ensures that, given investor attitudes to risk, total surplus is divided optimally. If the claims held by the original investors were not junior, the first goal would not generally be achieved. The reason is the debt overhang problem again: if y_1 and y_2 are small and initial investors have a senior claim to part of date 2 receipts, then it may be impossible to raise $i - y_1$ even if the investment is profitable.

Thus, even if investors are risk averse and markets are incomplete, the theory predicts that all claims issued by a firm should be subordinated.[15]

10.2.3   Asymmetric Information

Finally, what happens if the managers and the market do not have the same information at date 1? In particular, suppose that the manager learns the value of y_1, y_2, r, and i at date 1, but the market learns the value only of y_1 and i. Myers and Majluf (1984) have observed that under these conditions a manager of an initially all-equity firm who acts on behalf of initial shareholders may pass up some profitable investment projects if these can be financed only by issuing new equity at date 1. The reason is that if y_2 is high but the market does not realize this, then the new equity issue will be sold at a discount relative to its true value, which may cause a large enough dilution of the initial equity that the wealth of initial equity-holders falls even though the new project is profitable. In contrast, profitable projects will always be undertaken if they can be financed out of retained earnings or by issuing debt because no dilution of initial equity occurs in these cases.

The Myers–Majluf analysis suggests why a firm might issue senior debt in addition to equity. However, the effect disappears if the manager is paid according to equation (10.1).[16] This compensation package rewards the manager according to the *total* value of the firm at date 2, net of any cash inflows from date 1 security issues, rather than just the value of initial equity. In particular, it is clear from the formula that whether or not the manager has private information about y_2 and r, he will wish to invest if and only if $r > i$. Hence the conclusion that all-equity firms (or, if taxes or market incompleteness are important, firms with junior debt claims) are optimal is robust to the introduction of asymmetric information as long at the manager is offered a compensation package like that in equation (10.1).[17]

In one part of their article Myers and Majluf appear to contend that a compensation package like that in equation (10.1) may be undesirable because it gives the manager no direct interest in the price at which new equity is offered, thus perhaps providing an incentive to favour friends with sweetheart deals. Unfortunately, such deals seem hard to avoid if the manager has private information: even if the firm issues no new shares, he can always tell friends to buy equity when it is undervalued and sell when it is overvalued. Also the formula in (10.1) at least makes the manager interested in the *value* of new equity because if, say, the manager sells new equity at too low a price, he may fail to raise $(i - y_1)$ and may have to forgo the new project. Moreover, the formula could presumably be modified to encourage the manager to be interested also in the price of new equity; in particular, he could be penalized if the firm's equity price were to rise significantly soon after the new issue (that is, if he underprices the new equity). Another possibility is to insist that the manager must always raise new capital through a rights issue, in which case the price of new equity does not matter to initial shareholders as long as the project is financed.[18]

Two other arguments against equation (10.1) and in favour of the idea that the manager acts on behalf of initial shareholders should be mentioned. First, because as a practical matter management holds significant equity in the firm, its interests are often said to be automatically aligned (at least partially) with those of initial shareholders. Apart from not explaining *why* management has a significant equity interest, this argument seems to ignore the fact that in public companies, management can vary its equity holding according to its information. In particular, even if management holds significant equity, this should not stop it from letting the firm issue new equity when the equity is undervalued: after all, there is nothing to prevent management from keeping its overall equity interest constant by buying part of the new issue itself if it is underpriced, thus avoiding wealth transfers from management to new shareholders.[19]

Second, the assumption that management acts on behalf of initial shareholders is sometimes justified because management has a fiduciary duty to this group and shareholders typically have votes. But it is difficult to know how important fiduciary duty is as an influence on management in practice. The sometimes extraordinary lengths to which managers go to defeat high-price hostile takeovers suggest that it is often not a dominant force.[20] And from a theoretical point of view, it is not very satisfactory to take as a given the existence of fiduciary duty and the fact that shareholders have votes: one would like to explain these things. Furthermore, it is far from obvious how one can explain them without dropping the maintained hypothesis that managers are selfless.

10.3 WHAT AN AGENCY APPROACH CAN DELIVER

We can summarize the argument so far as follows. If there were no significant conflicts of interest between insiders and outsiders, capital structure would look very different. All debt issued by firms would be unsecured and subordinated, and firms would easily avoid financial distress and bankruptcy costs by arranging in advance with creditors that debt could be forgiven or postponed at the manager's discretion.[21] In such a world there would be no reason to give shareholders (or any other outside group for that matter) votes. Why not give all the votes to informed management and rely on it to seek appropriate merger partners or to vote itself out of office if a better management team appears?[22]

The conclusion I draw from this is that conflicts of interest between insiders and outsiders are crucial for understanding even the most basic aspects of capital structure. In spite of this, surprisingly few scholars have adopted an agency perspective. For example, tax theories of financial structure, probably the largest part of the literature on capital structure, never mention agency problems. And the many scholars (starting with Jensen and Meckling, 1976) who argue that debt is costly because it causes management to favour shareholders at the expense of creditors typically do not model the more basic conflict of interest between management and security holders as a whole.

In the past few years, examinations of the conflict of interest between insiders and outsiders have begun to appear, but they are still in their infancy. Two strands have emerged. One analyzes entrepreneurial firms, that are essentially owned and controlled by managers, who may, however, be prepared to give up some control to persuade an outside investor to provide financing.[23] The conflict of interest arises because management receives some benefits from running the firm that cannot be transferred to outside investors. This part of the literature typically studies the optimal allocation of control between management and a single outside investor but does not analyze the choice between publicly traded securities such as debt and equity.

The second strand of the literature focuses on public corporations, in which management has a relatively small profit stake and rarely has voting control. Since Jensen and Meckling's work it has been recognized that an agency problem exists under these conditions because many of the costs and benefits of management's actions are borne by outside investors rather than by management itself. However, what is not clear in Jensen and Meckling or in other initial analyses is why it makes sense to use financial structure to solve this agency problem.[24] In particular, why not simply put management on an optimal incentive scheme such as that corresponding to equation (10.1)?

Recently, scholars have tried to answer this question by being more specific about management's objectives. A traditional incentive scheme works well if agency problems arise only because management dislikes working hard. However, such a scheme is much less effective if the manager obtains large control rents from running the firm (control rents that cannot be charged for adequately ex ante, either because the manager has limited wealth or because he is risk-averse and the rents are uncertain). These control rents may represent the utility the manager gets from the job or from presiding over a large and perhaps growing empire, or they may represent the monetary and non-monetary perquisites the manager can get by virtue of his position of power. Incentive schemes may be less effective under these conditions because a *very* large incentive payment may be required to induce management to give up these control rents. It may be cheaper for investors to resort to mechanisms that force management to yield control or to curb its empire-building tendencies. Bankruptcy and takeover bids, both of which are intimately connected to a firm's financial structure, are examples of such mechanisms.

The idea that management likes to entrench itself and cares about the size of the empire under its control is, of course, not new. It was the basis of many early studies of management and is at the heart of Jensen's free cash flow hypothesis.[25] Moreover, the idea derives some empirical support from the fierce resistance of managers to many take-overs.[26] However, it is only very recently that the empire-building mo-tive has been incorporated into theoretical models of capital structure. As we shall see, a number of basic aspects of capital structure can be explained in this way.

I will proceed by modifying my earlier model in two ways. In the first variation, I introduce the possibility that a firm's existing assets have an alternative use at date 1 – in particular, that they can be liqui-dated.[27] However, for simplicity, I drop the assumption that there is a new investment opportunity at date 1. Under these conditions, debt may be useful to force the manager to liquidate the firm in a situation in which this is efficient but contrary to self-interest.

10.3.1   Variation 1

Suppose that $r = i = 0$, and that if a firm's assets are liquidated at date 1, they yield L in addition to the already realized date 1 return y_1. Assume that the manager and the market both learn y_1, L, and y_2 at date 1 (these may be uncertain ex ante, however). Efficiency dictates that liquidation should occur at date 1 if and only if $y_2 < L$. (I main-tain the assumption of a zero interest rate.) However, suppose that the manager obtains large private benefits of control from running the firm between dates 1 and 2 and will therefore resist liquidation if at all possible. Moreover, for simplicity assume these private benefits are sufficiently large that no feasible incentive payment can persuade the manager to yield control voluntarily.[28]

The sequence of events is illustrated in Figure 10.2. Given the large private benefits, the only way to get management to relinquish control at date 1 is through bankruptcy or takeover. I assume that no takeovers occur at date 1 because there are no potential acquirers and focus on bankruptcy.[29]

Assume that the firm's capital structure consists of equity and senior debt that is owed P_1 at date 1 and P_2 at date 2 (at the moment, I simply assume the debt to be senior; I consider why this might be desirable later). Suppose that the manager retains control if he does not default at date 1, but that default automatically triggers Chapter 7 bankruptcy, which in turn triggers complete liquidation of the firm. This sequence implicitly rules out renegotiation between creditors and the firm in or out of bankruptcy. Although the assumption of no renegotiation is strong, it is not unreasonable if creditors are dispersed: collective action problems can then make renegotiation difficult even under the supervision of a bankruptcy court. Given that default leads to bankruptcy and to the loss of control benefits, the manager never defaults voluntarily. Thus if $y_1 \geq P_1$, he will pay P_1 to creditors at date 1 and save $y_1 - P_1$; $y_1 - P_1 + y_2$ will then be available for creditors and shareholders at date 2. Thus the date 1 value of the firm (the value of debt *and* equity, including interest and dividend payments) will be $y_1 + y_2$.

But what if $y_1 < P_1$? If $y_1 + y_2 \geq P_1 + P_2$, the manager can still avoid default at date 1 by issuing $P_1 - y_1$ dollars of new junior debt due at date 2 and repaying this together with the senior debt P_2 out of date 2 income y_2. Thus the date 1 value of the firm is again $y_1 + y_2$. However, if $y_1 < P_1$, and $y_1 + y_2 < P_1 + P_2$, then the manager cannot avoid default and liquidation will occur. In this case, the date 1 value of the firm is $y_1 + L$, of which the creditors receive Min $(P_1 + P_2, y_1 + L)$ and shareholders the rest.

Denoting the firm's date 1 market value by V_1, we can summarize the above discussion as follows:

$$V_1 = \begin{cases} y_1 + y_2 & \text{if } y_1 \geq P_1 \\ & \text{or } y_1 < P_1 \text{ and } y_1 + y_2 \geq P_1 + P_2 \\ y_1 + L & \text{otherwise} \end{cases}$$

We are now in a position to discuss optimal capital structure. Suppose that capital structure is chosen at date 0 to maximize the total value of the firm.[30] If there is no ex ante uncertainty about y_2 and L, the first-best outcome can be achieved by setting $P_1 = 0$ if $y_2 > L$; and $P_1 > y_1$, $P_1 + P_2 > y_1 + y_2$ if $y_2 < L$.[31] The firm's date 0 market value is $V_0 = \text{Max }(y_1 + y_2, y_1 + L)$.[32]

Matters become more interesting if y_2 and L are uncertain. To simplify,

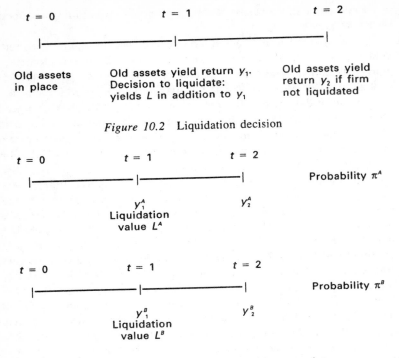

Figure 10.2   Liquidation decision

Figure 10.3   Liquidation decision with uncertainty

I will focus on the special case in which the vector (y_2, L) can take on just two values (y_2^A, L^A) and (y_2^B, L^B); see Figure 10.3.

Obviously, if $y_2^A \geq L^A$, $y_2^B \geq L^B$, the first-best outcome can again be achieved with no date 1 debt; if $y_2^A \leq L^A$, $y_2^B \leq L^B$, the first-best can be achieved with high levels of date 1 and date 2 debt. The interesting case is $y_2^A > L^A$, $y_2^B < L^B$ (or vice versa). I divide this case into three sub-cases.

(1) $y_1^A + y_2^A > y_1^B + y_2^B$. Here the first-best can again be achieved, for example, by setting $P_1 = y_1^A + y_2^A$, $P_2 = 0$. The reason is that the firm can avoid default in state A (by borrowing y_2^A) but not in state B. This is the efficient outcome.

(2) $y_1^A + y_2^A \leq y_1^B + y_2^B$, $y_1^A > y_1^B$. Now the first-best can be achieved by setting $P_1 = y_1^A$, P_2 very large. The reason is that the firm can avoid default in state A (by paying y_1^A) but not in state B. Again this is efficient.

(3) $y_1^A + y_2^A \leq y_1^B + y_2^B$, $y_1^A \leq y_1^B$. Now the first-best cannot be achieved. Given any value of P_1, P_2, default in state B occurs if and only if $y_1^B < P_1$ and $y_1^B + y_2^B < P_1 + P_2$. But these inequalities imply $y_1^A < P_1$ and $y_1^A + y_2^A < P_1 + P_2$, and hence default also occurs in state A. It is impossible to have liquidation in state B, where liquidation is efficient, without also having it in state A, where it is inefficient. Thus the choice is between having liquidation in both states or neither. The first, which can be achieved by setting P_1 and P_2 very large, is preferable to the second, which can be achieved by setting $P_1 = 0$, if and only if

$$\pi^A L^A + \pi^B L^B > \pi^A y_2^A + \pi^B y_2^B \tag{10.2}$$

This completes the analysis of optimal capital structure in the two-state case. The main difference relative to the case of perfect certainty is that interior solutions occur: it may be optimal to choose debt levels to take intermediate values rather than zero or 'very large'. Also, high debt sometimes leads to inefficient liquidation and low debt sometimes prevents efficient liquidation (see the third sub-case above).

Even this very simple model can explain why firms issue senior or secured debt. If P_2 were a junior claim, the firm would be able to issue debt senior to it at date 1 in the amount of y_2, and avoid bankruptcy whenever $y_1 + y_2 \geq P_1$. It is easy to check that in the second sub-case above, the first-best outcome is no longer achievable under these conditions.[33]

To summarize variation 1, if management cannot be trusted on its own accord to liquidate the firm, debt *can* help to put pressure on management. Moreover, in general, it is important that the firm's capital structure contain both short-term and senior, long-term debt; short-term debt to force management to pay out cash in the short run, leading in some circumstances to default and liquidation, and senior, long-term debt to prevent management from financing the payout by borrowing against long-run earnings.

10.3.2 Variation 2

The assumption in variation 1 that default and bankruptcy automatically lead to liquidation is strong. After all, Chapter 11 is specifically designed to avoid inefficient liquidation. The second variation of the earlier model avoids this assumption by considering firms that, although in financial distress, are not in danger of entering Chapter 7 bankruptcy or being liquidated.

In this variation the investment possibility i, r at date 1 is reintroduced.[34] However, I now suppose that L is so low that liquidation is no longer a viable alternative. So the firm must decide whether to expand at date 1 or to maintain the status quo. I also focus on long-term securities that pay out at date 2; in particular, I rule out short-term debt due at date 1. This assumption is restrictive but can be justified in the following way. Imagine that because liquidation is so unattractive, management can always default on short-term debt, declare Chapter 11 bankruptcy, keep creditors at bay, and run the firm as usual until date 2. Under these conditions, only long-term securities *can* have a role.[35]

And long-term securities do have a role. Suppose that management's empire-building tendencies mean that it always wants to make the new investment if at all possible (moreover, no incentive scheme can prevent this).[36] The only way to prevent management from expanding is to restrict access to capital. In other words, under the assumption that short-term debt is ineffective as a means of getting cash out of a firm, there is no way to stop management investing if $y_1 \geq i$. However, if $y_1 < i$, management needs to raise $i - y_1$ dollars from the date 1 capital market to invest. How easy or difficult this is depends on how much senior debt is already due at date 2.

To be specific, suppose that the firm's date 0 security structure consists of senior, long-term debt promising P_2 at date 2 plus equity.[37] Assume that management and the market observe y_2, r, and i at date 1. If $y_1 < i$, management will be able to raise the additional $i - y_1$ for investment if and only if

$$i - y_1 \leq y_2 + r - P_2 \tag{10.3}$$

This follows from the fact that, given that the manager will use the $i - y_1$ to invest, there will be $y_2 + r$ available at date 2 to be distributed to all security holders. Of this, P_2 has already been promised to date 0 creditors and the rest is available for new date 1 creditors. Thus the date 1 market value of the firm is

$$V_1 = \begin{cases} y_1 + y_2 + r - i & \text{if } y_1 \geq i \text{ or equation (10.3) holds} \\ y_1 + y_2 & \text{otherwise} \end{cases}$$

It is again straightforward to analyze the firm's optimal capital structure in this second variation. Suppose management always needs to go to the capital market to invest ($y_1 < i$). If there is no ex ante uncertainty

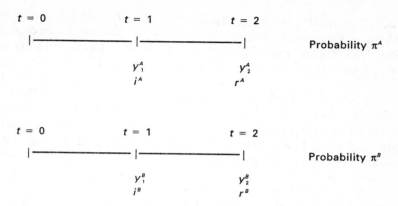

Figure 10.4 Investment decision with uncertainty

about y_2, i, and r, it is easy to achieve the first-best outcome. If $r > i$, set $P_2 = 0$; equation (10.3) is always satisfied and investment always takes place, which is efficient. In contrast, if $r < i$, set P_2 very large; equation (10.3) is never satisfied and investment never takes place, which is again efficient.

Matters become more interesting if y_2, r, and i are uncertain. To simplify, again suppose that (y_2, r, i) takes on just two values (y_2^A, r^A, i^A) and (y_2^B, r^B, i^B); see Figure 10.4. It is again trivial to achieve the first-best outcome with no debt if $r^A \geq i$ and $r^B \geq i^B$, or with very large debt if $r^A \leq i^A$ and $r^B \leq i^B$. The interesting case is when $r^A > i^A$ and $r^B < i^B$. I divide this into two subcases.

(1) $y_1^A + y_2^A + r^A - i^A > y_1^B + y_2^B + r^B - i^B$. Here the first-best can be achieved by setting P_2 somewhere between $y_1^B + y_2^B + r^B - i^B$ and $y_1^A + y_2^A + r^A - i^A$. Equation (10.3) is satisfied in state A but not in state B, and investment occurs only in state A, which is efficient.

In other words, the debt level is set somewhere between the maximized net value of the firm in state A and the maximized net value in state B. This gives management enough leeway to finance a profitable new investment in state A but prevents financing an unprofitable one in state B.

(2) $y_1^A + y_2^A + r^A - i^A \leq y_1^B + y_2^B + r^B - i^B$. The first-best is no longer achievable for any choice of P_2. The reason is that

$$i^A - y_1^A \leq y_2^A + r^A - P_2 \text{ implies that}$$

$$i^B - y_1^B \leq y_2^B + r^B - P_2$$

so it is impossible to have investment in state A without also having it in state B. Thus the choice is between having investment in neither state (set P_2 very large) or in both (set $P_2 = 0$). The first is preferable if and only if

$$\pi^A(r^A - i^A) + \pi^B(r^B - i^B) < 0$$

Again this second variation can explain why not all debt is subordinated. If the date 2 debt were junior, then from the point of view of management trying to raise capital at date 1, the debt would be equivalent to equity because it can always be diluted. In other words, one might as well set $P_2 = 0$, which is not generally optimal.

The lesson from this second variation complements that from the first. If management is interested in empire building, the danger for security holders is that it will try to raise capital for unprofitable investment projects by issuing claims against earnings from existing assets. Senior, long-term debt can be useful in constraining management: this debt mortgages part of long-term earnings and reduces management's ability to dilute claims against earnings from existing assets.

The two variations are similar in economic terms. In fact, because liquidation can be thought of as negative investment, the reader may wonder whether they are identical. This is not the case, however, at least in modelling terms. In the liquidation variation, short-term debt is crucial, and a position has to be taken on what happens if management defaults at date 1 (I assumed that this triggered Chapter 7 bankruptcy and liquidation). The second variation ignores short-term debt and so date 1 default is not even an issue.

10.3.3 Observed Patterns of Capital Structure

A great deal of empirical work has lately been done on capital structure. Although not all the findings agree, some robust observations ('stylized facts') have emerged. I will take these facts as a given in what follows and consider what light the theory I have described can throw on them.

The stylized facts are that profitable firms have low levels of debt; firms with a large proportion of tangible assets have high levels of debt; firms with stable cash flows have high levels of debt; debt-for-equity swaps raise share prices; equity-for-debt swaps lower share prices; pure equity issues lower share prices.[38]

All of these facts *can* be explained by at least one of the variations of the basic theory described above. However, not all are inevitable consequences of the theory. In some cases the theory predicts that reversals should also be observed.

Consider the relationship between profitability and debt level. Variation 1 can certainly explain why profitable firms (in particular, those with high y_2s) can have low debt. Suppose L is fixed, but y_2 varies across firms, and this variation is observable. If y_2 is large ($y_2 > L$ for sure), it is optimal to set $P_1 = P_2 = 0$; whereas, if y_2 is small ($y_2 < L$ for sure), it is optimal to set P_1 and P_2 very large. Firms whose main asset is human capital might be examples of those whose going concern value substantially exceeds their liquidation value. In contrast, firms whose main assets consist of natural resources might have going concern values close to, or sometimes less than, their liquidation value.

However, a small change in variation 1 could generate a positive relation between profitability and the debt level. Suppose that, on average, profitable firms have liquidation values that are high relative to profitability. That is, the more profitable the firm, the more likely it is to satisfy the condition $y_2 < L$. In such cases large debt levels will be required in order to trigger liquidation of profitable firms.

Variation 2 also does not clearly predict the relationship between profitability and debt. If a firm's profitability refers to the value of new investment, it is optimal for profitable firms to have low debt (if $r > i$ for sure, the optimal $P_2 = 0$). However, if profitability refers to the value of old investments, then it is optimal for profitable firms to have high debt. In sub-case 1 of the two-state case ($r^A > i^A$, $r^B < i^B$, $y_1^A + y_2^A + r^A - i^A > y_1^B + y_2^B + r^B - i^B$), the optimal P_2 lies between $y_1^B + y_2^B + r^B - i^B$ and $y_1^A + y_2^A + r^A - i^A$, and is thus increasing in $y_1^B + y_2^B$, $y_1^A + y_2^A$.[39]

Consider next the fact that firms with a large fraction of assets that are tangible have high debt. If tangibility is associated with high liquidation value, then variation 1 explains this fact rather clearly. Other things being equal, high L's make liquidation more attractive and so raise the optimal P_1, P_2 (it is more likely that $y_2 < L$ or that equation (10.2) will be satisfied). One possible offsetting effect is that firms with low L's (those whose main asset is human capital, for example) are arguably less likely to be sold off piecemeal in a Chapter 7 bankruptcy liquidation precisely because there would be such a great loss of value. If renegotiation can be relied on for such firms (in Chapter 11, say), it might make high debt *more* attractive when L is low. It is difficult to know how important this effect is in practice, however.

Variation 2 seems to have little to say about the relationship between debt and asset tangibility, because there is no obvious proxy for asset tangibility in this variation.

Consider now the relationship between debt and the stability of cash flows. The best way to understand this is to combine variations 1 and 2 in a very simple way. Suppose that liquidation and expansion are *both* options for the firm at date 1 but that expansion is never profitable ($r < i$ for sure). Suppose also that default at date 1 automatically triggers liquidation. Then the trade-off for initial security holders is between setting P_1, P_2 high to limit management's ability to expand, and setting P_1, P_2 low to avoid inefficient liquidation.

For example, assume y_1 and y_2 are perfectly certain and $y_2 > L$ for sure (so liquidation is always inefficient). Then the first-best outcome can be achieved by setting $P_1 = y_1$ and $P_2 = y_2$. The reason is that management never defaults, but because it has to pay out all its cash and its debt capacity is exhausted, it can never raise capital for unprofitable new projects. But if y_1 is uncertain, the first-best outcome is typically not achievable because it is impossible to prevent management from using current earnings for investment, and to exhaust the firm's debt capacity in all states of the world (this requires $P_1 \geq y_1$ and $P_1 + P_2 \geq y_1 + y_2$, for sure), without triggering inefficient liquidation in some states of the world (inefficient liquidation occurs whenever $P_1 > y_1$ and $P_1 + P_2 > y_1 + y_2$). So there is now a trade-off for initial security holders. If inefficient liquidation poses a greater threat to the firm's total value than does carrying out unprofitable new investments, the optimal debt level will fall as y_1 becomes more uncertain (to reduce the chance that $P_1 > y_1$ and $P_1 + P_2 > y_1 + y_2$). But if unprofitable new investments pose the greater threat, the optimal debt level will rise as y_1 becomes more uncertain (to reduce the chance that $P_1 < y_1$ or $P_1 + P_2 < y_1 + y_2$).

So the theory can explain why firms with stable cash flows have more debt but can also explain the opposite.

I next explore the results of the various event studies on the effects of different kinds of recapitalizations on share prices. I will concentrate on variation 1, although similar results could undoubtedly be obtained from variation 2. In much of what follows, the driving force behind a recapitalization will be the threat of a hostile takeover.

Debt-for-Equity Swaps Typically Raise Share Prices[40]

To see that variation 1 can explain this, suppose that the management obtains private information just after date 0 that a hostile takeover is imminent (it will occur at date 1/2, say). Assume for simplicity that as far as the market is concerned this is a very unlikely event, so the anticipation of it has no effect on market value. However, if the management signals the event through a recapitalization, then the market of course reacts.

Assume also that for unspecified reasons (for example, historical reasons) the firm initially consists of 100 per cent equity and that the hostile bid will succeed unless the management can convince the market that it will run the firm approximately efficiently (the idea is that management is safe if it is close to efficient, because there are some costs in making a bid).

Suppose it is known that for this firm $y_1 = 100$ and $L = 150$, as in Figure 10.5. In the absence of any action by the management before a bid is made at date 1/2, market participants will reason that, if the bid fails, the management will *not* liquidate at date 1 because, given that the firm has no outstanding debt, it will be under no pressure to do so.[41] Anticipating this, shareholders tender to the bidder and the bid succeeds.

To prevent this outcome, the management must bond itself just after date 0 to take efficient action at date 1. An obvious way to do this is to make a debt-for-equity swap.[42] For example, suppose the management issues new short-term debt promising 250 (that is, sets $P_1 = 250$ and $P_2 = 0$) and uses the proceeds to buy back equity. Because $y_1 < P_1$ and $y_1 + y_2 < P_1 + P_2$, the new debt guarantees that the firm will default at date 1 and be liquidated then, which is the efficient outcome. Thus the hostile takeover is thwarted, and the management retains control, if only until date 1.

What is the effect of the recapitalization on the value of equity? Before the recapitalization the equity was worth $y_1 + y_2 = 200$. Afterwards the total value of the firm is $y_1 + L = 250$. Given that all the capital raised by the new debt is used to buy back shares, all of this 250 accrues to initial shareholders. Thus the effect of the recapitalization is to raise the value of equity by 50.

Variation 1 is thus consistent with the apparent fact that debt-for-equity swaps raise the value of equity. However, I now show that, under a different information structure, variation 1 predicts that such swaps can reduce the value of equity.

Debt-for-Equity Swaps Can Lower Share Prices

Suppose that the vector (y_1, y_2, L) is known to take on two possible values. In Figure 10.6 state A is the good state and state B the bad

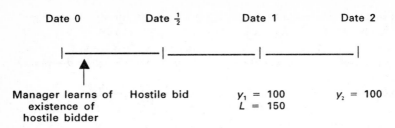

Date 0	Date $\frac{1}{2}$	Date 1	Date 2

Manager learns of existence of hostile bidder   Hostile bid $y_1 = 100$ $L = 150$ $y_2 = 100$

Figure 10.5   Recapitalization decision in face of hostile bid

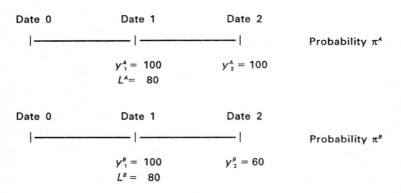

Date 0	Date 1	Date 2	
	$y_1^A = 100$ $L^A = 80$	$y_2^A = 100$	Probability π^A

Date 0	Date 1	Date 2	
	$y_1^B = 100$ $L^B = 80$	$y_2^B = 60$	Probability π^B

Figure 10.6   Liquidation versus continuation in good and bad states

state. Assume that, ex ante, π^A is very close to 1 and π^B is very close to zero. However, imagine that the management receives private information just after date 0 that in fact state B is sure to occur (the receipt of this information is very unlikely ex ante). This information will very shortly become available to the market, at date 1/4, say. In addition everyone already knows that a hostile bid will be made at date 1/2. Again assume that the firm is initially all equity. The information structure is shown in Figure 10.7.

Given that, in ex ante terms, state A is very likely, the management would have no incentive to deviate from the all-equity structure in the absence of the information that state B is going to occur (in this case it would adjust its estimate of π^A even closer to 1). The point is that an all-equity firm is under no pressure to liquidate at date 1. But, since π^A is close to 1, this outcome is approximately efficient, so the management is safe from a takeover at date 1/2. The market's ex ante valuation of the initial equity is therefore approximately $y_1^A + y_2^A = 200$.

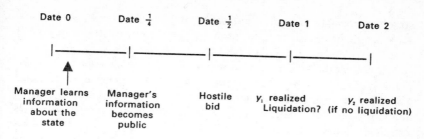

Figure 10.7 Recapitalization decision with hostile bid and uncertainty

The management, however, knows that the market will soon learn to its surprise that the bad state B is the true state. Given this, the management's job will be in jeopardy unless it can bond itself to liquidate at date 1, since in state B liquidation is efficient.[43] One thing the management can do is to make a debt-for-equity swap. For example, it might set $P_1 = 180$. This commits it to liquidation at date 1 in state B and thus thwarts the hostile takeover at date 1/2.

Of course, given this information structure, the management's recapitalization signals that it has learned unfavourable information about the state, in particular that state B will occur. The new debt, however, is riskless (because $y_1^B + L^B = 180$) and so sells for 180. Since all of this accrues to initial shareholders, the value of equity when the recapitalization is announced is also 180. This represents a drop in equity value from 200 even though the recapitalization is in security-holders' interests. The point is that bad news about the state signalled by the recapitalization offsets the increase in bonding.[44]

Thus variation 1 can explain not only the apparent fact that debt-for-equity swaps raise the price of equity but also the reverse.

Let us turn now to equity-for-debt swaps. These are not simply the opposite of debt-for-equity swaps because the debt-holders must be *persuaded* to sell their debt. Each small debt-holder always has the option to hold on to his debt and see it appreciate in value as others tender in the debt buyback.

Equity-for-Debt Swaps Typically Reduce the Price of Equity

It is easy to see that variation 1 can explain how equity-for-debt swaps can reduce the price of equity. Suppose that there are two states of the world, as in Figure 10.6, again with ex ante probabilities $\pi^A \simeq 1$, $\pi^B \simeq 0$. Now, however (for some historical reason), the initial capital structure consists of equity and senior debt promising $P_1 = 180$ and $P_2 = 0$. Suppose also that the probability of a takeover at any time is zero.

If a recapitalization is at all costly for the management (for example, if it requires effort), then management will not bother to recapitalize given the ex ante probabilities $\pi^A \simeq 1$, $\pi^B \simeq 0$ (in state A it will be able to avoid default by issuing \$80 of date 2 debt, and state B is extremely unlikely). However, suppose the management obtains private information at date 1/4 that $\pi^A = \pi^B = 1/2$. It is now in its interest to buy back some of the debt to avoid default and liquidation in state B. For example, suppose that the management issues new equity worth \$20 and uses it to buy back \$20 of debt (so that P_1 falls to $P_1' = 160$). Such a swap is feasible even if the market deduces from the swap that the management has learned $\pi^A = \pi^B = 1/2$. The reason is that existing debt-holders are indifferent between selling their debt back to the firm and not selling, since they are being offered one dollar for each dollar of debt, which is also what they get individually if they do not tender (with $P_1' = 160$, the firm's debt is riskless). Furthermore, after the swap, equity-holders receive $y_1^A + y_2^A - P_2' = 40$ in state A and $y_1^B + y_2^B - P_1' = 0$ in state B, so the market value of equity is 20. By issuing a large (or infinite) amount of new equity (in effect, overwhelming initial equity-holders), the management can indeed raise the \$20 necessary to buy back the debt.

Of course, this swap is very bad news for initial equity-holders, both because it signals that the bad state is more likely and because the extent of management bonding falls. The value of their equity falls to zero on announcement of the swap (their ownership stake in the firm will be infinitely diluted by the new equity issue). In contrast, before the recapitalization, when the market assumed $\pi^A \simeq 1$ $\pi^B \simeq 0$, the value of initial equity was approximately $y_1^A + y_2^A - P_1 = 20$.

Thus equity-for-debt swaps can reduce the price of initial equity. However, again the opposite can occur under a different information structure.

Equity-for-Debt Swaps Can Increase the Price of Equity

Suppose that the economy is again as in Figure 10.6. Now, however, the market thinks that $\pi^A \simeq 0$ and $\pi^B \simeq 1$, whereas management learns privately just after date 0 that $\pi^A = 0.9$, $\pi^B = 0.1$ (information that will become available to the market at date 1/4). Also assume it is known that a bidder will appear at date 1/2. (So the information structure is as in Figure 10.7.) Finally, suppose the initial capital structure of the firm is such that $P_1 = 180$ and $P_2 = 0$.

If state B were indeed very likely – as the market thinks – management would not wish to buy back a lot of debt at date 1/4, because this would commit it to an *inefficient* outcome at date 1 (the market knows that the management will never voluntarily liquidate then) and so a successful bid would occur at date 1/2. However, once the management learns that $\pi^A = 0.9$, $\pi^B = 0.1$, it may want to recapitalize, because if it buys back $20 of debt, it can avoid default in state B. Moreover, even though an inefficiency $L^B - y_2^B = 20$ is introduced in state B, the expected inefficiency as of date 1/2 is only $\pi^B \times 20 = 2$. So, as long as the bid costs exceed 2, the management will be safe from a date 1/2 bid even after the recapitalization.

The recapitalization works as before. The management issues new equity worth $20 and uses it to buy back $20 of debt. Creditors are indifferent between tendering and not tendering (they receive one dollar on the dollar either way because the firm is worth at least 160 in each state), whereas equity holders as a whole after the recapitalization receive $y_1^A + y_2^A - P_1' = 40$ in state A and $y_1^B + y_2^B - P_1' = 0$ in state B; that is, the value of all equity, using the newly signalled probabilities $\pi^A = 0.9$, $\pi^B = 0.1$, is $40 \times 0.9 = 36$. Because the value of new equity is 20, the value of initial equity is 16.

Before the recapitalization, the value of equity is $\pi^A(y_1^A + y_2^A - P_1) + \pi^B(y_1^B + L^B - P_1) \simeq 0$. Thus the recapitalization causes an *increase* in the value of equity even though it reduces the level of management bonding: the good news that state A occurs with probability 0.9 offsets the decrease in efficiency resulting from reduced bonding.

These last examples can throw light on one final kind of recapitalization: a pure increase in equity. Event studies find that this reduces the value of initial equity, and it is easy to see how. Simply take the first equity-for-debt example given earlier and note that, instead of using the $20 from the equity issue to buy back $20 of debt, the management could achieve exactly the same outcome by retaining the $20 in the firm and using it to repay some of the debt at date 1. The effect of this on the value of initial equity will be to reduce it (from $20 to zero), just as the event studies find.

On the other hand, the second equity-for-debt example also shows that new equity issues can sometimes *raise* the value of initial equity. Again let the management retain the $20 from the new equity issue and use it to repay some of the date 1 debt. Then the new equity issue causes the value of initial equity to rise from approximately zero to $16.

10.4 CONCLUSIONS

The many theories of capital structure – based on taxes, market incompleteness, asymmetric information, and so forth – are consistent with the apparent facts about capital structure that I have described in the previous section (see Harris and Raviv, 1991). However, these theories do not explain an even more basic aspect of capital structure: the widespread use of senior or secured debt. Only the approach that focuses on the conflict of interest between insiders and outsiders seems capable of explaining both sets of observations.

Although this agency (or managerial discretion) approach is still in its infancy, I have described a version of it that is consistent with the findings of a number of recent event studies (as well as with various other stylized facts). At the same time, to explain these findings, it was necessary to make specific assumptions about the structure of information faced by the firm's managers and the market. With different assumptions the approach predicts that reversals of these findings should be observed. I suspect this is a feature of *any* theory of capital structure. That is, it is hard to imagine how a theory could explain the apparent facts independently of information structure.

The agency approach could be extended in many ways. The two variations described in the previous section could be combined, the model could be generalized to more periods to obtain a richer theory of the maturity structure of debt, and the sharp distinctions supposed between debt and equity could be relaxed.

This last extension deserves some elaboration. In the model I used earlier, the distinction between debt and equity is stark: equity-holders are completely passive, and creditors automatically force a bankrupt firm into liquidation or prevent a financially distressed firm from raising new capital. In reality, of course, the picture is more complex. Equity-holders have votes that can be used to replace management, particularly when tendered to a hostile bidder.[45] Creditors do sometimes renegotiate their debt to avoid a firm's liquidation or allow new investments to be financed (perhaps via Chapter 11 bankruptcy). In future work it would be desirable to consider these possibilities and to understand their implication for the firm's choice of debt–equity ratio.

A related issue concerns the role of bankruptcy procedure. In this chapter, bankruptcy has, in effect, served as a punishment for managers of firms that have not paid their debts. This is questionable not only in positive terms but also from a normative point of view. Arguably, bankruptcy procedure should be designed more with the goal of maximizing the value of the firm than with punishing errant managers. Little work has been done on optimal bankruptcy procedures.[46] But it is to be hoped that the insights from the agency approach will be useful in guiding future work on this topic.

Finally, I should emphasize that, although I have advocated the agency approach over other approaches, such as those based on taxes or asymmetric information, I do not mean to suggest that these other approaches have nothing to offer. On the contrary, the agency approach could undoubtedly benefit greatly from being combined with them in future work.[47] One goal would be to explain observed variations in capital structure across industries and countries and over time. My point has simply been that trying to explain capital structure without being explicit about the conflict of interest between insiders and outsiders seems doomed to failure. The agency perspective is necessary for understanding capital structure, even if it may not by itself always be sufficient.

Notes

* This paper has been published in Margaret M. Blair (ed.) (1993), *The Deal Decade. What Takeovers and Leveraged Buy-outs Mean for Corporate Governance* (Washington DC: Brookings).

1. I thank Carliss Baldwin, Michael Brennan, Ian Cooper, Jim Poterba, Shan Li, Luigi Zingales, Jeff Zwiebel, and, especially, John Moore and Andrei Shleifer for helpful comments. I am also very grateful to John Moore for letting me include some of our unpublished joint work. Financial support from the National Science Foundation and the Center for Energy Policy Research at MIT is gratefully acknowledged.

2. For an excellent and comprehensive account of this literature, see Milton Harris and Artur Raviv (1991).

3. Clifford W. Smith, Jr. and Jerold B. Warner (1979) found that in a random sample of eighty-seven public issues of debt registered with the Securities and Exchange Commission between January 1974 and December 1975, more than 90 per cent of the bonds contained restrictions on the issuing of additional debt. Although the strength of such debt covenants declined during the 1980s, it is still very common for new public debt issues to contain some restrictions on new debt. See Richard Brook (1990).

   Another factor worth noting is that for US manufacturing companies traded on the New York and American stock exchanges (Compustat,

Primary-Supplementary-Tertiary file) the average ratio of secured debt to total debt ranged from 22 per cent to 33 per cent between 1981 and 1989 (author's calculations).

4. See Stewart C. Myers (1977). Some of the ideas in this section parallel those found in Philip H. Dybvig and Jaime F. Zender (1991).

5. In extensions, it would be important to allow for many managers, workers, and so forth.

6. Equation (10.1) also causes the manager to invest efficiently if r is uncertain at date 1, regardless of his attitude toward risk. This is because a risk-averse person is risk-neutral with respect to small bets and so, if θ is small, the manager will be interested in the expected net present value of investment. See Kenneth J. Arrow (1971).

7. When $y_1 + y_2 + r - d < i$ and $r > i$, it is in the collective interest of the initial creditors to forgive some of the initial debt d. However, if this debt is dispersed, it will not be in any creditor's individual interest to forgive or renegotiate debt and renegotiations are likely to break down. See, for example, Mark J. Roe (1987).

    The debt overhang problem disappears if the new investment opportunity can be spun off from the firm and financed as a separate corporate entity. However, this may be difficult to arrange to the extent that the same management team runs both firms and can use transfer pricing to reallocate profits between them. Under these conditions, the market can keep track only of total profits ($y_1 + y_2$ or $y_1 + y_2 + r - i$) and project-specific financing is impossible.

8. This means that the issues raised in Merton H. Miller (1977) do not arise.

9. I am ignoring the very small fraction of the firm's date 2 receipts used to compensate the manager.

10. In a multiperiod model in which further investment may occur at dates 2, 3, ... it would presumably be efficient to ensure that the debt issued at date 1 is also subordinated, in the sense that it would contain a covenant allowing the firm to issue debt senior to *it*.

11. PIK bonds, which give management the option of paying interest in cash or in additional securities, were in fact used extensively in LBOs during the 1980s. See Jeremy I. Bulow, Lawrence H. Summers, and Victoria P. Summers (1990).

12. In fact, before 1989, US corporations apparently faced few restrictions on their ability to use PIK bonds to wipe out taxable income. Since 1989 the Revenue Reconciliation Act has constrained them. See Bulow, Summers, and Summers (1990).

13. A person with a von Neumann–Morgenstern utility function evaluates a gamble in terms of the expected utility of its return.

14. An outcome is Pareto optimal if it is impossible to make some people better off without making others worse off.

15. Two points should be noted. First, there is an even simpler way to sustain the optimum if financial intermediaries can be created without cost: the firm issues 100 per cent equity, the manager is given the right to issue new equity or debt at date 1, and a financial intermediary repackages the net return R as the N securities $s_1(\cdot). \ldots . s_N(\cdot)$. For a discussion of practical examples of this kind of repackaging, see Robert C. Merton (1989).

Second, the analysis of optimal security structure when markets are incomplete becomes considerably more complicated when the return from the investment, r, is stochastic. The reason is that the optimal investment rule is no longer clear (it depends on attitudes toward risk) and must be derived endogenously along with the optimal sharing rules. I conjecture, however, that the main result – that all claims issued by the firm will be subordinated – generalizes.

16. This observation is also made by Dybvig and Zender (1991).

17. As far as I can see, this conclusion is also valid (at least approximately) in a multiperiod or infinite period context. The appropriate generalization of equation (10.1) is that the manager receives a small fraction θ of the total market value of the firm at date T (discounted to date 0), minus a fraction θ of any cash inflows to the firm at previous dates (discounted to date 0), plus a fraction θ of any dividends or interest paid at previous dates (discounted to date 0). Here T is the firm's last date in a finite horizon model and a far-off date if the horizon is infinite.

18. These arguments assume that it is always efficient for the manager to raise capital by issuing shares on the open market instead of borrowing or making private placements. Suppose, however, that borrowing or private placement is advantageous and it is difficult to measure objectively whether such deals are made on favourable terms. Shareholders may prefer to give the manager some equity in the firm rather than apply the formula in equation (10.1) to encourage him to make the effort to achieve a good deal. Under these conditions, the Myers–Majluf (1984) analysis may apply. However, this approach, by stressing the manager's effort, departs from the working hypothesis that the manager is selfless and his decisions are not costly to him.

19. This is a version of the Modigliani–Miller argument that investors can always undo a firm's financial structure by trading on their own account. If it is strapped for cash, management could always borrow to finance its purchases, using the acquired shares as collateral.

It is worth emphasizing that the assumption that management acts on behalf of shareholders is much less controversial in the case of a small private company in which management holds most or all of the equity and the equity cannot be easily traded.

20. See, for example, Macmillan's (unsuccessful) efforts to defeat Robert Maxwell, as described in Cynthia Crossen and Karen Blumenthal ('An Anti-Takeover Arsenal That Failed'), *Wall Street Journal*, 4 November 1988, p. B1.

21. A qualification should be made here. Some scholars have argued that even if the management is selfless, senior or secured debt or both may be useful as a way of bonding the firm if it engages in strategic behaviour in product markets or in bargaining with unions. See Carliss Y. Baldwin (1983), James A. Brander and Tracy R. Lewis (1986) and Enrico C. Perotti and Kathryn E. Spier (1991). Although strategic effects may well be important, however, it would be surprising if they alone could explain the widespread use of senior or secured debt or the variations in such debt across industries, countries, or over time.

22. Another qualification should be made. Giving votes to a dispersed group

of security-holders may increase management's bargaining power in negotiations with an acquirer. See Luigi Zingales (1991).

23. See, for example, Robert M. Townsend (1979), Douglas Gale and Martin Hellwig (1985), Oliver Hart and John Moore (1989), Philippe Aghion and Patrick Bolton (1992) and Douglas W. Diamond (1991).

Some of this literature is surveyed in Franklin Allen (1989).

24. See, for example, Stephen A. Ross (1977) and Sanford J. Grossman and Oliver D. Hart (1982).

25. On the early managerial literature, see William J. Baumol (1959), Robin L. Marris (1964) and Oliver E. Williamson (1964). On the free cash flow hypothesis, see Michael C. Jensen (1986).

26. See Michael J. Barclay and Clifford G. Holderness (1989) for additional empirical evidence that control rents are large.

27. This first variation is related to work by Rene Stulz (1988) and Guozhong Xie (1990). The present version is based on unpublished work that I have carried out with John Moore.

28. These private benefits are not modelled explicitly. One interpretation is that the manager obtains a great deal of utility from being in charge of an empire. Of course, in reality, managers also care about their wealth. Thus future studies ought to relax the assumption that incentive schemes have no role to play.

29. In principle the firm's owners could remove the manager in other ways — by firing him, for example. But in the present model there is no real distinction between bankruptcy and a management firing (bankruptcy triggers liquidation, which can be thought of as representing the value of the firm if the manager is fired). One arrangement that I rule out is a *contingent* liquidation or firing contract, one in which the owners specify that the manager is fired if and only if $y_2 < L$. A contingent contract is enforceable only if y_2 and L are *verifiable*, as well as being observable to the manager and the market; arguably this is not the case. (A variable is verifiable if it can be litigated over. Many variables are observable to certain parties but not verifiable. For example, in the hearings before the Senate Judiciary Committee, Judge Clarence Thomas and Professor Anita Hill both presumably knew whether Thomas had sexually harassed Hill, but neither was able to establish the truth objectively. A variable that is not verifiable cannot be the basis of an enforceable, contingent contract.)

30. One interpretation is that the choice is made before an initial date 0 public offering by the original owner, who wishes to maximize his total receipts in this offering. Another interpretation is that the threat of a hostile takeover forces management to maximize market value at date 0.

31. In what follows, the possibility that $y_2 > L$ will be important. One point of view is that $y_2 \leq L$ always because there is nothing to stop outside bidders from competing in a Chapter 7 liquidation for the right to run the firm as a going concern. Two justifications for not adopting this point of view can be given. First, there may be insufficient time for outside bidders to raise the financing for their bids in Chapter 7 liquidation. Second, if incumbent management has special skills, they may be the only party that can bid for the firm as a going concern, and although they may win the auction, they may end up paying the second highest value for the

firm's assets, represented by the (piecemeal) liquidation value of L.

32. In discussing optimal capital structure, I always treat the manager's private benefit of control as a pure rent that does not enter into the firm's market value. Thus the manager's private benefits do not affect the initial choice of capital structure.

33. To see this, note that to obtain the first-best outcome one must have default in state B, that is, $y_1^B + y_2^B < P_1$. But this implies $y_1^A + y_2^A < P_1$, that is, there will also be default in state A.

34. This variation is based on Oliver Hart and John Moore (1990).

35. Another justification for ignoring short-term debt is that much of the analysis that follows applies when the firm needs to go to the capital market to finance new investment ($y_1 < i$); under these conditions short-term debt as a means for getting cash out of the company has little value.

36. This is again an extreme assumption, but the main ideas of the analysis should apply when management is interested in both empire-building and financial compensation.

37. More general security structures, including debt of different seniorities, are considered in Hart and Moore (1990).

38. For discussion of these, see Harris and Raviv (1991), Ronald W. Masulis (1988) and Stewart C. Myers (1989). For original sources, see Paul Asquith and David Mullins, Jr. (1986), W. Carl Kester (1986), M. Long and I. Malitz (1985), Ronald W. Masulis (1980) and Sheridan Titman and Roberto Wessels (1988).

39. For more on this, see Hart and Moore (1990).

40. For a model close in spirit to this discussion, see David A. Butz (1990).

41. Assume that the chances of another bidder appearing later are negligible.

42. I assume that it is too late to make such a swap after the takeover bid is announced.

43. I assume that bonding must occur before the market learns the true state at date 1/4 and a fortiori before a bid occurs at date 1/2 (dates 1/4 and 1/2 might be very close together).

44. The idea that a managerial action that serves shareholders can cause a decline in share price because the action reveals bad news about the company is far from new. See, for example, Andrei Shleifer and Robert W. Vishny (1986).

45. Hostile takeovers played a background role in the analysis in the previous section.

46. An exception is Lucian A. Bebchuk (1988).

47. Asymmetric information played an important background role in the analysis of event studies in the previous section.

References

Aghion, P. and P. Bolton (1992) 'An Incomplete Contracts Approach to Financial Contracting', *Review of Economic Studies*, vol. 59, pp. 473–94.

Allen, F. (1989) 'The Changing Nature of Debt and Equity: A Financial Perspective', in R.W. Kopke and E.S. Rosengren (eds), *Are the Distinctions*

234 Game Theory, General Equilibrium, and Information

Between Debt and Equity Disappearing? (Federal Reserve Bank of Boston Conference Series 33) pp. 12–38.

Arrow, K.J. (1971) *Essays in the Theory of Risk Bearing* (Chicago: Markham Publishing).

Asquith, P. and D. Mullins, Jr. (1986) 'Equity Issues and Offering Dilution', *Journal of Financial Economics*, vol. 15, pp. 61–89.

Baldwin, C.Y. (1983) 'Productivity and Labor Unions: An Application of the Theory of Self-Enforcing Contracts', *Journal of Business*, vol. 56, pp. 155–85.

Barclay, M.J. and C. G. Holderness (1989) 'Private Benefits from Control of Public Corporations', *Journal of Financial Economics*, vol. 25, pp. 371–95.

Baumol, W.J. (1959) *Business Behaviour, Value and Growth* (London: Macmillan).

Bebchuk, L.A. (1988) 'A New Approach to Corporate Reorganizations', *Harvard Law Review*, vol. 101, pp. 775–804.

Brander, J.A. and T.R. Lewis (1986) 'Oligopoly and Financial Structure: The Limited Liability Effect', *American Economic Review*, vol. 76, pp. 956–70.

Brook, R. (1990) 'Debt Covenants and Event Risk: The Practitioner as a Source of Evidence', Working Paper 51, Columbia University Law School.

Bulow, J.I., L.H. Summers, and V.P. Summers (1990) 'Distinguishing Debt from Equity in the Junk Bond Era', in J.B. Shoven and J. Waldfogel (eds), *Debt, Taxes and Corporate Restructuring* (New York: Brookings) pp. 135–66.

Butz, D.A. (1990) 'Bust Up Takeover Bids and Asymmetric Information', University of California, Los Angeles.

Diamond, D.W. (1991) 'Debt Maturity Structure and Liquidity Risk', *Quarterly Journal of Economics*, vol. 106, pp. 709–37.

Dybvig, P.H. and J.F. Zender (1991) 'Capital Structure and Dividend Irrelevance with Asymmetric Information', *Review of Financial Studies*, vol. 4, pp. 201–19.

Gale, D. and M. Hellwig (1985) 'Incentive Compatible Debt Contracts: The One Period Problem', *Review of Economic Studies*, vol. 52, pp. 647–63.

Grossman, S.J. and O.D. Hart (1982) 'Corporate Financial Structure and Managerial Incentives', in J.J. McCall (ed.), *The Economics of Information and Uncertainty* (University of Chicago Press) pp. 107–37.

Harris, M. and A. Raviv (1991) 'The Theory of Capital Structure', *Journal of Financial Economics*, vol. 46, pp. 297–355.

Hart, O.D. and J. Moore (1989) 'Default and Renegotiation: A Dynamic Model of Debt', MIT Department of Economics Working Paper 520.

Hart, O.D. and J. Moore (1990) 'A Theory of Corporate Financial Structure Based on the Seniority of Claims', National Bureau of Economic Research Working Paper 3431.

Jensen, M.C. (1986) 'Agency Costs of Free Cash Flow, Corporate Finance and Takeovers', *American Economic Review*, vol. 76, pp. 323–9.

Jensen, M.C. and W.H. Meckling (1976) 'Theory of the Firm, Managerial Behaviour, Agency Costs and Ownership Structure', *Journal of Financial Economics*, vol. 4, pp. 305–60.

Kester, W.C. (1986) 'Capital and Ownership Structure: A Comparison of United States and Japanese Manufacturing Corporations', *Financial Management*, vol. 15, pp. 5–16.

Long, M. and I Malitz (1985) 'Investment Patterns and Financial Leverage', in B.M. Friedman (ed.), *Corporate Capital Structure in the United States* (University of Chicago Press).

Marris, R.L. (1964) *The Economic Theory of Managerial Capitalism* (Glencoe, Ill.: Free Press).

Masulis, R.W. (1980) 'The Effects of Capital Structure Change on Security Prices: A Study of Exchange Offers', *Journal of Financial Economics*, vol. 8, pp. 139–77.

Masulis, R.W. (1988) *The Debt/Equity Choice* (New York: Ballinger).

Merton, R.C. (1989) 'The Changing Nature of Debt and Equity: Discussion', in R.W. Kopcke and E.S. Rosengren (eds), *Are the Distinctions Between Debt and Equity Disappearing?* (Federal Reserve Bank of Boston Conference Series 33) pp. 44–8.

Miller, M.H. (1977) 'Debt and Taxes', *Journal of Finance*, vol. 32, pp. 261–75.

Myers, S.C. (1977) 'Determinants of Corporate Borrowing', *Journal of Financial Economics*, vol. 5, pp. 147–75.

Myers, S.C. (1989) 'Still Searching for Optimal Capital Structure', in R.W. Kopcke and E.S. Rosengren (eds), *Are the Distinctions Between Debt and Equity Disappearing?* (Federal Reserve Bank of Boston Conference Series 33).

Myers, S.C. and N.S. Majluf (1984) 'Corporate Financing and Investment Decisions When Firms Have Information That Investors Do Not Have'. *Journal of Financial Economics*, vol. 13, pp. 187–221.

Perotti, E.C. and K.E. Spier (1991) 'Capital Structure as a Bargaining Tool: The Role of Leverage in Contract Renegotiation', Harvard University Discussion Paper 1548.

Roe, M.J. (1987) 'The Voting Prohibition in Bond Workouts', *Yale Law Journal*, vol. 97, pp. 232–79.

Ross, S.A. (1977) 'The Determination of Financial Structure: The Incentive Signalling Approach', *Bell Journal of Economics*, vol. 8, pp. 23–40.

Shleifer, A. and R. Vishny (1986) 'Greenmail, White Knights and Shareholders' Interest', *Rand Journal of Economics*, vol. 17, pp. 293–309.

Smith, C.W. Jnr. and J.B. Warner (1979) 'On Financial Contracting: An Analysis of Bond Covenants', *Journal of Financial Economics*, vol. 7, p. 122.

Stulz, R. (1988) 'Managerial Control of Voting Rights: Financing Policies and the Market for Corporate Control', *Journal of Financial Economics*, vol. 20, pp. 25–54.

Titman, S. and R. Wessels (1988) 'The Determinants of Capital Structure Choice', *Journal of Finance*, vol. 43, pp. 1–19.

Townsend, R.M. (1979) 'Optimal Contracts and Competitive Markets with Costly State Verification', *Journal of Economic Theory*, vol. 21, pp. 265–93.

Williamson, O.E. (1964) *The Economics of Discretionary Behavior* (New York: Prentice-Hall).

Wilson, R. (1968) 'The Theory of Syndicates', *Econometrica*, vol. 36, pp. 119–32.

Xie, Guozhong (1990) 'Essays on the Theory of the Firm', PhD dissertation, Massachusetts Institute of Technology.

Zingales, L. (1991) 'Insiders' Ownership and the Decision to Go Public', Massachusetts Institute of Technology.

Part IV

Applications

11 Non-Hierarchical Aspects of the Internal Organization of the Enterprise: A Partial Survey in Comparative Perspective

Masahiko Aoki
STANFORD UNIVERSITY

11.1 INTRODUCTION

It has become evident that one of the fundamental causes of the failure of socialist economies was the incompatibility of centralized national planning with efficient systems of information transfer and incentives. But will problems associated with the former centrally planned economies be resolved if the monolithic, single-peaked, hierarchy of the national planning apparatus is replaced by multiple hierarchies of management and control which will compete in the product market and whose entry and exit will be controlled by the capital market? If we turn our eyes to market economies we find a variety of forms of internal structure and governance of enterprises as well as differences in the degree and methods of control by the capital market. Why does such a variety exist, and what are its implications for efficiency? Will enterprises of different national, cultural, and historical origins eventually converge to the ideal economists' model of a hierarchy exploiting economies of specialization, scope, and scale under the discipline of perfectly competitive markets?

In the last two decades, there has been a growing interest by economists in the 'theory of the firm'. Contractual theorists have shed important light on the incentive aspects of employment contracts as well as of capital market control over management. Transaction-cost

239

economics (pioneered by Coase, 1937 and revitalized by Williamson, 1975) has investigated conditions for comparative efficiency and the limits of hierarchical, as opposed to market, transactions. There have also been occasional attempts by economists to break open the black box of the 'firm' and to analyze the performance characteristics of stylized models of enterprise hierarchy.

But although their contributions have been significant in revealing and understanding the general nature of the enterprise, economists are still far from a full integration of the two approaches mentioned above. As we will see, a fundamental premise of the contractual approach (the Revelation Principle) leads to a theoretical construction in which the essence of the enterprise is captured by two-tier principal–agent contractual relationships, either investor–management or employer–employee. By reducing the, actually more complex, organizational structure of the enterprise, contractual theorists have been very successful in understanding the incentive aspects of some of its institutional arrangements, but at the cost of ignoring another important aspect of its internal organization: organizational coordination as opposed to market transaction (Coase, 1988). But whether (external) corporate control and internal coordination can be dealt with in complete isolation, for the purpose of understanding the nature and implications of a variety of organizational forms, may be doubted.

Transaction-cost economists have increasingly come to recognize the importance of the intermediate mode of transactions, between hierarchies and markets. But they appear to presume that this intermediate mode generally takes the form of contractual relations between enterprises, not within the enterprise (Williamson, 1985, 1991a). The mathematical analysis of hierarchical control and coordination has long been based on rather specific *ad hoc* models, and the treatment of internal hierarchy, and its assessment in comparison with other types of internal coordination mechanisms, has only recently been attempted.

It is this author's view that in assessing the comparative performance of different organizational forms of the enterprise in market economies, as well as deriving the implications for transforming/reforming socialist enterprises, a somewhat broader perspective is necessary, although various analytical concepts, tools, and results developed within the framework of the above-mentioned theories will undoubtedly provide valuable help. In presenting this view, I rely upon the observations of the following 'stylized facts' (to be elaborated later):

1. Rigid hierarchical structuring, as conceived in mathematical modelling by economists, is becoming increasingly obsolete not only as an economy-wide coordination mechanism but also as an internal control and coordination mechanism for large enterprises. Various forms of non-hierarchical coordination are supplementing and/or partially replacing hierarchical coordination within efficiency-oriented large enterprises.

2. Despite the possibility that diverse organizational forms may perform differently, contingent upon the technical and market conditions of a particular industry, a similar pattern of organizational form tends to appear across industries in one economy, while somewhat different patterns appear in other economies. For example, the organizational form α may be more efficient for industry A, while the form β may be more efficient for industry B. But we may observe that enterprises seem to cluster around the form α in one economy, while the form β is predominant in another. One implication of this could be that a dominant organizational form in each economy is becoming an important determinant of its comparative advantage, in lieu of its endowment of natural resources. Another implication may be that (internal) efficiency does not completely determine the choice of organizational form.

3. The market for corporate control has not been active in some large market economies, such as Germany and Japan, and is rapidly becoming a less active institution even in the United States. In Germany and Japan, employees' voices are reflected legally or implicitly when selecting top management. Thus, the corporate governance structure of the enterprise may not be completely controlled by external investors, at least in a non-negligible segment of market economies.

I believe that these stylized facts cannot be dismissed as aberration from the model of the enterprise as a pure functional hierarchy under the control of a perfectly competitive capital market. Fact 1 above is a natural response to today's state of competition among enterprises of different national origins, of the development of information and communication technology, of the higher level of aspiration, education, and training of organizational participants, etc. As an economist, I will not dismiss fact 2 as only culturally conditioned. It may foreshadow the existence of some kind of 'system effects' which could be expressed in economists' language. If so, enterprises in the transitional economies may not emulate a range of organizational forms from different economies. The design of an organizational form needs to be consistent with the design of other elements of the system (such as financial institutions) and of the social heritage. Fact 3 should encourage economists to re-examine critically the accepted formulation of the 'objective' of the firm as the maximization of its share price. The managements of enterprises in market economies may be pursuing more complex objectives, which then requires a more sophisticated analytical approach to issues of the behaviour (management decisions) and corporate governance of the enterprise.

The rest of this chapter is dedicated to a partial survey of the rather scarce literature relevant to the above-mentioned facts and their implications, and the main concern is *comparative*. The coverage of the literature is admittedly biased and far from complete (geographically somewhat Pacific-rim-centric because of my limited communication capacity). Section 11.2 examines the logic of the so-called Revelation Principle as an essential building block of the principal–agency theory of the enterprise and shows how it contributed to the reduction of the essentials of enterprise structure to the 'degenerate hierarchy' (Melumad, Mookherjee and Reichelstein, 1991), thus failing to capture an essential organizational aspect of the enterprise. Section 11.3 surveys the most recent literature on hierarchies as the internal organization of the enterprise. Section 11.4 briefly summarizes various real world facts about the internal structure of the enterprise which may not be captured by the traditional concept of hierarchies. The next two sections discuss conditions under which non-hierarchical coordination within the enterprise, such as horizontal coordination of parallel information processing, knowledge sharing, joint responsibility and help, on-site problem solving, etc., become informationally more efficient than hierarchical coordination (Section 11.5) and incentive compatible (Section 11.6). The next two sections deal with complementarities among business and internal organizational strategies of the enterprise (Section 11.7) as well as complementarities between these and external factor market institutions (Section 11.8). Section 11.9 discusses the implication of such complementarities for the nature of the corporate governance structure of the enterprise and the usefulness of the bargaining approach for analyzing the enterprise's behaviour under multi-stakeholder governance structure.

11.2 THE PITFALL OF THE REVELATION PRINCIPLE

The theory of principal–agent contracts has made remarkable progress in the last two decades and has had a considerable impact on the theory of the firm in general, and the theory of its internal structure specifically. Surveys of important contributions by Hart and Holmstrom (1987) and Holmstrom and Tirole (1989) and textbooks by Milgrom and Roberts (1992) and McMillan (1992) have helped to make this theory the common knowledge of students of economics and practitioners and to affirm that it has now the status of a 'paradigm'.

Despite its great achievements otherwise, one possible criticism (see Coase, 1988) of the principal–agency approach to the internal structure is that it has so far been preoccupied with incentive issues to the relative neglect of issues of organizational coordination. For this limitation the so-called 'Revelation Principle' (Myerson, 1979 and others) is responsible and must be critically examined.

Assume a standard framework of the principal to multi-agent relationships in which agents have acquired private information before contract and are limited in liability (ability to pay). Suppose that each agent learns the random quantity (ability, etc.) $z > 0$ prior to the choice of effort, where $\Pr (z = z_i) = p_i$, $i = 1, \ldots N$. The agent reports $z^\wedge$ to the principal and chooses effort e producing $x = ze$ at personal costs $C(e)$, or else quits, incurring cost $c(0) = 0$. The agent is paid $s(z^\wedge, x) \geq 0$. A contract specifies a level of output x_i that the agent is expected to produce in event z_i and the sharing rule $s(.\,, .)$. The revelation principle states that, without loss of generality, we may limit attention to contracts that make it optimal for the agent to be truthful and report $z^\wedge \equiv z$. The essence of a proof is easy to grasp. Given a sharing rule $s(.\,, .)$ in response to which the agent's optimal report and action are $z^\wedge = g(z)$ and $x = f(z)$ respectively, the new rule $s^*(z, x) \equiv s(g(z), x)$ provides the same pay and performance, making it optimal for the agent to be truthful. The same logic applies to the case where the outcome of agents' efforts are also confounded with the effect of stochastic events (hidden actions).

In the context of organizational design, the revelation principle implies that any non-cooperative equilibrium outcome of an arbitrary organization can be replicated by a centralized two-tier structure, wherein agents communicate their entire private information to the centre (principal) and there is no interaction among agents. Thus the organization structure becomes irrelevant and one can confine attention only to 'degenerate hierarchies' (Melumad, Mookherjee and Reichelstein,

1991) which have only two tiers without any horizontal interaction.

The revelation mechanism elicits the agents' information by providing choice. Information rents accrue to agents other than those with the lowest z. At the optimal grand contract, rents increase with the value of z. As a result, outputs are distorted, and contract output (in the absence of hidden action) is first-best efficient only for the agents with the highest z.

Now, suppose that some information is not observable to the principal, but is public among agents. It is claimed that, in this case, truthful information can even be *costlessly* elicited by the principal if agents do not collude. Information perfectly shared among agents is thus never private (Moore and Repullo, 1989). For example, consider a situation where efforts of agents are not directly observable by the principal but can be observed by all agents. Then the principal can contrive a multi-stage direct revelation mechanism (in which one agent reports to the principal about others' efforts, another agent accords or contests, and so on) that can elicit true information from agents by penalizing those who misrepresent. It is claimed that first-best efforts can thus be induced as a unique sequential equilibrium (Ma, 1988). There are no gains, therefore, for the principal from allowing agents' side-contracting (i.e., by delegating effort coordination to them and letting them reshuffle the sharing of outcome among themselves) even if there is private information among agents initially unknown to the principal.

However, it is obvious that, in reality, the internal organizations of large enterprises are characterized by multi-layered hierarchies in which agents are likely to be engaged in vertical and horizontal side trades of various kinds (pecuniary and non-pecuniary, implicit and explicit) not directly controllable by the principal. The revelation principle implicitly posits that there are no communication costs other than agents' incentives not to disclose private information without the provision of quasi-rents, and thus no other barrier to the transmission of private information. Even these incentive costs can be reduced to nil if information is completely shared among agents. But in reality, because of bounded rationality of the principal and agents, there can be many other barriers to communication. Agents' private information may take the form of expert knowledge which cannot be fully understood by others lacking the expertise. Some information may not be easily codifiable and may be impossible to communicate without noise, delay and reduction of its value, except through direct personal contact. Bounded rationality of the principal may make it impossible for him to communicate directly with all agents without causing excessive information overload.

McAfee and McMillan (1991b) recently recognized the limits of the degenerate model of internal organization, and built a multi-layered hierarchical model in which the revelation principle is successively applied from the bottom to intermediate levels to the top. They rationalize such an approach by positing, without explicit modelling, that there is a limit to the capacity of superiors to process truthfully revealed information from subordinates. Since at each level information rents need to be paid to subordinates, the multi-layered hierarchy incurs multiplying effects of information rents. The principal can retrieve some of these rents only at the expense of introducing a distortion, paying the agent less than the full value of his marginal product. As a result, the firm operates inefficiently. The degree of this inefficiency varies with demand elasticity and with the length of the hierarchy. The costs of the operating hierarchy thus create a limit to the size of the firm, depending on the state of market competition. However, information costs which render the two-tier degenerate organization impossible remain implicit in their model.

The implementation of a direct revelation mechanism *à la* Ma (1988), when mutual monitoring among agents is possible, is also likely to incur high communication costs in terms of time and effort. But even if there were no communication costs *per se*, the possibility of collusion, when communication channels are open among agents, may prevent implementation of the first-best revelation mechanism. The agents may find an effort constellation which they all prefer to the one the principal wishes to implement, and then collude in sending distorted messages to the principal at the communication stage in order to elicit their preferred choice. Itoh (1992b) has indeed shown for a specific model that the principal's attempt to prevent side-contracting by the design of a grand contract is abortive, when collusion at the communication stage is possible, in the sense that there does not exist any such contract which implements a given effort level with lower costs than optimal side contracts. Of course, writing and enforcing side contracts will not be costless either (Tirole, 1990). But Itoh's result is important in indicating that there are cases in which horizontal interactions among agents, and the delegation of effort coordination among agents, may become valuable to the principal (the organization). It is thus suggested that the explicit consideration of costs of communication and the possibility of lateral communication may lead to a richer theory of the internal organization of the enterprise.

11.3   RECENT THEORIES OF HIERARCHY

Traditionally economists have seen the essence of the internal organization of the enterprise as a functional hierarchy which may be characterized by such institutional features as (a) the specialization of operational activities; (b) the separation of coordination (managing) from operational activities (doing); and (c) the successive centralization of information through administrative layers. More formally, a hierarchy is defined as a set (called the tree) of half-ordered agents[1] having the following properties: (i) there is only one common superior (the root) to every agent; and (ii) any agent except for the root has at most one immediate superior through which it receives information and to which it reports.

The literature on hierarchy (excluding the vast principal–agency literature on degenerate hierarchies) may be roughly divided into two fields: one dealing primarily with the controlling aspect of hierarchies and the other with their coordination aspect. According to the former, a hierarchy is viewed as a mechanism in which a strategic decision made at the top level is decomposed through each successive level into a command for a specialized task to each operating unit at the bottom level. The major benefit is the utilization of economies of specialization in operating tasks. However, as the strategic decision is successively decomposed through hierarchical layers, the effectiveness of control is diluted because of the limited decision-making capacity of intermediate-level managers (Williamson, 1967; Beckman, 1977; Rosen, 1982), or their fixed set-up time (Keren and Levhari, 1979, 1983), or their limited ability to monitor subordinates' actions (Calvo and Wellisz, 1978; Qian, 1994).

In contrast to the first approach in which incentive issues are normally highlighted, either explicitly or implicitly, in the reduced-form cost/production function, the second approach adopts the 'team' framework in which agents are assumed to share an identical objective (thus incentive issues are assumed away), but are bounded-rational in information processing/communication/computation. Suppose that operational activities are performed by units at the bottom level, interconnected by technological input–output relations and jointly constrained by the availability of organizational resources. The technologies of operating units are subject to the influence of (mutually independent) random events. Depending on the realized values of random variables, the optimal assignment of tasks to each operating unit and the allocation of organizational resources to it may vary. Assuming that centralized information processing of random events is impossible, Cremer (1980) considers the problem of optimally decomposing the organization ex ante into divisions within which the coordination of operational tasks and the allocation of organizational resources may be done on the basis of ex post information.

Geanakoplos and Milgrom (1991) combine the quadratic production model of Cremer with the Bayesian learning of random events by managers (supervisors) at different levels. Managers are limited by their capacity to learn as well as by the time available for learning. The authors consider the problem of optimal structuring of a hierarchy and derive, *inter alia*, the following results: If firms have better prior information about their environments (as in a traditional industry where technology is fairly well known), a flatter hierarchy may be optimal. In the opposite case, where the prior uncertainty is great and the information-processing job is more difficult (as in a more rapidly evolving industry), firms should hire more able managers at higher levels and provide them with smaller areas of control, as there is more scope for good management to improve matters.

The most recent model by Keren and Levhari (1989), in a series of their works on hierarchy, is an attempt to synthesize the two aspects of hierarchies: controlling and coordinating. The top supervisor makes a central plan based on information at hand and the plan is gradually decomposed through intermediate levels to the operating level, as in the first approach. Information is initially collected at the operating level with a rich natural language of a range equal to the number of commodities involved, but information is aggregated (the number of individual messages is reduced) in the process of successive reporting to superiors. Time consumed in information processing (aggregation and reporting) and plan decomposition at each intermediate level is an increasing function of the range of messages that level receives and of its span of control. The payoff to the firm is a decreasing function of delay and of deviation from an optimal plan caused by reliance on coarser aggregated information in plan-making. However, the ability to rely upon coarse information enables the organization to delay the arrival of diminishing returns to scale resulting from its efficiency in the use of time. Keren and Levhari reached a somewhat different conclusion from Geanakoplos and Milgrom regarding the effect of increasing complexity of the organization's environment on the organizational structure. An increase in the range of natural language at the operational level may lead (or may not, depending on the parameter values of the model) to a flatter hierarchical structure, because the increased complexity raises the necessary coordination time per level so that it pays to reduce the number of tiers by increasing the span of control at each.

Melumad, Mookherjee and Reichelstein (1991), present a potentially rich model which combines consideration of incentive and information. Their model is the principal–agency type in which there is one principal and two agents who can communicate only imperfectly, for some reason other than incentive to distort information to their own advantage. Since the revelation principle does not hold, three-tier structures or communications among agents need to be considered as possible in addition to the degenerate two-tier structure. Melumad *et al.* modelled the agents' limited capacity for communication by the specification that agents are restricted to selecting messages from a message set which is coarser than the original space (e.g., the agents can communicate the value of a continuous variable only in terms of 'high', 'intermediate' or 'low' (Oniki, 1974, is a predecessor). In a two-tier hierarchy the principal collects imperfect information from both agents, but imperfection is symmetrical between agents. In the three-tier mechanism, however, the agent at the intermediate level does have precise information regarding its own technology, although imperfect information regarding the other, and is motivated by this biased information to assign more production to itself. But if the principal can monitor the production assignments, he can mitigate the loss of control and can benefit from delegating inter-agent coordination to that agent who has better information than has the principal, at least on its own technology. Melumad *et al.*'s model suggests one way to analyze nondegenerate hierarchies in the principal–agency framework.

11.4 NON-HIERARCHICAL ASPECTS OF INTERNAL ORGANIZATION

A highly developed form of hierarchy, in the context of the modern large enterprise, is conceived to be what Chandler (1966) and Williamson (1975) called the M-form structure. The enterprise organization is subdivided into multiple divisions engaged in different business lines, each of which internalizes functionally specialized departments such as sales/distribution, finance, manufacturing, supply procurement, design, etc. These departments are each hierarchically controlled by the responsible middle-manager. Each division is controlled by the top manager at the corporate headquarters who monitors division managers and allocates organizational resources. By internalizing certain functions of capital markets such as monitoring management (of divisions) and transferring financial resources to the most profitable uses, the large enterprise can save on transaction costs, while each division can enjoy the economies of specialization attributable to traditional hierarchies.

However, we are now witnessing the emergence of various forms of non-hierarchical organization as well as signs that rigid hierarchies, including the M-form, may be losing their effectiveness in the increasingly competitive global market environment, becoming obsolete under rapidly developing communication and information technologies, and/or not viable for political, social or other reasons. We may consider some of those signs and some questions which might motivate analytical inquiries into non-hierarchical structures:

(1) The M-form structure, if each division is organized tightly as a closed entity, may fail to capture certain economies which could result from closer relations among divisions as well as duplicating some costly activities. For example, when each division has separate sales departments, potential marketability of a system of complementary products made by different divisions may fail to be recognized; and the lack of horizontal interactions among research and development (R&D) departments of separate divisions may lead to costly duplication of research efforts.[2]

(2) In industries where competition in the market involves a variety of products manufactured in small or large batches through numerous production steps, market information must be rapidly channelled to production scheduling and procurement orders to minimize costs of unsold products, manufacturing and intermediate inventories, etc. Rigid adherence to ex ante plans prepared by the administrative apparatus must give way to flexible adaptation to emerging information. Thus to adapt to changing market conditions, horizontal, cross-functional coordination of sales, manufacturing and supply functions is developing in such industries (e.g. automobiles, metals, air lines) with the aid of computer networks and electronic data transmission systems.

It is also likely that these industries are the so-called 'stable-tech' industries (Chandler, 1992), in which the final product has remained much the same over time and competition is based largely on improvement and diversification of the existing products and processes. Here it is essential that R&D is closely linked with engineering, marketing, and supply so that new products attuned to changing market demands are made commercially available as quickly as possible.

Flexible adaptation also requires quick problem-solving, consistent with the goals of the organization, at the site where problems arise. For this, the 'Fordist' mode of organization (complete separation of 'doing' from information-gathering, problem-solving and coordinating) is not efficient. The delegation of problem-solving to the lower levels, enterprise-specific training programmes, the shop-level team approach, are some examples of better ways of coping with such needs (see Boyer's study (1991) for OECD for a summary of these phenomena in five advanced economies: United States, France, Japan, Germany, and Sweden).

(3) It is to be noted that the development of robotics and other computer-aided manufacturing systems has not replaced human skill, but rather facilitated increased integration of operational and problem-solving activities at the manufacturing site. Likewise, the development of computer networks and electronic data transmission systems makes possible the collective use of on-site information on a wider scale within organizations, which in turn requires of participants a broader knowledge of organizational procedure (e.g. security). It goes without saying that the development of computer-aided design and other experimental equipment has facilitated R&D strategies of faster product improvement. These technological developments in the sphere of manufacturing, marketing, design and engineering appear to be accompanied by closer non-hierarchical coordination among traditionally separate functions rather than by tighter hierarchical control. Is there any logical reason for it? (See Milgrom and Roberts, 1990b.)

(4) One fundamental source of the inefficiency of the former centrally planned economies seems to be that, during the long period of command economy, people's behaviour has been adapted to sequential information processing and that the practice of parallel information processing, which requires flexible horizontal coordination either through markets or within organizations, is now hard to learn. Thus delays in the changes in production patterns due to such inefficiencies may be responsible for shortages of particular goods. If one compares organizational practices in Russia and those in any advanced economies, one must be impressed by the flexibility, decentralization and informational efficiency of the latter. This not-so-novel revelation may imply, however, that the economists' traditional model of the internal organization of the enterprise as a vertical hierarchy, similar to the central planning apparatus in its essential working and different only in its size, has failed to capture some essential characteristics of business organization in advanced market economies.

(5) In the transforming/reforming socialist economies, the workers in the state-owned enterprise may have inherited socialist values of solidarity, compassion, egalitarianism, etc. Does this socialist heritage have any value for the development of a reformed work organization, possibly accompanied by appropriate group incentive schemes, to save on the costs of transition (Blinder, 1992), or is it counterproductive and should be relinquished in favour of promoting individual competition?

The real world thus seems to tell economists that we should begin earnest comparative examination of various non-hierarchical forms of internal organization of the enterprise. We will now survey the recent analytical literature on this subject, although it is as yet very scarce.

11.5 EFFICIENCY CONDITIONS FOR HORIZONTAL INTERACTIONS: THE TEAM APPROACH

This section compares hierarchical with non-hierarchical coordination. We consider first the team theoretic approach, focusing on the information aspect, and later the contractual approach, focusing on the incentive aspect. The team theoretic approach further divides into two themes: organizational structures as endogenous choice variables and comparison of different structures exogenously given.

A series of works by Radner, in cooperation with Van Zandt, consider the problem of designing an optimal information network when a given batch of information items needs to be processed and aggregated under a time constraint. It takes one unit of time to process one item. But there is an important non-convexity in communication costs, in the sense that it takes one unit of time for any agent to read a report from any other agent, irrespective of the number of previously processed items that the report contains. Because of the communication costs, it is optimal to have only one agent to do all the information processing if there is no time limit. But if there is an urgency constraint, it is efficient for several agents to collaborate in processing information items, because the time gained through parallel processing may outweigh the time lost through communication.

Radner (1992, 1993) showed that the efficient network to aggregate a given number of items with the minimum number of agents and subject to a given time limit is necessarily hierarchical. As expected, there is a tradeoff between the number of agents and delay, reflecting the tradeoff between serial and parallel processing. It is to be noted, however, that 'hierarchy' in his mathematical propositions refers to the (algebraic) tree structure of information networks and not necessarily to the authority structure of an organization in which the functions of managing and doing are separated. Indeed, in Radner's optimal hierarchical network, every agent, including the root of the tree, is engaged in processing information items (i.e., doing) and there is no agent exclusively specialized in reading reports from others.

Van Zandt (1991) and Radner and Van Zandt (1992) extend their analysis to a more realistic feature of organizations, where a cohort of information items arrives periodically, and derive an approximate formula for defining efficient tradeoffs between the number of agents and delay. They show that, in this case, a division of the information-processing function (doing) and the reading-adding function (managing) approximates efficiency (but agents processing information do not necessarily report to the same agents all the time). As the number of items increases indefinitely, the delay must also increase indefinitely, even if agents may be added without limit. Thus there emerge strong decreasing returns to scale, even though there is no fixed factor involved, though the existence of a fixed factor has long been envisaged as the cause of decreasing returns.

The model of Radner and Van Zandt is closely related to a recent development of computer science. Bolton and Dewatripont (1994) adapted their model to a more obviously economic context. They introduced gains from specialization explicitly, by letting the time required to process a given item be a decreasing function of the frequency with which this item is processed by the same agent. They found that if gains from specialization are very high, the 'regular' hierarchy (in which there is a complete separation between the two functions) is efficient. But if communication costs become very small, the 'assembly line' type of network becomes efficient; this being one in which every agent is engaged in both processing and receiving in information (except for the first agent in the line) and sending it (except for the last one). One may interpret the Bolton and Dewatripont result as implying that a traditional hierarchy, characterized by the separation of operating and managing, may not be efficient under advanced communication technology or agents' enhanced communication ability. The so-called *kanban* system (which was invented by a Japanese car manufacturer and is being widely used in assembly-line industries for reducing inventories of work in process) is analogous to the 'assembly line' network (Aoki, 1988).

In the same vein as Radner and Van Zandt, Marschak and Reichelstein (1992) deal with the efficient design of a network for the enterprise in which each agent (information processor) is also responsible for the final decision about some action variables. The only cost of information is that of communication, measured by the size dimensionality of messages, in the spirit of the Hurwicz-Reiter theory of comparative mechanism design. They show that, in general, the efficient means of communication are shadow prices of scarce goods and they derive certain conditions under which the efficient network mechanism using those communication media becomes hierarchical. These conditions exclude, however, the existence of 'public' goods used jointly by agents. If such public goods exist, a ring-like network becomes efficient in one of their examples.

The above writers treat the emergence of non-hierarchical structures endogenously, which may theoretically be the more satisfactory approach, although the analysis still remains at a highly abstract level. In contrast, Aoki (1986, 1990a) compares the relative informational efficiency of hierarchical and non-hierarchical structures which are modelled in a rather *ad hoc* way, but he is able to derive some empirically testable implications. In his model, hierarchy is identified with the mechanism in which the allocation of organizational resources is made on the basis of centralized (noisy or ex ante) information regarding events affecting shop-level costs. In horizontal coordination, operating units (shops) are engaged in learning by doing about their own environments and in utilizing processed information locally, at the sacrifice of gains available from the centralized use of information or operating efficiency derived from specialization. Hierarchy is more efficient if the environment is either very stable or highly volatile. In the former case, decentralized information processing will not generate information value exceeding the cost of sacrificing economies of specialization; in the latter, localized adaptation to environmental changes may yield unstable results. However, in the intermediate range, where changes in environmental variables are continuous and gradual, the horizontal mechanism may perform better, provided that the learning and communication capacities of operating units are sufficiently high. A similar conclusion is derived by Itoh (1987) in terms of the range of information processing at the lower level of hierarchy. In the intermediate range of uncertainty surrounding the enterprise, a broader range of information-processing capacity needs to be developed at the lower level; but the possibility of horizontal coordination of decisions at the lower level is not explicitly considered in his model.

The comparison of hierarchies and polyarchies by Sah and Stiglitz (1986 and 1988) may be seen as most relevant to a comparison of the centralized bureaucracy-controlled planning system with the multi-enterprise market system. But it may also provide building blocks for the comparison of alternative internal organizations of the enterprise. In the two-agents case, a hierarchy is defined as the decision-making structure in which the adoption of a project whose outcome is uncertain must be made unanimously by the two agents (the lower and higher bureaus). A polyarchy is the one in which either agent (division) can adopt a project independently of the other without communication. Specifically a 'coordinated' polyarchy, which is relevant to our current discussion, sets criteria for adopting projects so as to maximize the joint output. The coordinated polyarchy (the team) has more rigorous adoption criteria, because, as is intuitively clear, it is relatively more susceptible to error of Type-II (some projects that get accepted should have been rejected) in comparison with a hierarchy. Because of this conservatism, it performs better than a hierarchy if the signalling of the quality of a project is sufficiently bad and if the proportion of good projects in the initial portfolio is less than half. This may be interpreted as greater uncertainties favoring the decentralized system.

Cremer (1990) suggests a new exploration into the role of common knowledge in organizations. He argues that one important facet of many organizations is that there are many possible partners with whom agents have horizontal relationships and that these contacts change regularly because of job turnover, promotions, separations, etc. This imposes a great load on the bounded rationality of agents if they must adapt their behaviour to every one of these relationships. He compares the information efficiency of two types of organization, in which two agents are in charge of different decisions jointly affecting the payoff, designated undifferentiated and differentiated organizations. In the former, both agents base their decisions on the same noisy information about the organizational environment; in the latter each agent also makes use of a variable that provides specific information about his own productivity. The latter organization can increase the amount of knowledge embedded in the organization, but by so doing creates difficulty in coordinating it. As the need for coordination of the actions of two agents becomes sufficiently strong, and the individual specific components of productivity sufficiently small, and the noisy observations become relatively greater, the relative benefit of the undifferentiated structure increases. This suggests that for non-hierarchical coordination to be fruitful, the amount of common knowledge within the enterprise must be sizable, and this will limit the specialization of knowledge.

The works mentioned above initiated inquiries into a field of non-hierarchical coordination not then explored, but assumed away any possible incentive problem by adopting the team theoretic framework. This separation represents an infant stage of research in this field and it is now highly desirable to develop an integrated model of incentives and coordination, and analyze the way in which the organization is able to control the rules of games that the agents are playing among themselves. The next section deals with work on horizontal interactions among agents within a contractual framework in which issues of incentive play a prominent role.

11.6 EFFICIENCY CONDITIONS FOR HORIZONTAL INTERACTIONS: THE CONTRACTUAL APPROACH

There is a growing literature on collusion (side contracting) within organizations, or interactions among agents uncontrollable by the principal due to lack of information. This literature was initiated by a seminal work by Tirole (1986) and later extensively surveyed by Tirole (1990). He is concerned mainly with 'negative' collusion which is detrimental to the welfare of the principal, while we now turn to considering some recent work dealing with 'positive' collusion, such as peer coordination of efforts, mutual help and agents' joint responsibility for tasks.

Suppose that in the multi-agent framework, agents can monitor others' efforts without cost and write side contracts based on information commonly observable by them. This may correspond to situations where some implicit behavioural code emerges which governs organization members at the work place (Okuno-Fujihara, 1989), or the coordination of efforts is agreed among work units and carried out without default. Assume, however, that it is costly to communicate the monitored results to the principal, or that agents may collude in communicating distorted information to him, so that it does not benefit the principal to collect information regarding efforts. If no agents have private information, side contracting will not generally add to the principal's welfare (Varian, 1990; Holmstrom and Milgrom, 1990).

Holmstrom and Milgrom (1990) and Ramakrishnan and Thakor (1991) showed that if agents are specialized in separate tasks and their technologies are stochastically uncorrelated, there is benefit from mutual monitoring. The principal offers the same contract to a group of agents as he offers to independent agents and, under mutual monitoring, the agents will choose the same action as before, but the cost of risk bearing will be made lower by mutual reinsurance. The risk-sharing advantage can be obtained, however, precisely because agents can monitor each other's efforts. Otherwise, the reinsurance will dilute incentives and agents will shirk. If technologies of agents are correlated beyond a certain critical level, however, the benefit of side contracting vanishes and the principal will do better to prevent side contracting.

Macho-Stadler and Perez-Castrillo (1993), Ramakrishnan and Thakor (1991), and Itoh (1993) find a benefit from mutual monitoring when each agent can allocate his effort to his own task as well as to helping with the other's task. For the case of symmetric agents, Itoh (1992) shows that mutual monitoring is also beneficial in the context of team production where the principal cannot observe the output of each agent, so that only aggregate output can be contracted. When agents can side contract for interactive efforts, such as help, they are motivated to allocate a given level of efforts among tasks so as to minimize the total cost of efforts. Therefore, the set of practicable effort constellations under mutual monitoring shrinks as compared with a situation of no side contracting. Because of this cost, mutual monitoring of efforts and help is Pareto-superior only when agents are sufficiently similar in their aversion to risk and effort.

Considering that one of the essential features of hierarchies has been thought of as specialization in tasks, the question arises of when 'help', or joint assignment of tasks to multiple agents, is beneficial. Holmstrom and Milgrom (1991) have demonstrated for their linear multi-agent model that joint assignments are never efficient. The reason is that, since agents are assumed to have constant absolute risk aversion, they bear a fixed risk cost for each task to which they are assigned and for which they are rewarded at a fixed rate of commission. Therefore, if there are tasks to which two agents are jointly assigned, it is better to split the same tasks among the agents, without affecting the total efforts required of either agent or the total effort allocated to any task by each individual, and then to set each agent's commission rate at zero for tasks from which he is detached. By so doing, the risk that the agent must bear is reduced.

However, this result depends critically upon the assumption of perfect substitutability of efforts for different tasks in agents' costs. Itoh (1992) has examined the effect of an alternative assumption, that an agent's effort costs do not depend upon the total effort alone, but the agent's marginal disutility of helping others is zero when the initial level of help is zero, so that diverting a small amount of effort from its own tasks to helping others always improves an agent's welfare. Under this condition (which we will call the Itoh condition), he found that it is beneficial for the principal to promote mutual help through group incentives provided that technologies of tasks are relatively uncorrelated. By group incentives, is meant a reward system in which an agent's commission rates are positive for all the tasks in which he may be involved through either his own efforts or through help.

If tasks are highly correlated, it is better to isolate agents and reward them on the basis of relative performance even under the Itoh condition. It is well known that if tasks are sufficiently similar, in stochastic terms, the relative comparison of noisy outputs produced independently by each agent can be a good device for filtering out randomness and detecting hidden efforts of agents.

But under such relative performance evaluation, or 'tournament', each agent may not be generally interested in helping because it would only enhance the possibility of others winning. As Lazear (1989) showed, even negative help (i.e., sabotage) may be promoted. Garvey and Swan (1992) show, however, that a relative performance evaluation scheme may be effective in promoting help under Itoh's condition (and with the assumption of measurement error in assessing individual contributions to noiseless output) if the prize of winning a tournament is not fixed ex ante, but is known to be dependent upon the aggregate output. In this case, helping may increase the probability of another's winning, but also increase the level of the prize if one wins. However, unless there is a type of corporate governance structure which makes an output-contingent prize credible, the system may not work. It will not do so if the principal may renege on the promise of a bonus in the event of high output. The corporate governance aspect of the model is discussed in the next section.

We may now summarize the discussion of this chapter so far:

1. The relative efficiency of horizontal coordination versus hierarchical coordination depends upon the nature of the stochastic environment of the enterprise (e.g., product market, technology). The former is informationally more efficient when environmental variables are continually changing, while the opposite is the case when they are changing occasionally and drastically or are very stable.
2. The integration of the information-processing function and the coordination function may become informationally more efficient than their complete separation when communication technology and/or

human communication capacity among work units are improved.

3. Task coordination may be delegated to the lower level of hierarchy, where relevant information is located, if agents are relatively homogenous in their attitudes toward risk and effort as well as in their knowledge.

4. Even if each agent is individually motivated, help and joint task assignments may be beneficially motivated if agents can reduce effort costs by switching tasks marginally and technologies of tasks are stochastically uncorrelated.

11.7 COMPLEMENTARITIES AMONG ATTRIBUTES OF THE ENTERPRISE

The last three sections have indicated that types of organizational coordination somewhat different from rigid functional hierarchy are developing in practice and that there is a parallel, albeit embryonic, development of theoretical interest in non-hierarchical coordination. In this section it is suggested that the practical development of horizontal coordination is likely to be accompanied by complementary developments of other managerial practices, particularly in the sphere of human-resource management, and attention is drawn to a recent analytical development of comparative statics under complementarity.

Economists have long been accustomed to the dichotomy of transaction-governing institutions as markets and hierarchies (Williamson, 1975). Hierarchies are a mechanism for integrating well-defined specialized functions, while markets provide opportunities for hierarchies to employ the services of specialized skills necessary to perform those functions. Conversely, if there are markets within which agents possessing specialized skills are fluidly and competitively mobile, the organizational integrity and effectiveness of the enterprise may not be automatically assured. There must also be a force integrating individual agents having diverse skills, interests, etc. to achieve the enterprise's goals, and the centralization of information and decision-making serves that purpose. Thus, markets and hierarchies complement each other to enhance the productive use of specialized skills.

In the emergent non-hierarchical coordination, however, a concept of skill, somewhat different from the specialized functional one, may be gaining in importance. In horizontal coordination operating on reduced buffer inventories, it is not necessarily efficient, from the organization's standpoint, for each worker to devote his energy exclusively to minimizing local cost without paying attention to the compatibility of his work scheduling with those of neighbouring units. The range of information processing required may also be wider. For example, the manager of a design team for a new product in the R&D department may need to be familiar with the capability of the manufacturing plant: the foreman in the rolling mill at a steel plant may not only need to achieve the temperature of the rolling process specified by the engineering department but may also be expected to spot a possible cause of product defects which may have originated in the end process of the shop immediately upstream; the worker who is installing engines at an automobile assembly line may be expected to cooperate in repairing the broken machine at an adjacent work point in order to keep the line moving smoothly. Such coordinating/problem-solving tasks have been a separate function performed exclusively by superiors/engineers/specialists in traditional hierarchies, but may be more or less integrated with operating tasks in non-hierarchical coordination. Thus the kinds of skills more effective in horizontal coordination may be relatively wide-ranging, integrating specialized operational skills and communication/problem-solving capability, possibly at the sacrifice of deeply specialized functional skills. Following Koike (1988), we may call such skills the integrative skills.

Itoh's (1987) model captures the above connections between the nature of skill and that of the appropriate mode of coordination. Suppose that the top level of the enterprise processes information about its macro environment and gives a relevant instruction to the lower level. The lower level understands the instruction and makes a local operating decision on the basis of micro information which it gathers. The enterprise's payoff depends upon the precision of information processing at both top and low levels. It is assumed that the consistency of local decision-making with changing local environment depends on the information-processing capacity of the lower level, and that information-processing capacity at the lower level has to be accumulated before the value of the macro variable is known. But once investment in the capacity is made, the precision of lower level information processing depends on the realized value of the macro variable. In other words, the information-processing capacity of the lower level is specific to the macro environment. The question is then what type of information-processing capacity, general or specialized, deep or shallow, needs to be developed ex ante at the lower level.

Itoh shows that when the macro environment is very stable (the situation in which hierarchical coordination is informationally more efficient), specialized skill should be developed (i.e. information-processing capacity which is effective over a narrow range of micro-variables, but highly precise within that range). But if the macro variable changes continually (the situation in which horizontal coordination is informationally more efficient), it is better to invest in more general skills (information-processing capacity which is effective over a wide range). However, if the macro variable becomes volatile (the situation in which hierarchical coordination is better), it is not efficient to invest in information processing at the lower level ex ante. It is better for the top level to process macro information first, and only after macro information is refined should the top management employ an agent endowed with the specialized micro capacity attuned to the macro environment.

Unlike highly specialized skill, effective in traditional hierarchies, wide-ranging, integrative skill is unlikely to be developed fully through formal training prior to actual job experience and/or experience at other workplaces. Integrative skill is more or less specific to the environment of a particular workplace and can be learnt and developed by experiencing various interrelated jobs in that workplace: participation in an enterprise-wide project team, a quality control group, a formal training programme provided by the employing enterprise, etc. Also, as we have noted in the previous section, for the delegation of coordination to, and cooperation among, workers to be effective for the organization's purpose, the workers need to be relatively similar in attitudes to work and risk and in knowledge. However, such similarity may also be formed only through common work experience.

To develop this contextual form of integrative skills, and to the extent that the enterprise relies on non-hierarchical coordination, long-term association of the workers with the enterprise and a consistent approach to human-resource management by the enterprise will become necessary. The selection and internal allocation of workers needs to be done carefully from the organizational perspective, rather than solely on the basis of an evaluation by the immediate superior of the skill required for a certain specified function. The enterprise may assign the worker to different tasks over time, and/or assign a team of workers to the same task, to make them understand the context of their work process and develop similar attitudes and knowledge.

Since there can be no spot market evaluating the contextual aspect of integrative skill, the enterprise needs to develop an incentive system by which workers are evaluated over time for the combined development of contextual and specialized skills and rewarded accordingly.

For that purpose, the enterprise may develop its own promotion ladder, to serve as a route for the upward mobility of workers, in place of the competitive external market. If a worker shirks the development of contextual skill, then he may be dismissed, which would lead to a reduction of employment-continuation value to him equivalent to the present value of contextual skill potentially realizable by him at a later stage. Such a credible possibility of dismissal may serve to deter workers from shirking the accumulation of contextual skill.

The promotion ladder within the enterprise may be called the *horizontal* hierarchy in contrast to the functional hierarchy (the *vertical* hierarchy) which we have dealt with in previous sections (terminology of Stiglitz, 1975). The vertical hierarchy is the hierarchy of specialized functions, whereas the horizontal hierarchy is the stratification of status-wages as an incentive device. Although in practice they may be intertwined, the conceptual distinction is useful for the purpose of comparative study of the internal organization of the enterprise.

While non-hierarchical coordination requires an organizational approach to human-resource management implementing systematic assignments of tasks to the workers and managing the horizontal hierarchy as an incentive device, the existence of consistent human-resource management may, conversely, facilitate the maintenance of effective non-hierarchical coordination. Under such a scheme, management is willing to delegate decision-making and problem-solving to the lower level of hierarchy without the fear of losing control and being threatened by competition from below (Prendergast, 1991). If human-resource management consistently rewards those who have developed contextual skill, the workers will become 'voluntarily' compliant in their actions with the organization's goal.

The symmetric decentralization–centralization couplings as described above have been termed the 'Duality Principle' (Aoki, 1990b): the perfectly competitive, decentralized labour market tends to be associated with the hierarchical control of operations within the organization, on the one hand, and the evolution of non-hierarchical coordination tends to be associated with systematic human-resource management relying on horizontal hierarchy, on the other. Centralization and decentralization are complementary, in the sense that the benefit of an increase in decentralization (or centralization) of organizational coordination becomes greater if a concurrent change in human-resource management in the direction of stronger organizational control (or reliance on the labour market) takes place.

Milgrom and Roberts (1990) hold that the development of horizontal coordination among traditionally separate functions is a necessary organizational reaction to recent technological development, resulting from 'complementarities' among various new elements of an enterprise's strategy: new production strategy, such as the introduction of a flexible manufacturing system, marketing strategy with an increased emphasis on variety and quality and shorter product cycles, a new R&D strategy of faster and continuous product innovation, etc. For example, it may be unprofitable for an enterprise to purchase a flexible manufacturing system without changing its marketing and R&D strategies, or to adopt a new marketing or R&D strategy without introducing a flexible manufacturing system, but it may be highly profitable to adopt all of them together. The new technological developments referred to in Section 11.4, paragraph (3), above, and the resulting reduction in costs of manufacturing, information processing and communication, product design and development, certainly enhance the profitability of a corresponding strategy. But because of complementarities between various elements of strategy, all other elements of strategy may be affected by change in one. One troublesome consequence for the economic analysis of such a situation is the non-convexity inherent in complementarities. The optimal strategy cannot be found by successive small independent changes in each element. Exploiting a system of complementarities requires a changes in various aspects of business strategy and fast cross-functional coordination between manufacturing, supply, marketing, design and engineering. Thus the development of new technology not only facilitates but also requires closer cross-functional coordination.

A noteworthy contribution of Milgrom and Roberts is that they have gone beyond the description of possible complementarity relationships and developed a new mathematical technique of comparative statics (the supermodularity analysis) which can be applied to complementarity relationships involving non-convexity, indivisibility, and discontinuity (see Milgrom and Roberts, 1990a and 1990b, and Milgrom and Shannon, 1991). In cooperation with others (including Holmstrom; Meyer; Qian), they apply this technique to show why distinctly different clusters of enterprises' attributes appear and why they can be changed only in a coordinated way.

For example, Holmstrom and Milgrom (1994) asked why outside procurement tends to involve the use of piece-rate incentives, worker ownership of tools, and worker's freedom to choose the time and methods of production, while inside procurement tends to involve the use of a fixed wage, enterprise ownership of tools, and the supervision of workers. They examined conditions (a type of complementarity) under which the commission rates, the allocation of transferable returns, workers' control of non-transferable returns and activity, and monitoring intensity covary positively with changes in exogenous parameters in cross-sectional studies.

11.8 SYSTEM EFFECTS: WHY DO DIFFERENT INTERNAL STRUCTURES EXIST?

Milgrom and Roberts and their associates show how parametric changes in the 'external' factor market environment, brought about by technological progress, necessitate coordinated adjustments in complementary elements of business strategy and how these, in turn, require close horizontal coordination among traditionally separate 'internal' functions. The duality principle indicates, however, that the effectiveness of such horizontal coordination may be enhanced by the centralization of human-resource management within the enterprise (i.e., by insulating the internal organization from the competition of the external labour market).

Complementarities among horizontal coordination, internal human-resource management, and an imperfect labour market are exemplified by Prendergast's (1992) model. He recognizes that in Japan, where cooperation and coordination of work efforts among workers are relatively more prevalent than elsewhere, workers are promoted more slowly and treated in a relatively more egalitarian way in the early stages of their careers. In the USA, on the other hand, where functional hierarchies are relatively more common, able workers are recognized early and treated differently from others.

He traced the impact of the slow promotion system, versus the star system, on workers' incentives to learn. Suppose that the enterprise is informed of workers' potential values (abilities) at a relatively early stage of their careers, but the workers are not. The star system signals this information to the workers by early promotion of the most able. High ability workers are thus encouraged to collect skills, but others are discouraged, resulting in a suboptimal spread of skill among workers in their intermediate career stage. On the other hand, in the slow promotion scheme too many workers invest in skill collection in the expectation of possible promotion at a later stage of their careers. Prendergast argues however, that the biases in investment are not entirely inconsistent with the need of the system, since hierarchical coordination relies more on the information-processing capacity of the few elite, while non-hierarchical coordination relies relatively more upon the information-processing capacity of workers at the lower levels. It should be noted that the slow promotion scheme requires an imperfectly competitive labour market, since otherwise the ability of an employee can be signalled by an outside offer.

The working of horizontal coordination may require imperfect competition in the capital market also. Aoki (1992) captures the non-hierarchical nature of organizational coordination in a reduced form by assuming that a vector of efforts of the members of a work team determines the level of output jointly with a random variable, but the contributions of individual actions cannot be precisely measured either by the manager or by peers. If team output is to be shared among team members, possibly after payments of fixed obligations to outsiders, a well-known moral hazard (free-riding) results because a team member may equate its marginal cost of effort to its share of the marginal team output, rather than to the marginal team output itself. The idea of a third party's budget-breaking has been proposed by a few authors as a solution for this problem (notably by Holmstrom, 1982, and by McAfee and McMillan, 1991a).

In Holmstrom's model, the third party imposes substantial penalties on team members if team output falls short of a critical level. If the third party itself derives utility from the collection of penalty, however, it becomes interested in the team's production not meeting the critical level. There may then be morally hazardous agreement between the third party and a member of the team that the latter shirk in exchange for a promised share in penalties (Estrin and Kotwal, 1984). A similar problem exists for the McAfee–McMillan model. In their simplest model without adverse selection, each team member puts up a large sum of money, corresponding to the optimal output of the team less his own reservation wage, as a bond before team production takes place and he recovers later the total value of the actual realized output (not a share thereof) so that he is motivated to work up to the optimal level. However, the third party has to make up a large deficit at the optimal output level (equivalent to the total value of members' reservation wages) and it is not clear how the third party is motivated to accept such an arrangement ex ante. Moreover, the workers' wealth constraints may deter them from making such large investments upfront.

Aoki (1994) partially resolves these problems by devising a nexus of contracts involving two types of third parties: general investors and the (main) bank. The range of possible output of the team is divided into three regions: the upper team control region, the intermediate bank intervention region, and the low liquidation region. The general investors receive a fixed rate of return in the upper and intermediate regions, but nothing in the event of liquidation. In the upper region the bank does not receive any return (except for the fixed rate of return in its capacity as a general investor) and the team members are the residual claimants. If output falls short of the upper region, control rights shift to the bank as in an Aghion and Bolton (1992) model. In both intermediate and low regions, the bank becomes the residual claimant, while guaranteeing the minimum wage to the team members. In the lowest output region, the bank liquidates the team after the payment of the minimum wages to its members and assumes the loss (budget-breaking). The ousted worker is assumed to lose some employment-continuation value because of the imperfection of the labour market. The participation constraint, for the bank to earn a positive return ex ante, is imposed for the design of the nexus of contracts.

Under team production, this nexus of contracts cannot attain the first-best solution, but is superior as an incentive device to normal debt contracts because of the information-processing capacity of the bank to verify the final output of the team at the intermediate and lower range. The role of the bank, as a principal monitor whose action is contingent upon the state of output, may be seen as reflecting an aspect of bank–firm relationships observed in the bank-oriented financial system of Japan and, to some extent, of Germany also. It is to be noted that the higher the losses in employment-continuation value that the workers of liquidated firms are expected to suffer, the stronger is the incentive effect of the bank-oriented nexus of contracts. This suggests that the partially internalized capital and labour markets (i.e. the described nexus of team and bank contracts) are complementary in promoting team output (horizontal coordination). On the other hand, if all the markets for the services of the specialized functions comprising hierarchies are perfectly competitive, the maximization of the residual after contractual payments for those services is consistent with the hierarchies' internal efficiency. A perfectly competitive market for corporate control over the residual also serves that purpose, so that we may say that perfectly competitive labour and capital markets are complementary institutional frameworks for enhancing efficient hierarchical coordination.

Garvey and Swan (1992) proposed an interesting model of corporate governance structure building a bridge between financial contracts and employment contracts. As already indicated, they show that tournament with output-contingent prizes may promote help among workers; and the next question is what type of corporate governance structure can ensure credible management commitment to such a scheme, which may not be enforceable by a third party such as a court. If management is subject to the control of residual claimants (stockholders), there is no incentive for it to increase the level of prize ex post when the output level is high. However, suppose that the founder of the enterprise devises a corporate governance structure in which the standard bondholder, the stockholder, and the worker all have positive weights in management decision-making. If the weight given to the bondholder is higher than that of the stockholder, the management is more likely when output is high to meet its fixed obligation to the bondholder, and the stockholder's resistance to paying some portion of the residual to the worker is relatively weakened. The credible prospect of bonus will enhance workers' incentives to help and a Pareto-dominant combination of efforts and helping may be realized. The founder of the enterprise can profit by anticipating these results when establishing the corporate governance structure.

Possible complementarities between institutional features of the employment and financial structures of enterprises as described above may suggest a reason why in some economies (e.g., the USA and UK) hierarchical coordination is relatively more firmly established across industries, while in some other economies (e.g., Japan and, possibly to a lesser degree, Germany) non-hierarchical horizontal coordination is relatively more prevalent. As noted already, one type of intra-organizational coordination may be informationally more efficient for certain stochastic characteristics of the product market and technology of industry, while other types may be informationally more efficient for other characteristics. Yet, we do not necessarily observe that the same type of internal structure tends to appear in the same industry across different economies. This phenomenon may be due to 'systematic effects' (Williamson, 1991a): the effectiveness of an internal structure of the enterprise also depends on the nature of the institutional framework of labour and capital markets; and changes in the internal structure may be slow, if not impossible, unless there are corresponding changes in the factor market environments.

Systematic effects may also have important implications for transitional planned economies. Reforms of enterprise structures, financial institutions, employment practices, and inter-firm relationships may have to be made systematically and consistently. Otherwise, the effectiveness and internal efficiency of enterprise organization may not be secured, with adverse consequences for the macro-performance of the transforming/reforming economies. However, as Blinder (1992) has argued, it may be advisable to minimize the transitional costs of systematic change; and then complementary relations among time-dependent variables must be taken into account (Milgrom, Roberts and Qian, 1991). This implies that some kind of continuation from the socialist heritage, rather than a 'big bang' approach, may be advisable. In this perspective, the German–Japanese system which relies more on the coherent work group at the shop-floor level, the practice of long-term employment, the bank-oriented financial system, arbitrative corporate governance structures (to be discussed more in the next section), etc., may provide a model worth serious examination by transitional economies. There seems to be a wider gap between the institutional framework of traditional planned economies and that of the highly competitive Anglo-American market system and it is not clear that an attempt to jump from the former to the latter is the less costly.

Even leaving aside the urgent issue of transitional economies, the discussion so far may suggest that a general inquiry into organizational evolution in the presence of complementary clustering could be an extremely important subject of research. Boyer and Orlean (1991) explore in this direction. In a simple evolutionary game framework, they find that a superior convention is able to invade a population currently following an established inferior convention if this new convention can implement social filters to establish at the outset a critical mass of innovation and to realize benefits of interactions. This result is not striking, but the authors interpret the surprising success of the Japanese transplants in the UK and USA in this light. They note that those Japanese transplants adopted extremely careful human-resource management as a social filter through which the first workers are carefully selected according to their motivation and aptitudes and are trained systematically in-house, so that initial cooperation will not be destroyed by opportunistic, market-oriented behaviour of insiders. It may also be noted that those transplants are subsidiaries of large established enterprises so they are also insulated from capital market monitoring.

11.9   A VARIETY OF CORPORATE GOVERNANCE STRUCTURE AND THE BARGAINING GAME APPROACH

One important generic element of the enterprise is the centralized goal-setting (strategic management decision) for organizational coordination.

This does not mean that the enterprise is organized in a monolithic manner. Participants in an organization and sub-units of an organization will have diverse (and often conflicting) interests. But for an organization to be effective there must be certain unified goals to which organizational activities are directed and by which contributions of all participants are evaluated. Let us identify the structure through which the organizational goal is set, and by which the top management which makes such a decision (or at least sets the agenda for it) is selected, as the corporate governance structure. As Frank Knight (1920, p. 290) said, 'What we call "control" consists mainly of selecting someone else to do the "controlling"'.

Economists have normally assumed that the enterprise in market economies aims at maximizing profit (or the value of the enterprise, as the dynamic analogue of profit). As already pointed out, this seems to be an innocuous assumption consistent with internal and allocative efficiency in so far as the enterprise internalizes the classical mechanism of hierarchical coordination and operates in an environment of perfectly competitive product and service markets. However, we have observed that, to the degree that non-hierarchical coordination supplements or replaces hierarchical coordination, the relationship of the enterprise to the labour and capital markets may also change, because of system effects. Some human resources embodying contextual skills may become organizational resources more or less specific to the internal network of non-horizontal coordination, and their evaluation will not be completely conditioned by the labour market. The owners of such human resources may thus become in effect partners of the enterprise and participate in the sharing of residual. The enterprise becomes in effect 'the partnership' (Stiglitz, 1991, p. 18; Radner, 1992, section 6).

In fact we observe roughly two prototypes of the governance structure of large enterprises in developed market economies: the Anglo-American type and the German–Japanese type. Drastically simplifying, the corporate governance structure in the former type is dominated by the interests of stockholders who exercise their control through the market for corporate control (the takeover mechanism), the board of directors, direct intervention in the case of large stockholders, etc. In the latter, the market for corporate control is essentially inoperative, because of large blocks of stable stockholding and the concentration of proxy-voting rights by the financial institutions, as well as closed individual ownership in Germany.

But the reflection of workers' voices is implicitly or explicitly institutionalized in the corporate governance structure in both economies.

In Germany, workers' participation is statutorily institutionalized in the co-determination scheme in which the employees' representatives occupy half of the seats of the Ausichrat, charged with the important right of appointing top management (the members of the Vorstand). In Japan, new top management is selected by a retiring/retired CEO from the internal rank hierarchy of employees, if the enterprise is in a good financial state; only financial distress of the enterprise triggers the exercise of control by the main bank in a manner modelled by Aoki (see Aoki, 1992; also Aoki, 1984, part III for a detailed comparative description of the corporate governance structures).

However, the above proto-typical dichotomization is highly stylized and the distinction should not be so starkly drawn. Even in the USA, hostile takeover is rapidly becoming difficult because of anti-takeover measures (poison-pill) by managements; and recent changes in corporate statutes have changed the fiduciary duty of directors to various 'stakeholders' instead of solely to the stockholders. In Germany and Japan, the increasing reliance of large enterprises on bond-market financing may be weakening the monitoring capacity of the banks, although there is no sign of the market for corporate control becoming active. The implications of these changes are as yet debatable; and it is not the intention here to speculate on the issue of convergence versus difference of corporate governance structure in market economies, but only to suggest a theoretic approach to the market behaviour of enterprises which explicitly recognizes the diversity of such structures.

Allowing for the possibility of multi-constituent corporate governance structures, an appropriate modelling of the enterprise may not be as an entity maximizing a single objective, such as the value of the enterprise, managerial utility, or income per employee, but rather as a (bargaining) game among interacting multiple players (stakeholders) of the enterprise: different types of investors and the holders of organizational human resources each endeavouring to maximize its own objective (see Aoki, 1984 and 1988; Hart and Moore, (1990)). In fact, it can be shown that the neoclassical type of the enterprise maximizing a single objective function may be a special case of the broader bargaining approach.

In the simplest case, where there is only one type of homogeneous investor (stockholders) and only one type of holder of organizational human resources, their interactions within the enterprise may be captured as a two-person bargaining game. In this game, bargainable subjects may be considered to include not only distribution variables (such as wages and dividends) but also strategic management-decision variables (such as the level of employment, investment) that may affect the welfare of the representative employee in the absence of a perfectly competitive labour market and with the prospect of internal promotion along a horizontal hierarchy.

One type of modelling of enterprise bargaining in the neoclassical tradition has been to assume that strategic management decision variables belong to the prerogative of the management acting in the interest of investors (or in its own interest) and are not bargainable, or that even if bargainable, there is no corporate governance mechanism under which the management is committed to the bargained result (Grout, 1984). But to the extent that the workers become organizational resources specific to the enterprise, the corporate governance structure unilaterally dominated by stockholders (or managers) may be trapped in an inefficient 'short-termism' (see Aoki, 1988, ch. 4).

An alternative hypothesis worth examining is that both management, as the representative of the investors, and the body of employees are engaged in repeated bargaining over a wide range of subjects and reach an agreement characterized as a perfect subgame equilibrium; or that management assesses the relative bargaining strength boldness (Aumann and Kurz, 1977) of each body and proposes a set of 'equilibrating' values of variables such that, for any risk (probability) of disagreement which one party would dare to take in favour of another alternative, the other party would rather wish to stick to the proposed set (Rubinstein, Safra and Thomson, 1992). A subgame perfect equilibrium, or the equilibrium point proposed by management as above, will approximate the Nash bargaining solution.

If the payoff of the (multi-dimensional) bargain outcome for each partner is homogenous of degree one with respect to bargainable variables, and if the risk attitude of each partner in the bargaining process is represented by a cardinal utility function of its own payoff with constant elasticity less than one, the Nash bargaining solution can be located by the following simple decomposition rule (Aoki, 1984):

1. The relative distribution of surplus value of the enterprise among the investors and the employees is constant, irrespective of changes in external product market parameters, and solely determined by their attitudes toward risk of failure to agree.
2. The equilibrium management policy can be obtained by taking the average of the optimal policy to the investors and the optimal policy to the employees, with weights given by their respective distributive shares in surplus value.

Here 'surplus value' refers to value-added of the enterprise net of the sum of external opportunity wages of the employees. The richness of this rule can be seen by examining the case where the aversion to risk of employees is relatively high (so that the elasticity of the utility function is greater than one). In this situation, there is no participation in the surplus value by the employees and no weight is given to the policy optimal for the employees. In other words, the employees get only the equivalent of the opportunity wage available in the external market and in making strategic management decisions the management maximizes surplus value accruable to investors (i.e., profit). It is easy to see that the other extreme point, where no weight is given to the investors, corresponds to the case of the worker-controlled firm. Thus the bargaining-game approach may be considered as a more general theory of the enterprise, with the neoclassical theory of the single-objective maximizing enterprise as a special case. At the same time, the above dichotomization rule suggests a simple way in which the traditional theory of the enterprise may provide a useful reference point for analysis of the behaviour of the enterprise as partnership and of the implications of multi-stakeholder corporate governance structure.

As Radner (1992) notes, 'In fact, most organizations combine aspects of both the partnership and principal–agent models.' Although there has not yet been 'significant progress on more comprehensive models of the firm that combines these two submodels in a systematic way', the bargaining-game approach may provide a useful analytical building block toward that direction.

Notes

1. That is, given any two agents in the set, either of them is superior to the other or not comparable.
2. Ill-structured M-forms may entail another problem. The increasing diversification in the American economy to unrelated industries in the 1960s, and the divestitures of the 1970s, plus the subsequent institutionalization of markets for corporate control in the 1980s greatly increased the ease with which the modern enterprise could be restructured. These successive phenomena enabled some American companies to remain powerful competitors in the most dynamic and transforming industries of the late twentieth century (aerospace, chemicals, pharmaceuticals, computers, etc.), while having devastating effects on the competitive capability of some companies in other industries. Why such a difference? Chandler (1992), the foremost authority on American business history, argues that competitive

companies are those which have succeeded in long-term strategic moves under the leadership of professional managers with long experience in their companies and industries. But the rise in the 1980s of what Chandler called 'transaction-oriented' mergers and acquisitions carried out by financial specialists, as well as by senior corporate managers, for the short-term profits produced by the transactions themselves led to an unhealthy separation between the top managers at the headquarters and the middle managers responsible for the operating divisions. This conclusion suggests that centralized control of business strategy may not be carried out effectively in complete divorce from concrete operational knowledge of divisions.

References

Aghion, P. and P. Bolton (1992) 'An Incomplete Contract Approach to Financial Contracting', *Review of Economic Studies*, vol. 59, pp. 473–94.

Aoki, M. (1984) *The Cooperative Game Theory of the Firm* (Oxford: Oxford University Press).

Aoki, M. (1986) 'Horizontal vs. Vertical Information Structure of the Firm', *American Economic Review*, vol. 76, pp. 971–83.

Aoki, M. (1988) *Information, Incentives and Bargaining in the Japanese Economy* (Cambridge: Cambridge University Press).

Aoki, M. (1990a) 'The Participatory Generation of Information Rents and the Theory of the Firm', in M. Aoki, B. Gustafsson and O.E. Williamson, *The Firm as a Nexus of Treaties* (Place: Sage Publications) pp. 26–52.

Aoki, M. (1990b) 'Towards an Economic Model of the Japanese Firm', *Journal of Economic Literature*, vol. 28, pp. 1–27.

Aoki, M. (1994) 'Contingent Governance of Teams,' *International Economic Review*, vol. 35, pp. 657–76.

Aumann, R. and M. Kurt (1977) 'Power and Taxes', *Econometrica*, vol. 45, pp. 1137–60.

Beckman, M. (1977) 'Management Production Function and the Theory of the Firm', *Journal of Economic Theory*, vol. 14, pp. 1–18.

Blinder, A. (1992) 'Should the Former Socialist Economies Look East or West for a Model?, mimeo, Princeton University.

Bolton, P. and M. Dewatripont (1994) 'The Firm as a Communication Network', *Quarterly Journal of Economics*, vol. 109, pp. 809–39.

Boyer, R. (1991) 'New Directions in Management Practices and Work Organization: General Principles and National Trajectories', mimeo, CEPREMAP.

Boyer, R. and A. Orlean (1991) 'Why are Institutional Transformations So Difficult?', mimeo, CEPREMAP.

Calvo, G.A. and S. Wellisz (1978) 'Supervision, Loss of Control and the Optimum Size of the Firm', *Journal of Political Economy*, vol. pp. 943–52.

Chandler, A. (1966) *Strategy and Structure* (Cambridge, Mass.: Harvard University Press).

Chandler, A. (1992) 'Competitive Performance of U.S. Industrial Enterprises: A Historical Perspective', mimeo, Harvard University.

Coase, R. (1937) 'The Nature of the Firm', *Economica*, vol. 4, pp. 386–405.

Coase, R. (1988) 'Lecture 3 of "Three Lectures"', *Journal of Law, Economics and Organization*, vol. 4, pp. 3–47.

Cremer, J. (1980) 'A Partial Theory of the Optimal Organization of Bureaucracy', *Bell Journal of Economics*, vol. 11, pp. 683–93.

Cremer, J. (1990) 'Common Knowledge and the Co-ordination of Economic Activities', in M. Aoki, B. Gustafsson and O. Williamson (eds), *The Firm as a Nexus of Treaties* (Sage Publication), pp. 52–76.

Estrin, M. and A. Kotwal (1984) 'The Moral Hazard of Budget-Breaking', *Rand Journal of Economics*, vol. 15, pp. 578–81.

Garvey, G.T. and P.L. Swan (1992) 'The Interaction between Financial and Employment Contracts: A Formal Model of Japanese Corporate Governance', *Journal of the Japanese and International Economies*, vol. 6, pp. 247–74.

Geanakoplos, J. and P. Milgrom (1991) 'A Theory of Hierarchies Based on Limited Managerial Attention', *Journal of the Japanese and International Economies*, vol. 5, pp. 205–25.

Grout, P.A. (1984) 'Investment and Wages in the Absence of Binding Contracts: A Nash Bargaining Approach', *Econometrica*, vol. 52, pp. 449–60.

Hart, O. and B. Holmstrom (1987) 'The Theory of Contracts', in T. Bewley (ed.), *Advances in Economic Theory – Fifth World Congress* (Cambridge: Cambridge University Press) pp. 71–155.

Hart, O. and J. Moore (1990) 'Property Rights and the Nature of the Firm', *Journal of Political Economy*, vol. 98, pp. 1119–58.

Holmstrom, B. (1982) 'Moral Hazard in Teams', *Bell Journal of Economics*, vol. 13, pp. 324–40.

Holmstrom, B. and P. Milgrom (1990) 'Regulating Trade Among Agents', *Journal of Institutional and Theoretical Economics*, vol. 146, pp. 85–105.

Holmstrom, B. and P. Milgrom (1991a) 'Multi-Task Principal–Agent Analyses: Incentive Contracts, Asset Ownership and Job Design', *Journal of Law, Economics, and Organization*, vol. 7, pp. 24–51.

Holmstrom, B. and P. Milgrom (1994) 'The Firm as an Incentive System', *American Economic Review*, vol. 84, pp. 972–91.

Holmstrom, B. and J. Tirole (1989) 'The Theory of the Firm', in R. Schmalensee and R. Willig (eds), *Handbook of Industrial Organization*, vol. 1 (Amsterdam: North Holland).

Itoh, H. (1987) 'Information Processing Capacity of the Firm', *Journal of the Japanese and International Economies*, vol. 1, pp. 299– 326.

Itoh, H. (1991) 'Incentives to Help in Multi-Agent Situations', *Econometrica*, vol. 59, pp. 611–36.

Itoh, H. (1992) 'Cooperation in Hierarchical Organizations: An Incentive Perspective', *Journal of Law, Economics and Organization*, vol. 8, pp. 321–45.

Itoh, H. (1993) 'Coalitions, Incentives, and Risk Sharing', *Journal of Economic Theory*, vol. 60, pp. 410–27.

Keren, M. and D. Levhari (1979) 'The Optimum Span of Control in a Pure Hierarchy', *Management Science*, vol. 25, pp. 1162–72.

Keren, M. and D. Levhari (1983) 'The Internal Organization of the Firm and the Shape of Average Costs', *Bell Journal of Economics*, vol. 14, pp. 474–86.

Keren, M. and D. Levhari (1989) 'Decentralization, Aggregation, Control Loss and Costs in a Hierarchical Model of the Firm', *Journal of Economic Behavior and Organization*, vol. 11, pp. 213–36.

Knight, F. (1921) *Risk, Uncertainty, and Profits* (London: Houghton Mifflin).

Koike, K. (1988) *Understanding Industrial Relations in Modern Japan* (London: Macmillan).

Lazear, E.P. (1989) 'Pay Equality and Industrial Politics', *Journal of Political Economy*, vol. 97, pp. 561–80.

Ma, C. (1988) 'Unique Implementation of Incentive Contracts with Many Agents', *Review of Economic Studies*, vol. 55, pp. 555–71.

Macho-Stadler, I. and J.D. Perez-Castrillo (1993) 'Moral Hazard with Several Agents: The Gains from Cooperation', *International Journal of Industrial Organisation*, vol. 11, pp. 73–100.

Marschak, T. and S. Reichelstein (1992) 'Network Mechanisms, Informational Efficiency and Hierarchies', mimeo, University of California, Berkeley.

McAfee, R.P. and J. McMillan (1991a) 'Optimal Contracts for Teams', *International Economic Review*, vol. 32, pp. 561–77.

McAfee, R.P. and J. McMillan (1991b) 'Organizational Diseconomies of Scale', mimeo, University of California, San Diego.

McMillan, J. (1992) *Games, Strategies, and Managers* (Oxford: Oxford University Press).

Melumad, N., D. Mookherjee and S. Reichelstein (1991) 'Hierarchical Decentralization of Incentive Contracts', mimeo, Stanford University.

Meyer, M., P. Milgrom and J. Roberts (1992) 'Organizational Prospects, Influence Costs, and Ownership Changes', *Journal of Economics and Management Strategy*, vol. 1, pp. 9–35.

Milgrom, P. and J. Roberts (1990a) 'Rationalizability, Learning, and Equilibrium in Games with Strategic Complementarities', *Econometrica*, vol. 58, pp. 1255–77.

Milgrom, P. and J. Roberts (1990b) 'The Economics of Modern Manufacturing: Technology, Strategy, and Organization', *American Economic Review*, vol. 80, pp. 511–28.

Milgrom, P. and J. Roberts (1992) *Economics, Organization and Management* (New York: Prentice-Hall).

Milgrom, P. and C. Shannon (1994) 'Monotone Comparative Statics', *Econometrica*, vol. 62, pp. 157–80.

Milgrom, J., J. Roberts and Y. Qian (1991) 'Complementarities, Momentum, and the Evolution of Modern Manufacturing', *American Economic Review*, vol. 81, pp. 84–8.

Moore, J. and R. Repullo (1989) 'Subgame Perfect Implementation', *Econometrica*, vol. 56, pp. 1191–220.

Myerson, R. (1979) 'Incentive Compatibility and the Bargaining Problem', *Econometrica*, vol. 47, pp. 61–74.

Okuno-Fujiwara, M. (1989) 'On Labor Incentives and Work Norm in Japanese Firms, *Journal of the Japanese and International Economies*, vol. 4, pp. 367–84.

Oniki, H. (1974) 'The Cost of Communication in Economic Organization', *Quarterly Journal of Economics*, vol. 88, pp. 529–50.

Prendergast, C. (1995) 'A Theory of Worker Responsibility', *Journal of Labour Economics*, vol. 13, pp. 387–400.

Prendergast, C. (1992) 'Career Development and Specific Human Capital

Collection', *Journal of the Japanese and International Economies*, vol. 6, pp. 207–27.

Qian, Y. (1994) 'Hierarchy, Loss of Control, and a Theory of State Ownership in Socialist Economies', *Review of Economic Studies*, vol. 61, pp. 527–44.

Radner, R. (1993) 'The Organization of Decentralized information Processing', *Econometrica*, vol. 60, pp. 1109–46.

Radner, R. (1992) 'Hierarchy: The Economics of Managing', *Journal of Economic Literature*, vol. 30, pp. 1382–415.

Radner, R. and T. Van Zandt (1992) 'Information Processing in Firms and Returns to Scale', *Annales d'Economique et de Statistique*, vol. 25/26, pp. 265–98.

Ramakrishnan, R.T. and A.V. Thakor (1991) 'Cooperation versus Competition in Agency', *Journal of Law, Economics, and Organization*, vol. 7, pp. 248–83.

Rosen, S. (1982) 'Authority, Control, and the Distribution of Earnings', *Bell Journal of Economics*, vol. 13, pp. 311–23.

Rubinstein, A. (1982) 'Perfect Equilibrium in a Bargaining Model', *Econometrica*, vol. 50, pp. 97–110.

Rubinstein, A., Z. Safra and W. Thomson (1992) 'On the Interpretation on the Nash Bargaining Solution and its Extension to the Non-Expected', *Econometrica*, vol. 60, pp. 1171–86.

Sah, R. and J. Stiglitz (1986) 'The Architecture of Economic System: Hierarchies and Polyarchies', *American Economic Review*, vol. 76, pp. 716–27.

Sah, R. and J. Stiglitz (1988) 'Committees, Hierarchies and Polyarchies', *Economic Journal*, vol. 98, pp. 451–70.

Stiglitz, J. (1975) 'Incentives, Risks, and Notes toward a Theory of Hierarchy', *Bell Journal of Economics*, vol. 6, pp. 572–9.

Stiglitz, J. (1991) 'Symposium on Organizations and Economics', *Journal of Economic Perspectives*, vol. 5, pp. 15–24.

Tirole, J. (1986) 'Hierarchies and Bureaucracies: On the Role of Collusion in Organizations', *Journal of Law, Economics, and Organization*, vol. 2, pp. 181–214.

Tirole, J. (1990) 'Collusion and the Theory of Organization', mimeo, Massachusetts Institute of Technology.

Van Zandt, T. (1990) 'Efficient Parallel Addition', mimeo, Bell Laboratories.

Varian, H. (1990) 'Monitoring Agents with Other Agents', *Journal of Institutional and Theoretical Economics*, vol. 146, pp. 153–74.

Williamson, O.E. (1967) 'Hierarchical Control and Optimum Firm Size', *Journal of Political Economy*, vol. 75, pp. 123–38.

Williamson, O.E. (1975) *Markets and Hierarchies: Anti Trust Implications* (New York: Free Press).

Williamson, O.E. (1985) *The Economic Institutions of Capitalism* (New York: Free Press).

Williamson, O.E. (1991a) 'Comparative Economic Organization: The Analysis of Discrete Structural Alternatives', *Administrative Science Quarterly*, vol. 36, pp. 269–96.

Williamson, O.E. (1991b) 'Strategizing, Economizing, and Economic Organization', *Strategic Management Journal*, vol. 12, pp. 75–94.

Discussion

John McMillan

UNIVERSITY OF CALIFORNIA AT SAN DIEGO

Masahiko Aoki has been a pioneer in the use of ideas from principal–agent theory for understanding how real-world institutions work. His writings have shown that modern economic theory provides valuable insights into the incentive structure of the Japanese firm (Aoki, 1988, 1990). In this chapter, Aoki reverses the question, asking what the facts can teach us about theory.

Aoki's chapter gives a useful account of where we are in the theory of the firm. Modern, game-theory-based microeconomics has been remarkably successful in understanding the micro-details of organizational interactions: the dealings between one individual and another. (Consider, for example, why contracts usually do not offer marginal payment rates of 100 per cent: why would a principal deliberately distort an agent's incentives? Modern theory provides subtle and empirically relevant answers to this question, based on risk-aversion and private information.) But a firm consists of a network of such one-on-one interactions. Modern microeconomics has been less successful in aggregating the individual interactions into a full model of a firm, with both horizontal and vertical exchanges among the people in the firm.

Aoki's chapter lays out a research agenda for theorists. The key question is why there exist costs of hierarchy; what exactly it is that limits the size of organizations. Existing models (such as McAfee and McMillan, 1995) are, as Aoki correctly notes, based on *ad hoc* assumptions about communication possibilities. Completing the theory of the firm will require precise understanding of (i) horizontal relationships among people in the firm; (ii) what the costs of communication and control within the organization consist of; (iii) the nature of complementarities among different incentive devices; and (iv) how the objectives of the various stakeholders – workers, managers, shareholders – get aggregated into an overall objective function for the firm.

Aoki compares Japanese and US firms. One important lesson from such a comparison is that market economies come in a variety of forms: there is no uniquely optimal institution that solves the problems of incentive-system design. In a conference in Moscow it is appropriate to look also to another source of facts in institutional economics. The transitions of the once-planned economies of the former Soviet Union, Eastern Europe, and Asia represent a natural experiment in institutional design. Markets are being created where none existed before. The transition enables us to watch institutional evolution as it is taking place. The reformers are addressing problems of incentive-system design that parallel those being addressed by principal–agent theorists – albeit at a different level of abstraction. I shall discuss two examples of evolving institutions (taken from China, which has had the longest time to experiment of any of the transition economies).

Community-Owned Firms

In China's economic reforms, much of the dynamism has come from non-state-owned industrial firms. The entry of these new firms illustrates the vitality of market forces. Despite impressive impediments – little law of contract, weak property rights, underdeveloped capital markets – when the restrictions on the activities of non-state firms were loosened, a huge amount of entrepreneurial investment occurred, with striking success. The non-state sector now accounts for a half of China's industrial output.

The non-state firms have unusual ownership forms and organizational structure, as Byrd and Lin (1990) describe. These firms are mostly located in rural areas. Some are private, in roughly the Western sense. But most are publicly owned: they are run by communities of a few hundred or a few thousand people. (Community ownership served to mobilize capital when there was no financial system to which fledgling firms could go for funds.) Why are these firms not subject to the perverse incentives normally associated with publicly owned firms (in particular, China's giant state-owned firms)? The answer seems to lie, in part, in the smallness of the ownership unit. The product-market and capital-market disciplines facing these firms are strong enough to induce efficient operation, even with community ownership.

Product-market discipline comes in the standard form: most firms compete with other non-state firms, and in some cases state firms, to sell their outputs, and the competition is often fierce. The financial-market discipline is unusual. Most of the investment capital in established firms comes from the firm's own retained earnings and, to a lesser extent, loans from other firms. The other main source of capital is the community government. The community government monitors

its investments in firms. Operating on a local scale, it is better informed about a firm's potential than a provincial or national industrial
bureau controlling a state firm would be, and so has more effective
control. Since the community government's resources are limited, and
most of its revenue (needed, among other things, to pay the salaries of
the community-government officials) comes from these enterprises, it
is motivated to protect its investment by inducing the firm to maximize its profits. Workers' wages depend on their own output, via piece-
rates; and remuneration rates and employment levels follow the firm's
profits up and down. The manager's pay is linked to the firm's profit
and sales; a successful manager also enjoys the perquisites that come
from managing a large firm. The internal and external disciplines work
so effectively that the productive efficiency of these community-owned
firms, it has been estimated (Byrd and Lin 1990, ch. 11), is as high as
the productive efficiency of those rural firms that are privately owned.

Manager Auctions

Of the myriad of novel institutions being invented as the formerly
planned economies grope their way toward capitalism, one of the most
intriguing is that of managerial jobs in China's state-owned firms being put up for auction. In these manager auctions, potential managers
bid for the right to be the firm's top manager for a specified period of
time – typically three to five years. Each bid consists of a promise of
the amount of profits the firm will deliver to the government in each
year of the contract. Bids are made meaningful by requiring the successful bidder to post a security deposit – on average about 50 per
cent of the manager's annual income – to be forfeited in whole or part
if the promised profits are not forthcoming. The winning bidder is
chosen not only by how much profit he offers but also by an evaluation of his competence, his plans for the firm, and so on. The new
manager receives a contract that makes his pay vary with the firm's
financial performance. The bidders often include the firm's current top
manager; lower-level employees of the firm; officials from the minis-
try that regulates the firm; and outsiders who believe they can do a
better job than the incumbent. Before the bidding, the firm's accounts
are opened to anyone who might decide to bid. The winner is often
the previous manager: one survey found that the incumbent won 55
per cent of the auctions. It is not surprising that the incumbent has an
advantage in the bidding and often wins; what is noteworthy is that
this is not an overwhelming advantage, and the incumbent loses al-

most half of the time. Thus the auctions produce considerable turnover of management.

In a market economy, long-term observation of performance in mid-level managerial positions provides information about a potential manager's abilities. In the transition economy, observed performance is suspect, as it was not attained in a genuinely market setting. Anecdotal evidence has it that the bidding process has served to identify competent managers who were previously unknown to the industrial bureau; thus the auctions have succeeded in putting better people into management jobs.

The auctions also reveal information about the firm's potentialities. Post-auction productivity, according to a recent study (Groves *et al.*, 1992), significantly exceeds pre-auction productivity. And the increase is larger when the incumbent manager wins the auction than when someone else wins. This may look paradoxical; but it reflects the information-revealing role of the auctions. Suppose a firm's performance is only partly under the control of the manager; a firm may simply be inherently either a good or a poor performer. The incumbent manager of a firm that is performing poorly, having inside information, knows how much scope there is for improving its performance. Outside bidders cannot infer from the information available to them whether the firm's poor performance is the result of its inherently low productivity or slack management. Outside bidders therefore submit moderately high bids, to allow for the possibility that the firm may have either a high or a low potential. The incumbent manager will bid high if the firm has a good potential, and low if it has a poor potential. Thus incumbent managers tend to win the bidding for those firms that have good potential but have been underperforming; outside bidders tend to win those firms that have poor potential. Given that the post-auction managerial incentives are stronger than the pre-auction managerial incentives, all firms do better after the auction. But the biggest improvements will come in the firms with the highest potential; and these tend to be won by incumbent managers. Hence we observe that productivity increases most in those firms that incumbent managers win. The auction, therefore, reveals information about the firm's inherent productivity. The Chinese manager auctions have promoted more effective regulation by revealing information about the inherent productivity of the firm and by identifying hitherto unrecognized competent managers.

Conclusion

Innovative institutions are arising in the transition economies. Community ownership overcomes the problem of how to get entry of new firms before there exists a market-oriented financial system. Manager auctions provide information to correct the absence of track records for potential managers. These are probably temporary solutions to the peculiar problems of transition; perhaps, however, they are sustainable institutions. Observation of how institutions in practice solve problems of information and incentives, can provide, as Aoki suggests, both a check on existing principal–agent theory and ideas as to where the theorizing should go from here.

References

Aoki, Masahiko (1988) *Information, Incentives, and Bargaining in the Japanese Economy* (Cambridge: Cambridge University Press).

Aoki, Masahiko (1990) 'Towards an Economic Model of the Firm', *Journal of Economic Literature*, vol. 28, pp. 1–27.

Byrd, William and Qingsong Lin (eds) (1990) *China's Rural Industry* (Oxford: Oxford University Press).

Groves, Theodore, Yongmiao, Hong, John McMillan and Barry Naughton (1992) 'China's Evolving Managerial Labor Market', *Journal of Political Economy*, vol. 103, pp. 873–92.

McAfee, R. Preston and John McMillan (1995) 'Organizational Diseconomies of Scale', *Journal of Economics and Management Strategy*, vol. 4, pp. 399–426.

12 Patents as an Incentive System[1]

Suzanne Scotchmer

UNIVERSITY OF CALIFORNIA AT BERKELEY

12.1 INTRODUCTION

The modern justification for granting patents is that patents give firms an incentive to invest in research and development (R&D). It therefore seems important to understand how patent law performs as an incentive system, and how it could be improved. Perhaps the most convincing investigation into the effectiveness of patent law would be an empirical one. However, an empirical investigation seems unpromising, since patent systems in different countries are not substantially different, and, in any case, important inventions are patented worldwide so that the incentives for R&D do not depend on where a firm is domiciled. In this chapter I will undertake the more limited task of trying to expose conceptually some shortcomings of patent law as an incentive system.

By definition, the best incentive system for supporting research would be that designed by a 'mechanism designer', as in the procurement literature. Such an incentive system would impute larger powers to government than the patent system does; in particular through the ability to identify potential R&D projects, to tax optimally and to contract with the researcher prior to his investment. This chapter discusses patents as an incentive system, maintaining the fundamental premise of patent law that revenues will be given through monopoly protection and that the patent authorities cannot tailor the extent of this protection (either through patent length or patent breadth) to specific aspects of the project, e.g., according to an ex ante negotiation in which the researcher is asked to estimate the costs. Patent protection can depend at most on ex post verifiable aspects of the research environment as a whole. My object is to point out ways in which the patent system diverges from an optimal incentive system given these constraints. I first discuss research environments assuming that innovations are 'isolated', and then the important circumstance that R&D is cumulative in the sense that innovators build on each other's achievements.

12.2   ON ISOLATED INVENTIONS

12.2.1   Single Innovators

With no *ex ante* uncertainty about the costs or benefits of R&D, and if the value of the patent were unrestricted, then the optimal patent policy might be obvious: choose the efficient research project and firm, and grant a patent that lasts exactly long enough to cover the costs of R&D. Since monopoly pricing imposes a social cost, the optimal patent life is the smallest one that gives the inventor enough incentive to invest. However, there are at least two problems with this answer. First, if the patent life cannot reflect R&D costs, the solution is not available. Nordhaus (1969) argued that nevertheless a finite patent life is optimal. Although a finite patent life discourages research when R&D costs are high, this loss is compensated by shortening the duration of the monopoly when R&D occurs. Second, the patent life is not the only patent variable that determines per-period profit. Broadening the patent will permit higher per-period profit and the life can then be shortened without discouraging R&D.

Since there is an obvious social improvement to be made by letting the patent life or breadth depend on R&D costs, it is worth setting forth the possible reasons why this is not done. The most obvious reasons are, first, firms' incentives to overstate their costs, and, second, the accounting problem of how to allocate overhead costs to different projects in a diversified firm. But even if we take the optimistic view that R&D costs are observable *ex post*, there is a third problem that relates to *ex ante* uncertainty. Even good projects sometimes fail, and firms will not undertake R&D if costs are reimbursed only if the project is successful.

Suppose that *ex ante* costs and benefits of a research project are given by probability distributions (F,H), where F is a distribution of the per-period social benefits, say s, and H is the distribution of costs, say c. The profitability of the patent in each time period will typically be less than the social value of the invention, s, and we shall refer to it as $\pi(s)<s$. Here we are taking the breadth of the patent to be fixed. The revenue earned by the firm will be $\Pi(s,T) = \int_0^T \pi(s)e^{-rt}dt$, where T is the patent life and r is the social rate of discount.

It seems obvious that if the patent life could reflect the realized social benefits and costs, the optimal patent life would be the one that gives the firm zero profit; that is, it satisfies $\Pi(s,T) - c = 0$. However there is a problem with this rule. The supports of the distributions F and H might be such that $\Pi(s,\infty) = (\pi(s)/r) < c$ for some (s,c) even if the project were *ex ante* efficient. To compensate for these 'unlucky' states of the world, it is necessary to give the inventor strictly positive profit whenever feasible, in such an amount that ex ante expected profit is zero, $E_F\Pi(s,T) - E_H c = 0$. But now the optimal patent life depends on *ex ante expectations* about costs and benefits, and not on *ex post realized* costs and benefits, even if the latter are observable. *Ex post* observability does not help very much. We are forced either to a system where the patent life is chosen according to an overall expectation of the benefits and costs (F,H) themselves or to some very different system in which R&D firms are given incentive to reveal their private information before the contract is made. However, incentives are costly. In the procurement literature, the firm's incentive to reveal its expected costs accurately depends on the threat that if costs are reported high, the project may be cancelled or reduced. Thus, beneficial projects may be cancelled.

The second problem in establishing the optimal patent life is that simultaneously one must establish the patent breadth. The boundaries of markets are fuzzy, and the profitability of the patent depends on its breadth. Klemperer (1993) studied the tradeoff in protecting profit between a long patent or a broad patent in a model where imitators can enter the market costlessly with close substitutes. Assuming that consumers have heterogeneous tastes, he showed conditions on elasticities of substitution under which each is best. In order to implement Klemperer's rules, the patent length and breadth must depend on detailed aspects of market demand or consumers' tastes and on the form of competition between firms. Such conditions fall entirely outside the spirit of patent laws as currently constituted, in which patent protection depends only on verifiable, technical aspects of the invention, and not on the (possibly fickle) market.

12.2.2 Interactions Among Firms

The optimal design of patent incentives takes on new dimensions when we consider interactions among competing R&D firms. We may note three problems: first, firms may have different expectations about the costs and benefits of an R&D programme ('pessimists' and 'optimists');

second, firms may have different research strategies or abilities, and decentralized patent incentives do not permit them to share information and delegate efficiently; and third, patent races change firms' incentives to invest when rates of investment are endogenous. Some, but not all, of these problems can be resolved through research joint ventures.

Optimists and Pessimists

So far we have assumed that a firm will respond to patent incentives by investing if $E_F\Pi(s,T) - E_H c \geq 0$, and that this is efficient since it implies that $E_F(s/r) - E_H c > 0$. But efficiency is not obvious, since the distributions (F,H) might only reflect the lunatic optimism of a single individual. In what sense, if at all, do we think that $E_F(s/r) - E_H c > 0$ should be the efficiency criterion? Clearly that would be the criterion if everyone agreed on the costs and benefits (F,H). But what if there is disagreement?

A modern approach to disagreements is to say that firms start with a 'common prior' over the costs and benefits of a particular research agenda, and the 'idea' (F,H) is a 'posterior' based on superior information.[2] If so, other individuals with the same information would presumably agree with it, and then the efficiency criterion $E_F(s/r) - E_H c \geq 0$ is convincing.

But suppose two individuals have different random draws of information, say (F,H) and (F',H'), where $E_{F'}\Pi(s,T) - E_{H'}c < E_{F'}(s/r) - E_{H'}c < 0 < E_F\Pi(s,T) - E_H c < E_F(s/r) - E_H c$. If individuals naively respond to decentralized patent incentives without noticing the investment strategies of other firms, then the firm with the idea (F,H) will invest and the other will not. But such an investment plan is not what a mechanism designer or social planner would do. The mechanism designer would aggregate the two random draws of information into a single posterior distribution, and decide whether to invest according to that posterior. Under the decentralized incentives of patent law, there is no natural way to share information. One possibility is that (as in the literature on rational expectations) firms might try to infer other firms' information by observing their investment strategies. Such a model has recently been investigated by Minehart and Scotchmer (1995).[3]

This coordination problem could possibly be solved within the framework of patent law by granting a patent life T such that $E_{F'',H''}[\Pi(s,T) - c] = 0$, where the distributions (F'',H'') are the posteriors that aggregate the information of the firms. At most one firm – the more optimistic firm – would invest. If two firms invested, each firm would face a probability of one-half of winning the patent and each firm's expected profit would be negative. However, the problem discussed in the section 12.2.1 is compounded. Not only must the patent life depend on *ex ante* expectations about costs and benefits rather than *ex post* realized costs and benefits, but in addition, it must aggregate the information of several firms, and some kind of *ex ante* communication is required to accomplish this.

Avoiding Duplication of Research Strategies

Even when firms have the same information, patent incentives may lead to inefficiencies through patent races. The literature has produced two views of patent races: that they inefficiently duplicate costs, and that they efficiently encourage higher aggregate investment. Of course such duplication is a form of higher aggregate investment, so these two views obviously presume different models of R&D. Inefficient duplication arises where R&D costs have a large fixed component (i.e. the natural interpretation of the model above is that the cost c is fixed, and if two firms invest, the total cost is $2c$). Investment by two firms is inefficient and we have noted above that this problem could be solved by restricting the patent life.

The concern with duplication suggests a broader question: If firms have different research strategies or research abilities to achieve the same end, which firms should invest? We might want several firms to pursue strategies that are complementary, in the sense of having complementary risk characteristics. This problem was first studied by Wright (1983), who compared 'patents, contracts and prizes' as methods to encourage or discourage entry of firms with different research lines. Wright assumed that the firms had different research strategies, so that duplication was not an issue; the only issue was how many firms would participate. Dasgupta and Maskin (1987) and Bhattacharya and Mookerhjee (1986) have also investigated parallel research lines, but in more specific models. Equilibrium strategies differ from efficient ones in various ways. Allen (1991) provides an abstract discussion of research agendas in which the research output is a partition of an information space. She does not investigate what would happen under decentralized patent incentives, but observes that a coordinated research strategy would make sure, as a minimum, that investments would partition the space differently. In all these cases, a mechanism designer would give firms incentive to report their research abilities and choose the efficient combination of strategies, which may be different from those in a patent race. If firms cannot observe each other's strategies, then the decentralized incentives of patent law, in which each firm stands to win the same patent, will typically not lead to efficiency. For example, there will be no way to guarantee that a strategy is not duplicated.

Delegation to the Least-Cost Firms

Patent races also fail to coordinate research efficiently when firms have different research costs. Suppose the project is worth s, and the expected R&D costs of firms A and B are $c_a < c_b$. Efficiency requires that firm A invest, and not firm B. The efficient patent life would just cover the costs c_a, and only firm A would invest. But without some coordinating mechanism, the private information on costs cannot be made public. If the patent life is established outside such a mechanism, neither firm A nor firm B knows which firm has lower costs, and even if they did know, the patent might be valuable enough to inspire an inefficient patent race.

Endogenous Rates of Investment

Participation of many firms may be efficient if there are no fixed costs of R&D, and if there is no cumulative learning within each firm. These are the two premises of the patent-race literature based on the Poisson R&D process, in which patent races may actually improve efficiency because they accelerate innovation. The patent-race literature based on the Poisson model focuses on the fact that R&D investment is a flow over time. Since the patent value is less than the social value, the marginal benefit of increasing the aggregate rate of investment is greater to a social planner than to a single private firm. As a consequence a single private firm would invest too slowly and delay the invention.

Patent races speed up the rate of investment, and in conjunction with a well-chosen patent life may therefore overcome the tendency toward under-investment (see Reinganum, 1992, for a survey of this subject). In the familiar Poisson technology under a concavity assumption, efficiency demands the participation of many firms: dividing a fixed rate of investment among several firms stochastically decreases the waiting time. For this reason, and also because the total rate of investment will be higher in a patent race, patent races stochastically reduce the time until the invention; and this may be a social improvement.

However, the optimal patent value does not simply reflect *ex post* verifiable R&D costs. Let us consider the obvious possibilities. Suppose, first, that the patent life is chosen so as to reimburse the aggregate expected R&D costs of the firms in the race, when they invest at the efficient rate. Then if all firms invest at the efficient rate, they will have equal probabilities of winning the patent, and will make zero expected profit. However, this will not be an equilibrium. A firm can make positive expected profit by reducing its rate of investment. Suppose, instead, that the winning firm is given a patent that reimburses its actual accumulated R&D costs. Then only one firm will race, since otherwise the firms will make negative expected profit, and the advantages of a patent race are then undermined. Even if investment by only one firm was efficient, the policy of reimbursing actual accumulated costs would suffer the problem identified in Section 12.2.1. There may be 'unlucky' states of the world where it is impossible for a patent to reimburse costs.

Research Joint Ventures

If the only problem of organizing research among many firms was to prevent duplicated effort, a patent value that reimbursed *ex ante* expected costs of one firm would solve the problem, since only one firm would invest, and it does not matter which firm. But whenever there is asymmetric information, either about costs and benefits or about other firms' research strategies or abilities as discussed above, the decentralized incentives of patent law fail because each firm's efficient strategy depends on the other firms' private information, and there is no obvious way to make the information public. Research joint ventures might permit firms to share their information, and thus invest efficiently.

If joint ventures had available all the power and the same objectives as a mechanism designer, then the inefficiencies due to decentralization would vanish. However, joint ventures face three constraints not faced by the mechanism designer. First, joint ventures must balance their budgets, whereas a mechanism designer can transfer funds between projects. Second, joint ventures face more stringent individual rationality constraints than the mechanism designer (as follows). And third, the objective of the joint venture is profit, not efficiency.

A research firm will participate only if participation provides at least as much expected profit as non-participation. The firms' reservation utilities are zero in the case of mechanism design; there is no patent protection, and unless a firm participates it will not be rewarded for discovery. In the case of joint ventures, the alternative to joining the venture is to race against it, with the prospect of achieving the innovation first and receiving the lucrative patent. (Without patent protection, the joint venture itself would not invest because it would subsequently face imitation by non-member entrants, and could not make positive net profit.) Thus, the joint venture must distribute expected profits so that each firm expects to earn at least as much by participation as it would in the race.

Participation constraints and the balanced-budget constraint restrict the set of outcomes that can be implemented when there are also incentive constraints. As a consequence of this general principle, not all the outcomes that can be implemented by a mechanism designer can be implemented by a joint venture. The implementable outcomes have not been studied in all the coordination problems mentioned above; however, they have been studied for R&D contexts where firms differ in their costs or abilities, and firms' rates of investment cannot be contracted on (Gandal and Scotchmer, 1993). In a model based on the Poisson technology, where each firm's probability and time of success depends on all the firm's abilities and rates of investment, Gandal and Scotchmer argue that if only rates of investment are unobservable or only abilities are unobservable, then first-best rates of investment can be implemented by a joint venture with participation constraints and budget balance. But if both rates of investment and abilities are unobservable, then first-best rates of investment *might* be implementable, but not with both participation constraints and budget balance. In such a case, the mechanism designer can implement better outcomes than can a joint venture.

Thus joint ventures might not be able to implement all the outcomes available to a mechanism designer, and cannot necessarily organize research efficiently. But in addition they might not *want* to implement efficient outcomes, since joint profit might not be maximized by efficient rates of investment, even if implementable. As mentioned above if the private value of the patent is smaller than the social value, rates of investment that maximize joint profit are smaller than the efficient rates. Thus, even if the joint venture has the ability to coordinate firms' research efforts efficiently, it will not do so. In fact the public interest might be better served by prohibiting the joint venture, since the joint venture would reduce investment. The latter argument implies, among other things, that the optimal patent value and the right antitrust stance toward joint ventures – whether or not they should be permitted – cannot be disentangled. If joint ventures are permitted, then the patent value must be large in order to avoid inefficient delay. If joint ventures are disallowed, the patent life must be shorter in order to avoid over-investment.

Thus, while joint ventures can ameliorate some of the losses from decentralized patent incentives that were mentioned above, they cannot accomplish everything a mechanism designer could accomplish. Like a mechanism designer, joint ventures have an incentive to delegate effort to least-cost firms, to aggregate firms' information about the costs and benefits of R&D, and to choose investment portfolios with attractive risk profiles. However, they may inefficiently reduce aggregate investment relative to what would happen in a patent race, since the private value of the patent is typically less than the social value.

12.3 THE PROBLEMS OF CUMULATIVE RESEARCH AND IMITATION

The problems are compounded when research is cumulative, in the sense that inventions of one inventor become a foundation for second-generation inventions by other inventors. Second-generation products are of at least three types: accessories, improvements, and applications. An *accessory* may be defined as a new product that can be sold to the consumer separately from the initial product, but is mainly useful when used together with it. An example might be software designed for a particular patented computer. An *application* involves a new use for the product that was not described in the initial patent claims. For example, laser surgery is an application of laser technology. An *improvement* comprises an innovation that cannot be sold separately from the original product but must be integrated into it (e.g., an automatic switch that shuts off an iron). Improvements and applications have similar strategic consequences, but differ in how we think of the bundling. A basic technology is bundled into the application, whereas an improvement is bundled into the basic technology.

When more than one firm is involved in developing a technology, a new problem arises: how to divide the joint profit between the sequential innovators. Suppose that the private value of the initial invention is (x/r), and that a firm other than the first patent-holder will have an idea (s, c_2) for a second-generation product, say an application, where s is the per-period value of the application and c_2 is its cost. Its social value is (s/r). If the first invention costs c_1, the social value of the first product is $(x/r) - c_1 + E_{F,H}\max\{0,((s/r) - c_2)\}$, where (F,H) are the distributions of s and c_2 respectively, known prior to investment in the first product. The second-generation product is facilitated by the first product, and its expected surplus $E_{F,H}\max\{0,((s/r) - c_2\}$ must therefore be counted as part of the value of the first product. Even if the first product has negative social value as a stand-alone product (i.e., if $(x/r) - c_1 < 0$), investment might be justified by the prospect of second-generation products. To give the first innovator sufficient incentive to invest, he must collect some of the profit from second-generation products.

If the firms could coordinate their efforts before the first investment, then a benevolent mechanism designer would have the first firm invest if $(x/r) - c_1 + E_{F,H}\max\{0,((s/r) - c_2) > 0$, irrespective of who the second firm might be. If the revenue was granted through monopoly protection, the efficient patent life T would satisfy $E_{F,H}[\Pi(x,T) + \Pi(s,T) - (c_1 + c_2)] = 0$.[4] (For simplicity, we will assume that the first and second innovations are invented more or less contemporaneously.) But without the mechanism designer, the efficient outcome is difficult to achieve. The second firm may be unknown at the time of the first investment, and then it is difficult for the first and second innovators to make a private agreement to invest, even if the monopoly duration T would yield positive expected joint profit. In what follows we assume that such deals cannot be made. The problem then arises that once the first investment has been made, the sunk costs of the first investment become irrelevant to bargaining over the incremental profit of later investments. Because of this, the profit from subsequent investments may not be divided in a way that reimburses costs to the first innovator.

Patent law establishes (i) whether the second-generation product infringes the first patent, (ii) whether the second product is itself patentable, (iii) the length of the first patent, and (iv) the length of the second patent if patentable. In patent law, infringement is a matter of the first patent's *breadth*. Whether the second-generation product infringes the previous patent depends on the claims permitted in the previous patent. Whether the second product is patentable depends on whether the investor has made an 'inventive step' that is not 'obvious'. The second product could be patentable but not infringing, infringing but not patentable, both patentable and infringing, or neither patentable nor infringing.

Three ideas about the optimal policy emerge. First, provided more than one firm is capable of developing the second-generation product, at least as much profit is transferred to the first innovator if the second-generation product is unpatentable and infringes the first patent as if the the second-generation product is patentable, whether or not it infringes the first patent. Second, if either the second-generation product is patentable, or if 'ideas are scarce', so that only one firm has the ability to develop each second-generation product, there is no patent policy in which all the profit from second-generation products is transferred to the first patentholder. The monopoly will therefore have to persist longer in order to stimulate R&D than if all research was concentrated in one firm, namely the T that satisfies $E_{F,H}[\Pi(x,T) + \Pi(s,T) - (c_1 + c_2)] = 0$. Third, patents must last longer when *ex ante* agreements between the patentholders are prohibited than when they are permitted. The main message here is that it is difficult to transfer profit to the first innovator, and patent lives could be shorter if a central authority could support the basic investment directly, or consolidate all the costs and benefits of R&D in one firm so as to avoid the subsequent problem of dividing profit.

The arguments for these ideas are very simple. For simplicity consider the case that $x = 0$: the basic research has no commercial value other than facilitating applications. We will let T_1 and T_2 represent the lives of the two patents respectively. The monopoly on the application can be supported in each time period either with an exclusive licence from the first patentholder or with its own patent. Thus the monopoly on the application lasts a duration $T = \max\{T_1, T_2\}$, and the total profit available from an application with social value s is $\Pi(s,T)$.

To see the first point above, suppose the application or new product is not patentable ($T_2 = 0$), and that the 'idea' is available to several firms. Prior to investment in the second product, the first patentholder can auction the right to an exclusive licence on the first patent and collect all its expected surplus $\Pi(s,T_1) - c_2$, where $T_1 = T$ is the length of the time profit is protected through an exclusive licence on the first patent. The application will be invented if $\Pi(s,T_1) - c_2 \geq 0$, and the first patentholder will earn profit $\Pi(s,T_1) - (c_1 + c_2)$.

The first patentholder's ability to extract all the profit might be undermined if the second product is patentable, because then a losing bidder who didn't get the exclusive licence might invest anyway and receive the patent on the second innovation. The first patentholder and winning bidder would be blocked from marketing the improvement or application even if they later achieved it. They would be forced to negotiate with the new patentholder *ex post*. Suppose that in this (*ex post*) negotiation each of the two blocking patents gets one-

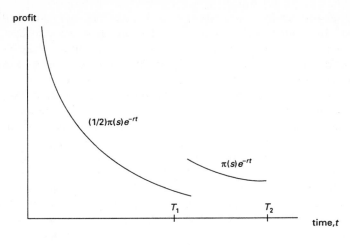

$(1/2)\pi(s)e^{-rt}$

$\pi(s)e^{-rt}$

T_1

T_2

time, t

Figure 12.1

half the surplus over which they are bargaining. This prospect might provide the losing bidder expectation of positive profit. Since the winning bid in the *ex ante* auction will be the difference in expected profit between winning and losing the bid, and since patentability may reduce this difference, patentability may reduce the first patentholder's profit. (For an elaboration of this argument, see Scotchmer, 1996.)

Continuing with the second point, the first innovator's ability to extract all the profit is also undermined if only one firm has the ability to develop the second product, or perhaps only one firm has the 'idea' for it, so that that firm has ex ante bargaining power as well as ex post bargaining power (Green and Scotchmer, 1995). The division of profit between the two firms will be determined by their licensing agreement, and the terms of this agreement will depend on whether it is made before investing in the application (*ex ante*) or after (*ex post*). The bargaining positions for an *ex ante* agreement are determined by what would happen otherwise, and we therefore consider what would happen if the firms had to rely on *ex post* licensing. Figure 12.1 shows firm 2's discounted per-period profit if the first patent lasts until T_1 and its own profit lasts until T_2. Since the firms own blocking patents on the application, it is reasonable that their bargain splits its value, and therefore the per-period revenue of firm 2 while both patents are in effect is $(1/2)\pi(s)$. During periods when only one patent is in effect, that patentholder earns all of $\pi(s)$. (If $T_1 < T_2$, then there is a period when firm 2 does not need to license, and if $T_1 > T_2$ there is a period when firm 1 does not need to license and earns $\pi(s)$.) Firm 2's total discounted profit is the integral under the curve until T_2, minus c_2. This profit may be positive, in which case there is no reason to license *ex ante* rather than *ex post*. If it is negative, firm 2 will nevertheless earn non-negative profit because it would not invest without an *ex ante* agreement. An ex ante agreement is negotiated before costs c_2 are sunk, and the firms share $\Pi(s,\max\{T_1,T_2\}) - c_2$, which might be positive even if firm 2's expected profit with *ex post* licensing would be negative. (In the ex ante agreement, firm 1 shares the costs c_2 as well as the profits $\pi(s)$.) It follows from these arguments that whether the firms license *ex ante* or *ex post*, firm 2 may make positive profit, and will not make negative profit. Thus if the patent life provided exactly zero profit in total $\Pi(s,T) - (c_1 + c_2) = 0$, firm 1 would make negative profit, and anticipating this, would not invest. Our second conclusion follows.

The third conclusion is that the monopoly distortion must last longer when *ex ante* agreements are not allowed. Suppose we want to ensure that both innovators cover their costs. Without *ex ante* agreements, the integral under the curve to T_1 in Figure 12.1 represents the first innovator's revenues, and the integral to T_2 represents the second innovator's revenues. If $c_1 < c_2$, we want $T_1 < T_2$, and if $c_1 > c_2$ we want $T_1 > T_2$. If patent lengths could depend on costs, we could ensure that each innovator earned exactly zero profit, and the same patent lives would be optimal whether we permitted *ex ante* agreements or not. However, as stressed above, patent lives cannot depend on R&D costs, and in particular T_1 cannot depend on c_2, since the first patent is granted before the idea (s,c_2) is known.

Suppose therefore that patent lives cannot reflect costs. As above, firm 2 will in general make positive profit if it invests, whether or not *ex ante* agreements are permitted, as discussed above. Eliminating *ex ante* agreements would discourage the development of some second products: those for which $\Pi(s,T) - (c_1 + c_2) \geq 0$ but firm 2's revenue after *ex post* licensing would not cover the costs c_2. To restore the incentive for investment in such products, we would have to increase T_2. If $T_2 < T_1$, such an increase would reduce the profit of firm 1, and to restore firm 1's profit we might also have to increase T_1. Thus, if we want to sustain a given level of R&D, patent lives must in general be longer when *ex ante* agreements are prohibited than when they are permitted.

The above paragraph suggests that *ex ante* agreements serve the public interest. This is surely true when second-generation products do not compete with first-generation products in the market. *Ex ante* agreements increase investment in second products.

But the welfare effects of *ex ante* agreements are murkier when second-generation products compete with first-generation products in the market. Such agreements then create a monopoly where competition would otherwise prevail. The monopoly increases joint profit in each period and permits a shorter patent life, but since the monopoly is distortionary, it might be better to let the firms compete in each period and extend the patent life for a longer period. Katz and Ordover (1989) discuss this issue, and argue that the one clear context where joint ventures should be permitted is where products are complements. In the case of 'applications' above, the products are neither complements nor substitutes, but the same argument applies.

Finally, a social cost of patent incentives that would be avoided if R&D were subsidized directly is that firms try to invent around the patent. This problem has been explored by Gallini (1992), who points out that costs of imitation cap the patentholder's profit, and that to protect profit patents should discourage imitation. An interpretation of this result is that patents should be on products rather than processes.

12.4 CONCLUSION

Patent law is a decentralized system of incentives that promotes competition for new products. But in innovation, as in other economic endeavours, economists have recently realized that competition can be destructive, and that mechanisms with greater ability to coordinate firms' efforts might be superior. I have described some coordination failures that arise from the decentralized incentives of patent law. Some of these failures arise because the patent value can, at best, depend on *ex post* observations of a firm's R&D costs, rather than on *ex ante* expectations about these costs, or on *ex ante* negotiations with the R&D firm which is given incentive to state its expected costs honestly. Other failures arise because firms cannot observe each other's private information about costs and benefits of research or private information about research strategies and abilities. Even if the private information were shared in a research joint venture, the joint venture's profit incentive under patent law might not lead to efficient investments. Finally, patent law's effectiveness in encouraging sequential innovation is limited by the firms' inability to make agreements among all potential innovators before the initial investment.

Notes

1. I thank Eddie Dekel, Joseph Farrell, John Geanakoplos, Ben Hermalin and Jacques Thisse for helpful discussion and comments.
2. We notice that the paradigm of common priors is unsatisfying because it leaves no room for 'imagination', as it identifies information about the costs and benefits of a known research programme with an 'idea'. One might argue that the act of imagination is in conceiving a research programme itself, not in having information on its costs and benefits.
3. Choi (1991) studies a slightly different problem where firms in a patent race have symmetric information but are unsure of the costs of innovation. Each firm updates its beliefs according to both firms' lack of success.
4. This notation assumes that the first product and second product serve different markets. If they served the same market, then we should write $\Pi(x + s,T)$ for the joint profit, and $\Pi(x + s,T) - \Pi(x,T)$ for the incremental profit provided by the second good instead of $\Pi(s,T)$.

References

Allen, Beth (1991) 'Choosing R&D Projects, An Informational Approach', *AEA Papers and Proceedings*, vol. 81, no. 2, pp. 257–61.

Choi, Jay P. (1991) 'Dynamic R&D Competition under "Hazard Rate" Uncertainty', *The Rand Journal of Economics*, vol. 22, no. 4, pp. 596–610.

Bhattacharya, Sudipto and Dilip Mookherjee (1986) 'Portfolio Choice in Research and Development', *The Rand Journal of Economics*, vol. 17, pp. 594–605.

Dasgupta, P. and E. Maskin, (1987) 'The Simple Economics of Research Portfolios', *Economic Journal*, vol. 97, pp. 581–95.

Gallini, Nancy T. (1992) 'Patent Policy and Costly Imitation', *The Rand Journal of Economics*, vol. 23 no. 1 pp. 52–63.

Gandal, Neil and Suzanne Scotchmer (1993) 'Coordinating Research through Research Joint Ventures', *Journal of Public Economics*, 1993.

Green, Jerry and Suzanne Scotchmer (1995), 'On the Division of Profit Between Sequential Innovators', *Rand Journal of Economics*, vol. 26, pp. 20–33.

Katz, Michael (1986) 'An Analysis of Cooperative Research and Development', *The Rand Journal of Economics*, vol. 17, no. 4, pp. 527–43.

Katz, Michael and Janusz Ordover (1989) 'R&D Cooperation and Competition', M.N. Baily and C. Winston (eds), *Brookings Papers on Economic Activity*, pp. 137–204.

Klemperer, Paul (1993) 'On the Optimal Length and Breadth of Patent Protection', *The Rand Journal of Economics*, (spring 1993).

Minehead, Deborah and Suzanne Scotchmer (1995) 'Ex Post Regret and the Decentralised Sharing of Information', Boston University, Department of Economics, Industrial Studies Program, Working Paper 58.

Nordhaus, William, (1969) *Invention, Growth and Welfare* (Cambridge, Mass.: MIT Press).

Reinganum, Jennifer (1989) 'The Timing of Innovation: Research, Development, and Diffusion', in R. Schmalensee and R. Willig (eds), *Handbook of Industrial Organization*, vol. 1 (New York: North Holland).

Scotchmer, Suzanne (1996) 'Standing on the Shoulders of Giants: Cumulative Research and the Patent Law', *Journal of Economic Perspectives*.

Scotchmer, Suzanne (1991) 'Protecting Early Innovators: Should Second Generation Products be Patentable', forthcoming *The Rand Journal of Economics*.

Wright, Brian (1983) 'The Economics of Invention Incentives: Patents, Prizes and Research Contracts', *American Economic Review*, vol. 73, pp. 691–707.

13 Empirical Studies of Product Markets

Alan Kirman
GREQAM, EHESS AND UNIVERSITY OF AIX-MARSEILLE
and

Louis Phlips
EUROPEAN UNIVERSITY INSTITUTE, FIESOLE

13.1 INTRODUCTION

In their introduction to the *Journal of Industrial Economics*' special issue on 'The Empirical Renaissance in Industrial Economics', Bresnahan and Schmalensee (1987) recall that industrial economics started as a distinct field of economics with a series of book-length case studies of particular industries under the impulse of Edward Chamberlin and Edward Mason. The idea was that the profession would learn about imperfectly competitive markets by induction from an accumulation of detailed studies of particular product markets. Knowledge of the facts would lead to theoretical hypotheses. These hopes did not materialize.

After the war, the availability of simple econometric techniques and government-supplied data (mainly census data) led to a long wave of industry-level cross-section studies 'testing' the structure–conduct–performance paradigm and a virtual disappearance of case studies. The search was for general objective relations between profits, prices, wages, and so on and market structure. In the 1970s, however, dissatisfaction became widespread: it was gradually recognized that these studies lacked sound theoretical foundations, that the industry-level data at hand were not appropriate and that more sophisticated econometric techniques would not suffice to uncover the basic truths one was looking for (see Schmalensee, 1988).

Then, in the 1980s, came the invasion of the field by game theorists. As a result, 'Industrial Organization has become a fairly theoretical field in recent years. At first sight, even a theorist should regret the very high ratio of theory to evidence in a field in which theoretical models are often lacking in generality and in which practical implications are so crucial' (Tirole, 1988, p. 3). The overflow of theoretical papers was perhaps an inevitable reaction to the earlier simple empiricism. In any case, it is beginning to show its usefulness for the analysis of actual markets. In the last few years, there has indeed been an 'empirical renaissance', characterized by empirical work based on explicit theoretical modelling, using new sets of data (especially data on individual firms) and exploiting the latest advances in econometric method.

This chapter is devoted to some of these new developments. As its title indicates, we shall focus on studies of particular product markets and completely neglect papers that study multiple industries. To keep our topic within limits, we also exclude agricultural products and natural resources, whether exhaustible or renewable. (This eliminates crude oil, but not gasoline, and does not eliminate salt, which is a manufactured product.)

13.2 THE RELEVANT MARKET

'Let producers A and B be located in the same geographic market.' 'Let producers A and B produce two varieties of the same product.' That is about all duopoly theory has to say about the market or the products for which it is supposed to be relevant. The determination of the real world 'market' or 'product' is supposed to be an empirical question. Yet, this determination is a condition *sine qua non* for any empirical study of a product market.

Anybody who got dirty hands trying to make such a determination will agree with Horowitz (1981) that 'the market concept is indeed imprecise, and that economists are far better equipped to discuss markets than they are to discover them. . . . The problem of discovering the relevant geographic market is at least as vexing as that of discovering the relevant product market.' Admittedly, spatial price theory defines neat market areas for geographically dispersed firms. However, price discrimination allows oligopolistic or monopolistic firms to invade their competitor's market areas, so that the high degree of overlap and cross-hauling tends to obviate the usefulness of this literature for practical applications. (See Elzinga and Hogarty, 1973 for an early discussion, and Thisse and Vives, 1988 for a recent game-theoretic approach.) In practice, the best guide is still good common sense and a detailed institutional knowledge.

However, some statistical tests are available. They concentrate on the analysis of price data, since the basic principle is still Cournot's: in a market, prices should take the same level throughout with ease and rapidity. The problem is how to translate this in terms of observed prices.

A natural thing to do is to examine price correlations between varieties of the (supposedly) same commodity or two geographic areas. This was done as late as 1985 by Stigler and Sherwin. The pitfalls are too numerous however. First, correlation may be spurious, if there is a common trend, for example. Second, small correlations do not imply that there is not a single market: consider the case where the two prices tend to equality but may differ at any point in time. Third, high correlations may be observed between separate markets, for example if the price in one market is a ceiling to the price in the other. Clearly, the time dimension (and lagged reactions in particular) has to be taken into account. That is why Horowitz (1981) and Howell (1982) use a first-order autoregressive model of the price differences allowing adjustment to a common long-run price.

Slade (1986a), however, sees no reason to suppose that price differences are stable or that a particular adjustment process is followed. She proposes a test that is not based on a particular model of price formation but simply formalizes the idea that two areas (or product varieties) are not common when the price in one area (or for one variety) is exogenous to the other.

In the simple case where there are two regions ($j = 1,2$), the test implies running the following four regressions:

$$p_t^j = \sum_{i=1}^{n_1^j} a_{ij} p_{t-i}^j + g_1^j(z_t) + \varepsilon_t^j \tag{13.1}$$

$$p_t^j = \sum_{i=1}^{n_2^j} c_{ij} p_{t-i}^j + \sum_{i=1}^{n_3^j} d_{ij} p_{t-i}^k + g_2^j(z_t) + \eta_t^j \tag{13.2}$$

where $j = 1,2$, $k = 2,1$, ε^j and η^j are disturbance terms with zero means such that each is uncorrelated with the right-hand-side variables in its respective equation and z_t is a vector of exogenous variables whose exogeneity is *not* to be tested. The joint hypothesis to be tested is that (i) the coefficient vectors d are zero; (ii) p^1 and p^2 are not contemporaneously correlated, and (iii) the covariance between η_t^1 and η_t^2 is zero. The $g_m(z_t)$ are specified as quadratic functions of time.

Slade (1986b) uses this test pairwise on the wholesale prices of gasoline in cities in Southeastern USA, the Northeast and between the East and West coasts to conclude that the Southeast is a local geographic market that is loosely connected to the Northeastern seaboard but entirely separate from the West coast.

Spiller and Huang (1986) go one step further. They propose a maximum-likelihood methodology to estimate the probability of arbitrage and the required arbitrage costs for a pair of regions. Two regions belong to the same market if, when the price in one region exceeds the other, the given prices in the two locations are linked by binding arbitrage conditions such that, if one price should increase, arbitrage would take place. Arbitrage costs thus reflect the maximum differential that can develop between prices. When the price differential is smaller, prices can vary independently of each other. The wholesale gasoline prices in the Northeast of the USA turn out to be such that (a) city-pairs with high probability of being in the same market are those that are nearby; (b) city-pairs with low probabilities are more distant, and (c) city-pairs requiring arbitrage in a north-to-south direction have lower probabilities of being in the same market than city-pairs requiring arbitrage in the opposite direction.

Tests such as those discussed are clearly most useful in offering objective answers to the vexing problem, which pervades most antitrust discussions, of determining the relevant market.

13.3   THE DEMAND FOR PRODUCTS

There is a long tradition in economics of estimating demand equations for specific products or groups of products. In the nineteenth century there was a very active debate over the nature of demand and little concern about its estimation. Until Marshall, there was considerable discussion as to the correct definition of demand for a single commodity. However, in the more formal literature there was convergence on the rather abstract Walrasian notion that demand simply represented the quantity that an individual would purchase at given prices which he was unable to influence. The subsequent theoretical literature concentrated largely on the extension of the analysis to interdependent markets and the problem of demand systems rather than single demand equations, still maintaining the abstract Walrasian approach. Until recently, the idea that demand should be treated in this way has not really been challenged either in the economic or in the econometric literature.

Once the twentieth-century literature had converged on this precise theoretical definition, econometricians concentrated on more sophisticated techniques for the estimation and identification of demand systems (for a detailed account of this evolution, see Morgan, 1990). The agreed definition was retained, that of competitive demand, concerning the quantities of goods an individual would buy at a given price were he constrained only by his income. In Working's (1927) paper the conceptual nature of demand and supply is not questioned. The only real problem for him is that of which is changing.

Let us return now to the implicit assumptions underlying the usual empirical analysis based on Walrasian demand theory. The first of these arises if one accepts that the market in question can essentially be thought of as functioning 'competitively'. The problem is then one of identification; in this case, separating out supply changes from demand changes. In a truly Walrasian, or Arrow–Debreu, world such a distinction could, of course, not be made, since all transactions over time represent one supply and one demand decision taken in some initial period. However, this problem is usually circumvented in the empirical literature by making an implicit assumption of stationarity – that the market is somehow repeated over time. This should, of course, be tested; but it does mean that one can talk of successive observations. However, in this case the appropriate theory is that referred to as temporary general equilibrium theory. The problem with this is that short-run demand loses many of the properties of its Walrasian counterpart. For example, it does not satisfy homogeneity or the Weak Axiom of Revealed Preference (see, e.g., Grandmont, 1983).

However, one may also question the appropriateness of treating purchases as being a direct expression of competitive demand. This clearly depends on the organization of the market. In particular, in many of the markets discussed in this chapter, there is no obvious reason to believe that transactions reflect anything corresponding to the standard theoretical idea of competitive demand. If successive lots of a good are auctioned, for example, there is no theoretical reason to believe that the average price will correspond to the competitive price that would have cleared the same market. There are many examples of markets in which trades are made after pair-wise bargaining or in which traders are dispersed geographically or have imperfect information. In all of these the idea of a single equilibrium price makes little sense.

There are further difficulties with trying to estimate empirical demand functions based on standard utility maximization. The first of these is the problem of aggregation. Even if individuals' demand functions satisfy certain properties, it is by no means necessary that these properties carry over to the aggregate level (see, e.g., Sonnenschein,

1972; Mantel, 1976; and Debreu, 1974). Indeed there is no direct, formal connection between micro-and macro-demand behaviour without extremely restrictive assumptions (see e.g. Deaton, 1986). A second difficulty is that the data for most empirical demand estimations are not obtained at the consumer level. If the purchaser of a good is not in fact the final consumer, one would have to show that properties of individual demand carry over to properties of quantities purchased by an intermediary at different prices. If one considers the simple case of a purchaser who has a monopoly locally of the product that he buys, then it is easy to construct examples in which this will not be the case. This question was raised by Working (1927) and mentioned again in the classical studies of the demand for individual products by Schultz (1938) who, although using individual properties of demand, made his estimations using data for farm prices and not shop prices.

All of this suggests that one should view with a great deal of scepticism efforts to use empirical demand estimation as a way of testing specific characteristics of micro-economic utility maximizing behaviour. As Keuzenkamp and Barten (1991) show, and as one might expect from the discussion above, the track record of attempts to 'verify' such a basic condition as the homogeneity requirement for demand systems is very poor. Marschak's (1943) study of the demand for meat is an early example of the rejection of the hypothesis of homogeneity and increasingly sophisticated analysis has done little better. Yet, as Samuelson (1947) predicted, the consequences of this for economic theory have not been significant.

A more pragmatic approach is to look at empirically estimated 'demand equations' as revealing interesting properties of consumption expenditure rather than as tests of particular tenets of utility theory. In particular, estimates of own and cross-price elasticities and of income elasticities are of interest for a variety of reasons. With this in mind a number of recent studies are worth mentioning.

In studying the consumption of, and expenditure on, tea in the UK using over sixty years of pre-war data, Nguyen and Rose (1987) found evidence of price inelasticity and of steadily decreasing income elasticity. They attribute this to a variety of factors such as demographic and organizational changes and changes in social habits, and point out the obvious consequences for the expansion of tea production in the developing countries. This study produces more evidence for one of the main explanations for the apparent decline in the terms of trade of the developing countries, that the elasticity of demand for their products is low and declining.

Another reason for being interested in demand elasticities is that, if they differ across groups, they can be used as a basis for price discrimination, something we shall come back to in a later section. As an example of this, Tremblay (1985), by estimating a firm demand function for US beer producers, was able to show the existence of demand asymmetries across 'strategic groups' which could account for differences in the strategic behaviour of regional and national beer producers.

The way in which the evolution of demand for a particular product in a particular country affects the development of the producing industry is of considerable interest but often requires long time series. A striking example of such a study is Larsen and Nilsson's (1984) examination of the production and consumption of bicycles in Denmark over ninety years. They document extensively the various factors which have influenced the purchase of bicycles during that time and, as is sometimes the case, their historical analysis provides insights which a more sophisticated econometric analysis might not have revealed.

A number of policy measures depend crucially for their effect on the responsiveness of demand. A good example of this is the recent concern with the evolution of diet, its impact on health and the use of policy measures to modify that evolution. A series of studies, often using a rather restrictive specification for the demand system, the so-called Almost Ideal Demand System (AIDS) of Deaton and Muellbauer (1980), has tried to analyze the nature and source of changes in the relative demand for meat and chicken products: Eales and Unnevehr (1988), Braschler (1983), Haldacher *et al.* (1982), Hudson and Vertin (1985); and for food fats and oils, Gould *et al.* (1991). In all these contributions the changing demographic structure seems to have played an important role, but to what extent this is due to the differential impact of health considerations on different segments of the population is difficult to assess. An earlier study which seemed to point in the opposite direction to those mentioned is that by Luttrell (1969) where demand for meat was found to be 'accelerating' and, although costs were decreasing, both prices and consumption had increased. This could be claimed to provide evidence for the later shift in demand resulting from greater awareness of health problems in the 1980s.

One further example of an investigation of the structure of the demand for a particular product which has quite general implications is Planting's (1982) look at the explanation for the changing seasonality in the consumption of gasoline in the USA. He emphasizes the importance of seasonal differences in price elasticities and suggests that these have been too frequently ignored in the analysis of economic time series.

In concluding this somewhat cursory examination we concur with Gilbert (1991) in suggesting that one of the important roles of empirical studies of demand is in measuring certain parameters, such as elasticities, and that undue priority has been given in the literature to the testing of often intrinsically untestable theoretical propositions. The very use of the term 'demand' itself may have contributed to the sterility of the debate and may help to explain the relative paucity of empirical studies of the consumption of specific goods in the major economic journals.

13.4 CONJECTURAL VARIATIONS AND MARKET POWER

A 'conjectural variation' is a conjecture, made by a firm, that a one-unit change in its output leads to a change of γ in its competitors' total output. A value of $\gamma = -1$ indicates that the firm is a price taker, while $\gamma = 0$ indicates Cournot behaviour. Collusion implies $\gamma = N - 1$, where N is the total number of firms. A methodology that assumes that firms maximize profits under the assumption that their rivals will react according to their conjecture is an attempt to model dynamic interactions in a static framework. From a game-theoretic point of view, such a methodology is not satisfactory since in a static game firms cannot react to one another, by the very timing and information structure of the game (Tirole, 1988, p. 244). Nevertheless, conjectural variations are often used in practice and sometimes interpreted as reduced form parameters[1] from the equilibrium of some unknown dynamic game (Schmalensee, 1989, p. 650).

We wish to emphasize that, whatever their theoretical interpretation, empirical measures of conjectural variations have a different meaning. They do not measure what firms believe will happen but how firms actually behave (possibly as a result of their expectations). As explained in great detail by Bresnahan (1989) in his extensive survey of empirical studies of industries with market power, they are measuring departures from perfectly competitive behaviour, that is, the extent of market power. As such, they are directly related to the Lerner index.

Bresnahan's argument is as follows. (We simplify his notation to abstract from problems of econometric estimation.) Let $p_t = p(q_t)$ be the instantaneous inverse market demand function, with $q_t = \Sigma_i \, q_{it}$ ($i = 1, \ldots, N$). Then the equality of firm i's marginal revenue and marginal cost can be written as

$$p_t = c_{it} - \frac{dp_t}{dq_t} q_{it} \tag{13.3}$$

where c_{it} is marginal cost. To allow for price-setting or quantity-setting conduct, (13.3) is generalized to

$$p_t = c_{it} - \frac{dp_t}{dq_t} q_{it} \theta_{it} \tag{13.4}$$

where $\theta_{it} > 0$ is a parameter that measures the competitiveness of oligopoly conduct. As θ_{it} moves further from 0, the conduct of firm i moves further from the conduct of a perfect competitor. Particular specifications of θ_{it} correspond to particular theories. For example, $\theta_{it} = 1$ is implied by Cournot–Nash equilibrium in a one-shot game (or monopoly if there is only one firm in the market). As θ_{it} rises, the price-cost margin ($p_t - c_{it}$) and the Lerner index rise. During periods of collusion, θ_{it} is larger than during price wars.

The crucial point is that θ_{it} can be redefined as

$$\theta_{it} = 1 + \gamma_i \tag{13.5}$$

where γ_i may be a function of the firm's own quantity, all other firms' quantities or other relevant variables. Consequently, $\theta_{it} = 1$ corresponds to $\gamma_i = 0$, while $\gamma_i = -1$ indicates perfectly competitive behaviour.

Many difficulties in the literature arise from a failure to understand the preceding argument. No harm is done when $\gamma_i = 0$ is identified with Cournot–Nash equilibrium, or when $\gamma_i = -1$ is called perfect competition. But what if it turns out that $\gamma_i = N - 1$? This corresponds to collusive joint profit maximization of N identical firms and $dq_j/dq_i = 1$. What is measured is the collusiveness of conduct, *not* how other firms react when firm i deviates from a collusive equilibrium. Note that in a collusive equilibrium there are no deviations: expectations about the reactions of other firms deter i from deviating, so that these reactions are not observed.

Geroski *et al.* (1985), Bresnahan (1989) and Martin (1993) discuss the estimation procedures of the empirical contributions by Iwata (1974) on the Japanese flat glass industry, Cubbin (1975) on the UK car industry, Gollop and Roberts (1979) and Roberts (1984) on firms in the US coffee roasting industry, Bresnahan (1980, 1981) on the American automobile industry, Appelbaum (1979, 1982) on textile, rubber, electrical machinery and tobacco, Porter (1983b) on railroads, Spiller and Favaro (1984) on the Uruguayan banking sector, Suslow (1986) on aluminium, Martin (1988) on four medical–surgical supply companies and four US motor vehicle producers, and Liang (1989) on the US breakfast cereal industry.

The main conclusions are that (a) there is substantial market power in the industries studied, which are typically highly concentrated industries or markets with dominant firms, and (b) this power results from anti-competitive conduct. These conclusions cannot be generalized, however. Indeed, these industries were selected either because cartels were known to exist or because good statistical data were available, which in turn may be a result of the presence of anti-competitive conduct. How the detected market power can be explained in terms of the evolution of (or differences in) market structure remains an open question: here, cross-sectional studies in the spirit of Sutton's (1991) book may be called for.

13.5 PRICE DISCRIMINATION

Price discrimination, unlike some of the topics dealt with in this chapter, has given rise to a substantial body of empirical literature, including a number of studies of specific markets, and a full account of both the economic theory and details of business practices may be found in Phlips (1983). Price discrimination can be defined, in general terms, as the sale of units of goods to different customers at prices which differ by more than the difference in the delivered cost of those units. From a strictly formal point of view, such a definition is devoid of content since only units of a homogeneous good delivered at the same time and place are considered as the same commodity and therefore in a competitive framework should have the same price. However, in practice, a much less tight definition of good is used and, for example, price discrimination is said to occur if two versions of the same car are sold at prices which differ by more than the differences in the cost of producing and delivering those two versions. The practical difficulties with this are obvious and arise frequently when discriminatory practices are challenged in the courts. Returning, for a moment, to the strict definition, the existence of discrimination is incompatible with first-best efficiency. The recognition of this has led to legislation (such as Article 86 of the Treaty of Rome) against discriminatory practices, particularly by 'dominant' firms. As a result of this, there is a large number of case studies of price discrimination in different markets. The main aim of many of these studies has been to establish whether in the particular case in question practices corresponding to those defined in law as discriminatory are present (for a discussion of this type of problem, see Posner, 1974, 1976; and Bork, 1978). We, however, shall confine our attention here to those papers which apply economic theory, and particularly recent development of theory, to empirical markets. Furthermore, we will consider not only the classic situation in which consumers are divided into groups according to their different demand characteristics and different prices are charged to different groups, but also cases in which firms may charge different prices to separate but identical groups of consumers. In the latter case the discrimination may arise from the structure of the supply side rather than that of the demand side.

The standard classification of discrimination by a monopolist is due to Pigou (1932) and is based on the degree of subdivision of the market and the possibility of extracting consumer surplus. Another is that given by Schneider (1952) who distinguishes between discrimination on the basis of the type of user, the use to which the product is put and geographical location – charging by country of destination, for example. More recently, considerable attention has been paid to the possibility of price discrimination in oligopolistic and monopolistically competitive situations. (For theoretical analysis with a duopoly see, for example, Gabszewicz and Thisse, 1980; Shaked and Sutton, 1982, and, for the multi-firm case, Katz, 1984; Borenstein, 1985; and Holmes, 1989.)

A first class of empirical contributions is that which looks at the discrimination between users or consumers of some good or service provided by a monopoly such as a public utility. The electricity industry has been the subject of extensive investigation in this regard. An essential problem for such an industry is that of spreading its fixed costs between users. Neufeld (1987) gives an account of how the demand charge rate structure was introduced. This principle, which relates an individual's charge to his own peak consumption, has been considered as a misapplication of the peak-load pricing scheme and thus representing an inefficient discrimination between different users. However, Neufeld argues that it was actually sustained as a sophisticated system for profit-maximizing price discrimination in the face of competition from isolated plants. Eckel (1987) criticizes peak-load pricing itself (see Bailey, 1972; Boiteux, 1949; and Wenders, 1976) and rate of return regulation as being socially inefficient. She claims that social efficiency requires that differences in customer class demand patterns be taken into account. However, it is by no means clear that the particular schedules actually charged to different customer classes by utilities achieve efficiency rather than profit maximization, and how this should be decided is discussed by Eckel.

Similar problems arise in other fields. For example, the sophisticated systems for pricing for telephone calls (see Billera *et al.*, 1978) or for airport landing charges (see Littlechild and Thompson, 1977) based on the Shapley value from cooperative game theory, provide a 'fair' attribution of overheads in determining different prices for the same good to different consumers. Of course, it can be argued that a landing by a 747 has a higher marginal cost than that of a light aircraft, but there is still discrimination in the technical sense since the differentials in the Shapley prices far exceed the differences in marginal cost. In industries where marginal costs are low relative to fixed costs almost all solutions proposed necessarily contain an element of discrimination.

Another area in which price discrimination is claimed to exist extensively is that of international trade. Where markets can be effectively separated by legal or non-tariff barriers, it is common to find the same physical product being sold at very different prices in different markets. This has been a source of interest in the European Community since such practices are, in principle, ruled out under the Treaty of Rome.

The pharmaceutical industry has been frequently cited as an extreme example of such practices. Schut and Van Bergeijk (1986) claim that there is a close positive correlation between per capita gross national product and the price charged for a given drug. Zanon (1981) discusses the use of discounts for large-scale purchases which effectively allows companies to discriminate through exclusive importers.

A second industry which has attracted interest is automobile manufacture. Price differentials are maintained in many countries by the existence of voluntary export controls. However, even within the EC substantial differences exist between pre-tax prices for the same car. A number of explanations have been advanced for this. Arbitrage is by no means trivial for the individual, and professional arbitrageurs who both import and service cars are ruled out by the exclusive dealership arrangement. Although simple discrimination by demand is suggested by many authors, Kirman and Schueller (1990) suggest that the price differences reflect, in part, the market structure with domestic producers playing the role of leader in their own country. Thus countries with higher-cost domestic producers have higher prices, even with identical demand. In addition, countries with no domestic producers have lower prices and pre-tax prices are lower in countries with higher taxes, a conclusion also reached by Murfin (1983, 1987). All this follows from the analysis of a simple one-shot non-cooperative game. Mertens and Ginsburgh (1985) confirm that price differences are not due to product differentiation but are mainly the result of discrimination. However, interestingly, Davidson *et al.* (1989) show that the welfare effects of lowering discrimination in this market are highly ambiguous and this reflects other theoretical results.

A further question raised here is to what extent do car manufacturers or other exporters discriminate by not passing exchange rate changes through to prices. Mertens and Ginsburgh (1985) and Kirman and Schueller (1990) both show that prices do not reflect, even in the longer term, exchange rate changes and are fixed with respect to local cars in domestic currency terms. Knetter (1989) shows that both US and German exporters maintain price differentials and that there is incomplete pass-through. All of this confirms the theoretical findings of Hens, Kirman and Phlips (1991) who show that, in an oligopolistic situation, exchange rate changes may actually result in perverse price changes (i.e. an increase in the price of the exports of a devaluing country). This leads to a serious problem in predicting the effects of a devaluation in the presence of oligopolistic competition.

In other areas also, attention has been focused on price discrimination in multi-firm settings. Shepard (1991) shows how price discrimination is practised by service stations offering both full service and self-service gasoline and suggests a method for detecting which part of price differences is due to discrimination and which to cost. Her analysis raises the question of what happens if the choice of full service, self-service, or dual functioning is made endogenous rather than exogenously given. Wolinsky (1987) gives a theoretical explanation of the empirical fact that manufacturers market the same good under different brand names and price discriminate in so doing. He cites the selling of 'own brand' products by chain stores as an example.

An interesting example of price discrimination, which directly concerns the academic economist, is that practised by scientific journals. Joyce (1990) confirms an old argument that photocopying has increased price discrimination and shows that the more copied a journal is, the greater is the discrimination between institutions and individuals.

In concluding this section, it should be noted that there is a strong school of thought, represented by a recent paper by Lott and Roberts (1991), which argues that much of apparent price discrimination can be cost explained. Some of their arguments are persuasive, others less so. The observation that consumer reports find Sears tyres manufactured by Michelin of lower quality than those marketed by Michelin itself may, in reality, say more about the tests used by consumer reports than about product differentiation. Although these reservations should be noted, few would doubt empirical evidence for the existence of price discrimination on a large scale.

13.6 TACIT COLLUSION AND THE 'FOLK THEOREM'

As we have said, it would not be possible to give an adequate account of empirical work on product markets without taking into consideration the theoretical revolution that has occurred in recent years in the field of industrial economics. Sophisticated models derived from noncooperative game theory have been developed to characterize the behaviour of agents and firms in different market structures. Furthermore, and this is what concerns us here, the analysis has been made dynamic through the use of repeated games, supergames, and differential games. However, the empirical verification of some of the major theoretical results of the 'new industrial economics' has developed remarkably slowly, though there are obvious reasons for this. In most cases the empirical testing of a theoretical proposition using a repeated game, for example, requires the use of extremely precise data on prices for a particular product of a specific industry. Furthermore, this data has to be collected over a relatively long time period. There are not many examples in the literature of the construction of such data sets.

To see what form empirical verification of theoretical propositions might take and the difficulties involved, we shall consider a standard problem, that of tacit collusion among producers or sellers. A standard argument has been that the existence of profits, in an oligopolistic situation, above those which would be obtained in the Nash equilibrium of the corresponding one-shot game, is prima facie evidence of collusion. Some such argument underlies much antitrust legislation, although the reference point, even in explicitly oligopolistic situations, is often referred to, misleadingly, as the 'as if competitive' one. (An explicit account of the empirical problems involved in using this approach for specific markets, such as that for synthetic fibres, is given by Albach and Klote 1973.)

However, as soon as the game in question is considered in a dynamic setting, the theoretical basis for this conclusion is undermined by the well-known 'Folk Theorem' from game theory. Put very loosely, a version of that theorem is that in a stationary oligopolistic situation in which players are impatient (i.e. they discount the future) all the 'cooperative' solutions of the one-period game are Nash equilibria of the overall non-cooperative game.

There are many models which use one-shot games, but for many economic situations these are inappropriate. The advantage of the repeated game or, in the case where the one-shot game changes from period to period, of the supergame approach, is that short-term punishments can be used to enforce more cooperative solutions. Thus one would observe outcomes in the dynamic approach which achieve better payoffs for all parties than the security levels guaranteed at the mini max solution of the one-shot game. As has been mentioned, the empirical testing of certain characteristics of the strategies involved in markets to see whether they correspond to those predicted in the theory is an awesome task, if only because of the types of data required.

In two recent papers, Slade (1991, 1992) has done this. In the first, she studies the market for saltine crackers in a small US town. She uses weekly data to test two standard simplifying hypotheses used in dynamic differential games: first, that competition can be studied in terms of single strategic variables such as prices or advertising; second, that the class of equilibrium studied is often restricted, to Markov-perfect or memory-less equilibria for example. Using modified versions of standard causality/exogeneity tests, she strongly rejects the strategic independence of choice variables. Thus it is not, as one might expect, acceptable to study competition from an individual choice point of view. As to the memory-less assumption, she finds that it is appropriate for price choice but not for advertising. The finding for pricing choices is in part one of interpretation. When the lagged variables do have an effect this is attributed to the fact that prices are not changed in every period. The latter problem is a standard one in many econometric examinations of empirical price data. The choice of when to change prices should be made endogenously (see Cecchetti, 1986, for a study of the frequency of magazine price changes). The discrete nature of these changes might lead one to doubt the appropriateness of the differential game approach.

In the second paper, Slade (1992) studies price wars amongst gasoline stations on a stretch of highway in Vancouver. The assumptions made are that there are N firms selling a differentiated product, each firm i faced with a demand curve

$$q_{it} = a_t - b_t p_{it} + d_t \sum_{j \neq i} p_{ji}$$

All have a common discount factor d and are assumed to choose strategies of the form

$$p_{it} = p_t^* + R_t \sum_{j \neq i} (p_{jt\text{-}1} - p_t^*) \qquad (13.6)$$

where R_t is the slope of the intertemporal reaction function and p_t^* the stationary equilibrium price corresponding to the period t parameters. If all the parameters were constant it is easy to see that the subgame perfect stationary equilibrium price for all players would be

$$p^* = \frac{a + bc - (N - 1) \, \delta \, d \, c \, R}{2b - (N - 1) \, d \, (1 + \delta \, R)}$$

In this case with $R_t = R$, then $R = 0$ corresponds to Bertrand–Nash, while $R = d = 1$ corresponds to joint monopoly or perfect collusion.[2] This work is closely related to an earlier paper by Slade (1987) in which she came to the conclusion, using the same data, that the reaction function approach was more appropriate than using discontinuous punishment strategies.

The essential problem tackled by Slade is that of allowing for changes over time in the demand parameters. Thus her work differs from the literature already discussed in Section 13.4, where the models are static, the data correspond to stable demand and the purpose is to test the deviation of prices from non-competitive and competitive norms. Slade's purpose is to examine those periods, 'price wars', which correspond to the triggering of punishment strategies and are the result of exogenous demand shocks.[3]

Her findings are that the parameters of firms' strategies do change over time but that the process generating these changes is stationary, that firms react asymmetrically to other firms' price changes and finally that the steady state equilibrium payoffs are above those for the Bertrand–Nash solution.

Two comments are in order. First, if the distribution of the demand shocks were stationary, as her analysis suggests, allowing a richer strategy set might have eliminated price wars altogether. Thus one is led to wonder how much the results depend on that restriction. Second, the asymmetry of the reactions evokes the old 'kinked demand' curve notion which, as Slade points out, has been revived in repeated game models by Anderson (1983) and MacLeod (1985).

Another empirical study of tacit collusion in a repeated game context is that by Rees (1993). He studies the salt duopoly in the UK in which the two participants have fixed capacity constraints and imports are effectively excluded. He finds that profits were above those of the Nash equilibrium for the one-shot game and suggests that the strategies employed be assimilated to those involving retaliation which can sustain one of the equilibria of a repeated game. He rejects the hypothesis that the two salt firms had arrived at a Nash bargaining solution or at the joint monopoly solution of the one-shot game. It should be pointed out, however, that neither of these possibilities would be inconsistent with the Folk Theorem type of result (see Abreu, 1986, 1988; and Fudenberg and Maskin, 1986). The problem with Rees's analysis is that there are only five annual observations. Much of his discussion is based on additional information supplied by the report of the Monopolies and Mergers Commission. He mentions that price changes were always closely synchronized, though neither producer was directly identified as a 'leader'.

This brings us to a last observation on the problem of tacit collusion. A number of empirical studies have postulated the existence of a leader–follower situation. Two classic studies by Tennant (1950) and Nicholls (1951) of the interwar US cigarette industry revealed a picture of fluctuating prices followed by a situation of price leadership and stable uniform prices. Strategic behaviour later seems to have been confined to advertising (see Schmalensee, 1972). A modern analysis would insist on the repeated game aspect of this situation. Furthermore it would point out that price leadership can itself be an equilibrium situation (see, e.g., Deneckere *et al.*, 1992, who introduce customer loyalty as one possible endogenous determinant of a price leadership equilibrium).

The same observation applies to other empirical analyses where price leadership is assumed rather than explained. Examples are Merrilees's (1983) examination of the Australian newspaper industry, Gisser's (1986) study on price leadership in US manufacturing industries, and Kirman and Schueller's (1990) investigation of the European car market.

From the evidence of this section, one might be led to the conclusion that the Folk Theorem type of result is very negative for empirical work. Since almost any situation can be sustained as an equilibrium of a repeated game, and many such situations can be sustained by a variety of strategies, the only criterion seems to be that profits should exceed those of the security level, or the Nash equilibrium of the one-shot game where that equilibrium is unique. Thus not even joint profit maximization is evidence of explicit collusion. In particular, players may be using very sophisticated strategies which will never actually be observed. Thus it may well be that the industry remains in a steady state with punishment only existing as a threat. The way round this in some of the papers already cited is to postulate external shocks which initiate changes in behaviour thereby revealing the strategies in use. This, however, raises the difficult question of how to distinguish between equilibrium strategies and adjustment to those strategies.

Although it is difficult to envisage what it is that one might observe that would be inconsistent with even relatively simple equilibria of a repeated or super game, this does not mean that we cannot learn anything from the actual outcomes observed empirically. A first step is to follow Slade in the papers cited and to test some of the simplifying assumptions used by game theorists to restrict the class of strategies allowed.

Secondly, from the welfare point of view, one positive aspect that might seem to emerge from all this is that welfare-diminishing highly profitable outcomes are only a subset of the many possible equilibria. However, as Salop (1986) points out, citing several specific empirical examples, there is a growing awareness in the legal and in the economic literature of the existence of contractual arrangements between buyers and sellers to facilitate oligopolistic coordination. These arrangements may therefore provide evidence of deliberate collusive selection of particular outcomes, and this in turn may provide the empirical way to eliminate some of the excessively large class of solutions produced by the Folk Theorem type of result. This will, in turn, depend on our ability to identify econometrically particular collusive equilibria, and a step in this direction has been made recently by Gasmi *et al.* (1992), using the soft-drink market as an example.

13.7 THE LEMONS PRINCIPLE AND EFFICIENCY

Bond (1982) provides what seems to be the first empirical test of Akerlof's (1970) Lemons Principle, according to which bad products drive out good products as the result of asymmetric information, because buyers only know the average quality but not the quality of an individual product. Bond considered the (American) market for used pick-up trucks, because there the demand is mainly non-commercial. Trucks were from one to five years old, to give time for the lemons effect to occur.

The measure of quality chosen is the amount of maintenance required on a truck, with a lemon being a truck that requires significantly more maintenance. Buyers should have difficulty in evaluating future maintenance from inspecting the truck, and the lemons principle implies that the proportion of trucks that required major engine maintenance should be higher for trucks that have been purchased used than for trucks that have been purchased new, after controlling for lifetime mileage and model year. Tests on group means indicated almost no support for the lemons principle in any of the model years and equally strong support for the hypothesis that trucks in the used market are superior. A logit model relating maintenance and lifetime mileage was also estimated, but no significant differences between new and used trucks were found.

Two years later, Pratt and Hoffer (1984) introduced two refinements to Bond's analysis. First, they notice that the survey used by Bond does not contain data on expenditure for maintenance, so that the relative cost of repairs could not be taken into account: only differences in frequencies of maintenance were accounted for. Second, Bond treated the lemon characteristic as permanent, in that he compared trucks acquired new with trucks acquired used. To the contrary, a comparison of trucks purchased used during a specific time period with those *held* during that period (whether acquired as new or used) would capture a basic feature of a lemons market, namely the fact that the owner of a good-quality product is less likely to sell it. The latter group should contain relatively more of the good-quality trucks. With this sort of grouping, it is no longer necessary to correct for lifetime mileage or vehicle age which are known to the buyer and thus do not affect the buyer–seller informational asymmetry.

The appropriate test is then to check whether average maintenance expenditure is larger on vehicles that were recently traded within a period than on trucks that were not traded recently. The null hypothesis that there is no difference, that is, that the market for used trucks is not a lemons market, was rejected: the market for used pick-up trucks now appeared as a lemons market!

Bond's reply was immediate and challenged this conclusion, criticizing Pratt and Hoffer for throwing away information on age and lifetime mileage that is available to the buyer. Bond's argument is this:

If 3-years-old trucks with average usage vary widely in quality and the variations cannot be observed by potential buyers, then those of lower quality will obtain the same price as those of higher quality and adverse selection will result. However, the fact that a 4-years-old truck becomes too costly to operate and is sold by its owner, while a 3-years-old truck owned by the same owner is not, is not necessarily related to the market for lemons because the buyer can observe the difference in age and anticipate costlier repairs. (Bond, 1984, p. 801)

Reestimating this model using the Pratt–Hoffer definitions, but correcting for differences in age and lifetime mileage, Bond (1984) finds no difference in maintenance for trucks less than 10 years old. But he found more frequent repairs among trucks more than 10 years old that have been traded recently. The differences found by Pratt and Hoffer thus arose from the inclusion of very old trucks in their sample and from their failure to control for differences in characteristics that buyers can observe.

Very old trucks are generally not sold by dealers, while most trucks in the 1–10-years-old category are sold by dealers. This tends to confirm Bond's earlier conclusion that the absence of a lemons market can be explained by the existence of counteracting institutions, such as warranties, that reduce or eliminate the asymmetry in information.

A logical next step is to ask whether, in the absence of adverse selection, equilibrium prices of consumer durables such as cars reflect all available information about future service flows and maintenance cost, as suggested by the user cost approach to the pricing of durables (see Stokey, 1981, for example). Emons and von Hagen (1991) test this idea for the German automobile market where public information about the reliability of all cars of the same vintage class and make is available. They find that the hypothesis that consumers rationally use public information cannot be rejected empirically and thus they corroborate related findings by Daly and Mayor (1983), Hartman (1987) and Kahn (1986), who demonstrated that used-car prices in the US reflect market information about increasing energy and fuel cost and product recalls.[4] Another finding is that while economic depreciation of a new car amounts to about one-third over the first two years of its life, the depreciation is negligible between the ages of two and four years. Novelty effects are completely exhausted after two years and the services of cars of these vintages are regarded as perfect substitutes.

The underlying theory can be summarized as follows. Utility is derived from the flow of services of a car rather than the car itself. Therefore demand depends on the user cost (rental price) of these services, which measures physical decay and loss of novelty effects. This cost, γ_t, differs from type to type but is the same for all cars i of a given type. The equilibrium price a consumer is willing to pay is the price p_{it} such that

$$\gamma_t = p_{it} - \delta E p_{it+2} + \delta E c_{it} \tag{13.7}$$

The right-hand side of (13.7) is the cost of holding a car for 2 years, which is the sum of the expected capital loss ($p_{it} - \delta E p_{it+2}$) and the expected cost of maintenance $\delta E c_{it}$, where the discount factor is $\delta = (1 + r)^2$.

Prices of different vintage classes of the same type are related through the depreciation factor ρ_t, such that

$$\gamma_t = \rho_t \gamma_{t-2} \qquad (t = 2, 4, \ldots, T) \tag{13.8}$$

Consumer expectations of the selling price obey

$$E p_{it+2} = p_{t+2} + \varepsilon_{it} \tag{13.9}$$

where p_{t+2} is the observed current average price of all vehicles of the same type which are two years older than the car a consumer considers buying. The term ε_{it} is the expected individual deviation, due to the consumer's particular way of driving and is zero on average. Consumer expectations of the cost of maintenance depend on the available public information about the reputation of the various brands and on regularly published official indices of technical quality. Private information again leads to individual deviations which sum to zero.

Under these assumptions, the structure of the observed quality indices is shown to induce a distribution of equilibrium capital losses and thereby of equilibrium prices. This is tested empirically using a regression of capital losses on the linearized cost expectation function per type.

13.8 AUCTION MARKETS

Economic theory distinguishes two polar cases: 'independent-private-value' auctions on the one hand, and 'common-value' auctions on the other. In the former, also called Vickrey auctions, each buyer is supposed to know with precision how much the object being auctioned is worth to him or her, but is ignorant about the others' private values. The individual private values are independent and thus convey no information about any other buyer's value. In common-value auctions, the item to be auctioned has a single objective value, but no one knows it. Bidders have differing estimates, based in part on private information but also on publicly available information. Recent advances in the integration of formal theory and empirical analysis are most noticeable in the study of common-value auctions. To these we turn first.

The work on US federal auctions of drilling rights on the Outer Continental Shelf is exemplary. In their 1987 paper, Hendricks, Porter and Boudreau collect statistical regularities about these auctions, for which a very rich data set is available.[5] These numbers provide considerable support for the assumptions and predictions of the first-price,[6] sealed-bid, common-value model. Hendricks and Porter (1988) go one step further and build a formal bidding model with asymmetric information,[7] whose empirical predictions are tested.

The emphasis is on 'drainage sales', that is, the simultaneous auction of tracts which are adjacent to tracts on which oil (or gas) deposits have already been discovered, as opposed to 'wildcat sales' of tracts in areas that have not been drilled. In the latter, information is symmetric, since bidders only have seismic information which has essentially the same precision for all firms. In the former, firms which own adjacent tracts can obtain information about the drainage tract that is being auctioned from their own on-site drilling on neighbour tracts. A neighbour firm is therefore better informed than non-neighbour firms.

A naive model might predict that non-neighbour firms will not bid in drainage sales. If this were the case, however, the neighbour firm would correctly anticipate this strategy and bid the reservation price (announced by the government) when worthwhile. But then the non-neighbours could bid slightly more and earn positive profits on average. In equilibrium, therefore, non-neighbour firms must participate in the auction. However, since neighbour firms know their estimates of the true value of the tract, the non-neighbour firms must use mixed strategies (pure strategies would be predictable and imply a certain loss) in order to have positive expected profits on some tracts. On average, though, their expected profits are zero in equilibrium, and this condition determines the equilibrium strategy of the neighbour firms.

The equilibrium properties of the model imply a number of empirical predictions:

1. The event that no non-neighbour firm bids occurs more frequently than the event that no neighbour firm bids. In fact, at least one neighbour firm participated in 83 per cent of the auctions, and at least one non-neighbour firm participated in 68 per cent of the auctions.
2. The neighbour firm wins at least one-half of the tracts. In fact, it won 62 per cent of the tracts it bid for, paying about 56 per cent of the ex post value of the tracts.
3. Expected profits to non-neighbour firms are zero. Average profit for non-neighbour winners was in fact virtually zero. As predicted by the model, it was positive on tracts which received a neighbour bid and significantly negative on tracts which received no neighbour bid.
4. Being better informed, neighbour firms should make earnings above average. That is what happened.
5. If only public information is taken into account, so that tract valuations are symmetric, then the distribution of the bids of the neighbour firm and that of the maximum of the bids by non-neighbours should be approximately the same. Maximum likelihood estimates of the joint distribution of these bids confirm this.
6. The estimates also show that the informed bid (that by the neighbour firm) is essentially independent of the number of uninformed bids, as predicted by the model.
7. The informed bid is an increasing function of the public signal (when a larger signal is good news), that is, of the profitability and the value of the adjacent tract.

Further findings are compatible with the hypothesis that neighbour firms did not compete against each other. Two-thirds of the sample of drainage sales had multiple neighbour firms. Competition among these should have tended to eliminate information rents. Yet these rents were positive and large. There were 74 tracts with multiple neighbour firms, but only 17 tracts had multiple neighbour bids. Furthermore, net profits were not significantly lower on tracts with multiple neighbours than on tracts with one neighbour firm. Finally, the bids of neighbour firms were strictly decreasing with the increasing number of such firms. All this suggests that neighbour firms coordinated their bidding decisions and submitted one serious bid on tracts considered worthwhile.

Before turning to private-value auctions, a word should be said about the 'winner's curse' which is said to occur frequently in common auctions. One way of defining it is to say that the winner is nearly certain to have overestimated the true value and therefore to have bid too high. Some descriptive studies of offshore leases[8] suggest that, in this sense, the winner's curse does exist. This in turn suggests that winners were not able to correct their profit maximizing bids to allow for it, that is, they did not optimize correctly. Consequently, to evaluate the existence of the curse and to evaluate the size of the overbidding empirically, an equilibrium bid function that can be estimated econometrically is needed.

Thiel (1988) works out such a function on the assumption that the winner overbids because he overestimates the true value (not because he overestimates the opponents' bids). Any bidder avoids the curse in equilibrium using a valuation function whose expectation, conditional on winning, is an unbiased estimate of the value. Thiel uses the theory of order statistics to derive a functional form that is linear in the parameters and estimates this by linear least squares on data for highway-construction auctions. Unfortunately, Levin and Smith (1991) show that this potentially most useful approach applies only in special cases that are of limited practical interest and arise only under circumstances that are unlikely in the real world.

In the area of private-value auctions, solid links between theory and estimation have also been slow to emerge. Until the end of the 1980s, empirical work mainly aimed at testing basic, rather common-sense, propositions, as is emphasized by MacAfee and MacMillan (1987). This may result from the fact that each prediction of auction theory is based on a set of restrictive assumptions, which are not likely to be satisfied simultaneously in reality. For example, Vickrey's result that the expected revenue is the same for English, second-price sealed-bid, Dutch and first-price sealed-bid auctions[9] disappears if there is risk-aversion, or if the private values are correlated. Revenue equivalence has been tested using US Forest Service sales of contracts for harvesting timber, since during one year both sealed-bid and open auctions were used. Mead *et al.* (1984) find that sealed-bid auctions yield significantly greater revenue. Correcting for selection bias and making a distinction between the actual number of active buyers (which is known) and the number of bidders as defined by theory, Hansen

(1985, 1986) finds that revenue equivalence cannot be rejected. What, however, if the valuations were in fact correlated, as is likely to be the case? Then theory predicts that the open auctions should have yielded the highest revenue!

Another favourite proposition is that the winning bid increases with the number of bidders. This is indeed the case in auctions for tax-exempt bonds, timber and off-shore drilling rights, according to Brannman *et al.* (1987). Note, however, that individual bids might decline as the number of bidders rises, if it were true that firms try to avoid the winner's curse: the more bidders, the more each bidder may want to correct his bid downwards (see Gilley and Karels, 1981; and Hendricks, Porter and Gertler, 1986).

Several interesting issues arise that are outside standard auction theory. One such issue is information acquisition in auctions that are repeated. Consider the common case of a government procurement agency that buys equipment or awards projects through first-price sealed-bid auctions at regular time intervals. Typically, it is badly informed about the evolution of production costs and about the number of active bidders in any period. On the other hand, it has an incentive to buy more or less today, depending on whether the current price is lower or higher than tomorrow's expected price. To hold auctions frequently is a way of acquiring relevant information. Feinstein, Block and Nold (1985) show that bidders, once they become aware of this, have an incentive to collude in order to misinform the agency, thus skewing its intertemporal allocation to their advantage. To show this, they first describe how the agency uses past data to improve its forecasts. They then show the means by which a cartel can manipulate these forecasts to its advantage, and they also derive the optimal short-run and long-run cartel policy such that the cartel's presence will remain undetected. It is possible for a cartel to follow a policy that takes the profit of intertemporal demand allocation away from the agency and yet confirms the agency's belief that it faces a competitive market! Three strategic variables are identified about which the cartel misinforms the government: (i) the mean of the sealed bids submitted by cartel members; (ii) the variance of the sealed bids submitted by cartel members; and (iii) the number of long-run market suppliers. A case study of highway-construction contracts shows that cartels increase this mean, reduce this variance and reduce the number of actual bidders. The details of a practical procedure used to this effect by a cartel of Belgian firms that supply the government through first-price sealed-bid auctions can'be found in Phlips (1988, pp. 120–1).

Corresponding mechanisms used in English and second-price sealed-bid auctions by cartels (called 'rings') are analyzed by Graham and Marshall (1987). Interviews with bidders who regularly participate in rings and with auctioneers who regularly fight rings provided the following description of collusive behaviour:

> First, a member of a ring never enters a truly competitive bid against another ring member. Second, rings employ procedures that ensure that the ring will win an item more highly valued by a ring member than by any non-ring bidder. Third, an item won by a ring becomes the property of the ring itself; the ultimate ownership of the item is determined in a secondary auction commonly known as a 'knock-out', which is separate from the main auction and involves only ring members. Fourth, the gains obtained by the coalition are shared by all ring members rather than accruing to only the winning bidder or some subset of ring members. Fifth, auctioneers respond to the presence of coalitions by establishing higher reserve prices. (pp. 1218–19)

The collusive strategies of the coalition are shown to represent a non-cooperative equilibrium.[10]

To fight rings, auctioneers have other means. In his study of wine auctions, Ashenfelter (1989) notes two practices that are unexplained by auction theory. One is that auctioneers are very secretive about whether and at what level they may have set a reserve price; another is that the identity of the purchaser is not revealed. The secrecy about reserve prices may serve to thwart rings: some sellers may prefer to have their goods sold later rather than risk a ring bidding to depress the price. By not revealing the identity of the purchaser, the auctioneer creates incentives for the ring members to deviate from the collusive agreement.

Finally, a breakthrough on the econometric front has to be mentioned. Laffont, Ossard and Vuong (1991) developed a general simulation-based econometric methodology for the empirical study of theoretical auction models, both private-value and common-value. They apply it to daily sales at the Dutch auction of eggplants in Marmande, France and are able to provide estimates of the parameters that characterize the distribution of the unobserved private values. In particular, an estimate is given for the (unknown) number of bidders (i.e. the size of the market) as opposed to the (observed) number of active participants.

13.9 CONCLUSION

In concluding it is worth reiterating what we said at the outset. Progress in applying recent developments in theory to empirical studies of product markets has been far outstripped by those developments themselves. While there are many obvious reasons for this – model limitations, unrealistic assumptions about consumer characteristics or market structure, inappropriateness of definitions, and in particular, difficulties in obtaining data – none of these can justify the failure to pursue the two missions of empirical work, to confront the theory with the facts, and simply to establish salient facts about the way in which economies actually work. As should be apparent from this survey, however, there are encouraging signs of efforts to bridge the, until recently, widening gap between theory and empirical work in the area that we have considered.

Notes

1. Cabral (1991) shows that in linear oligopolies and for an open set of values of the discount factor, there exists an exact correspondence between the conjectural variations solution and the solution of a quantity-setting repeated game with minimax punishments during T periods.
2. Compare the discussion in Section 13.4.
3. In her model, unlike that of Porter (1983a), and Green and Porter (1984), all relevant variables are observable and price wars are not triggered by cheating, which cannot be directly detected.
4. Other applications of the user cost approach include Berkovec (1985), Bresnahan and Yao (1985), and Wykoff (1973).
5. For each tract, this set includes: date of the lease sale; location, water depth and acreage; which firms bid and the value of their bids; number and data of any wells that were drilled; and the annual production if any oil or gas was extracted. The drilling and production data can be used to calculate ex post value for each tract. Tracts are typically in a square grid pattern but vary in size.
6. In a 'first-price' auction, the highest bid is the price paid by the winner.
7. Based on Engelbrecht-Wiggans, Milgrom and Weber (1983).
8. See Capen, Clapp and Campbell (1971), Hendricks, Porter and Boudreau (1987), and Thaler (1988). Other studies suggest that oil firms avoid falling victims to the curse: see Mead *et al.* (1984), and Hendricks, Porter and Gertler (1986). See also Ashenfelter and Genesove (1992) on real-estate auctions.
9. In an English auction the bids are publicly made and are ascending. In a second-price auction, imagined by Vickrey (1961), the player with the highest bid is the winner but pays the second-highest bid. In a Dutch

auction descending prices are announced and the winner is the first who accepts the current price.
10. See also the recent paper by Porter and Zona (1993) on detection of bid rigging in procurement auctions. The data indicate that the bids of non-cartel firms were related to cost measures while the higher cartel bids were not.

References

Abreu, D. (1986) 'External Equilibria of Oligopolistic Supergames', *Journal of Economic Theory*, vol. 39, pp. 191–225.
Abreu, D. (1988) 'On the Theory of Infinitely Repeated Games with Discounting', *Econometrica*, vol. 56, pp. 383–96.
Akerlof, G. (1970) 'The Market for "Lemons": Quality Uncertainty and the Market Mechanism', *Quarterly Journal of Economics*, vol. 84, pp. 488–500.
Albach, H. and N. Kloten (1973) *Preispolitik auf dem Farbstoffmarkt in der EWG* (Tübingen: J.C.B. Mohr (Paul Siebeck)).
Anderson, G. (1983) 'Quick-Response Equilibrium', mimeo, Department of Economics, University of California, Berkeley.
Appelbaum, E. (1979) 'Testing Price Taking Behavior', *Journal of Econometrics*, vol. 9, pp. 283–94.
Appelbaum, E. (1982) 'The Estimation of the Degree of Oligopoly Power', *Journal of Econometrics*, vol. 19, pp. 287–9.
Ashenfelter, O. (1989) 'How Auctions Work for Wine and Art', *Journal of Economic Perspectives*, vol. 3, pp. 23–36.
Ashenfelter, O. and D. Genesove (1992) 'Testing for Price Anomalies in Real-Estate Auctions', *American Economic Review, Papers and Proceedings*, pp. 501–5.
Bailey, E.E. (1972) 'Peak-Load Pricing Under Regulatory Constraint', *Journal of Political Economy*, vol. 80, no. 4, pp. 662–79.
Berkovec, J. (1985) 'New Car Sales and Used Car Stocks: A Model of the Automobile Market', *Rand Journal of Economics*, vol. 16, pp. 195–214.
Billera, L.J., J. Heath and D.C. Raanan (1978) 'Internal Telephone Billing Rates: A Novel Application of Non-Atomic Game Theory', *Operations Research*, no. 27, pp. 956–65.
Boiteux, M. (1949) 'La tarification des demandes en pointe: Application de la théorie de la vente au coût marginal', *Revue générale de l'électricité*, vol. 58, pp. 321–40. Translated as 'Peak Load Pricing', *Journal of Business*, vol. 33, no. 2 (April 1960), pp. 157–98.
Bond, E.W. (1982) 'A Direct Test of the "Lemons" Model: The Market for Used Pickup Trucks', *American Economic Review*, vol. 72, pp. 836–40.
Bond, E.W. (1984) 'Test of the "Lemons" Model: Reply', *American Economic Review*, vol. 74, pp. 801–4.
Borenstein, S. (1985) 'Price Discrimination in Free-Entry Markets', *Rand Journal of Economics*, vol. 16, no. 3, pp. 380–97.
Bork, R.H. (1978) *The Antitrust Paradox* (New York: Basic Books), p. 397.

Brannman, L., J.D. Klein and L.W. Weiss (1987) 'The Price Effects of Increased Competition in Auction Markets', *Review of Economics and Statistics*, vol. 69, pp. 24–32. Reprinted in L.W. Weiss (ed.), *Concentration and Price* (Cambridge, Mass.: MIT Press, 1989, pp. 67–84).

Braschler, C. (1983) 'The Changing Demand Structure for Pork and Beef in the 1970s: Implications for the 1980s', *Southern Journal of Agricultural Economics*, no. 15, pp. 105–110.

Bresnahan, T.F. (1980) 'Three Essays on the American Automobile Oligopoly', unpublished Ph.D. dissertation, Princeton University.

Bresnahan, T.F. (1981) 'Departures from Marginal-Cost Pricing in the American Automobile Industry: Estimates for 1977–78', *Journal of Econometrics*, vol. 17, pp. 201–27.

Bresnahan, T.F. (1987) 'Competition and Collusion in the American Automobile Industry: The 1955 Price War', *Journal of Industrial Economics*, vol. 35, pp. 457–82.

Bresnahan, T.F. (1989) 'Empirical Studies of Industries with Market Power', in R. Schmalensee and R. Willig (eds), *Handbook of Industrial Organization*, Vol. II (Amsterdam: North-Holland), ch. 17.

Bresnahan, T.F. and R. Schmalensee (1987) 'The Empirical Renaissance in Industrial Economics: An Overview', *Journal of Industrial Economics*, vol. 35, pp. 371–7.

Bresnahan, T.F. and D.A. Yao (1985) 'The Nonpecuniary Costs of Automobile Emissions Standards', *Rand Journal of Economics*, vol. 16, pp. 437–55.

Cabral, L.M.B. (1991) 'Conjectural Variations as a Reduced Form', mimeo, Faculty of Economics, New University of Lisbon, October.

Capen, E.C., R.V. Clapp and W.N. Campbell (1971) 'Competitive Bidding in High-Risk Situations', *Journal of Petroleum Technology*, vol. 23, pp. 641–53.

Cecchetti, S.G. (1986) 'The Frequency of Price Adjustment. A Study of the News-Stand Prices of Magazines', *Journal of Econometrics*, vol. 31, pp. 255–74.

Cubbin, J. (1975) 'Quality Change and Pricing Behaviour in the United Kingdom Car Industry', *Economica*, vol. 42, pp. 45–58.

Daly, G.D. and T.H. Mayor (1983) 'Reason and Rationality During Energy Crises', *Journal of Political Economy*, vol. 91, pp. 168–81.

Davidson, R., M. Dewatripont, V. Ginsburgh and M. Labbe (1989) 'On the Welfare Effects of Anti-Discrimination Regulations in the EC Car Market', *International Journal of Industrial Organization*, vol. 7, pp. 205–30.

Deaton, A.S. and J. Muellbauer (1980) *Economics and Consumer Behaviour* (Cambridge: Cambridge University Press).

Debreu, G. (1974) 'Excess Demand Functions', *Journal of Mathematical Economics*, vol. 1, pp. 15–23.

Deneckere, R., D. Kovenock and R. Lee (1992) 'A Model of Price Leadership Based on Consumer Loyalty', *Journal of Industrial Economics*, vol. 40, no. 2, pp. 147–56.

Eales, J.S. and L.J. Unnevehr (1988) 'Demand for Beef and Chicken Products: Separability and Structural Change', *American Journal of Agricultural Economics*, August, pp. 521–32.

Eckel, C.C. (1987) 'Customer-Class Price Discrimination by Electric Utilities', *Journal of Economics and Business*, February, pp. 19–33.

Elzinga, K.G. and T.F. Hogarty (1973) 'The Problem of Geographic Market Delineation in Antimerger Suits', *Antitrust Bulletin*, no. 18, pp. 45–81.

Elzinga, K.G. and R.A. Rogowski (eds) (1984) 'Relevant Markets in Antitrust', *Journal of Reprints for Antitrust Law and Economics*, vol. 14, no. 2.

Emons, W. and J. von Hagen (1991) 'Asset Prices and Public Information. An Empirical Investigation in the Market for Automobiles', *European Economic Review*, vol. 35, pp. 1529–42.

Engelbrecht-Wiggans, R., P.R. Milgrom and R.J. Weber (1983) 'Competitive Bidding and Proprietary Information', *Journal of Mathematical Economics*, vol. 11, pp. 161–9.

Feinstein, J.S., M.K. Block and E.C. Nold (1985) 'Asymmetric Information and Collusive Behavior in Auction Markets', *American Economic Review*, vol. 75, pp. 441–60.

Fudenberg, D. and E. Maskin (1986) 'The Folk Theorem in Repeated Games with Discounting or with Incomplete Information', *Econometrica*, vol. 54, pp. 533–54.

Gabszewicz, J.J. and J-F. Thisse (1980) 'Entry (and Exit) in a Differentiated Industry', *Journal of Economic Theory*, vol. 22, pp. 327–38.

Gasmi, F., J.J. Laffont and Q. Vuong (1992) 'Econometric Analysis of Collusive Behavior in a Soft Drink Market', Document de Travail 16, Institut d'Economie Industrielle, Toulouse.

Geroski, P.A., L. Phlips and A. Ulph (1985) 'Oligopoly, Competition and Welfare: Some Recent Developments', in P.A. Geroski, L. Phlips and A. Ulph, (eds), *Oligopoly, Competition and Welfare* (Oxford: Blackwell), pp. 1–18.

Gilbert, C.L. (1991) 'Do Economists Test Theories? – Demand Analysis and Consumption Analysis as Tests of Theories of Economic Methodology', in N. de Marchi and M. Blaug (eds), *Appraising Economic Theories* (Edward Elgar), ch. 4.

Gilley, G.W. and G.V. Karels (1981) 'The Competitive Effect in Bonus Bidding: New Evidence', *Bell Journal of Economics*, vol. 12, pp. 637–49.

Gisser, M. (1986) 'Price Leadership and Welfare Losses in U.S. Manufacturing', *American Economic Review*, vol. 76, pp. 756–67.

Gollop, F.M. and M.J. Roberts (1979) 'Firm Interdependence in Oligopolistic Markets', *Journal of Econometrics*, vol. 10, pp. 313–31.

Gould, B.W., T.L. Cox and F. Perali (1991) 'Demand for Food Fats and Oils: The Role of Demographic Variables and Government Donations', *American Journal of Agricultural Economics*, February, pp. 212–21.

Graham, D.A. and R.C. Marshall (1987) 'Collusive Bidder Behavior at Single-Object Second-Price and English Auctions', *Journal of Political Economy*, vol. 95, pp. 1217–39.

Grandmont, J.M. (1983) *Money and Value* (Cambridge: Cambridge University Press).

Green, E.J. and R.H. Porter (1984) 'Noncooperative Collusion under Imperfect Price Information', *Econometrica*, vol. 52, pp. 87–100.

Haldacher, R.C., J.A. Craven, K.S. Huang, D.M. Smallwood and J.R. Blaylock (1982) *Consumer Demand for Red Meats, Poultry and Fish* (Washington,

D.C.: US Department of Agriculture, Econ. Res. Serv., NED), September.

Hansen, R.G. (1985) 'Empirical Testing of Auction Theory', *American Economic Review*, AEA Papers and Proceedings, vol., 75, pp. 156–9.

Hansen, R.G. (1986) 'Sealed-Bid Versus Open Auctions: The Evidence', *Economic Inquiry*, vol. 24, pp. 125–42.

Hartman, R.S. (1987) 'Product Quality and Market Efficiency: The Effect of Product Recalls on Resale Prices and Firm Valuation', *Review of Economics and Statistics*, vol. 69, pp. 367–72.

Hendricks, K. and R.H. Porter (1988) 'An Empirical Study of an Auction with Asymmetric Information', *American Economic Review*, vol. 78, pp. 865–83.

Hendricks, K., R.H. Porter and B. Boudreau (1987) 'Information, Returns, and Bidding Behaviour in OCS Auctions: 1954–1969', *Journal of Industrial Economics*, vol. 35, pp. 517–42.

Hendricks, K., R.H. Porter and P.J. Gertler (1986) 'Bidding Behavior and Joint Venture Formation in OCS Auctions', mimeo, SUNY Stony Brook.

Hens, T., A. Kirman and L. Phlips (1991) 'Exchange Rates and Oligopoly', EUI Working Paper ECO No. 91/42, Florence, Italy.

Holmes, T.J. (1989) 'The Effects of Third-Degree Price Discrimination in Oligopoly', *American Economic Review*, vol. 79, pp. 244–50.

Horowitz, I. (1981) 'Market Definition in Antitrust Analysis: A Regression-Based Approach', *Southern Economic Journal*, vol. 48, pp. 1–16.

Howell, J. (1982) 'An Examination of the Dynamic Behavior of Cross-Regional Price Differences in Regular and Unleaded Gasoline', mimeo, US Federal Trade Commission.

Hudson, M.A. and J.P. Vertin (1985) 'Income Elasticities for Beef, Pork and Poultry: Changes and Implications', *Journal of Food Distribution Research*, no. 1, pp. 25–85.

Iwata, G. (1974) 'Measurement of Conjectural Variations in Oligopoly', *Econometrica*, vol. 42, pp. 947–66.

Joyce, P. (1990) 'Price Discrimination in "Top" Scientific Journals', *Applied Economics*, no. 22, pp. 1127–35.

Kahn, J.A. (1986) 'Gasoline Prices and the Used Automobile Market: A Rational Expectations Asset Price Approach', *Quarterly Journal of Economics*, vol. 101, pp. 323–39.

Katz, M.L. (1984) 'Price Discrimination and Monopolistic Competition', *Econometrica*, vol. 52, no. 6, pp. 1453–71.

Keuzenkamp, H.A. and A.P. Barten (1991) 'Rejection Without Falsification. On the History of Testing the Homogeneity Condition in the Theory of Consumer Demand', mimeo, Department of Economics, Tilburg University and Catholic University Leuven.

Kirman, A. and N. Schueller (1990) 'Price Leaderhip and Discrimination in the European Car Market', *Journal of Industrial Economics*, vol. 39, pp. 69–91.

Knetter, M.M. (1989) 'Price Discrimination by U.S. and German Exporters', *American Economic Review*, vol. 79, no. 1, pp. 198–210.

Laffont, J.-J., H. Ossard and Q. Vuong (1991) 'Econometrics of First-Price Auctions', Institut d'Economie Industrielle, Document de travail 07, Université des Sciences Sociales, Toulouse.

Larsen, H.K. and C.-A. Nilsson (1984) 'Consumption and Production of Bicycles in Denmark 1890–1980', *Scandinavian Economic History Review*, vol. 32, no. 3, pp. 143–58.

Levin, D. and J.L. Smith (1991) 'Some Evidence on the Winner's Curse: Comment', *American Economic Review*, vol. 81, pp. 370–5.

Liang, J.N. (1989) 'Price Reaction Functions and Conjectural Variations: An Application to the Breakfast Cereal Industry', *Review of Industrial Organization*, vol. 4, pp. 31–58.

Littlechild, S.C. and G.F. Thompson (1977) 'Airport Landing Fee: A Game Theoretic Approach', *Bell Journal of Economics*, vol. 8, pp. 164–204.

Lott, J.R. and R.D. Roberts (1991) 'A Guide to the Pitfalls of Identifying Price Discrimination', *Economic Inquiry*, vol. 24 (January), pp. 14–23.

Luttrell, C.B. (1969) 'Meat Prices', *Federal Reserve Bank of St. Louis Review*, August, pp. 24–8.

MacLeod, W.B. (1985) 'A Theory of Conscious Parallelism', *European Economic Review*, vol. 27, pp. 25–44.

Mantel, R. (1976), 'Homothetic Preferences and Community Excess Demand Functions', *Journal of Economic Theory*, vol. 12, pp. 197–201.

Marschak, J. (1943) 'Money Illusion and Demand Analysis', *The Review of Economic Statistics*, pp. 40–8.

Martin, S. (1988) 'The Measurement of Profitability and the Diagnosis of Market Power', *International Journal of Industrial Organization*, vol. 6, pp. 301–21.

Martin, S. (1993) *Advanced Industrial Economics* (Oxford: Blackwell), forthcoming.

McAfee, R.P. and J. MacMillan (1987) 'Auctions and Bidding', *Journal of Economic Literature*, vol. 25, pp. 726–31.

Mead, W.J., A. Moseidjord and P.E. Sorensen (1984) 'Competitive Bidding under Asymmetric Information: Behavior and Performance in Gulf of Mexico Drainage Lease Sales 1959–1969', *Review of Economics and Statistics*, vol. 47, pp. 505–8.

Merrilees, W.J. (1983) 'Anatomy of a Price Leadership Challenge: An Evaluation of Pricing Strategies in the Australian Newspaper Industry', *Journal of Industrial Economics*, vol. 31, pp. 291–311.

Mertens, Y. and V. Ginsburgh (1985) 'Product Differentiation and Price Discrimination in the European Community: The Case of Automobiles', *Journal of Industrial Economics*, vol. 34, pp. 151–66.

Morgan, M.S. (1990) *The History of Econometric Ideas* (Cambridge: Cambridge University Press).

Murfin, A. (1983) 'Tax Rates and Price Levels in the European Motor Industry', *Fiscal Studies*, vol. 4, no. 1, pp. 44–7.

Murfin, A. (1987) 'Price Discrimination and Tax Differences in the European Motor Industry', in S. Crossen (ed.), *Tax Coordination in the European Community* (London: Kluwer Law and Taxation), pp. 171–94.

Neufeld, J.L. (1987) 'Price Discrimination and the Adoption of the Electricity Demand Charge', *Journal of Economic History*, September, pp. 693–708.

Nguyen, D.T. and M. Rose (1987) 'Demand for Tea in the UK 1974–1983: An Econometric Study', *Journal of Development Studies*, vol. 24, no. 1, pp. 43–59.

Nicholls, W.H. (1951) *Price Policies in the Cigarette Industry* (Nashville: Vanderbilt University Press).

Phlips, L. (1983) *The Economics of Price Discrimination* (Cambridge: Cambridge University Press).

Phlips, L. (1988) *The Economics of Imperfect Information* (Cambridge: Cambridge University Press).

Pigou, A.C. (1932) *The Economics of Welfare*, 4th edn (London: MacMillan).

Planting, R. (1982) 'Prices and Seasonality – The Case of Motor Gasoline', *Business Economics*, vol. 17, no. 1, pp. 56–8.

Porter, R.H. (1983) 'A Study of Cartel Stability: The Joint Executive Committee, 1880–1886', *Bell Journal of Economics*, vol. 14, pp. 301–14.

Porter, R.H. and J.D. Zona (1993) 'Detection of Bid Rigging in Procurement Auctions', *Journal of Political Economy*, vol. 101, pp. 518–38.

Posner, R.A. (1974) 'Exclusionary Practices and the Antitrust Law', *University of Chicago Law Review*, p. 510.

Posner, R.A. (1976) *Antitrust Law* (Chicago: The University of Chicago Press), pp. 125 ff.

Pratt, M.D. and G.E. Hoffer (1984) 'Tests of the Lemons Model: Comment', *American Economic Review*, vol. 74, pp. 798–800.

Rees, R. (1991) 'Collusive Equilibrium in the Great Salt Duopoly', *Economic Journal*, vol. 103, pp. 833–48.

Roberts, M.J. (1984) 'Testing Oligopolistic Behaviour: An Application of the Variable Profit Function', *International Journal of Industrial Organization*, vol. 2, pp. 367–83.

Salop, S.C. (1986) 'Practices that (Credibly) Facilitate Oligopoly Co-Ordination', in J.E. Stiglitz and G.F. Mathewson (eds), *New Developments in the Analysis of Market Structure* (Cambridge, Mass.: MIT Press), ch. 9, pp. 265–90.

Samuelson, P.A. (1947) *Foundations of Economic Analysis* (Cambridge, Mass.: Harvard University Press).

Schmalensee, R. (1972) *The Economics of Advertising* (Amsterdam: North-Holland).

Schmalensee, R. (1988) 'Inter-Industry Studies of Structure and Performance', in R. Schmalensee and R.D. Willig (eds), *Handbook of Industrial Organization* (Amsterdam: North-Holland).

Schmalensee, R. (1989) 'Industrial Economics: An Overview', *Economic Journal*, vol. 98, pp. 643–81.

Schneider, E. (1952) *Pricing and Equilibrium* (London: William Hodge & Co.).

Schultz, H. (1938) *The Theory and Measurement of Demand* (Chicago: Chicago University Press).

Schut, F.T. and P.A.G. Van Bergeijk (1986) 'International Price Discrimination: The Pharmaceutical Industry', *World Development*, vol. 14, no. 9, pp. 1141–50.

Shaked, A. and J. Sutton (1982) 'Relaxing Price Competition Through Product Differentiation', *Review of Economic Studies*, vol. 49, pp. 3–13.

Shepard, A. (1991) 'Price Discrimination and Retail Configuration', *Journal of Political Economy*, vol. 99, no. 1, pp. 30–53.

Slade, M.E. (1986a) 'Conjectures, Firm Characteristics and Market Structures: An Empirical Assessment', *International Journal of Industrial Organization*, vol. 4, pp. 347–70.

Slade, M.E. (1986b) 'Exogeneity Tests of Market Boundaries Applied to

Petroleum Products', *Journal of Industrial Economics*, vol. 34, pp. 291–303.

Slade, M.E. (1987) 'Interfirm Rivalry in a Repeated Game: An Empirical Test of Tacit Collusion', *Journal of Industrial Economics*, vol. 35, pp. 499–516.

Slade, M.E. (1991) 'Equilibrium Solution Concepts in Dynamic Games: An Empirical Analysis of Price and Advertising Competition', Discussion Paper no. 91–02, University of British Columbia, Department of Economics.

Slade, M.E. (1992) 'Vancouver's Gasoline Price Wars: An Empirical Exercise in Uncovering Supergame Strategies', *Review of Economic Studies*, vol. 59, pp. 257–76.

Sonnenschein, H. (1972) 'Market Excess Demand Functions', *Econometrica*, vol. 40, pp. 549–63.

Spiller, P.T. and E. Favaro (1984) 'The Effects of Entry Regulation on Oligopolistic Interaction: The Uruguayan Banking Sector', *Rand Journal of Economics*, vol. 15, pp. 244–54.

Spiller, P.T. and C.J. Huang (1986) 'On the Extent of the Market: Wholesale Gasoline in the Northeastern United States', *Journal of Industrial Economics*, vol. 35, pp. 131–45.

Stigler, G.J. and R.A. Sherwin (1985) 'The Extent of the Market', *Journal of Law and Economics*, no. 28, pp. 555–85.

Stokey, N.L. (1981) 'Rational Expectations and Durable Goods Pricing', *Bell Journal of Economics*, vol. 12, pp. 112–28.

Suslow, V.Y. (1986) 'Estimating Monopoly Behavior With Competitive Recycling: An Application to Alcoa', *Rand Journal of Economics*, vol. 17, pp. 389–403.

Sutton, J. (1991) *Sunk Costs and Market Structure* (Cambridge, Mass.: MIT Press).

Tennant, R.B. (1950) *The American Cigarette Industry* (New Haven, Conn.: Yale University Press).

Thaler, R. (1988) 'The Winner's Curse', *Journal of Economic Perspectives*, vol. 2, pp. 191–202.

Thiel, S.E. (1988) 'Some Evidence on the Winner's Curse', *American Economic Review*, vol. 78, pp. 884–95.

Thisse, J.-F. and X. Vives (1988) 'On the Strategic Choice of Spatial Price Policy', *American Economic Review*, vol. 78, pp. 122–37.

Tirole, J. (1988) *The Theory of Industrial Organization* (Cambridge, Mass.: MIT Press).

Tremblay, V.J. (1985) 'Strategic Groups and the Demand for Beer', *Journal of Industrial Economics*, vol. 34, pp. 183–98.

Vickrey, W. (1961) 'Counterspeculation, Auctions, and Competitive Sealed Tenders', *Journal of Finance*, vol. 16, pp. 8–37.

Wenders, J.T. (1976) 'Peak Load Pricing in the Electricity Industry', *Bell Journal of Economics*, vol. 7, no. 1, pp. 232–41.

Wolinsky, A. (1987) 'Brand Names and Price Discrimination', *Journal of Industrial Economics*, vol. 35, pp. 255–68.

Working, E.J. (1927) 'What Do Statistical "Demand Curves" Show?', *Quarterly Journal of Economics*, vol. 61, pp. 215–35.

Wykoff, F.C. (1973) 'A User Cost Approach to New Automobile Purchases', *Review of Economic Studies*, vol. 40, pp. 377–90.

Zanon, L. (1981) 'Price Discrimination and *Hoffmann-La Roche*', *Journal of World Trade Law*, July-August, pp. 305–22.

14 The Labour Supply of Lone Mothers in Denmark and the United Kingdom[1]

Nina Smith,

CENTRE FOR LABOUR MARKET AND SOCIAL RESEARCH, AARHUS

Ian Walker,

KEELE UNIVERSITY

and

Niels Westergård-Nielsen

CENTRE FOR LABOUR MARKET AND SOCIAL RESEARCH, AARHUS

14.1 INTRODUCTION

In most countries income support is targeted on low-income households by 'means testing' welfare payments. The result is that many low-income households face a situation where an increase in gross income generates little, if any, increase in net income. Their incomes are 'taxed' at the margin at a very high rate while their average tax rate is low, or even negative. Since households headed by lone parents constitute a large proportion of low-income households, this group is particularly interesting for investigating the potential adverse work incentives that the welfare system can produce. In the USA, lone parenthood is thought to be the major determinant of poverty (see Knieser, McElroy and Wilcox, 1988) while in the UK lone parents have, over recent years, become an increasingly important client group for income-support schemes (see Ermisch and Wright, 1989a).

Thus, lone parents are a major client group for social welfare systems throughout Europe and one which is growing, since the number of lone parents has risen rapidly in recent years.[2] Since we know from the labour supply literature that the sensitivity of women to fiscal incentives is somewhat higher than that of men, the existence of a sizeable group of women facing high marginal rates of 'tax' constitutes an important potential source of inefficiency.

In the UK, the lone-parent population represented 10 per cent of all families with children in 1975 and 16 per cent in 1990. There are now more than one million lone parents of which close to 10 per cent are fathers and 7 per cent are widows.[3] In Denmark, it is estimated that in 1974 there were approximately 70 000 lone parents and in 1986 the number was 97 000, amounting to 14 per cent of all households with children of which 84 per cent were headed by females, and 7 per cent by widows (estimates by Thaulow and Gamst, 1987, based on survey data).

In Denmark, 40 per cent of the lone-parent households received social welfare (*bistandshjoelp*) in 1986, and about one-third of the disposable income of lone parents came from social transfers, including unemployment benefits. For households with two parents the same figures were 4 per cent for households with two members in the labour force and 8 per cent for households with one member in the labour force. In the UK the picture is, if anything, even more dramatic. In 1986, 55 per cent of lone parents were in receipt of the main welfare benefit for those with low incomes (Income Support, formerly known as Supplementary Benefit) compared with 7 per cent of two-parent families; and 39 per cent of normal net income for lone-parent households came from social security benefits compared with 7 per cent for married couples with children.

Earlier Danish studies of the economic status of lone parents have demonstrated that the marginal increase in disposable income for lone parents who supply additional labour is equal to, or close to, zero over large ranges of their budget constraints.[4] High marginal tax rates were noted in a survey of five countries, including the UK, in Brown (1989). In the USA, Moffit (1992) notes that the operation of the AFDC system (aid for parents with dependent children) imposes penal rates on lone parents. The question therefore arises whether lone parents would become less dependent on the welfare system if the tax rates they face, including reductions in public transfers, could be reduced.

In Denmark, the main forms of welfare payments for low-income families are housing subsidies for those in rented accommodation, child benefits, child-care subsidies, primarily for those with pre-school children, and social welfare which provides a minimum income for those whose incomes are sufficiently low. In the UK, the main benefits are Income Support, which provides a minimum income (plus housing costs) for those on low incomes, Family Credit (a wage subsidy for those who work and have low incomes), and Housing Benefit (a rent subsidy for those not on Income Support but who nevertheless have high housing costs relative to their incomes). Note that there is no nation-wide subsidy scheme for child-care in the UK, although there are some subsidized nurseries operated by local authorities, who may give preference to lone mothers over married mothers in allocating their scarce places.[5]

These various forms of income support are clearly more important for lone mothers than they are for married couples, since eligibility is largely determined by household income. Because the great majority of married mothers have working husbands and may often work themselves, forms of income support are less likely to be relevant for couples (at least at the margin). Thus, this chapter concentrates on the sensitivity of the labour supply behaviour of lone parents to the nature of the tax and income-support systems in the UK and Denmark.

The empirical approach in this chapter is to attempt to capture the broad features of labour supply by assuming that choices are limited to discrete alternatives of not working, working part-time, or working full-time. This considerably simplifies the complications associated with non-linearities induced by the tax and welfare systems. In Section 14.2, we describe the main features of the relevant components of the Danish and UK welfare and the tax systems, and in Section 14.3 an empirical model is presented. Section 14.4 describes the two data sources used in the study which, for Denmark, is a cross-section of lone parents drawn from Danish register data, and for the UK is pooled cross-sections for a number of years drawn from the UK Family Expenditure Survey. A preliminary description of the labour market behaviour of lone parents is also given in Section 14.4. The observed hours and earnings distributions for lone parents are contrasted with those for married women with dependent children. In Section 14.5 we apply to our data the framework in Section 14.3 which models the discrete choices between working and not working, and between working part-time and full-time. Section 14.6 uses the Danish and UK estimates to simulate the impact of replacing all means-tested benefits for lone parents by a lump-sum transfer. The predicted behavioural effects are so pronounced that the implication for the net income distribution is perverse: net income inequality as measured by the Gini co-efficient actually falls in response to such a change. This, of course, shows just how poor a measure of welfare net income could be in the face of either time-series or cross-section differences in incentive structures.

14.2 LONE MOTHERS AND THE TAX AND TRANSFER SYSTEMS IN DENMARK AND THE UK

The tax system in Denmark is well known for its steep progression, suggesting that high marginal rates are most relevant to the higher end of the earnings distribution. However, for households with low incomes there may be the possibility of entitlement to either a housing subsidy or a subsidy for child-care costs or both. The day-care subsidy is available for those aged below 75 with children, while the housing subsidy is available for those living in rented accommodation. Furthermore, low-income families were entitled to a means-tested child subsidy in 1985, which is the year studied in the empirical analysis below. Individuals with no other income, who are not eligible for unemployment payments or public pensions, may receive social welfare. The level of the subsidies depends on household incomes as well as on the costs of housing and the availability and costs of child-care.

The housing subsidy is given as a subsidy to rents up to a certain maximum which depends on the number of children. An 'ideal' rent is defined as 15 per cent of the taxable income up to a certain income and 25 per cent thereafter. The subsidy is calculated as 75 per cent of the difference between this ideal rent and the actual, and is illustrated in Figure 14.1.

Lone parents were in 1985 entitled to an annual child subsidy of DKK 6000 for one child and DKK 9800 for two children; and this is three times higher for single parents than for couples. The subsidy is decreased by 6 per cent for income above DKK 187 000, and the effects are illustrated in Figure 14.2.

A third subsidy is the subsidy for institutionalized child care illustrated in Figure 14.3. Though all Danish day-care institutions are heavily subsidized by the local authorities, low-income families are entitled to a subsidy to child-care payments. Child-care was free in 1985 if annual taxable income (regulated by the number of dependent children in the household) was less than DKK 40 000. If the taxable income was above 40 000, the subsidy was decreased by 1 per cent for each extra DKK 1000 of taxable income (following a 5 per cent reduction as income rose from DKK 40 000 to 41 000).[6]

Finally, if the disposable income of the lone parent household was below about DKK 60 000, the household may have been entitled to social welfare. It is very difficult to describe briefly the rules of the social welfare system and its dependency on household income because the basic principle of the system is that social welfare depends

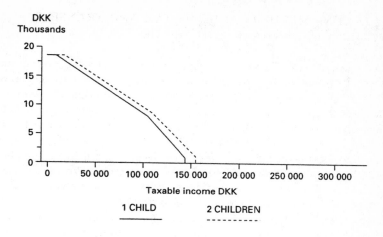

Figure 14.1 Housing subsidy 1985 – Denmark

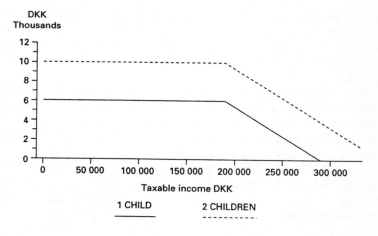

Figure 14.2 Child subsidy 1985 – Denmark

on a comprehensive evaluation of the circumstances of the household, and no specific rules for the administration of social welfare were laid down in 1985. The general principle is that more help should be given to formerly well-functioning families with temporary economic problems than to families with permanent problems. In the former case the maximum amount of social welfare paid in cash to a lone-parent household in 1985 was about DKK 30 000 plus DKK 11 300

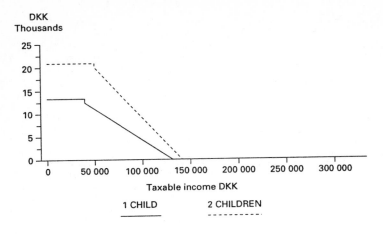

Figure 14.3 Child-care subsidy 1985 – Denmark

for each child. Further, the social security office might pay different 'necessary' expenses, especially housing expenditures, telephone bills, etc., for families with temporary economic problems.[7] The maximum total amount of social welfare for households on temporary help could usually not exceed the after-tax value of the maximum unemployment insurance payments in the year. In 1985 the maximum was between DKK 60 000 and 72 000, depending on the local area tax rate. If the household received social welfare for more than nine months, the total payment was reduced to about DKK 40 000 plus 6800 for each child, and no 'necessary' expenses were paid by the social security office. If the household earned some income, the social welfare was reduced by 100 per cent of such earnings. Social welfare payments are not taxable.

In 1985 there were 5 tax brackets in the Danish income-tax system. The marginal tax rates on taxable income were nil up to DKK 20 300, 33.7 per cent up to 22 700, 48.1 per cent up to 111 300, 62.5 per cent up to 182 600 and 73.3 per cent thereafter.[8]

There are three main elements in the UK welfare system[9] that are relevant to the labour supply choices of lone mothers. (i) The Income Support (IS) – formerly Supplementary Benefit (SB) – system of social assistance provides a minimum income depending on the household's demographic profile, and also covers housing costs in many circumstances. (ii) Housing Benefit (HB) is a means-tested payment which depends on the demographic composition of the household and is related to the household's rent and rates (but does not cover mort-

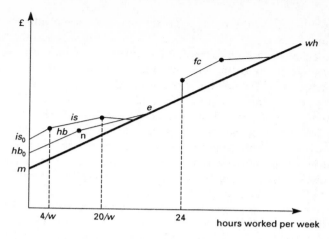

Figure 14.4   Hypothetical budget constraint (UK welfare system)

gage payments). It is not typically paid to those on IS because the IS system compensates for housing costs (in the form of the confusingly named Certificated Housing Benefit) at least as generously as standard HB. (iii) Family Credit (FC) – formerly Family Income Supplement (FIS) – is a benefit whose value is 70 per cent of the difference between a 'prescribed amount' (which depends on the demographic composition of the household) and actual income, but can be paid only if hours of work are at least 24 per week.

Each of these benefits is individually relatively simple but they interact in a complicated way. For example, FC is treated as income in the calculation of HB but HB is not relevant to the calculation of FC. Moreover, it is possible to be in receipt of FIS and HB and to have a positive liability for income tax and social security contributions (called National Insurance (NI)) on one's earnings. Thus a poverty trap exists whereby the marginal tax rate that an individual faces on an additional £1 of earnings can come close to, but not exceed, 100 per cent.

Figure 14.4 illustrates the complicated nature of the UK welfare system. The bold line gives the gross budget constraint, i.e. the constraint in the absence of a tax/benefit system: its intercept is given by the level of maintenance received, m, and its slope is the gross wage, w. The line labelled *is* shows the post-IS constraint. At zero hours of work household income and consumption is given by is_0 which is the IS *scale rate* for this household type plus housing costs less any unearned income including maintenance. At £4 of weekly earnings (shown as an arbitrary point on the hours axis) the marginal wage falls to $0.5w$ until earnings reach £20 (the so-called tapered disregard) and thereafter the marginal wage becomes zero. IS entitlement is the vertical distance between the bold line and the line *is*. However, the household may be entitled to HB in the absence of IS. Thus, on top of gross income, given by the height of the bold line, the household would receive rent and rate relief. The separate components of HB are means-tested at different rates and the rate on each depends on whether income is above or below some needs allowance which depends on household composition. If income was exactly equal to the needs allowance then the amount of relief would be 60 per cent of rates and, if applicable, rent. The effect of the HB scheme on the gross constraint is given by the line labelled *hb* in Figure 14.4, where the vertical distance between the two lines gives the amount of entitlement. The most HB one could receive was 100 per cent of rent and rates, in which case there would be a parallel section to the *hb* line; a kink occurs at the needs allowance, *n*, and entitlement is eventually exhausted at the point labelled *e*. Finally, Family Credit is payable once weekly hours reach 24, provided that income has not reached the prescribed amount (which depends on the number of children). This is shown as the line labelled *fc* which may have a parallel section since there is a maximum amount followed by a section with slope $0.7w$, because the implicit tax rate on FIS is 70 per cent. It is quite possible for FIS and HB to be payable simultaneously, and for the tax and social security contribution scheme (not illustrated) to apply as well.

14.3   EMPIRICAL MODEL

The literature on the estimation of models of labour supply behaviour is voluminous. An issue that has attracted a great deal of attention is the econometric complications induced when individuals face budget constraints that are nonlinear, and especially when they are non-convex. A nonlinear, but convex, budget constraint is generated by a progressive tax system. Non-convexities are generally due to welfare benefits being withdrawn as income rises. The appropriate econometric modelling of labour supply models when budget constraints are non-convex is difficult to implement and has generally required the use of a functional form for the hours equation or the utility function which is simple and restrictive. Thus, for example, a linear labour supply equation (Hausman, 1981; and Blomquist, 1983) or a CES specification for preferences (Zabalza, 1983) have proved popular.

The existing literature often attempts to model desired hours of work and treats labour supply as a continuous variable (with censoring below zero). However, casual empiricism suggests that individuals may not, in any cross-section, be observed to be working their desired hours of work. There may be institutional or technological reasons for individuals to be unable to choose any particular level of hours of work except by moving from one job to another, which may involve considerable costs. Moreover, there may be relatively few job opportunities available in certain ranges of the hours distributions because of nonconvexities in firm's cost functions resulting from start-up costs, nonlinear pay-roll taxes, etc. Thus, many individuals are likely to be out of long-run equilibrium, in the sense that they would prefer different hours at the present wage but that the current job is the best available option. Dickens and Lundberg (1985) and van Soest, Woittiez and Kapteyn (1990) have recently emphasized this aspect of labour supply by showing that conventional labour supply models are quite poor at fitting actual cross-section hours distributions. Indeed, a discrete choice model may be a better approximation to reality than a conventional continuous-hours model.

If labour supply can only be varied discretely so that the only possible levels of labour supply are h_1 hours per year (part-time), h_2 hours (full-time) or zero hours (non-participation), then the labour supply decision can, at least implicitly, be characterized by

$$h = h_j \quad \text{if} \quad U(h_j, y_j) > U(h_k, y_k) \quad \text{and}$$

$$\max(U_j, U_k) > U(0, y_0) \quad j, k = 1, 2 \tag{14.1}$$

where y is consumption, and h is hours of work. y is given by $y = wh + \mu - T(wh + \mu)$ where $T(.)$ is the tax/benefit function which indicates the amount of tax net of benefit receipts payable at any level of income, and μ is unearned income. This problem is essentially a polychotomous discrete choice model based on random utility differences, and the model could be made operational by an appropriate choice of $U(h,y)$ to derive the structural parameters that charaterize preferences. However, in this chapter we have adopted an alternative reduced form approach, where participation and the choice between part-time and full-time work conditional on participation is modelled as a bivariate Probit with an appropriate correction for the resulting selection bias associated with the estimation of the part-time/full-time

340

Applications

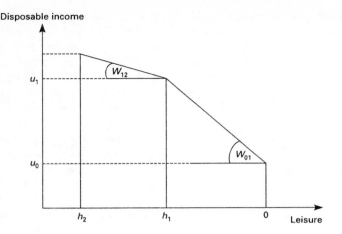

Figure 14.5 Stylized budget constraint for the 3-state model

choice on a sample of participants. The empirical model is illustrated in Figure 14.5.

The participation decision is determined by the height of the 'budget line' in the three states 0, h_1, h_2, corresponding to non-participation, part-time participation, and full-time participation, respectively. Thus, the decision to participate depends on the disposable income as non-participant as well as the increment in disposable income from being either a part-time or a full-time participant.

We assume that the probability of labour force participation can be represented by the latent variable

$$Y_{1i}^* = \delta_1 Z_{1i} + \delta_2 w_{01i} + \delta_3 w_{12i} + \delta_4 y_{0i} + \varepsilon_{1i} \qquad (14.2)$$
$$= X_{1i}\beta_1 + \varepsilon_{1i}$$

where we assume that $\varepsilon_{1i} \sim N(0,\sigma_1^2)$ and $w_{ij}, \forall i, j$ is the average increase in disposable income per hour's work when changing the state from i to j. Z_1 is a vector of individual characteristics that affect preferences. The participation state is represented by the dichotomous variable $Y1$ such that $Y_{1i} = 1$ if $Y_{1i}^* > 0$ (participation), or $Y_{1i} = 0$ (non-participation).

The choice between part-time and full-time participation is represented by the latent variable

$$Y_{2i}^* = \gamma_1 Z_{2i} + \gamma_2 w_{12i} + \gamma_3 y_{1i} + \varepsilon_{2i}$$
$$= X_{2i}\beta_2 + \varepsilon_{2i} \tag{14.3}$$

ε_{1i} and ε_{2i} are assumed to be bivariate normal distributed with $Corr(\varepsilon_{1i}, \varepsilon_{2i}) = \rho$. Z_2 a vector of individual characteristics that influence the choice between part-time and full-time work[10]. The dichotomous variable Y_2, corresponding to Y_2^*, is defined by $Y_2 = 1$ if $Y_{2i}^* > 0$ (full-time), or $Y_{2i} = 0$ (part-time).

We only observe the preferences between part-time and full-time participation if the individual is a participant. Hence, we treat the estimation problem as a bivariate Probit model with self-selection. The probability of observing individual i as non-participant is given by

$$P(Y_{1i} = 0) \; P(Y_{1i}^* \leq 0) = P\,(\varepsilon_{1i} \leq -\, X_{1i}\beta_1)$$
$$= \Phi\!\left(\frac{-X_{1i}\beta_1}{\sigma_1}\right) \tag{14.4}$$

where Φ is the standard normal distribution function. The probability of observing individual i as a part-time participant is

$$P(Y_{2i}^* < 0) \, - \, P(Y_{1i}^* < 0 \wedge Y_{2i}^* < 0)$$
$$= \Phi\!\left(\frac{-X_{2i}\beta_2}{\sigma_2}\right) \, - \, \Phi_2\!\left(\frac{-X_{1i}\beta_1}{\sigma_1}, \frac{-X_{2i}\beta_2}{\sigma_2}, \rho\right) \tag{14.5}$$

where $\Phi_2\,(.,\,.;\rho)$ is the bivariate standard normal distribution function. Finally, the probability of observing individual i as a full-time participant is given by

$$P(Y_{1i}^* > 0 \wedge Y_{2i}^* > 0) = 1 \, - \, \Phi\!\left(\frac{-X_{1i}\beta_1}{\sigma_1}\right)$$
$$- \, \Phi\!\left(\frac{-X_{2i}\beta_2}{\sigma_2}\right) \, - \, \Phi_2\!\left(\frac{-X_{1i}\beta_1}{\sigma_1}, \frac{-X_{2i}\beta_2}{\sigma_2}, \rho\right) \tag{14.6}$$

Hence, the likelihood function is given by

$$L = \prod_{i=1}^{N_0} \Phi\left(\frac{-X_{1i}\beta_1}{\sigma_1}\right) \prod_{i=N_0+1}^{N_1} \left\{ \Phi\left(\frac{-X_{2i}\beta_2}{\sigma_2}\right) \right.$$

$$\left. - \Phi_2\left(\frac{-X_{1i}\beta_1}{\sigma_1}, \frac{-X_{2i}\beta_2}{\sigma_2}, \rho\right) \right\}.$$

$$\prod_{i=N_1+1}^{N} \left\{ 1 - \Phi\left(\frac{-X_{1i}\beta_1}{\sigma_1}\right) - \Phi\left(\frac{-X_{2i}\beta_2}{\sigma_2}\right) \right.$$

$$\left. + \Phi_2\left(\frac{-X_{1i}\beta_1}{\sigma_1}, \frac{-X_{2i}\beta_2}{\sigma_2}, \rho\right) \right\} \qquad (14.7)$$

where the first N_0 observations are non-participants, the following N_1 observations are part-time participants and the last $N - N_0 - N_1$ observations are full-time participants.

Identification in models such as this is a controversial question. The problem is to identify the parameters of each equation and this can only be achieved if there is at least one variable which can legitimately be excluded from each equation. The matrices Z_1 and Z_2 could contain, at least some, different variables to capture the impact of sociodemographic characteristics. For example, one might be willing to assume that local labour market conditions affect only participation but not the split between part-time and full-time employment. However, ideally identification should be achieved by natural exclusion restrictions and in this empirical example we assume that Z_1 and Z_2 contain the same variables. Thus, we rely here on the economic structure of the model which dictates that participation depends on y_0, w_{01} and w_{12} but, conditional on participation, full-time work depends only on y_1 and w_{12} but not on y_0 or w_{01}. This is a natural exclusion restriction and will succeed in identifying the model provided that there is independent variation in these variables (i.e. provided they are not closely correlated with the included variables y_1 and w_{12}). In fact $y_1 = y_0 + 25w_{01}$ so that we rely on w_{01} and w_{12} being independent of one another. Clearly w_{01} and w_{12} are only independent of one another to the extent that there is independent variation in the tax rates on part-time and full-time earnings. Here, the fact that budget constraints are quite complicated comes to our assistance.

We use predicted gross wages to generate w_{01} and w_{12}. The wage equations are quite conventional and we considered the usual problem of selection bias arising from estimating the equation over a sample of participants only using a reduced form Probit participation equation to generate the Inverse Mill's Ratio, following the usual Heckman (1976) two-step technique. We exploit the fact that our data include y_0, which we use as a determinant of participation but not of wages.

14.4 DESCRIPTION OF DATA

14.4.1 Denmark

The Danish data are drawn from the Danish Longitudinal Data Base (LDB) which itself is a 5 per cent sample (240 000 individuals) of the Danish adult population, originating from Danish administrative registers.[11] The sub-sample used in this study is a cross-section from 1985 of all lone parents having children aged less than 18 years. Married or unmarried but cohabiting men and women from the master sample are included in some of the tables below in order to contrast the group of lone parents with these groups.[12]

The labour supply of the individuals is not directly observable but is calculated on the basis of annual payments to the Supplementary Pension Scheme (ATP), which are related to the number of employed hours during the year and the unemployment insurance payments during the year. A non-participant is defined as a person supplying less than 200 hours of labour during the year. Part-time is defined as being in the range 200–1400 hours annually, and full-time participation is defined as more than 1400 hours annually. The maximum of 1400 hours for the part-time employed is chosen because it corresponds to the maximum hours (6 a day) for normal part-time contracts within the public sector. The distribution of the three labour market states across the sample is shown in Figure 14.6.

The columns in Figure 14.6 show that the labour supply of lone mothers is somewhat different from the labour supply of married/cohabiting mothers. More lone mothers are in full-time jobs and fewer are in part-time jobs, suggesting that the total economic situation of the household matters in the supply decision. The figure also reveals that only about 12 per cent of lone fathers work less than full-time and we have dropped this group from further investigation because of its heterogeneity and small size.

The presence of small children in a lone-parent household may be a major impediment to labour supply by the mother. Figure 14.7 confirms that this is in fact the case. For this reason, the variables for children are divided into dummy variables which emphasize the age of the youngest child. Since higher numbers of children in all ages are also expected to influence the labour supply decision, a variable 'child > 2' takes the value 1 if the woman has more than two dependent children.

The economic variables are used to compute the budget lines and hence the income levels in each of the three states, non-participation,

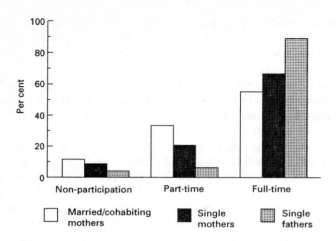

Figure 14.6　Participation rates for persons with children – Denmark

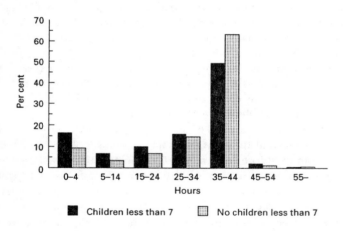

Figure 14.7　Distribution of hours for lone mothers by age of youngest
child – Denmark

part-time participation, and full-time participation. First, a wage equation
is estimated that takes into account the selection bias associated with
using a sample of participants only. The predicted wage rate for each
state is then used to form wage income in each state. Finally, this
wage income is used together with the information on the family
characteristics and unearned income to calculate tax and benefits in
the three states, using the rules as they are described in Section 14.2.

The information on benefits comes from different sources, since all details are not directly available in LDB. The potential child subsidy in each of the three states is calculated as a function of the potential taxable income in the corresponding three states. Information on average values for day-care and housing expenditures for lone parents come from a report by the Danish Minister of Economics (1987) where these averages are calculated for different groups of lone parents. Based on these figures, the individual potential housing and child-care subsidies are calculated by applying the appropriate rules. Expenses for institutionalized day-care (which is subsidized by municipalities to the extent of two-thirds on average) is considered as an expenditure related to working part-time or full-time. Thus, it is assumed that non-participants with pre-school children do not incur such expenditure.

The evaluation of social welfare in the three participation states is not straightforward, because of the lack of definite rules. If the person has unearned income, receives a housing or day-care subsidy, or has other sources of income, the social welfare is reduced by the full amount of such receipts. Therefore, we assume that in the non-participation state, social welfare tops up disposable income to DKK 50 000. The maximum level of DKK 50 000 is chosen, partly because it corresponds to the maximum level for social welfare and partly because it is equal to the maximum observed value of social welfare in the sample.

Based on these variables and unearned income we calculate the weekly disposable income y_0, y_1, and y_2 in the states as non-participant, part-time participant, and full-time participant, respectively. The values of y_j ($j = 0, 1, 2$) are defined as the sum of average weekly unearned income plus predicted weekly wage income in the three states (0 hours, 1200/45.2 hours, and 1808/45.2 hours, respectively)[13] minus the calculated average weekly net tax payment (net of subsidies and social welfare in the state concerned). The wage variable w_{01} is defined as the average net wage per hour's employment in part-time work, while w_{12} is the net wage per hour for full-time workers. Graphically y_j corresponds to the height of the budget line in state j, as explained in Section 14.3, and w_{01} and w_{12} are the slopes calculated by $w_{01} = (y_1 - y_0)(h_1 - h_0)$ and $w_{12} = (y_2 - y_1)(h_2 - h_1)$ where $h_0 =$, $h_1 = 1200/45.2$, and $h_2 = 1808/45.2$.

14.4.2 The UK

In order to address the determinants of labour force participation and welfare dependency empirically, the UK Family Expenditure Survey data sets for 1979 to 1988 were pooled. This provides a reasonable sample size to allow an econometric model of labour supply decisions to be estimated. The sample consists of 2933 lone mothers.

In addition to significant changes across time, there are also differences at a point in time in the behaviour of different types of lone mother. In particular, the age of the youngest child is very important. Figure 14.8 shows the breakdown in labour force status by age of youngest child, where non-participation is zero normal weekly hours and earnings, part-time is normal earnings positive and normal hours between 1 and 31 inclusive, and full-time is normal earnings positive and normal hours at least 32. Having a pre-school child (i.e. one aged 0–4) has a dramatic impact on labour force participation, while the effect of having the youngest child in the 5-to-10-year-old group is smaller, relative to having the youngest child aged 11 to 16.[14]

Figure 14.9 shows the effect of maintenance receipts on labour force status. The group who receive maintenance are much more likely to work than the group who do not, while for those that do work maintenance is likely to result in the undertaking of part-time rather than full-time work. The treatment of maintenance by the tax/welfare system is quite complicated: as far as Supplementary Benefit (SB) is concerned, maintenance is treated as any other source of unearned income and is effectively taxed at 100 per cent; Housing Benefit (HB) also treats maintenance as income but the tapers are much less severe; Family Income Supplement (FIS) treats regular maintenance as income and imposes a 50 per cent taper on it; there is no National Insurance (NI) liability of maintenance.

The effect on net income of receiving an additional £1 of maintenance is zero for most non-participants on SB, but positive for full-time workers and, to a lesser extent, for part-time workers. Thus, maintenance receipt encourages participation, but because of the income effect of the additional income on labour supply we might expect that, conditional on working at all, the impact of maintenance would be negative.

Finally, Figure 14.10 shows the significance of whether or not the lone mother is a householder (i.e. is the head of household). Such individuals will typically be the only adult in the household, while non-householders necessarily live with other adults, often their parents.

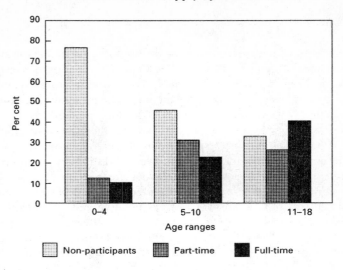

Figure 14.8 Labour force status by age of youngest child – UK

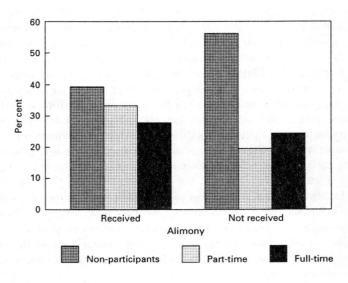

Figure 14.9 Labour force status by maintenance receipt – UK

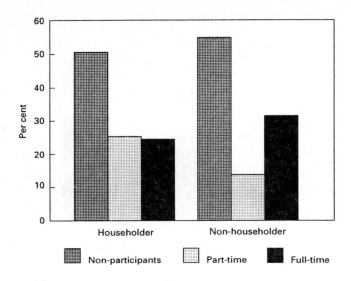

Figure 14.10 Labour force status by householder status – UK

Non-householders will have very different housing costs from those of householders and their SB entitlements are correspondingly lower. On the other hand, non-householder lone parents are quite different people from householder lone parents: they tend to be younger, to have fewer children, and to have younger children. In addition, such women may find it easier to work, to the extent that they have access to child—care from other household members. Figure 14.10 shows that non-householders are a little less likely to work, but if they do then they tend to work full-time. But how much of the observed net effect is due to each of the influences listed above is impossible to deduce from our data.

In order to address the question of the effects of economic opportunities on labour market behaviour we need to compute exactly what these opportunities might be. This involves computing the level of tax liabilities and benefit entitlements at each of the potential labour market states. Since the wage available to non-participants is unknown, this requires that estimates of the wage equation relevant to each labour market state be used to compute earnings at each point. Given these earning levels, tax and benefits are calculated assuming that individuals commanded their predicted wages at the alternative values of hours of work.

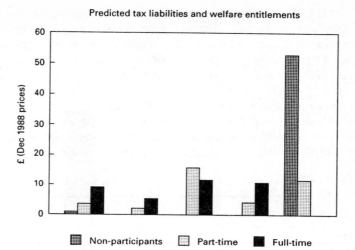

Figure 14.11 Predicted tax liabilities and welfare entitlements per week – UK

The data were inflated to December 1988 prices and the mean levels of SB, FIS, HB, NI, and tax are given in Figure 14.11 for three specific levels of weekly hours: 0, 25 and 40.

SB entitlements at zero hours are quite large because there are no earnings to offset entitlements at this point; HB entitlements are zero at this point since SB typically covers housing costs; FIS entitlements are zero for hours below 24. At part-time hours, earnings are such as to exhaust most SB entitlements, HB is now more important, and FIS entitlements are now large. At full-time hours, SB entitlements are zero, FIS is zero, and HB entitlements are much smaller, but tax and NI liabilities are much higher. The overall levels of net weekly income (given the wage predictions) are £89.34 at the non-participation point, £116.83 at the part-time point, and £127.37 at the full-time point (December 1988 prices).

14.5 RESULTS

The model has been estimated on 4004 lone mothers for Denmark and 2933 for the UK. The results are given in Table 14.1.

The wage coefficients are significantly positive (with the exception of w_{12} in the UK participation equation) and the income coefficients are significantly negative.[15] The age group indicators generally have significantly negative coefficients. The omitted age group is women aged 35–39 years. The lowest participation is found for the youngest and the oldest women. The youngest of those working are also most likely to prefer part-time work.

In Denmark, small children have no significant effect on the probability of participation but, conditional on participation, do increase the likelihood of working full-time rather than part-time. Having many children (3 or more) has a clear negative effect on the participation

Table 14.1 Estimated coefficients: Bivariate probit with self-selection[16]

	Denmark		UK	
Participation	Coeff.	Std.error	Coeff.	Std.error
Constant	−0.155	0.222	0.247	0.262
$y_0/100$	−0.094	0.015	−0.286	0.108
w_{01}	0.050	0.003	0.758	0.035
w_{12}	0.051	0.003	−0.043	0.038
Youngest child 0–2	0.543	0.099	−1.168	0.106
Youngest child 3–6	0.507	0.083	–	–
Youngest child 3–4	–	–	−0.829	0.115
Youngest child 5–10	–	–	−0.328	0.073
Child > 2	−0.668	0.096	–	–
Part/full-time				
Constant	1.170	0.204	0.851	0.329
$y_1/100$	−0.073	0.010	−0.139	0.134
w_{12}	0.057	0.006	0.145	0.047
Youngest child 0–2	0.234	0.096	−0.208	0.202
Youngest child 3–4	–	–	−0.735	0.191
Youngest child 3–6	0.519	0.081	–	–
Youngest child 5–10	–	–	−0.472	0.096
Child > 2	−0.050	0.102	–	–
Rho	−0.596	0.162	−0.183	0.128
Log-likelihood	−2905		−2442	
No. of obs.	4004		2933	

Notes: Both models include regional and age group dummy variables in both equations. The UK model also includes year dummies and the unemployment rate since it uses pooled data over time and dummy variables to capture maintenance receipt and head of household, while the Danish model includes union membership dummies in the full-time/part-time equation only and dummy variables for sickness and owner occupation.

probability but has no significant effect on the choice between full-time and part-time. Being a house- or flat-owner decreases the likelihood of participation as well as the likelihood of full-time working; and this is most probably because this variable catches some unmeasured wealth effect. Living outside Greater Copenhagen means a higher probability of participation but a lower likelihood of working full-time. The sickness variable, which is a rather crude measure of bad health, indicates that persons who have received sickness benefits are less likely to hold full-time jobs.

It is also found that the probability of working full-time versus part-time is not influenced in any significant way by the specific unemployment insurance fund variables.

The correlation between the error terms in the participation relation and the full-time relation is estimated to be significantly negative, implying that unobserved factors that increase the probability of participation also decrease the probability of full-time participation.

14.6 INEQUALITY AND SOCIAL WELFARE

It has become commonplace to compare inequality over time and across countries on the basis of net income. Part of the aim of such studies is to comment on the impact of differences in tax and social welfare systems in reducing inequality. However, when net income is itself endogenous, via the labour supply decision, this methodology is potentially suspect. Here we use our estimates to indicate what impact social welfare systems might have on income inequality. A reasonable presumption is that social welfare systems reduce income inequality and the precise magnitude is an empirical question. Table 14.2 shows the effect of removing the social welfare system in each country and replacing it with a system of equal lump-sum transfers. The figures show the effects averaged across the three groups in the observed data where both the pre- and post-reform figures have been evaluated in terms of expected values from the estimated parameters. UK income figures are in £ a week while the Danish figures are DKK000s a year.

Notice that without a labour supply effect (columns 2) the expected net income of those observed in the non-participation (NP) category (y_0) falls dramatically, while the effect is smaller for the part-time (PT) category (y_1) and the effect for full-time workers (y_2) is positive. Thus, net income inequality, measured by the commonly used Gini coefficient, rises markedly. However, the effect on labour supply is

Table 14.2 Simulating the abolition of the welfare system

| | Denmark | | | UK | | |
	1 *Pre- reform*	*2* *Post- reform* *(fixed h)*	*3* *Post- reform*	*1* *Pre- reform*	*2* *Post- reform* *(fixed h)*	*3* *Post- reform*
NP	.24	.24	.04	0.59	0.59	0.27
PT	.22	.22	.10	0.22	0.22	0.18
FT	.54	.54	.86	0.18	0.18	0.644
y_0	53.5	24.9	91.6	116.1	63.7	127.4
y_1	83.6	81.2	100.2	152.6	127.9	148.7
y_2	100.5	110.6	107.3	178.1	177.4	160.1
Gini coeff.	0.145	0.167	0.128	0.127	0.155	0.111

also quite marked: the expected proportion of the NPs in the post-reform data is much lower than in the pre-reform data and the expected number of PTs is also lower, while the expected number of full-time workers (FTs) is higher. This is not surprising, in view of the estimates. However, the effect on the Gini coefficient of taking impacts on labour supply into account is so large that it more than counteracts the results calculated with no labour supply effects. That is, inequality falls once labour supply effects are taken into account.[17]

14.7 CONCLUSION

This chapter has analyzed the labour supply of lone mothers in Denmark and the UK emphasizing the tax and benefit schemes that are especially relevant for this low-income group. In Denmark, despite the fact that the implicit tax rate is close to 100 per cent in certain parts of the income distribution, labour force participation rates of lone mothers are relatively high while in the UK low participation is the rule.

In the econometric analysis we include the progressive income-tax schemes, the day-care subsidy, child-care subsidies, housing subsidies and social welfare payments in a discrete choice supply model, explaining non-participation, part-time participation, and full-time participation.

Wage effects on labour supply appear to be smaller in Denmark than in the UK but the most substantial difference between the estimates is the effect of children. In the UK there is a dramatic effect of pre-school children on participation, while this is not the case in Denmark. This is consistent with the extensive availability of child-care in Denmark.

The main significance of the analysis is illustrated by some simulation results which show the impact of abolishing the social welfare systems in the two countries. In both Denmark and the UK we show that, in the absence of labour supply effects, such a policy would induce a dramatic increase in equality; but once the labour supply effects are taken into account there is actually a decrease in inequality. This suggests that it is likely to be inappropriate to compare inequality across countries and across time without taking into account the behavioural implications of the tax and social welfare systems.

Notes

1. We are grateful to the Danish Social Research Council and the British Council for financial support to facilitate the authors' collaboration on this project. Helle Engelund, Hanne Vajhøj, Mikael Kristensen and Leif Husted have provided excellent research assistance on the project. An earlier version of the paper was presented at the ESPE 91 conference.
2. See Ermisch (1991) for details.
3. See Haskey (1991) for estimates of the number of UK lone parents from a number of sample surveys including the Family Expenditure Surveys used here.
4. Thaulow and Gamst (1987). However, none of these studies model the supply decision or estimate the supply effects of the tax and transfer system for lone mothers.
5. See Cohen and Clarke (1986) for an international perspective on child-care.
6. It is also possible to get a subsidy to child-care after school hours. This is, however, not included here since there were relatively few such places and it would be difficult to predict who would receive such a benefit. However, these places are relatively cheap, compared to day-care places.
7. As there were no general rules, it is difficult to give exact figures. The figures mentioned here, and the figures used in the empirical model, refer to the rules which were used in a small number of experimenting municipalities (forsøgskommuner) where the evaluation principle was abandoned and the social welfare was paid according to some specific rules.
8. As the income tax consists of taxes to the state as well as local taxes which differ between municipalities, the figures are average marginal tax rates for the whole country.
9. The terminology here relates to the pre-April 1988 welfare system. In April 1988, SB was replaced by Income Support, and FIS by Family Credit. The general structure of the welfare system remained unchanged but the disregard of child-care expenses that was a feature of the SB system was dropped from the Income Support scheme. Much further detail can be found in papers in Dilnot and Walker (1990).

10. For non-participants a number of labour market variables relevant to the choice between part-time and full-time work are not observed. As examples, we do not observe the membership of a trade union for most non-participants, and the replacement ratio from Unemployment Insurance benefits is by definition set to zero if the person is not a member of a UI-fund. The sickness variable only catches health conditions for persons who are eligible for unemployment benefits. Among the non-participants, we only observe these variables for individuals who are insured against unemployment and are 'full-time unemployed'.

11. A detailed description of an earlier version of the LDB sample is given in Westergård-Nielsen (1984).

12. Self-employed persons, assisting wives (wives employed in firms owned by their husbands) and pensioners are excluded from the sample. The two former groups are excluded because we are not able to calculate a labour supply for these persons. The exclusions leave us with 4067 lone mothers (and 570 lone fathers) who are not cohabiting, and in the following analyses we drop a further 63 observations because of missing information on some variables, leaving us with 4004 lone mothers.

13. In general, all annual variables are transformed into average weekly variables by dividing by 45.2 since this was the standard number of weeks in 1985 used by the administrative registers.

14. Up to 18 if in full-time education. The data tell us whether or not children attend full-time or part-time nursery although the difference in the labour market status across these categories is very small.

15. Note that the interpretation of the coefficients on the economic variables depend on the currency units – £1≈DKr10.

16. Estimated by the Newton-algorithm in LIMDEP v6.0.

17. The same is also true if Atkinson measures are used, except at high degrees of inequality aversion.

References

Blomquist, N.S. (1983) 'The Effect of Income Taxation on the Labour Supply of Married Men in Sweden' Journal of Public Economics, vol. 22, pp. 169–197.

Brown, J.C. (1989) 'Why don't They Go To Work: Mothers on Benefit?' Social Security Advisory Committee Research Paper 2 (London: HMSo).

Cohen, O. and K. Clarke (1986), *Children and Equal Opportunities*, Equal Opportunities Commission (London: HMSo).

Danish Minister of Economics (1987) *Lovmodellen* (Copenhagen: Danish Government Publishing Office).

Dickens, W. and S. Lundberg (1985) 'Hours Restrictions and Labour Supply', NBER Working Paper 1638, Harvard.

Dilnot, A.W. and I. Walker (1990) *The Economics of Social Security* (Oxford: Oxford University Press).

Ermisch, J. and R. Wright (1989a) 'Welfare Benefits and Lone Parents' Employment', NIESR Working Paper, London.

Ermisch, J. and R. Wright (1989b) 'The Interpretation of Negative Sample Selection Effects in Wage Offer Equations', mimeo, Birkbeck College, London.

Ermisch, J. (1991), *Lone Parenthood: An Economic Analysis* (Cambridge: Cambridge University Press).

Haskey, J. (1991) 'Estimated Numbers and Demographic Characteristics of One-Parent Families in Great Britain', *Population Trends*, vol. 65, pp. 35–48.

Hausman, J. (1981) 'Labour Supply', in H. Aaron and H. Pechman (eds.), *How Taxes Affect Behaviour* (New York: Brookings Institution).

Heckman, J. (1976) 'Sample Selection Bias as a Specification Error', *Econometrica*, vol. 47, pp. 153–62.

Knieser, T.J., M.B. McElroy and S.P. Wilcox (1988) 'Getting into Poverty Without a Husband, and Getting out With or Without', *American Economic Review (Papers and Proceedings)*, vol. 78, pp. 86–90.

Moffit, R. (1992) 'Incentive Effects of the U.S. Welfare System: A Review', *Journal of Economic Literature*, vol. 30, pp. 1–161.

Thaulow, I. and B. Gamst (1987) *Enlige forsørgere mellen selvforsørgelse og bistandshjælp* (Copenhagen: Socialforskningsinstituttet Publikation).

Van Soest, A., I. Woittiez and A. Kapteyn (1990) 'Labor Supply, Income Taxes, and Hours Restrictions in the Netherlands', *Journal of Human Resources*, vol. 25, pp. 517–58.

Walker, I. (1990) 'The effect of Income Support Measures on the Labour Market Behaviour of Lone Mothers', *Fiscal Studies*, vol. 11, pp. 55–74.

Westergård-Nielsen, N. (1984) 'A Danish Longitudinal Database', in G. Newman and N. Westergård-Nielsen (eds), *Studies in Labour Market Dynamics* (Amsterdam: Springer-Verlag).

Zabalza, A. (1983) 'The CES Utility Function, Nonlinear Budget Constraints, and Labour Supply', *Economic Journal*, vol. 93, pp. 312–30.

15 Competition and Cooperation Among Producers: Cournot Revisited

Christian Schmidt
UNIVERSITY OF PARIS-DAUPHINE

15.1 OLD READINGS AND RECENT RE-WRITINGS OF COURNOT[1]

Cournot's name is generally associated with the analysis of monopoly and for a long time the approach adopted by the author of *Recherches sur les principes mathématiques de la théorie des richesses* (1838) was seen as an essay in the progressive generalization from a detailed study of monopoly to one of the market economy in general (Roy, 1933; Lutfalla, 1938).[2] This general belief, underpinning the dominant interpretation of this work, has had a definite influence on the understanding of its analyses. For example, the criticisms, often divergent, of his treatment of duopoly made by the first generation of economists and mathematicians interested in economics (Bertrand, 1883; Edgeworth, 1891 and 1897; Fisher, 1899; Pareto, 1911) are partly explained by this widespread, but in our opinion largely inexact, view of Cournot's approach.[3]

It now seems that these misinterpretations can be regarded as having been dissipated, more than a century after the publication of *Recherches sur les principes mathématiques de la théorie des richesses*, thanks to game theory and, in particular, to the definition of non-co-operative equilibrium that it has introduced. This contribution by Nash (1951, 1953), now regarded as an essential source of renewal of economic theory, rapidly opened the way to a re-reading of Cournot which has tended to reverse previous assessments of the contribution made to the subject by *Recherches sur les principes mathématiques de la théorie des richesses* (Mayberry, Nash and Shubik, 1953). The accent is now being placed on his analysis of duopoly, extended to the cases of oligopolies, and on the original manner in which he dealt with the market. This rediscovery of Cournot has crowned the work of re-examination carried out especially by Shubik on the basis of Nash's research programme. It has produced definitions that have now become common in the current literature on game theory relating to the Cournot–Nash models and equilibria.[4]

This brief reminder of the change in the way Cournot's work has been received by economists inevitably raises questions of broader scope in the minds of those who deal with the history of thought. One of these questions concerns the links between the formal instrument used in analysis and the economic content of the phenomenon it is meant to apprehend. For example, it is the analytical formulation chosen by Cournot to represent the relations between the quantities D_1 and D_2 and the price in the duopoly case (Cournot [1838], 1974 edition, p. 130)[5] that lies at the origin of the erroneous economic interpretation of Cournot by Bertrand (1883, p. 297). On the same lines, it was by making a slight reformulation of Cournot's system of equations that Pareto drew the conclusion that the problem dealt with by Cournot by means of his duopoly model is not that of competition between two producers but that of a very special form of alternative monopoly (Pareto, 1911, in Lutfalla (ed.), 1938, pp. 254–5). In addition, the formulation using discrete terms, more familiar to non-cooperative game theoreticians than formulations in terms of a continuum, are not relevant for representing situations such as those described by Cournot, where the strategies of the players are characterized in terms of the quantities of the product in question, but without requiring recourse to the concept of a mixed strategy in the sense used in game theory. This transposition of Cournot's initial algebraic formulation into the mathematical mould of non-cooperative games has turned out to be necessary in order to bring out the original economic content of his treatment of duopoly.

Detailed consideration of this first question leads on to a second more particular question of the exact effect of this rewriting of Cournot's work in game-theory terms on the intelligibility of its economic content. At first sight, it seems to introduce a breach in the interpretation of *Recherches sur les principes mathématiques de la théorie des richesses*. It was, in fact, by searching for an economic significance in the mathematical system developed by Cournot that the first generation of mathematical economists, using a variety of arguments, reached the conclusion that it was impossible to develop a theory of competition starting from monopoly. But a fresh look at Cournot's system of equations in the light of game-theory reasoning has led a later generation to find in it the seeds of a strategic theory of competition between producers.

Deeper reflection reintroduces an element of continuity into this story. The solution of the duopoly model conceived by Cournot in chapter VII is in fact a unique and stable Nash equilibrium. But this result is not unrelated to the particular constraints imposed by Cournot on his model, where costs are zero, where the demand functions of the differential equations inversely link quantities to prices and where the price is determined by the sum of the quantities placed on the market by the two producers. These demand functions are sometimes treated as being linear;[6] and it turns out, in some cases, that simply abandoning the assumption that the demand functions are linear is enough to call into question the result of Cournot's model (Friedman, 1977 and 1989; Rasmussen, 1989). Moreover, the inversion of the economic mechanism as suggested by Bertrand, so that the strategies of the two producers are based on the prices and not on the amounts, leads, with the same constraints on costs and on the demand functions, to a result that is mathematically equivalent (the existence of an unique and stable Nash equilibrium as the solution of the system). But the economic significance is altered, since the equilibrium point corresponds in this case to a situation in which the prices of the two producers are zero.[7] The new formal framework offered by game theory has therefore made it possible to refine the distinction between the theoretical component of a general nature presented by Cournot and its specific contingent component, the latter being dependent on the economic assumptions chosen. It remains to be seen whether this latter component reflects only a concern for mathematical simplification or has more fundamental economic significance.

As for the problem initially raised, concerning the relations between the mathematical formalism and the economic content of the results it enables one to achieve, the example of the non-identical twins formed by Cournot's and Bertrand's duopoly games brings out, first, the semantic nature of the economic distinction between prices and quantities. For the game theoretician, what is involved is simply a variant on the familiar 'prisoner's dilemma'. The interpretation of the difference between the two assumed strategies and their outcomes is not the concern of the mathematician, but exclusively that of the economist, once one goes beyond the common formal structure and considers the economic assumptions used in each construction.

This conclusion leads on to examination of one final question. The differences between the successive readings of Cournot by mathematical economists are not explained only by the progress in mathematics in the intervening periods. It seems that Bertrand chose prices as the controlling variables for the two duopolists with the aim of refuting the economic relevance of Cournot's mathematical system: Cournot's equations as reinterpreted by Bertrand lead to an equilibrium solution deprived of all economic significance, in that prices are zero. On the other hand, Shubik's rehabilitation of Cournot duopoly is largely attributable to the fact that the treatment he proposes for competition between two producers of the same product leads to a solution that is economically significant and is even comparable with certain properties of the competitive market,[8] and so increases the relevance of a strategic approach to the market. In other words, the technical arguments put forward, while clearly linked to the advances made in mathematics, are never totally without reference to a more general context of *a priori* conceptions which in fact determine the interpretations contained in the various rereadings and rewritings. It then becomes legitimate to ask about the biases that are inevitably introduced.

The aim of this chapter is, first, to identify some of the biases contained in the retrospective analyses of duopoly and oligopoly that are attributed to Cournot. To do this, we confront the *a priori* ideas on which these analyses are based with the place and significance of these subjects in *Recherches sur les principes mathématiques de la théorie des richesses*. This exercise will then lead on to sketching out the main lines of an original research programme into Cournot regarding the relationship between the nature of the goods produced and the economic consequences of the way their production is organized. A final section briefly discusses some of the further investigations which might contribute to progress in industrial economics.

15.2 MONOPOLY, DUOPOLY AND COMPETITION

In the various interpretations of Cournot duopoly recalled earlier, none of the authors mentioned was genuinely concerned to reconstitute the place occupied by the examination of this situation in the totality of the analysis developed by the author of *Recherches sur les principes mathématiques de la théorie des richesses*. For the first group, it seemed to be self-evident that it was one stage in Cournot's efforts to construct an economic theory of wealth, taking the analysis of monopoly as the starting point. For the second group, duopoly manifestly provided the beginnings of an outline of a theory of wealth based on an analysis of different types of market. What is the truth concerning these preconceived ideas?

It is true that chapter VII ('De la concurrence des producteurs' – 'on competition between producers'), where the case of duopoly is introduced, constitutes merely a simple application of the fundamental concepts introduced at an earlier point in the analysis, especially in chapters IV ('Loi du débit') and V ('Du monopole'). While this tends to support the first group's reading of the duopoly analysis, it still does not go so far as to validate the idea that, for Cournot, duopoly is the necessary transition in the extension of the economic theory of monopoly to that of the competitive market. This oversimplified version of Cournot's general plan of work can be refuted by two arguments taken from his book. First, the theory of producer monopoly, set out in chapter V, rests on the hypothesis of competition between the purchasers of a good of which the monopolist is the seller (Cournot, p. 100). Second, the examination of competition between two producers of a homogeneous good, which provides the guiding thread for the Cournot duopoly model, is undertaken on the basis of a 'fonction du débit' whose formulation is the inverse of that used in the analysis of monopoly (Cournot, p. 130).

The implication of the first of these arguments is easily demonstrated. In the absence of the assumption of competition between purchasers, it is not possible to determine the equilibrium monopoly price using what Cournot calls the 'Loi du débit' (Cournot, p. 94, equation (1)). For Cournot, monopoly is not a category that logically precedes competition, since the situation of monopoly production analysed in chapter V simultaneously introduces a seller's monopoly and competition between purchasers. what is special about Cournot's approach is not that it starts from monopoly, but rather that it reserves the analyses of monopoly and competition to the producer group only. This feature distinguishes it from the way in which Edgeworth, in particular, tackled these same questions.

It is doubtful, on the other hand, whether Cournot himself grasped the full implication of the second argument. Certainly, the terms in which he introduces the inversion in the formulation of the demand functions, when he starts to deal with the question of competition between two producers, makes one sceptical:

Au lieu de poser comme précédemment $D = F(p)$, il nous sera commode d'employer la notation inverse $p = f(D)$; et alors, les bénéfices des propriétaires (1) et (2) seront exprimés respectivement par $D_1.f(D_1$

$+ D_2$), $D_2.f(D_1 + D_2)$, c'est-à-dire par des fonctions dans chacune desquelles entrent deux variables D_1, D_2. (Cournot, p. 130)

From a formal point of view, all that happens is an inversion in the notation of the 'débit' function, but it is possible to argue about what he meant by 'commode' ('convenient'). Maintaining the initial notation used in the analysis of producer monopoly would have meant leaving prices as the control variable in the case of competition between two producers. There is no intuitive or analytical objection to this; it is worth noting that Bertrand advocated proceeding in this way in his approach to duopoly. But adjustment by means of price makes it impossible to move progressively to the case of indefinite competition (chapter VIII) by increasing the number of producers, since the non-cooperative equilibrium is attained when prices are zero irrespective of the number of competitors. To be more precise, the elimination of profit, assuming indefinite competition, takes place at equilibrium in the case of Bertrand-style duopoly, when the pair of non-cooperative equilibrium strategies corresponds to zero values of price.

The inversion of the mathematical notation of the 'loi du débit', when Cournot moves from the analysis of monopoly to that of competition between producers, therefore turns out to be necessary for the economic significance of competition between producers to be understood as Cournot intends. As prices and quantities do not carry equivalent and interchangeable information (Schmidt, 1985), it is not surprising that they do not lead to the same results when one or other of them uniquely characterizes all the game strategies, even though these are themselves identical (cf. Cournot and Bertrand duopolies).

It would seem, however, that Cournot applied this semantic difference between prices and quantities in a different way. After deriving his equations with respect to quantities (Cournot, p. 13, equations (1) and (2)), he in fact returns to derivation with respect to price when he sums these two equations in order to obtain the prices (Cournot, p. 133, equations (3) and (4)).[9] What interests him is not so much the comparison of the trading adjustment mechanisms as identifying analytically what distinguishes the monopoly situation (or the collusion situation) from that of competition between producers.

But in favour of the second interpretation of Cournot, mentioned at the beginning of this section, it has to be said that he introduces his duopoly analysis at the beginning of chapter VII, which is entirely devoted to the analysis of competition between producers. Here, duopoly finds itself treated as the simplest case of competition between producers of a homogeneous good. Perhaps even more interesting is the fact that Cournot chooses the special case of duopoly to expound an analytical criterion permitting a precise discrimination between situations in which competition between producers prevails and ones in which there is an agreement between them, a case which then resembles that of monopoly. For Cournot, the essence of competition has to be sought in the way that producers of the homogeneous good make their calculations when each one tries to maximize his income 'de son côté' (i.e. individually). He is at pains to underline the point in the following words:

> Nous disons chacun de son côté et cette restriction, comme on va le voir, est bien essentielle; car s'ils s'entendaient pour obtenir le plus grand revenu, les résultats seraient tout autres et ne différeraient pas, pour les consommateurs, de ceux qu'on a obtenus en traitant du monopole. (Cournot, p. 130)

This comment takes on added significance when it is transcribed in the language of game theory.[10] For Cournot, in fact, the essence of competition lies in the non-cooperative nature of the game in which two independent producers confront each other. It is therefore not compatible with the possibilities of there being an understanding between the two producers, as portrayed by a cooperative game, whose economic consequences would amount to a monopoly situation. In other words, the dividing line between competition and monopoly in this case coincides exactly with the classical distinction in game theory between non-cooperative and cooperative games (Schmidt, 1990). The reason why Cournot chose the particular case of duopoly to introduce this criterion, with its wider significance, was simply because duopoly allows no ambiguity. With two producers, exclusive sellers of a homogeneous good, two and only two situations are conceivable: either there is no understanding between them and there is therefore competition, or there is an understanding and the cooperation between them is seen from the outside as a monopoly.

This interpretation finds confirmation in the terms used by Cournot at the end of chapter VII when raising the question of the reasons why producers in a competition situation do not come together, since this would enable each of them to derive a larger profit than can be obtained from non-cooperative equilibrium. To answer this question, he in fact reverts to the initial case of producer duopoly, which he deals with exactly as in the prisoner's dilemma, by showing the instability in such a game of the pair of cooperative strategies, even though this would correspond to an optimal situation as defined by Pareto. It is in the particular framework of duopoly that he sets out the precise nature of the problem, since he writes at the end of the chapter:

> En d'autres termes, cet état ne sera pas une situation d'équilibre stable et, bien que plus favorable aux deux producteurs, il ne pourra subsister à moins d'un lien formel. (Cournot, p. 134)

This means that, for Cournot, two producers are in a competitive situation when they produce a homogeneous good in identical conditions and are not linked together by any *'binding agreement'*, to use the term applied in defining cooperative games. One can safely assume that this is the sense intended by Cournot in his expression *'lien formel'*. In his treatment of duopoly, therefore, Cournot has not only anticipated there being an economic interpretation of the distinction between cooperative and non-cooperative games, but he even understood its true significance (binding nature of the agreements entered into), something that the game theoreticians failed to do initially (Binmore and Dasgupta, 1987; Harsanyi and Selten, 1988; Binmore, 1990).

In grasping the significance of competition by means of non-cooperative games between producers of a homogeneous good, where each of them chooses in a rational manner the quantities he decides to put on the market (the quantities delivered by the others being given), Cournot is bound to consider what he calls 'indefinite competition' as a limiting case of the competitive process (chapter VIII). This particular case arises when no variation in the quantity of the good delivered by any one of the individual producers has any incidence on the price (Cournot, p. 143). This means that the calculation method which, for Cournot, characterizes competition between producers of a homogeneous good, loses its relevance under the hypothesis of indefinite competition. Strictly speaking, this régime of indefinite competition, which is the same as what would later be called 'pure and perfect competition', thus falls outside the scope of competition in the precise sense used by Cournot. It is somewhat surprising, therefore, that this theoretical singularity does not trouble the author of *Recherches sur les principes mathématiques de la théorie des richesses*, who merely contents himself with treating indefinite competition as an observable reality, which he introduces in the following manner:

> Cette hypothèse est celle qui se réalise dans l'économie sociale pour une foule de producteurs et pour les productions les plus importantes.

Elle réintroduit dans les calculs une grande simplification, et c'est à en développer les conséquences que ce chapitre est destiné. (Cournot, p. 143)

To propose as the guiding thread of Cournot's thought the search for a typology of markets, as do the advocates of the second interpretation of his treatment of duopoly, seems to be virtually contradicted by this quotation. At the very least, it raises doubts concerning the validity of the parallels often drawn between the treatment of competition developed by Cournot and the intuitively similar concept of imperfect competition (Robinson, 1933). The question of the affinity of Cournot's concept with the notion of monopolistic competition introduced by Chamberlain (1933) is more complicated. It is true that, for Cournot, competitive equilibrium does not exclude profits for the producers (indeed, quite the contrary) and that it is always possible to interpret his competitive equilibrium in terms of monopolistic competition, if one considers that this epithet designates only the power that each producer exercises individually over the price. In this sense, competition and monopoly power are not self-contradictory for Cournot; again, quite the contrary. But this conclusion does not lead in Cournot's thinking to the idea of a relationship between some measure of the degree of monopoly and the types of competition. On the one hand, we have seen that, for Cournot, it is the alliance between producers and not the competition between them that produces a monopoly situation. Cournot indeed notes the inconsistency between the effects of monopoly in his sense and the régime of indefinite competition (Cournot, p. 146). There is a terminological ambiguity here which it is important to clear up. For Cournot, competition necessarily implies the producer's power to influence price. If he decides to call it 'monopoly effect', it is clear that the competition mechanism according to Cournot is, by definition, monopolistic. On the other hand, if the term 'monopoly' is reserved for a type of organization of production identified by its calculus, competition and monopoly become mutually exclusive. In these circumstance, it is possible to consider that indefinite competition does not form part of the analysis of competition, for the first reason, and yet does not come under monopoly, for the second. This means that, if one adheres strictly to the definitions he lays down, Cournot's ideas include neither a continuum ranging from monopoly to indefinite competition via monopolistic competition, nor any notion of intermediate régimes between monopoly and competition.

As a consequence, it is no more true to say that the place occupied by the analysis of producer monopoly in Cournot's general approach justifies interpreting his analysis of duopoly as a simple extension to competition, than it is to claim that the disturbing similarity observed between his treatment of competition and the modelling of competition in the form of a non-cooperative game means that Cournot can be considered to have made a start on defining a typology of markets. To understand what Cournot was trying to show by means of his explanation of duopoly and producer competition, it is necessary to reconstitute the complete research programme contained in all three chapters (VII, 'De la concurrence' (on competition); VIII, 'De la concurrence indéfinie' (on indefinite competition); and IX, 'Du concours des producteurs'), as these constitute a single whole, relating to a single scientific subject. This is what we propose to do here.

15.3 SUBSTITUTION, COMPLEMENTARITY AND MODES OF PRODUCTION

A close reading of *Recherches sur les principes mathématiques de la théorie des richesses* reveals that the competition introduced in chapter VII represents only one aspect of the analysis. The other is described in chapter IX, where Cournot concentrates on exploring a system in which two producers each produce a good that is linked to the other, in a relationship of strict complementarity, in the production of a third good (Cournot, p. 156). There is a striking affinity between his duopoly model and this other model, which he calls 'concours des producteurs'. The demand functions are of the same form, as are the initial assumptions concerning costs. The 'loi du débit' applied to the two models enables him to show, using the same line of reasoning, that in both cases the income available to the producers acting individually ('chacun de son côté') is less than the income that would result from their joining forces (Cournot, p. 160).[11]

The economic significance of this formal similarity requires some explanation. Let us consider the alternative situations envisaged by Cournot for the producers in the duopoly case – competition or understanding. Just how these are to be transposed to the case of 'concours de producteurs' is not immediately obvious. The existence of two producers, each of whom controls the production of a different good, seems in fact to exclude competition between them if the goods they produce are complementary. But to go no further than this remark would be failing to understand Cournot's particular approach. What characterizes this mode of production for him is, as we have seen, not conflict between the producers but rather the fact that each producer is trying 'individually' to maximize his income (Cournot, p. 130). This mode of production, which leads to competition when applied to producers of a homogeneous good (competition as examined in chapters VII and VIII), can also be seen when each producer enjoys the monopoly of a product, and when their products contribute jointly and exclusively to the production of a third product. In this case Cournot talks of 'division des monopoleurs' which he contrasts with their 'association' (Cournot, p. 161). Competition between producers and 'division des monopoleurs' then comes down to a single mode of organization of production decisions, with the difference between them corresponding merely to the relationship between the goods produced by the producers in the two different cases.

This conclusion leads to an extension of the information supplied by Cournot on the definition of the set of products in the two cases he is analysing. At first sight, duopoly and competition involve only one good, whereas 'concours des producteurs' needs at least three: one produced by each of the monopolists and a third obtained by combining fixed quantities of the first two. It will be seen, however, that Cournot chooses to introduce his study of duopoly by considering two different sources with identical quality (Cournot, p. 129). Translated into contemporary economic terms, these sources are two perfectly substitutable goods. Furthermore, the three goods used in the analysis of 'concours des producteurs' are not treated on the same level. He takes into account only the variations in quantities of the two goods produced by the monopolists, while the demand function leading to the definition of the price is introduced only for the composite good (Cournot, pp. 156–7). One can therefore take it that through 'concours des producteurs', Cournot is in fact analyzing the case of two goods that are intrinsically complementary, as demonstrated by the formulation of the demand function $D = F(m_1 \cdot p_1 + m_2 \cdot p_{2)}$, where m_1 and m_2 represent the proportions of the two goods being considered and p_1 and p_2 their prices.[12] Lastly, the producer of the third good is absent in the formulation of the problem of 'concours des producteurs', so that what we have in this case is a two-player game.

Thus Cournot reduces the analysis of duopoly to the solution of a system in which one wants to determine the profits of the two producers and the prices of their perfectly substitutable products on the basis of an exogenous demand function. Similarly, the study of 'concours des producteurs', for Cournot, is equivalent to solving a system in which the unknowns also include the profits of the two producers of goods which, in this case, are intrinsically complementary, and also the price of the good resulting from their linear combination on the basis of the same exogenous demand function.[13] This is why the two models proposed by Cournot can be regarded as being intended to identify the properties of the two modes of organization of decisions on production, taking two extreme types of relations between the goods produced. In the duopoly case, the two goods are perfectly substitutable, while in that of 'concours des producteurs', they are strictly complementary.

These clarifications demonstrate the single logical structure that underpins chapters VII, VIII and IX of *Recherches sur les principes mathématiques de la théorie des richesses*. Cournot is concerned with seeking and comparing the equilibria associated with two modes of production, in one of which the producers are liable to reach an understanding, and, in the other, they are not. To achieve this, he successively envisages two extreme economic hypotheses, one in which the goods produced are perfectly substitutable and one in which they are fully complementary. He first approaches each of them using a simplified model, with identical mathematical characteristics,[14] before going on to discuss their generalization, by increasing the number of producers in the first case and by increasing the number of intermediate products in the second and then introducing production costs. The research programme can be summarized in Figure 15.1, where M_1 and M_2 correspond to the models developed at the beginning of chapters VII and IX respectively.

The contemporary retranslations of M_1 and M_2 into non-cooperative-games terms yield one interesting preliminary result. As the games are non-cooperative, and given the constraints introduced by Cournot in his chosen demand functions, there exists in both cases a single non-cooperative equilibrium, E_1 in M_1 and E_2 in M_2. These two equilibria are less attractive for each of the two producers than the cooperative equilibrium that would result from their association: E_3 in M_1 and E_4 in M_2. In sum, association between producers is a mode of production which always benefits the producers, whether their activity involves substitutable goods, as in M_1, or complementary goods, as in M_2. But these equilibrium positions that are beneficial to the producers are not naturally attainable by them in a system where the decisions of individual producers are completely decentralized, hence the dominance of E_1 over E_3 in M_1 and of E_2 over E_4 in M_2 (Cournot, pp. 160–1). The contradiction between, on the one hand, the constraints that are inherent

		Substitutable	Complementary
Mode of organization of the producers	Separate	E_1	E_2
	In association	E_3	E_4
		M_1	M_2

Figure 15.1 Economic nature of the goods produced

Producer of *b*

		Acting individually	In association
Producer of *a*	Acting individually	$\pi a_1 = \pi b_1$	$\pi a_2,\ \pi b_2$
	In association	$\pi a_3,\ \pi b_3$	$\pi a_4 = \pi b_4$

Figure 15.2

in the type of game in which the producers define their own strategies (non-cooperative games) and, on the other, their shared interest in the solution corresponding to association (cooperative games), comes back in the first case to a prisoner's dilemma situation between the two competing producers and, in the second, to an absence of coordination between the two producers supplying inputs into the final product.

The payoff matrix illustrated in Figure 15.2 can be applied to the non-cooperative game situations described by models M_1 and M_2. Each producer has two strategy options: to act individually or to achieve an understanding. Let us suppose that they both choose the optimal strategy, in other words the one that ensures them maximum profits. The payoff values are constituted by the profits of each of the two producers. Using the particular assumptions chosen by Cournot (Cournot, pp. 131–3, equations (1), (2), (3), (4), and pp. 156–61 (a), (b), (c), (d)), it can be deduced that $\pi a_1 = \pi b_1$ and $\pi a_4 = \pi b_4$ and that $\pi a_4 > \pi a_1$ and $\pi b_4 > \pi b_1$ in the two games corresponding to M_1 and M_2.[15] These relations hold good whether the strategies are defined in terms of quantity of or price. But it will be recalled that the values of $\pi a_1 \ldots \pi a_4$ and $\pi b_1 \ldots \pi b_4$ differ in the two cases, as regards M_1 (Cournot duopoly and Bertrand duopoly). This difference disappears in M_2.

The M_1 and M_2 models have another, more subtle, common characteristic, which emerges clearly when they are transposed into non-cooperative-game terms. While the two producers are the only actual players, the determination of the equilibrium solutions of the system introduces in both cases the demand functions of the products. The intervention of consumers is therefore essential, because this is needed for the full solution of the models; but, at the same time, the consumers are not treated as being players in the game. In economic terms, this means that, in the phenomena Cournot is trying to analyze, the consumers are regarded as being exogenous in relation to the decision-makers and their behaviour is considered merely as part of the *a priori* information available to the two producers. It will be seen that this special representation of the duopoly and 'concours de producteurs' situations has fostered some of the fallacious interpretations of Cournot's thinking that were denounced earlier.

Let us look in more detail at the implications of this for M_1, the model which has attracted most attention from commentators. While the model does not explain the interactions between producers and consumers, each of the producers knows with certainty the aggregate demand function of the consumers, since it is on the basis of this information that he seeks to maximize his profits through his choice of the quantities of the product he will deliver.[16] By posing the problem of producer decisions in this manner, Cournot reduces the uncertainty of the system to each producer's lack of knowledge of the quantities of the product that will be delivered by the other. This reasoning lays the ground for a later formalization in game-theory terms.

The analysis of duopoly proposed by Cournot in fact suggests a complex process in which each of the two producers reacts not only to the strategic movements of the other but to the indirect consequences of those movements generated through consumer demand. But Cournot does not develop such an argument. The particularity of this approach to the problem seems to have escaped the notice of Bertrand, who fails to understand how the quantities offered on the market by the two producers can be treated as independent variables (Bertrand, 1883, p. 299). Pareto, for his part, although denouncing Bertrand's error, assimilates the control variables of the system (the quantities delivered by the producers) to simple independent variables (Pareto, 1911, in Cournot, Lutfalla (ed.), 1938, pp. 253–5). Lastly, Shubik (1959) is unable to decide whether Cournot-duopoly should be given a static or a dynamic interpretation. A dynamic interpretation would require not only the introduction of an additional assumption, concerning the conditions for the adjustment of the quantities delivered by each producer to the information he obtains from knowing the quantities delivered by the other, but also the incorporation in the game of the strategic reaction of the consumers (Shubik, 1959). In our view, the complete description of duopoly in dynamic terms is not the aim of the Cournot model, any more than the dynamics of 'concours des producteurs' is the object of the second model. For this reason, it is probably more in keeping both with Cournot's intentions and with the requirements of game theory to treat both of them a single-move strategic games (Friedman, 1977).

It can be interesting, nevertheless, to extend the analysis of the question dealt with in Cournot's duopoly model by transforming the interpretation of the strategic options open to the producers of the two perfectly substitutable goods, designated as *a* and *b*, in such a way as to introduce the first move into the analysis. It will then be seen that the producer making the first move should be able to impose on the second producer a non-cooperative equilibrium that is more favourable to himself than to his competitor (Stackelberg equilibrium). This is equivalent to replacing the first ('individual') option by the option consisting of taking the initiative by making the first move, the second option being merely to refuse to take this initiative. If both take the initiative simultaneously, we revert to a Nash game. It is more difficult to interpret the situation in which neither takes the initiative, but it is reasonable to think that this leads to a Pareto solution.[17] The set of situations resulting from the games that are possible under this interpretation are summarized in Figure 15.3, where I and $\bar{I}$ respectively represent the two strategic options just described.

The absence of the consumers from the game in which the M_1 and M_2 models are treated does not mean that consumers play no part in Cournot's research programme; indeed, quite the contrary. First, it is with reference to the consumers that the relationship is defined between the two types of good being considered, and it is precisely this relationship that constitutes the difference between the two models. This reference is direct in M_1 and indirect in M_2, where the complementarity of the two goods results in the first place from their productive combination. But one may consider that this productive combination has economic significance only insofar as it is a response to a demand, and this restores the reference to the consumers in the case of 'concours des producteurs'. Moreover, it is from the viewpoint of the consumers that Cournot assesses the consequences in terms of the general welfare resulting from the various equilibrium situations identified by his analysis.

Producer of *b*

	l	$\bar{l}$
Producer of *a* *l*	Nash equilibrium	Stackelberg equilibrium to the advantage of a
$\bar{l}$	Stackelberg equilibrium to the advantage of b	Pareto equilibrium

Figure 15.3

To be more precise, the equilibria E_1 and E_3 in M_1 and E_2 and E_4 in M_2 correspond not merely to the payoffs in the games but also to the resulting prices of the good from the two perfectly substitutable sources in the M_1 case and from their productive combination in M_2. The consumers whose interests represent general welfare obviously have an interest in seeing that the good should be as cheap as possible. This plausible hypothesis makes it possible to interpet the price of this good as an index of consumer satisfaction and this leads Cournot to the discovery of a second important result. Whereas the interests of the producers are opposed to those of the consumers when they produce substitutable goods (M_1), they operate in the same direction when they produce complementary goods (M_2) (Cournot, p. 160). This is why the solution of cooperation (treated as a monopoly) which forms a Pareto optimum in the producer duopoly game is not a social optimum, whereas the merger of the two separate producers in the 'concours des producteurs' game is, on the contrary, indeed a social optimum.

The demonstration of the first result relating to perfectly substitutable products is well known to contemporary duopoly theoreticians and needs no discussion within the narrow framework of the assumptions used in the Cournot model. However, the second, concerning strictly complementary products, has received little attention and its economic interpretation is not intuitively obvious. Cournot examines the derivatives of the profit functions with respect to price when the producers operate 'individually' (non-cooperative game) and when there is an understanding between them (cooperative game). With costs zero and a demand function $D = F(p)$ where $F'(p) < 0$, the maximum value of the derivative of the profit function is always higher in the case of non-cooperative equilibrium than it is in the case of cooperative equilibrium (Cournot, pp. 147–59). One can therefore conclude that in c's model of complementary products, $p_1^* > p_2^*$, where p_1^* represents the price of the composite good under non-cooperative equilibrium and p_2^* the price associated with cooperative equilibrium (see Annex). This does not prevent $\pi_2^* > \pi a_1^* + \pi b_1^*$, where π_2^* is the value of the equilibrium monopoly profit resulting from the association of the producers of a and of b, and πa_1^* and πb_1^* are the values corresponding respectively to the equilibrium profits of the producers of a and b acting individually. As the monopoly equilibrium is equivalent to the equilibrium of a cooperative game between the producers of a and b, the two producers have an interest is reaching an understanding, which is also for the greater benefit of the consumers of the composite good.

The economic interpretation of this mathematical result can be represented in the following terms. The sum of the profits that the two producers are capable of deriving from the delivery of goods a and b, when they choose their strategies independently, is limited by the constraint inherent in the exclusively complementary use made of their output. To avoid the risk that a part of this quantity remains unused, they are each obliged to deliver a quantity that is lower than they would deliver if they were able to coordinate their action. The result is a higher price to the consumers, by reason of the shape of the demand function of the composite good. But this price will never be sufficient to compensate for the loss of profit generated by the reduction in the quantities traded separately by each producer, the profit being understood as (price × quantity traded). This means that their total profit is less than they would have obtained by reaching an understanding.

This interpretation leaves one question unresolved and presents a major difference from the case of the perfectly substitutable goods analyzed in the duopoly model. When Cornot argues on the basis of an understanding between the two producers, he is able to assimilate this situation to that of a monopolist maximizing his profit and to exclude from his model the examination of the way in which this profit is shared between the two (allied) producers, exactly as in the duopoly model. This is no longer the case when the two producers are supposed to be acting independently and individually, since the model must be able to determine the profit of each producer, and this requires an additional item of information in the 'concours des producteurs' model. Nothing in the Cournot model makes it possible to write $\pi a_1^* = \pi b_1^*$, contrary this time to the case of the duopoly model, where this equality could result from the assumption of competition between two producers of equal strength operating in identical conditions (Cournot, p. 133). Cournot is aware of this objection, as is shown by the following comment on the equality he postulates between the profits of the two producers of the complementary goods *a* and *b*:

Dans l'hypothèse purement abstraite qui nous occupe, les bénéfices se partageraient également entre les deux monopoleurs; et en effect il n'y aurait aucune raison pour que le partage fût inégal au profit de l'un plutôt qu'au profit de l'autre. (Cournot, pp. 159–60)

This difference from the producer duopoly model brings out the particular nature of the problem posed to the producers in the two cases. Under 'concours des producteurs', the Pareto sub-optimality of the Nash equilibrium is the simple consequence of a lack of coordination between them. When there is understanding between the two duopolists, it is a direct effect of the competition between them. This is why the comparison with the prisoner's dilemma holds only in this latter case.

Taking this observation a stage further makes it possible to specify the difference between the problems encountered by the producers in the two models. The sub-optimality of the Nash equilibrium in the non-cooperative game of model M_2 is simply the consequence of a lack of coordination in deciding their strategies. Since their interests converge, neither can gain an advantage at the expense of the other. The sub-optimality of the Nash equilibrium in the non-cooperative game of model M_1 has a different origin. The interests of the duopolists are this time partly divergent and there are situations in the system that give an advantage to one at the expense of the other. This time, it is their competition which explains this property. It can therefore be concluded that only the producer duopoly case and, more generally, that of competition as defined by Cournot, can be assimilated to a prisoner's dilemma. The case of understanding between monopolists must rather be regarded as a game of Schelling-type pure coordination (Schelling, 1960).

This difference between the two models finally leads to a more profound interpretation of the relation between prices and quantities. As we have seen, the duopoly model has differing economic significance depending on whether the duopolists define their strategies in terms of price or of quantity. But the same is not true of the 'concours des producteurs' model, where, on the contrary, the two strategic variants lead to identical economic results. Cournot had himself correctly grasped this difference, because he differentiates the profit functions of the two producers with respect to price in m_2: $d(paDa)/dpa = 0$; $d(pbDb)/dpb = 0$ (Cournot, p. 157) instead of differentiating them with respect to quantities, as in M_1. By proceeding in this way, Cournot is treating the 'concours des producteurs' case as a direct extension of his monopoly model (chapter V), as is justified when one recalls that the two producers of the complementary goods are monopolists. When the competition is between producers of substitutable goods, the situation is no longer the same and Cournot opts for an inversion of the relationship. This choice can be explained either by a desire to underline the opposition between monopoly and competition (see Section 15.2) or as a simple matter of convenience.

From a more general point of view, the information transmitted by Cournot's two models concerning the relation between prices and quantities brings us back to the initial question of the links between the mathematical formulation and its economic interpretation. The inversion of the function linking quantity to price makes no difference to the economic result when the products are complementary, but it transforms it when the products are substitutable. In the former case, the economic phenomenon described by the model is independent of the choice of strategic variable associated with the producers; it is critically dependent on it in the latter case. This absence of symmetry therefore suggests that the answer to the question depends on the nature of the relation between the goods produced.

15.4   ELABORATION, MISUNDERSTANDINGS AND LINES OF RESEARCH

The results presented and discussed here come uniquely from an elaboration of chapters IV, V, VII, VIII and IX of *Recherches sur les principes mathématiques de la théorie des richesses*. But they have been exploited neither by Cournot himself, their 'discoverer', nor by the later interpreters of his thinking. Reflecting on this observation reveals an opportunity for the historian of economic thought to make a positive contribution to economic analysis. We shall first try to explain why the economic implications of the properties demonstrated by Cournot and recapitulated here have not been fully worked out.

One may suppose that Cournot considered his work as a kind of ground-clearing of the possibilities offered by a particular branch of mathematics, namely analysis, to clarify certain fundamental concepts of political economy (Cournot, p. 33). To put it more precisely, Cournot should now be recognized as the real pioneer of qualitative analysis applied to economics.[18] He explains himself on this point in the preface to his book, where he indicates that he is in no way trying to introduce numerical calculation into economics, but is concentrating on the relations between arbitrary economic magnitudes, which he intends to examine by way of functions which satisfy certain conditions capable of being formulated either qualitatively (the signs of the derivatives) or quasi-qualitatively (existence of extreme values) (Cournot, pp. 31–3). In fact the backbone of his work is formed by the 'loi du débit', which he formulates by means of a continuous demand function subject to a small number of conditions that are immediately translatable into economic terms (chapter IV). This he then uses to re-examine the fundamental notions of economics. With a touch of malice, he in fact warns the reader of the surprises in store for him, when he writes at the end of this preface:

> Peut-être remarqueront-ils dans son exposé des premières notions sur la concurrence et sur le concours des producteurs, certaines relations assez curieuses, à les envisager sous le point de vue purement abstrait, indépendamment du but d'application que l'on se propose. (Cournot, p. 34)

This says it all. The choice of the two examples is not a matter of chance and yet Cournot's scientific treasure long remained hidden.

The main reason for this has to be sought in the manifest lack of interest of his successors in his analysis of 'concours des producteurs'; but they destroy the harmony of our author's work by thus ignoring one of the two aspects of his research.[19] However, the causes of this lack of interest are not the same for the different generations of economic theoreticians who have looked into Cournot's work.

The first generation of mathematical economists tended to neglect the 'concours des producteurs' case by erroneously interpreting it as a badly posed problem of bilateral monopoly (Zawadzki, 1914). Admittedly, both in 'concours des producteurs' and in bilateral monopoly we have two monopolists each controlling one of two goods which in combination are the subject of a demand. But the analogy stops there. The two goods in the 'concours des producteurs' case are in no way substitutable, as they are in bilateral monopoly, but are strictly oligopolistic, and the phenomenon studied by Cournot is not exchange between the two monopolists but the effect of the organization of their respective productions on the price of the composite good that results from their combined activities. If one is looking for a study of bilateral monopoly in chapter IX, devoted to 'concours des producteurs', one is clearly not going to find it. This misunderstanding has been an important factor in the neglect of chapter IX by this generation of Cournot's readers.

The neglect of the 'concours des producteurs' case by contemporary economists trained in game theory has its origin in other considerations. Their re-reading of Cournot is linked, as we have seen, to the emergence of Nash's research programme and this programme tends to assimilate the whole class of non-cooperative games to one particular category of these games, namely 'contests' (to use the terminology proposed by Binmore in Binmore and Dasgupta, 1986). While it is not difficult to treat as a contest the game which opposes the duopolists and, more generally, the competing producers in M_1, this is no longer possible in the 'concours des producteurs' case, where no contest is involved. In M_2, as we have seen, the interests of the two producers are in fact strictly convergent; hence the difficulties encountered by contemporary theoreticians in describing 'concours des producteurs' in terms of a non-cooperative game.

More generally, the method followed by Cournot is somewhat perplexing, consisting as it does of analyzing the impact of the mode of production on the profits of the producers and on the prices of the goods produced using only the demand function, with production costs introduced only at a later stage as a complication in the initial models:

> Nous avons examiné jusqu'ici comment la loi de la demande, pour chaque denrée en particulier, combinée avec les circonstances de la production de cette denrée, en déterminait le prix et réglait les revenue des producteurs. (Cournot, p. 191)[20]

The result of this is that the properties demonstrated by Cournot concerning the economic consequences of the mode of production of substitutable and complementary products are based not on the quantities produced but on the quantities delivered by the producers (initial assumption of zero cost). The first generalization of Cournot's results consists of reintroducing a cost constraint into these models, in other words an analysis of the production itself. By exploring in this direction for duopoly and oligopoly, the contemporary theoreticians of industrial economics have shown, among other things, that

Cournot's non-cooperative game could either (a) have no equilibrium solution (Roberts and Sonnenschein, 1976; Novshek, 1985) or (b) on the contrary, have several equilibria (Shubik, 1970; Rasmusen, 1989). We therefore now know that the Cournot production duopoly model, with a Nash non-cooperative equilibrium that is unique, stable and sub-optimal, constitutes a highly special case, even within the family of models where the control variables are the quantities produced and delivered to consumers.[21]

There is a second set of possible extensions to Cournot's research programme which has yet to be undertaken. These concern the 'concours des producteurs' model. The implications of the results demonstrated by Cournot are different in this case from those of duopoly and competition, not only from a normative standpoint but also from a positive standpoint. It can, in fact, be accepted that the producers of perfectly substitutable goods are participants in a non-cooperative game, on condition that they operate in an economic universe characterized by having a very large number of competitive consumers, as the behaviour of the latter can then be reduced (as a first approximation) to an aggregate demand function. But this argument is not immediately transposable to the case of producers of strictly complementary goods for exclusive use. Whether their interaction should be represented in the framework of a non-cooperative game remains an open question. We have already seen that this non-cooperative game is in no way a contest. The further examination of the special case of 'concours des producteurs' therefore leads to a re-examination in more detail of the economic interpretation of the dividing line between a cooperative and a non-cooperative game.

The 'concours des producteurs' model, as formulated by Cournot, takes into account only the strategies of the two producers who control the strictly complementary goods. Their interaction manifests itself exclusively through the consequences of these strategies for the quantities of the composite good delivered to consumers. As an intuitive illustration, Cournot takes the example of two producers of primary goods which enter into the exclusive composition of an intermediate composite good (Cournot, p. 156). The Cournot model can be taken a stage further by treating the producer of this intermediate good as a third player. This new form of the game would make it possible to analyze the interactions between the strategies of the non-competing players and those of their customer and so to deduce, along the lines of the research programme initiated by Cournot, certain conclusions regarding the mode of production and the economic impact on consumers.

This transformation of the initial 'concours des producteurs' model can thus lead one to pose the problem of mergers and integrations of firms in the framework of Cournot's general reasoning.

More generally, the abstract viewpoint deliberately chosen by Cournot led him in his *Recherches sur les principes mathématiques de la théorie des richesses* to give preference to the analysis of the economic consequences of the mode of production that are associated with the types of inter-producer games in two extreme cases — those where the goods produced are *perfectly* substitutable and those where they are *completely* complementary (cf. M_1 and M_2). A natural extension of this investigation is to apply Cournot's analytical structures to the intermediate cases.

This line of research nevertheless requires a certain clarification of concepts. We must point out that the two models implicitly used by Cournot are not on the same level. The 'concurrence des producteurs' is defined in a first-level model (pure substitutes), while the 'concours des producteurs' is introduced in a second-level model (intrinsic complements and a compound good). As for competition, the existence of several producers of the same good (or of perfectly substitutable goods), who are decentralized and independent (i.e. with no possibility of concluding binding agreements)[22] is sufficient to mean competition between them, assuming rational behaviour. Where does this leave the competition concept, when the goods produced are only imperfectly substitutable? One might use the term 'incomplete competition' for this type of situation, to avoid confusion with the quite distinct concept of 'imperfect competition' (see pp. 364–5 above). In any case, the delimitation of the competitive space as understood by Cournot needs a prior investigation of the relevant sets of goods, which in turn leads to closer examination of the procedures for the identification of these goods.

Turning to the definition of 'concours des producteurs': this is based on the intrinsically complementary nature of the goods each of which is produced exclusively by a single producer. The manner in which Cournot introduces the idea of complementarity into his analysis implicitly recalls, not the definition that was subsequently to be proposed in the framework of the theory of demand, but the later definitions drawn from the theory of linear programming (Morishima, 1979). This reinterpretation has made it possible, as Morishima has pointed out, to build a bridge between demand theory, which was initially built up from the customer, and the theory of the firm, which developed quite separately (Morishima, 1979, p. 149). It can therefore be used for the immediate generalization of the notion of 'concours des producteurs' to the cases of final goods that are intrinsically complementary. But such a classification is not by itself sufficient to describe the whole process of 'concours des producteurs' as suggested by Cournot's formulation.

Even so, the most fertile extension of Cournot's research programme as regards industrial economics consists of transforming its field of application: (i) by relaxing the initial assumption that identifies each production centre with a particular product; (ii) by making the relationship between activity and product more explicit. Broadening would have the effect of achieving compatibility between the competitive and 'concours des producteurs' relations as defined by Cournot. It would then make it possible to derive, along the lines set out in *Recherches sur les principes mathématiques de la théorie des richesses* the economic properties of the modes of production that can be logically associated with a wide variety of possible situations.

ANNEX: THE 'CONCOURS DES PRODUCTEURS' MODEL

LET:

a and b be two goods which contribute exclusively to the production of a third, in the respective proportions m_a and m_b ($m_a + m_b = 1$);
D the demand for the composite good;
p its price;
D_a and D_b the quantities of a and b, respectively, delivered by their producers;
p_a and p_b their prices;
π_a and π_b the corresponding profits.

Moreover, let F be the demand function ($D = F(p)$ or, $p = \phi(D)$).
From the above definitions, we can derive the following equalities:

$$p = m_a \cdot p_a + m_b \cdot p_b;$$
$$D_a = m_a \cdot D = m_a \cdot F(m_a \cdot p_a + m_b \cdot p_b);$$
$$D_b = m_b \cdot D = m_b \cdot F(m_a \cdot p_a + m_b \cdot p_b);$$
$$\pi_a = p_a \cdot D_a;$$
$$\pi_b = p_b \cdot D_b.$$

Let case 1 be that in which each producer maximizes his own profit acting individually (non-cooperative game), and case 2 that in which both agree to maximize their joint profit (cooperative game).

In case 1, writing first-order conditions for maximization gives:

$$F(p) + p_a \cdot (dF(p)/dp_a) = 0$$
$$F(p) + p_b \cdot (dF(p)/dp_b) = 0$$

That is,

$$F(p) + p_a \cdot (dF(p)/dp) \cdot (dp/dp_a) = F(p) + m_a \cdot p_a \cdot (dF(p)/dp) = 0$$
$$F(p) + p_b \cdot (dF(p)/dp) \cdot (dp/dp_b) = F(p) + m_b \cdot p_b \cdot(dF(p)/dp) = 0$$

which leads to:

$$m_a \cdot p_a = m_b \cdot p_b = p/2$$

and the condition for p:

$$H_1(p) = 2F(p) + p \cdot (dF(p)/dp) = 0.$$

The first-order condition for case 2 can be written:

$$H_2(p) = F(p) + p \cdot (dF(p)/dp) = 0$$

The demand function being non-negative for any value of p,

$$H_1(p) \geq H_2(p).$$

On the other hand, since production of all goods is assumed to have zero cost, no profit function can take on negative values. Moreover, at zero price, profit obviously vanishes. This means that unless the demand function vanishes for any value of p, profits take on positive value for $p = 0^+$ in case 1 as well as in case 2.

Assuming the existence of equilibrium in case 1 and in case 2, let p_1^* and p_2^* denote the values of p which maximize π_a and π_b respectively in case 1 (Nash equilibrium) and in case 2 (Pareto equilibrium).

It stems from the above that:

  (i) for $p < p_1^*$, $H_1(p) > 0$ and
  (ii) for $p < p_2^*$, $H_1(p) > 0$

If $p_2^* > p_1^*$, then $H_2(p_1^*) > 0$. But this is impossible, since, by definition, $H_1(p_1^*) = 0 \geq H_2(p_2^*)$.

Hence, $p_1^* \geq p_2^*$.

Now let π_1^* and π_2^* be the sum of the profits at the equilibrium price associated with case 1 and case 2, respectively.

$$\pi_1^* = p_1^* \cdot F(p_1^*) \leq \text{Max } p \cdot F(p) = p_2^* \cdot F(p_2^*) = \pi_2^*.$$

Note that the formulation chosen for the problem is to put $d\pi_a/dp_a = p_a + D_a \cdot dp_a/dp_a$, in accordance with that originally used by Cournot (pp. 197–8). One can also write $d\pi_a/dD_a = D_a + p_a \cdot dD_a/dD_a$ without altering the two demonstrated results. When a and b are strictly complementary goods, therefore, the choice of the adjustment variable has no effect on the economic consequences of the calculations made by the two producers.

Notes

1. Certain terms which have specific connotations in Cournot's analysis and which were not adopted by later economists – 'concours des producteurs', 'loi du débit', 'fonction du débit', etc. – have been left in French in the text that follows.
2. It will be noticed that this interpretation does not coincide with the outline adopted by Cournot in the progress of his analysis. The chapter devoted to indefinite competition (chapter VIII) in fact precedes that dealing with 'concours des producteurs' (chapter IX). Remembering that Cournot's intention was to proceed from the simple to the composite using a Cartesian approach, G. Lutfalla attributes this anomaly to the fact that the order of the chapters in the published work is not that in which Cournot originally dealt with them. But he produces no proof of this (G. Lutfalla, Introduction to his edition of *Recherches sur les principes mathématiques de la théorie des richesses* (1938), pp. xv–xvi. See Note 14).
3. Most of these criticisms concerned the solution proposed by Cournot to the problem of duopoly. For these authors, either the problem was indeterminate, or its solution had no economic significance, or it was incorrectly posed. But these criticisms were indirectly aimed at Cournot's whole intellectual approach.
4. It was Shubik who originated these appellations. During the 1950s, he gave the name 'Nash–Cournot solution' to the point of non-cooperative equilibrium in a game in which each producer chooses the quantity delivered on the market, with the quantity delivered by the other producer taken as given. He later proposed a distinction between the Nash–Cournot model which he contrasts with that of Bertrand and the Nash–Cournot equilibrium which he contrast with that of Walras. For a detailed study of this last point, see Novshek and Sonnenschein (1978, 1985, 1987).
5. All future references in the form (Cournot, p. . . .) in the text are to the 1974 edition of this work unless otherwise indicated.
6. It will be noted, however, that in Cournot's original formulation the demand function associated with the 'loi du débit' is not subject to any linearity constraint (Cournot, pp. 93–8).
7. In the formulation of duopoly suggested by Bertrand, the Nash equilibrium point is that where $pa = pb = 0$, with a slight fall in price leading for both producers to a discontinuous change in their respective shares of the market. It is worth noting, however, first that Bertrand never constructed the model that has been attributed to him and, second, that it is not so much the mathematical result as the economic interpretation placed on the model constructed from Bertrand's suggestions that may seem surprising.
8. Shapley and Shubik, in their attempt to clarify the term 'competition',

point out that the use of the epithet 'competitive' applied to the concept of equilibrium describes, paradoxically, a situåtion in which there is no interaction between the competitors. If, for them, the approach adopted by Cournot provides the basis for one of the three possible concepts of competition, there is then nothing to distinguish perfect competition from a régime of administered prices. But they maintain, contrary to ourselves, that the three approaches are convergent (Shapley and Shubik, 1967, pp. 67–8).

9. An ambiguity remains, however, in Cournot's commentary on the equations he uses for obtaining the definition of the strategies of the two producers through derivation with respect to quantities ($D_1F(D_1 + D_2)$), $D_2F(D_1 + D_2)$, because he writes: 'Le propriétaire 1 ne peut influer directement sur la fixation de D_2, tout ce qu'il peut faire c'est, lorsque D_2 est fixé par 2, de choisir pour D_1 la valeur qui lui convient le mieux, ce à quoi il parviendra en modifiant le prix' (Cournot, p. 130). This discrepancy between his mathematical formulation and the literary part of his interpretation did not escape the attention of Shubik (1989, p. 122).

10. 'De son côté/'individually' – signifies that each producer takes as given the strategic choice made by the other. This interpretation was clarified only retrospectively, using the Nash definitions, and this formulation of Cournot's has been at the origin of an obscure debate on the independence of the decisions of the two producers (cf. Bertrand, 1883; and Pareto, 1911). Here again, it was Shubik (1959) who underlined the importance of this pronouncement of Cournot's.

11. The result demonstrated by Cournot applies to all the profits available to the two producers and not directly to the profits allocated individually to one or the other. In the case of association between the producers, there is no explanation as to the distribution of this higher profit between the two producers. As regards the equality of profits, this results from the special assumptions chosen by Cournot for the duopoly model, while in the association model it is simply postulated.

12. According to this formulation, $m_1 \cdot p_1$ and $m_2 \cdot p_2$ are to be understood in the same manner as the budget constraint in the traditional theory of the consumer.

13. This is the only point at which the linearity property appears in the 'concours des producteurs' model.

14. With the exception that he uses, as we have seen, the inverse formulation of the demand function in the duopoly model and reverts to the initial formulation in the 'concours des producteurs' model.

15. Moreover, $\pi a_2 > \pi a_4 > \pi a_1 > \pi a_3$ for producer 1 and $\pi b_3 > \pi b_4 > \pi b_1 > \pi b_2$ for the producer 2 in model M_1, hence its interpretation in terms of the prisoners' dilemma.

16. It is important to point out that the strategic variables in the duopoly game corresponding to M_1 are the quantities delivered by each producer to the consumers and not the quantities produced. It seems difficult to interpret M_1 as a market model in the manner envisaged by Shubik, for example, because of the absence of any role for the consumer. On the other hand, the economic argument drawn from the existence of long-term production programmes on the part of firms to justify the definition

of producer strategies in terms of quantities, used by Friedman (1977) among others, seems no more acceptable. In any case, it is understandable that the very special treatment reserved by Cournot for the analysis of duopoly should have perplexed successive generations of economists.

17. Suppose, for example, that each one associates with his decision not to make the first move the threat to revert to 'individual' action; if the other were to decide to take the initiative that would give him the advantage (mutual dissuasion). It can then be argued that they would be in a certain sense obliged to reach an understanding, depending on examination of the credibility of their reciprocal threats.

18. By 'qualitative analysis' is meant the identification of economic properties that do not depend on the values of the variables being examined, but only on their direction of change. It is true that Cournot's research is not 'qualitative' on this definition, but *Recherches sur les principes mathématiques de la théorie des richesses* contains several notes proving that the objective he assigned to economic theory was of this nature.

19. Guitton notes perceptively in his preface to the re-edition of *Recherches sur les principes mathématiques de la théorie des richesses* that Cournot had no followers of his distinction between 'competition' and 'cooperation' among producers (Guitton, 1974, p. 19). Quite apart from questions of terminology, it has to be admitted that this distinction has not been correctly understood until now.

20. This introduction to chapter XI ('Du revenu social' – 'on social income'), where Cournot's method is summarized, presents the interest of underlining the link between two of its special features, which appear independent of each other at first sight. On the one hand, he centres his analysis on the manner in which the law of demand for individualized products determines the modes of relationship between the producers, on which in turn depend their prices and profits. The production process is treated as a 'circumstantial' datum, on the same level as taxation (a production cost for the producers). On the other, the totality of Cournot's argument is conducted in terms of partial equilibrium. The same reason finally leads the author to take as given the 'circumstances of production' and the 'quantities and prices of other produce and the incomes of other producers' (Cournot, p. 191). He is fully aware of this dual limitation and indicates a way of getting round it by examining, in particular, the case of the appearance of a new product in the economic macrocosm being studied (pp. 209–12). It was especially by taking this viewpoint a stage further that Novshek (1980) and Novshek and Sonnenschein (1978) proposed a linkage between Cournot's partial equilibrium and Walras's general equilibrium.

21. This conclusion could lead to a reduction in the scope of the results demonstrated by Cournot, by considerably limiting their generality. But such a conclusion would be tainted by retrospective bias. When resituated in the context adopted by Cournot himself, this should not be regarded as restrictive, in that he was not aiming to derive a general theory, which seemed to him an unattainable goal and perhaps not even a desirable one.

22. The competition between producers is therefore for Cournot the result of

a simultaneous satisfaction of several objective conditions concerning (a) the economic definition of the goods produced, (b) the respective positions of the producers and (c) the content of the information available to them. The same is obviously true of the identification of the situation corresponding to 'concours des producteurs'. But systematic study of this point has yet to be carried out.

References

Bertrand, J. (1883) 'Théorie mathématique de la richesses sociale et recherches sur les principes mathématiques de la théorie des richesses', *Journal des savants*, no. 499 (4 September).

Binmore, K. (1990) *Essays on the Foundations of Game Theory* (Oxford: Basil Blackwell).

Binmore, K. and P. Dasgupta (1986) *Economic Organisations as Games* (Oxford: Basil Blackwell).

Binmore, K. and P. Dasgupta (1987) *The Economics of Bargaining* (Oxford: Basil Blackwell).

Chamberlain, E.H. (1933) *The Theory of Monopolistic Competition: A Re-Orientation of the Theory of Value* (Cambridge, Mass.: Harvard University Press).

Cournot, A.A. [1838] (1938) *Recherches sur les principes mathématiques de la théorie des richesses*. New Edition (1938) with introduction and notes by G. Lutfalla (Paris: Marcel Rivière).

Cournot, A.A. [1838] (1974) *Recherches sur les principes mathématiques de la théorie des richesses*. Preface to 1974 edition by H. Guitton (Paris: Calmann-Lévy).

Edgeworth, F.Y. (1891) 'Teoria para del monopolio', *Giornale degli Economisti*.

Edgeworth, F.Y. (1897) 'La théorie mathématique de l'offre et de la demande et le coût de production', *Revue d'économie politique*, vol. 10.

Fisher, I. (1899) 'Cournot and Mathematical Economics', *Quarterly Journal of Economics*, no. 119.

Friedman, J.W. (1977) *Oligopoly and the Theory of Games* (Amsterdam: North Holland).

Friedman, J.W. (1989) 'Duopoly', in *The New Palgrave* (London: Macmillan).

Guitton, H. (1968) 'Antoine-Augustin Cournot', in *The International Encyclopaedia of the Social Sciences*, vol. 3 (New York: Macmillan and Free Press).

Guitton, H. (1974) Preface to the 1974 edition of *Recherches sur les principes mathématiques de la théorie des richesses* (Paris: Calmann-Lévy).

Harsanyi, J.C. and R. Selten (1988) *A General Theory of Equilibrium Selection in Games* (Cambridge, Mass.: MIT Press).

Lutfalla, G. (1983) Introduction and notes to the new edition of A.A. Cournot, *Recherches sur les principes mathématiques de la théorie des richesses* (Paris: Marcel Rivière).

Mayberry, J.P., J.F. Nash and M. Shubik (1953) 'A Comparison of Treatment of a Duopoly Situation', *Econometrica*, vol. 21.

Morishima, M. (1979) 'Separability and Intrinsic Complementarity', in *Theory* of Demand: Real and Monetary (Oxford: Clarendon Press).

Nash, J.F. (1951) 'Non-Cooperative Games', Annals of Mathematics, vol. 18.

Nash, J.F. (1953) 'Two-Person Cooperative Games', Econometrica, vol. 21.

Novshek, W. (1980) 'Cournot Equilibrium with Free Entry', Journal of Economic Theory, vol. 19, no. 2.

Novshek, W. (1985) 'On the Existence of Cournot Equilibrium', Review of Economic Studies, vol. 52, no. 1.

Novshek, W. and H. Sonnenschein (1978) 'Cournot and Walras Equilibrium', Journal of Economic Theory, vol. 19, no. 2.

Novshek, W. and H. Sonnenschein (1987) 'General Equilibrium with Free Entry: A Synthetic Approach to the Theory of Perfect Competition', Journal of Economic Literature, vol. 25 (September).

Pareto, V. (1911) 'Economie mathématique', in Encyclopédie des sciences mathématiques.

Rasmussen, E. (1989) Games and Information (Oxford: Basil Blackwell).

Roberts, J. and N. Sonnenschein (1976) 'On the Existence of Cournot Equilibrium Without Concave Profit Functions', Journal of Economic Theory, vol. 13.

Robinson, J. (1933) The Economic of Imperfect Competition (London: Macmillan).

Roy, R. (1933) 'Cournot et l'école mathématique', Econometrica, no. 1.

Schelling, T.C. (1960) The Strategy of Conflict (Cambridge, Mass.: Harvard University Press).

Schmidt, C. (1985) La Sémantique économique en question (Paris: Calmann-Lévy).

Schmidt, C. (1990) 'Game Theory and Economics: An Historical Survey', Revue d'économie politique, no. 5.

Shapley, L.S. and M. Shubik (1967) 'Concepts and Theories of Pure Competition', in M. Shubik (ed.), Essays in Mathematical Economics in Honor of Oskar Morgenstern (Princeton: Princeton University Press).

Shubik, M. (1955) 'A Comparison of Treatment of a Duopoly Problem', Econometrica, vol. 23.

Shubik, M. (1959) Strategy and Market Structure (New York: John Wiley).

Shubik, M. (1970) 'A Further Comparison of Some Models of Duopoly', Western Economic Journal, no. 6.

Shubik, M. (1989) 'Antoine-Augustin Cournot', in Game Theory in the New Palgrave (London: Macmillan).

Zawadzki, W. (1914) Les mathématiques appliquées à l'économie politique (Paris: Marcel Rivière).